ENVIRONMENTAL DISPUTE RESOLUTION IN INDONESIA

For my fellow travellers – Samali, Niluka and Rama

Cover illustration: Gold mine in West Kalimantan, 2005 (photograph by Fridus Steijlen)

VERHANDELINGEN
VAN HET KONINKLIJK INSTITUUT
VOOR TAAL-, LAND- EN VOLKENKUNDE

259

DAVID NICHOLSON

ENVIRONMENTAL DISPUTE RESOLUTION IN INDONESIA

KITLV Press
Leiden
2009

Published by:
KITLV Press
Koninklijk Instituut voor Taal-, Land- en Volkenkunde
(Royal Netherlands Institute of Southeast Asian and Caribbean Studies)
PO Box 9515
2300 RA Leiden
The Netherlands
website: www.kitlv.nl
e-mail: kitlvpress@kitlv.nl

KITLV is an institute of the Royal Netherlands Academy of Arts and Sciences (KNAW)

Research for this book was funded by the Royal Netherlands Academy of Arts and Sciences in the framework of the Scientific Programme Indonesia-Netherlands.

Cover: Creja ontwerpen, Leiderdorp

ISBN 978 90 6718 326 0

Contents

Acknowledgements

Writing a book can often feel like a solitary task, but I was fortunate to undertake this research not alone but within the framework of the Indonesia Netherlands Study on Environmental Law (INSELA) project. I found our annual conferences in both Holland and Indonesia, and the opportunity to prepare and present an annual paper, both a support and stimulus for the direction of my own research. I would like to thank all my co-researchers on both the Dutch and Indonesian sides of the project for their collegial and academic support at various times throughout the duration of the project.

Prior to joining the INSELA project, I commenced post-graduate research at Murdoch University, where I was based at the Asia Research Centre. I am most grateful for the support of the centre during that period and also the feedback and assistance I received from a number of people at the time including Richard Robison, Kanishka Jayasuriya, Gitte Heij and Carol Warren.

Once in Holland, under the auspices of INSELA, a good part of my time was spent working on the thesis that led to this book in the attic of the Van Vollenhoven Institute, then located on the Rapenburg. I would like to acknowledge the support of the Institute and the assistance offered by all concerned (both academic and administrative staff) to myself and my family during our stay in Holland and throughout the duration of the project. Particularly thanks go to my co-researchers for their feedback, comments and companionship along the way including Julia Arnscheidt, Nicole Niessen, John McCarthy and other participants. Thanks also to Albert, Cora and Sylvia for their able research assistance at various stages and to Nel, Mariaane, Kari and most recently Jan Van Olden for administrative help along the way.

Whilst in Jakarta I was particularly grateful for the hospitable and friendly assistance offered to me by the various members of the Indonesian Centre for Environmental Law (ICEL). This assistance included access to the centre's extensive library resources, numerous discussions on various issues and assistance in the practicalities of doing research in Jakarta and beyond. Particularly I would like to acknowledge the support, comments and/or assistance I received at various stages from Mas Achmad Santosa, Wiwiek

Awiati, Asep Warlan Yusuf, Takdir Rahmadi, Indro Sugianto, Siti Megadianty Adam, Ari Mochammed Arif, Hanif and Achmad Soleh.

Whilst researching in Solo I was generously assisted by Adi Nugroho of Gita Pertiwi, and Bapak Mutakin of Lembaga Studi Lingkungan; and I acknowledge the time and assistance provided to me by Goenawan Wibisono, Sri Hardono and various officials of Bapedal Karanganyar. In Semarang I would like to acknowledge the support of the Legal Aid Institute of Semarang, particularly the assistance I was given by Tandiono Bawor Purbaya and Poltak Ike Wibowo in researching the Kayu Lapis Indonesia dispute. In Kudus I was generously assisted by the Indonesian Foundation for Legal Service (YAPHI) whilst researching the Babon River case and in particular acknowledge Bambang, Lala and Yusuf for the assistance they gave me. Whilst in Pekalongan I was most grateful for the assistance and hospitality of Bapak Ismar during my stay there.

As may be at least partially evident from the preceding paragraphs, the research undertaken for this thesis and book involved a considerable amount of travel not only in Indonesia but also between the Netherlands and Australia. I was fortunate not to have to undertake this journey alone, but to have the constant companionship and support of my wife Samali and my children Niluka and (for part of the time at least) Rama. Samali, my heartfelt appreciation for your unwavering support throughout our extended adventure around the world and through all the packing, unpacking, relocating, cultural adjustments and all the other myriad challenges of living far from home in a foreign country. Thanks for being there and sharing the journey with me. Niluka and Rama, it certainly wouldn't have been the same without you along for the ride! Niluka, I remember your ecstatic joy at waking up to fresh snow at Christmas whilst living in Leiden. Rama, how can I forget you bouncing along in an Indonesian *selendang* being fed mango pieces in the tropical heat? Thanks for being your wonderful selves and making it all so much fun.

List of abbreviations

ADR	Alternative dispute resolution
AJA	Administrative Judicature Act
APHI	Assosiasi Pengusaha Hutan Indonesia, Indonesian Forestry Entrepreneurs' Association
BAPPENAS	Badan Perencanaan dan Pembangunan Nasional, the National Development Planning Agency
BATNA	Better alternative to a negotiated agreement
BOD	Biological Oxygen Demand level (of water)
BPPI	Badan Penelitian dan Pengembangan Industri – Industry Research and Development Institute
CELA	Course on Environmental Law and Administration
COD	Chemical Oxygen Demand level (of water)
DPRD	Dewan Perwakilan Rakyat Daerah, Regional Legislative Assembly
EIA	Environmental impact analysis
EMA	Environmental Management Act (Indonesia)
ICEL	Indonesian Centre for Environmental Law
INSELA	Indonesia-Netherlands Study on Environmental Law and Administration
IPTN	PT Industri Pesawat Terbang Nusantara, the company to which funds were transferred from the Indonesian government's State Reafforestation Fund
IPTN case	Another name for the Reafforestation Funds case
KKL	Konsorsium Korban Limbah, Consortium of Waste Victims, an environmental advocacy group comprising members of the Ngringo community and NGO workers in their dispute with PT Palur Raya
KKLB	Kerukunan Korban Limbah Kali Banger, Association of Banger River Waste Victims
KMPL	Kelompok Masyarakat Peduli Lingkungan, farmers' advocacy group, formed from the Mangunharjo and Mangkang Wetan communities against PT KLI
KPPT	Kelompok Pemantau Pencemaran Tyfountex, Tyfountex Pollution Monitoring Group, a community group comprising members of Gumpang village and neighbouring villagess
LBHS	Lembaga Bantuan Hukum Semarang, Semarang Legal Aid Institute

LKMTL	Lembaga Kesejahteraan Masyarakat Tambang dan Lingkungan, Institution for the Welfare of Mining Community and Environment, a Dayak villagers' community organization
LSL	Lembaga Studi Lingkungan, a community and environmental advocacy organization
NGO	Non-government organization
PPIPL	Pusat Pengembangan Informasi dan Penaatan Lingkungan, Environmental Monitoring and Information Centre of the Central Environmental Impact Agency
PT IACI	PT Indo Acidatama Chemical Industry
PT IIU	PT Inti Indorayon Utama, a North Sumatran pulp and paper factory
PT IKPP	PT Indah Kiat Pulp and Paper company
PT IMI	PT Indonesia Miki Industries, a group of industries comprising: PT Sumbertex (textile and plastic rope/nets producer); PT Miki Indo Industri (MSG, noodles, coffee and glucose); and PT Batang Alun (saccharin and cyclamate).
PT IPU	PT Indo Perkasa Usahatama company, land developers
PT KEM	PT Kelian Equatorial Mining, a subsidiary of international mining giant Rio Tinto
PT KLI	PT Kayu Lapis Indonesia, a large wood-processing factory near Semarang, Central Java
PT PIM	PT Pupuk Iskandar Muda, owner of a liquid gas-processing factory in Northern Aceh
PT SDC	PT Semarang Diamond Chemical, a calcium citrate industry located on the Tapak River
PT SSS	PT Sarana Surya Sakti, factory in Surubaya
WALHI	Wahana Lingkungan Hidup Indonesia, Indonesian National Forum for the Environment
YAPHI	Yayasan Pengabdian Hukum Indonesia, Indonesian Foundation for Legal Service
YLBHI	Yayasan Lembaga Bantuan Hukum Indonesia, Indonesian Legal Aid Foundation

Introduction

Environmental disputes in Indonesia

In a world of diminishing resources, exponential population growth and rapid development, environmental disputes are increasingly common phenomena. Indonesia has proven to be no exception to this global trend. Indeed environmental problems and related conflict in Indonesia have frequently assumed international dimensions. Forest fires of unprecedented scale, uncontrolled logging of old growth rainforest and the environmental fallout from some of the world's largest mines are just some of the environmental issues that have held the international spotlight in Indonesia. An even more profuse range of environmental controversies frequents the pages of the Indonesian press, including the dumping of industrial and hazardous waste, the overexploitation of natural resources, illegal logging in national parks, air pollution in overcrowded cities and flooding and landslides caused by deforestation. Within each of these complex environmental issues is a host of interrelated human disputes involving local communities, companies, local, regional and national government agencies, environmental organizations, security forces and many other parties each with their own views, interests and agenda. Such disputes, if left unresolved, can spiral into wider social conflict and exacerbate environmental degradation. In Indonesia, as in many other countries, effective mechanisms for the resolution of environmental disputes are urgently needed. This book, developed from research conducted under the auspices of the Indonesia-Netherlands Study on Environmental Law and Administration (INSELA), endeavours to address this need via a thorough documentation and analysis of the practice of environmental dispute resolution in Indonesia. The main question addressed in this book is thus: to what extent have the formal (legally prescribed) mechanisms for environmental dispute resolution (that is, litigation and mediation) actually been effective in resolving environmental disputes?

Academic context

Research on this topic would appear to fill several significant gaps in the existing academic literature. The majority of environment related academic research to date in Indonesia has been from either an environmental studies, political science or public policy perspective.[1] Whilst there has been one useful overview of environmental regulations in Indonesia (Warren and Elston 1994:74), there have been few studies from a social-legal perspective of environmental law (or dispute resolution) and its implementation.[2] The INSELA project, of which this research formed a part, was intended to address this gap in the current academic literature relating to environmental law and its implementation in Indonesia. In addition, this current volume seeks to add to the growing academic fields of environmental public interest law and environmental dispute resolution. The field of environmental public interest law concerns primarily the increasingly common phenomenon of environmental public interest litigation and the legal framework within which it occurs. Whilst the early literature in this area was largely American based, over the last several decades an increasing number of comparative perspectives have become available from a range of jurisdictions.[3] Nonetheless, there have not been any detailed English language studies of environmental public interest litigation or citizen-initiated enforcement of environmental law in Indonesia. Indonesian language studies of environmental law and its application are, of course, more numerous. Academic studies have provided some useful overviews of laws and associated regulations, but for the most part have not encompassed detailed examination of judicial interpretation of environmental law, nor of the surrounding social-political context and its interaction with legal processes.[4] The bulk of Indonesian language commentary on environmental public interest law and its application has originated from environmental non-government organizations (NGOs) active in the area, principally the Indonesian Centre for Environmental Law (ICEL), the Indonesian Forum for the Environment (WALHI) and the Indonesian Legal Aid Foundation

1 See Aden 1975:987; Adicondro 1998:29-70; Aditjondro and Kowalewski 1994:381-95; Barber 1989:423; Parnwell and Bryant 1996; Cribb 1990:1123-35; Dauvergne 1994:497-518; Dauvergne 1998:13-20; Hardjono 1986:3-13; Hirsch and Warren 1998:325; Lucas 1998:229-61; Lucas and Arief Djati 2000:8; MacAndrews 1994:85-103, 369-80; Potter 1996:9-37.

2 A few exceptions in this respect include Otto 1997:21-62; Mas Achmad Santosa 1990:1-150.

3 A useful and comparative commentary on this area of law is Robinson and Dunkley 1995:342. Other references include: Cassels 1989:495; Chopra 1992:8; Cottrell 1993:102-26; Cranston 1997:233-55; Desai 1993:27-40; Denvir 1976:1133; Kramer 1996:1-18; Lau 1995:49-50; Gomez and Cottrell 1994:237; Harding 1992:231; Peiris 1991:66; Micklitz and Reich 1996:445; Susman 1994:57-103.

4 Leading Indonesian texts on environmental law include: Hamzah 1995:332; Koesnadi Hardjasoemantri 1991, 1993:358; Daud Silalahi 1992:294; Rachmadi Usman 1993:277.

(YLBHI).[5] The work of these organizations has been documented in a diverse array of case notes, practitioner reflections, press releases, newsletters, seminar papers and short articles, much of which has been invaluable in the course of the present study.[6] However, more detailed and comprehensive studies, incorporating theoretical and comparative perspectives, have to date been lacking.

Literature on environmental mediation or alternative dispute resolution also had its roots in the United States, where informal modes of dispute resolution gained popularity as an alternative to litigation in the late 1970s onwards. As in the case for environmental public interest law, the literature has had a strong practitioner focus, although more recently attempts at more detailed theoretical formulations have been made.[7] Whilst the practice of environmental mediation has spread outside Western countries to the developing world, there have been relatively few studies on the application of Western derived approaches to environmental mediation in countries such as Indonesia.[8] Indonesian language commentaries on environmental mediation are limited, but include a useful compilation of case studies sponsored by the Ford Foundation, to which reference is made in the course of Chapter IV (Mas Achmad Santosa, Takdir Rahmadi and Adam 1997:190). To date, however, the available literature has lacked a comparative, theoretically-based study of both litigation and mediation as approaches to environmental dispute resolution, which the present study attempts to remedy.

Methodology

The research methods employed for this study have combined legal and social-scientific approaches. The theoretical discussion of environmental dispute resolution in Chapter I draws upon academic literature in the field of environmental mediation and litigation. Chapter I also includes an overview of environmental disputes in several sectors, which is based upon a compilation of written materials, including Western and Indonesian

5 These studies are referred to in subsequent chapters and generally originate from public interest environmental lawyers such as Mas Achmad Santosa (Indonesian Centre for Environmental Law).

6 Specific sources from the Indonesian Centre for Environmental Law (ICEL) and other NGOs are referred to where relevant in subsequent chapters. ICEL also publishes a useful information bulletin on environmental law and advocacy titled *Hukum dan Advokasi Lingkungan* and until 1999 published an environmental law journal (*Jurnal Hukum Lingkungan*) in Indonesian and English.

7 On this point see O'Leary 1995:17-36 and Blackburn 1990:151-70.

8 The few studies that have been done include: Moore and Mas Achmad Santosa 1995:23-9; Moore 1998:160-95; Takdir Rahmadi 1998:34-6; Mas Achmad Santosa 1996.

academic literature, press clippings and reports by several environmental organizations.[9]

Chapter II provides an overview of environmental litigation in Indonesia, focusing on the legal framework and its interpretation by Indonesian courts. The primary legal sources for this chapter are the various Indonesian environmental laws and regulations discussed and the transcripts of judicial decisions from environmental cases. Copies of judicial transcripts on environmental cases were not always easy to find, due to the absence of a judicial reporting service specific to the area of environmental law. The majority of transcript copies were obtained from legal practitioners or NGOs active in the field of environmental law and advocacy. Where I refer to a judicial decision, I am referring unless otherwise noted to a copy of the judicial transcript from that decision. The discussion in Chapter II covers all civil and administrative environmental cases in Indonesia from 1982-2002 for which I have been able to obtain information. Nonetheless, the lack of reliable judicial reporting systems in Indonesia means that, whilst the chapter is illustrative, it cannot claim to be absolutely comprehensive and inclusive of all relevant environmental cases in this period. The commentary and analysis of judicial interpretation in this chapter is also based upon a range of secondary materials including press clippings, practitioner commentaries and interviews.

The four case-studies of environmental litigation and mediation discussed in Chapters III and V are based on a compilation of written materials and interviews. Written materials were of a diverse nature, including correspondence, press releases, newspaper clippings, case notes, institutional reports, photographs, and minutes of meetings gathered during the course of field visits. Interviews were conducted during several visits to Indonesia in July 1997, October 1999, May 2000 and a more extended period of field research from August 2000 until June 2001. I have also conducted several follow-up interviews in June and November 2003.[10] During these periods of field research I was based in either Jakarta or Yogyakarta and often travelled to other locations throughout Java, particularly Semarang, Kudus and Pekalongan. My fieldwork and empirical research were thus Java-centred and also mainly focused on industry-related disputes, which were the most common in these areas. Interviews were generally semi-structured according to questions I had previously prepared, although usually they were conducted flexibly to allow the conversation to take its own course. Interviews were conducted with a range of actors in the selected case studies and in relation

9 Including the Indonesian Forum for the Environment (WALHI), the Indonesian Centre for Environmental Law and the London based International Campaign for Ecological Justice in Indonesia.

10 Follow-up interviews in November 2003 were conducted by phone from Perth, Australia.

to environmental dispute resolution in general. My primary sources in this respect included local, regional and national environmental organizations involved in environmental disputes or advocacy; representatives from communities who had suffered environmental damage or pollution; legal aid practitioners involved in environmental litigation or mediation; journalists who had researched or written about high-profile environmental disputes; governmental officials from environmental agencies at the national, provincial and district level; legal academics; judges and industry representatives.

Interviews were also a source of information for several of the cases included in the overview of mediation in Chapter IV. The chapter is primarily literature-based however, as it seeks to provide an overview of reported, high profile environmental mediation cases to date in Indonesia. The overview draws upon a diverse literature including published Indonesian language studies of environmental mediation, practitioner commentaries and articles and press reports. This chapter also reflects a Java and industry-related focus, although I have included one mining dispute (the KEM dispute) located in Kalimantan. The bias of the chapter toward Java and industry-related disputes is not a comment on the lack of disputes in other areas or sectors in Indonesia. It is rather a reflection of the focus of my own empirical research, which was Java and industry related, and the focus of the available literature on environmental mediation in Indonesia, upon which I drew in compiling the overview.

Overview of book

As explained above, this research is undertaken within the broader framework of the Indonesia-Netherlands Study on Environmental Law and Administration in Indonesia (INSELA), the aim of which was to analyse environmental law and management in Indonesia from both an empirical and normative perspective and to make recommendations on the basis of that analysis. The central research question addressed by the INSELA project was as follows: What have been the consequences of the enactment and implementation of the 1997 Law on the Environment and its predecessor of 1982 for environmental management in Indonesia, and to what extent may certain legislative and policy measures, notably regarding harmonization of legislation and the decentralization of management, contribute to increased effectiveness and legal certainty in the protection of the environment?

In addressing this broad research agenda, the project was further divided into four sections: Part A focusing on national environmental and sectoral legislation and policy, Part B on decentralization and local management institutions, Part C on environmental law enforcement and dispute settlement, and Part D on diagnosis, comparative research, recommendations and interventions. Whilst this book addresses research questions within all of these parts, our particular focus is on Part C, relating to legal mechanisms for environmental dispute resolution. Specifically, this book examines the legal framework and legally prescribed mechanisms for environmental dispute resolution in Indonesia, namely litigation and mediation. We shall examine the extent to which such mechanisms have been effective in resolving environmental disputes, and the factors (both legal and non-legal) influencing the outcomes of litigation and mediation in environmental disputes. Finally, we shall make recommendations based on our analysis for the further development and improvement of environmental dispute resolution in Indonesia.

Chapter I begins with a discussion of theoretical perspectives on environmental disputes and environmental dispute resolution, particularly litigation and mediation, illustrated in parts with references to the Indonesian context. The discussion of litigation and mediation defines the functions, objectives and necessary conditions of these two approaches to environmental dispute resolution. This theoretical discussion provides an evaluative framework that is referred to in subsequent chapters, particularly the conclusion (Chapter VI).

Chapter II presents a detailed study of environmental litigation in Indonesia, providing an overview of the environmental legal framework relevant to litigation and considering how key provisions have been interpreted and applied by Indonesian courts in environmental cases. The overview covers a twenty-year period, dating from 1982, when the first Environmental Management Act was enacted, to 2002. The chapter seeks to evaluate salient trends in judicial decision-making and the success of private and public interest litigants in obtaining environmental justice in this period.

In Chapter III, our examination of environmental litigation is further developed in a more detailed study of two particular cases; the Banger River dispute, and the Babon River dispute. The two case studies provide more insight into the history of the disputes, efforts to resolve the dispute before commencing litigation, and the actual process of litigation. The case study approach taken in this chapter, and later in Chapter VI, is intended to provide a more empirically grounded, politically contextualized consideration of litigation's role in resolving environmental disputes.

In Chapter IV the focus shifts to environmental mediation, with an overview of the use of mediation in Indonesia to resolve environmental disputes to date. The chapter examines the legal, institutional and cultural framework for mediation in Indonesia and includes an overview and analysis of reported mediation cases, in order to assess relevant trends in the process and outcomes of mediated environmental disputes to date. Again, the overview does not purport to be comprehensive, but rather is a selection of relatively high-profile environmental disputes in which a formal process of mediation was undertaken. The aim of the chapter is to identify common trends, issues, problems and outcomes in applying mediation to environmental disputes in Indonesia.

In Chapter V, a more in-depth examination of mediation is undertaken in two case studies of environmental mediation, the Palur Raya dispute and the Kayu Lapis Indonesia dispute. Each case study provides a detailed description and analysis of the mediation process, considering the different variables influencing the course of mediation with reference to the theoretical framework introduced in Chapter I. In the concluding Chapter VI, we endeavour to synthesize the insights gained from our overview and case-based analysis of environmental litigation and mediation. The chapter evaluates the outcomes of both approaches to environmental dispute resolution and considers the extent to which they have facilitated access to environmental justice in practice. The chapter then provides a concluding analysis of the legal and non-legal variables that have most noticeably influenced the process and outcomes of environmental litigation and mediation, referring to the theoretical framework elaborated in Chapter I. On the basis of this analysis, the chapter also endeavours to make recommendations to improve the effectiveness of environmental dispute resolution in Indonesia.

A note on the currency exchange rate

At the time of writing the book the exchange rate between the US dollar and the Indonesian rupiah was approximately US$ 1: Rp 7,500. At the present time (2009) the exchange rate is approximately US$ 1: Rp 10,000.

CHAPTER I

Environmental dispute resolution
Theoretical and Indonesian perspectives

Environmental disputes

What do we mean when we talk about an 'environmental dispute'? In the literature on mediation and environmental dispute resolution we find a number of different definitions. Christopher Moore defines environmental disputes as 'tensions, disagreements, altercations, debates, competitions, contests, conflicts, or fights over some element of the natural environment' (Moore 1998:160-95). J.W. Blackburn and W.M. Bruce define 'environmental conflict' as arising: 'when one or more parties involved in a decision-making process disagree about an action which has potential to have an impact upon the environment' (Blackburn and Bruce 1995:1-2). Lawrence Susskind refers to environmental disputes as 'disagreements among stakeholders in a range of public disputes which involve environmental quality or natural resource management' (Susskind and Secunda 1998:160-95). Gail Bingham, in her review of a 'decade of experience' in resolving environmental disputes, does not define 'environmental dispute' but categorizes the disputes reviewed into six broad categories: land use, natural resource management and use of public lands, water resources, energy, air quality and toxics, which she further subdivides into 'site-specific' and general policy categories (Bingham 1986:30).

For our purposes we shall limit the scope of both 'environmental' and 'dispute', so as to more clearly define our research focus. At its broadest, 'environmental' is an expansive concept that might connote any element of the natural environment including issues of natural resource management, energy generation, development, and industrialization. Indeed the term 'environmental' may even be understood to extend beyond the natural environment to encompass aspects of the man-made or built environment, as in the case of heritage conservation or 'environment' as it is used in the context of planning law. Our focus will be more specific, in part due to the more specific definition of environmental dispute in the Indonesian Environmental Management Act (EMA) 1997, which limits itself to disputes relating to the incidence or suspected incidence of environmental pollution or damage. For our purposes then, an 'environmental' dispute is a dispute that relates in some way to the incidence, or suspected incidence of environmental pollution or damage of some kind.

What then do we refer to as a 'dispute'? Moore's definition quoted above is a broad one, encompassing conflict of seemingly any nature. In contrast, Henry Brown and Arthur Marriot define a dispute as 'a class or kind of conflict which manifests itself in distinct, justiciable issues' (Brown and Marriott 1999:2). In a similar vein, James Crowfoot and Julia Wondolleck distinguish the specific nature of a 'dispute' from the more general, non-specific nature of 'conflict', which they describe as 'the fundamental and ongoing differences, opposition, and sometimes coercion among major groups in society over their values and behaviours toward the natural environment'. A 'dispute' is not distinct from the conflict process, but rather it is a specific, identifiable part of it, namely a 'specific conflict episode that is part of a continual and larger societal conflict' (Crowfoot and Wondolleck 1990:17-31). Guy Burgess and Heidi Burgess make a similar distinction, characterising environmental conflict as centring on entrenched, long-term differences between opposing groups' underlying values and beliefs on the proper relationship between human society and the natural environment (G. Burgess and H. Burgess 1995:101-20). Examples of environmental conflict include

> The deep ecology/fair use conflict [...] hunters and those favoring biodiversity and 'watchable wildlife'; solitary wilderness trekkers and mountain resort patrons, pro- and antigrowth factions; advocates of a 'small is beautiful', low consumption lifestyle and proponents of a more materialistic 'good life'; and advocates of tight pollution control requirements based upon the belief that human life is priceless and persons wishing to take a hard look at the economics of pollution control (G. Burgess and H. Burgess 1995:101-20).

Environmental conflict, as it is defined here, is largely value-based and group-centred in nature, and thus less susceptible to resolution. By contrast, disputes are characterized more by their specificity, which ultimately renders them more susceptible to adjudication and resolution. W. Felsteiner, R. Abel and A. Sarat (1980:631-54) have characterized the emergence of a dispute as involving three stages: 'naming, blaming and claiming'. 'Naming' involves the identification of a particular experience as injurious. 'Blaming' involves the attribution of that injury to the fault of another individual or social entity, whilst the third stage, 'claiming', occurs when a remedy is claimed from the person or entity believed to be responsible for the injury. Finally, a claim is transformed into a dispute when it is wholly or partly rejected. Thus it is the specific and particularized nature of a dispute, centring upon a particular claim, which make it justiciable and more amenable to resolution via methods such as litigation or mediation.

There is, nonetheless, a close relationship between environmental conflicts and disputes. Broader, value- or interest-based conflicts between groups in society may contribute to a pattern of ongoing disputes that relate to more particular circumstances, claims or policies. Individual disputes may well be susceptible to resolution, however the more general and diffuse process of environmental conflict is likely to continue through subsequent disputes (G. Burgess and H. Burgess 1995:101-20). The scope of this book is limited to environmental disputes and their resolution and does not extend to an investigation of their antecedents or the broader processes of environmental conflict that may underlie them. However, discussion of the broader dynamics between conflicting groups in some cases may influence the dispute resolution process and so may be the subject of commentary in later chapters.

Environmental disputes may be further categorized as either private or public interest. Private interest environmental disputes relate to damage to an individual's or group's property or person, caused as a result of a polluting or environmentally damaging activity in a particular location. In contrast, the central issue of public interest environmental disputes is the impact of environmentally damaging or polluting activities on the 'public interest' in environmental preservation. Where severe, such damage may threaten essential environmental functions integral to the continued functioning of the ecosystem. Preservation of environmental functions is ultimately necessary for human survival and, in Indonesia, the 'public interest' in such preservation is recognized by article 4 of the EMA 1997, which states the 'preservation of environmental functions' to be one of the 'targets of environmental management'.[1] In a public interest environmental dispute, the claimant's primary objective is protection of this public interest in environmental preservation. The respondents in environmental public interest disputes frequently include government agencies responsible for environmental protection, and may also include private industries. Environmental public interest disputes may also be site specific or may concern more general issues of policy.[2]

In practice, private and public interest claims may overlap and be pursued within a single dispute (Robinson 1995a:294-326). For instance, victims of environmental pollution themselves may not only pursue compensation of

1 Article 1(5) defines 'preservation of environmental functions' as 'a set of efforts to maintain the continued supportive and carrying capacities of the environment'.

2 See for instance the Reafforestation case (Chapter II) which concerned the transfer of monies from a Reafforestation Fund to an aircraft manufacturing company.

personal damage, but also may advocate restoration of their local environment of which they are a particle. Nonetheless, the two objectives and their respective remedies remain distinct in character. In any case, the predominant character of an environmental claim as public or private can usually be determined according to the identity of the claimant. Where the claimant is an individual or group that has suffered direct, personal loss because of environmental pollution or damage then the claim may be considered predominantly private interest in character. Where the claimant is an organization purporting to represent the public interest in environmental preservation then the claim is predominantly public interest in character. Separation of private and public interest objectives in environmental disputes will assist us at a later stage in assessing the effectiveness of the respective dispute resolution processes in meeting those respective objectives.

Approaches to dispute resolution

A commonly adopted categorization in mediation literature divides approaches to processing and resolving disputes into three broad categories: power-based, rights-based and interest-based (Boulle 1996:350; Fisher and Ury 1991:200; Ury, Brett and Goldberg 1986:3-10). In a power-based approach, the disputing parties resolve their conflict through a contest of strength, which may encompass tactics such as lobbying, use of political influence, demonstrations, industrial action or physical force. Power-based approaches would also encompass criminal or administrative enforcement of law or sanctions through the state apparatus, a process which rests on the power of the state.[3] When a power-based approach is taken, the most powerful party typically wins. In a rights-based approach the dispute is adjudicated by an authoritative institution or individual such as an administrator, court, tribunal or arbitrator. The outcome of the dispute is determined according to the law, written policy or societal norms upon which the adjudicating body bases its decision. Litigation, like arbitration or a process of tribunal review, is a rights-based approach to dispute resolution. Finally, in an interest-based approach, such as mediation or negotiation, the conflicting parties negotiate, with or without third party assistance, in order to reach a voluntary settlement amenable to both parties' interests. The outcome is determined by the respective interests of the parties and their willingness to compromize in order to resolve the dispute at hand.

3 Although criminal and administrative enforcement would more correctly be understood as a combination of power-based and rights-based approaches, as it is not a case of arbitrary power (although sometimes this may be the case), but rather state power exercised according to certain rules.

The three approaches to dispute resolution described above are roughly comparable to Donald Black's three styles of 'social control', which may also be understood as approaches to conflict management.[4] The 'penal' style is a state initiated process of punishing or penalising offenders in some manner for acts considered blameworthy or morally repugnant. A penal approach is often taken in situations where the relational or social distance between victim and offender, or between offender and state, is large.[5] A penal approach to conflict management and/or social control could generally be equated with or at least encompassed within the category of 'power-based' approaches discussed above. The 'compensatory' style is a victim initiated process where a victim claims payment of compensation by a violator. This style is focused more on the proper redress of harm rather than the punishment of wrongdoing. A compensatory style is more commonly used where the relational distance is of an intermediate nature.[6] A compensatory style may be equated for our purposes with a rights-based approach to dispute resolution through litigation, where harm is redressed according to an established set of legal principles. The 'conciliatory' style involves a third party to the dispute who helps the disputing parties negotiate a mutually acceptable resolution to the dispute; a style comparable to the interest-based approach to dispute resolution described above. As the conciliatory style is consensual and not coercive, it is most effective where the relational distance between the disputants is close, involving multiple and lasting ties. Where these ties are disrupted then both parties will possess sufficient incentive to seek resolution of the conflict.[7]

This book focusses on the latter two styles, compensatory and conciliatory, equating with rights-based and interest-based approaches to dispute resolution, which for our purposes refers to the processes of litigation and media-

4 Bedner and Van Rooij 2001:1. See also the seminal work Black 1976:40-7, and an elaboration of Black's theory in Horwitz 1990:312.

5 Black describes relational distance as the degree to which people participate in one another's lives. The closest relationships involve total interpenetration, the most distant none at all. Relational distance may be measured by, for instance, the scope, frequency and length of interaction between people, the age of their relationship, and the nature and number of links between them in a social network. Relational distance is a variable affecting both the quantity of law used in a social setting and the style of social control: Black 1976:40-7.

6 Yet Black still equates a compensatory style with a penal style in that both are accusatory, having a complainant and a defendant and ultimately a winner and a loser. Whereas a conciliatory style is remedial in nature, focusing on restoring social harmony and repairing social bonds: Black 1976:40-7.

7 However, whilst Black makes a link between a conciliatory style and close relational distance, it should be noted that mediation and conciliatory forms of dispute resolution have been applied with success to a range of modern environmental disputes (see further discussion of this below) where there is often considerable relational distance between the disputants.

tion as applied to environmental disputes. Penal styles of social control, such as the prosecution of criminal offences or enforcement of administrative sanction, and power-based or political modes of conflict resolution are not directly in the scope of this study. Nonetheless, we shall not discount such modes of social control and dispute resolution as they may have an important, albeit indirect effect, on the commencement, process and outcome of litigation and mediation. Indeed, as we shall see in subsequent chapters, environmental disputants may pursue each approach at different stages or a combination of approaches in any one dispute. In the course of a single environmental dispute, parties might first seek to consolidate their power bases and resolve the matter in their favour through a political contest. If a stalemate is reached, negotiation or mediation could be attempted, which if unsuccessful might result in a final stage of litigation to resolve the dispute. Alternatively, the interaction of these different approaches may be contemporaneous, as in the case where the dynamics of a 'power-based' struggle influence the process and outcome of a rights-based/compensatory or interest-based/conciliatory approach to dispute resolution.

The interaction of these different approaches to dispute resolution will be explored in more detail in later chapters. For now, our focus turns to our main subject, the processes of litigation and mediation. In this section we undertake a theoretical overview of litigation and mediation, considering the objectives, functions and necessary conditions for these different approaches to dispute resolution. We also attempt to define an evaluative framework to be applied in later chapters when we shall consider the effectiveness of litigation and mediation in resolving environmental disputes in Indonesia.

Environmental litigation

Definition of environmental litigation

Environmental litigation may be defined for our purposes as an environmental dispute (see definition above), which has resulted in one or more parties commencing legal proceedings in a civil or administrative court.[8] With the globalization of modern environmental law, facilitated by international agreements such as the Stockholm and Rio Declarations, environmental litigation has become increasingly common in a range of jurisdictions. Legislative provisions defining environmental rights, and stipulating grounds for environ-

8 Criminal proceedings, which are initiated and conducted by the state prosecutorial agency, are thus excluded from the scope of the present research.

mental damage compensation, environmental restoration, and legal standing for environmental organizations, are now found in a diverse range of Western and developing countries.[9]

Objective of litigation 1: dispute resolution

From a claimant's perspective a primary function of environmental, or for that matter other types of litigation, is dispute resolution. Indeed dispute resolution, and dispute processing, has been generally regarded by social-legal scholars as a distinguishing and central function of courts across different societal contexts.[10] Disputes are resolved, or more accurately determined, by the court's authoritative application of state law to the particular circumstances of a case, which provides a final determination of the rights, remedies and relationship of disputing parties. 'Resolution' of a dispute, in the judicial sense, is thus focused on application of the law rather than reconciliation of the concerns, interests or longer term relationship of the disputing parties, a fact that has led some scholars to question the suitability of courts for dispute resolution (Cotterrell 1992:222). Nonetheless, research has tended to vindicate the value of courts as dispute resolution institutions, and indeed an authoritative application of law may be a particularly suitable approach to resolving a dispute where the parties' interests are irreconcilable through more 'consensual' approaches to dispute resolution such as mediation (Cotterrell 1992:222).

Objective of litigation 2: law enforcement

What is apparent from this discussion is that courts as an institution and the process of litigation therein serve a dual function: resolving conflict between individual disputants on the one hand but on the other hand applying and enforcing legal norms. It is well recognized that the consistent application of legal norms by courts plays an important role in maintaining social order, legal certainty and the legitimacy of a regime (Shapiro 1981:17). Martin Shapiro, for instance, has argued persuasively that the conflict resolution function of courts must be seen as interdependent with their social control and law-making functions (Shapiro 1981:1-10). Courts may thus play an important role in not only resolving disputes but also in applying or enforc-

9 Public interest environmental law and litigation in a wide range of countries including the US, UK, Australia, South Africa, India and the European Union are discussed in: Robinson and Dunkley 1995:342. For an interesting collection of articles on environmental litigation in countries including the UK, US, Canada, Ukraine, Georgia, Denmark, Australia, France and Italy see also: Deimann and Dyssli 1995:343.

10 Walker (1980:301) states 'the function of the court is to decide disputes'. See also the comparative model of a court in Becker 1970:26.

ing law. This 'enforcement' role of the courts may provide a useful adjunct to administrative law enforcement, particularly in the environmental field. There are a number of reasons justifying such a 'dual approach' to enforcement, perhaps the foremost amongst which is the frequent failure of government agencies to effectively enforce environmental law. Enforcement failure may occur for a number of reasons, including a lack of resources or political will. Furthermore, from a purely practical perspective, private citizens, who may initiate suits for environmental enforcement, are more likely to be directly affected by pollution and thus better situated to detect potential violations of environmental law. In this respect, citizens have been described as 'omnipresent, motivated and uniquely interested in environmental quality' and thus 'one of a nation's greatest resources for enforcing environmental laws and regulations' (Roberts and Dobbins 1992:531).

Objective of litigation 3: environmental justice

As discussed, the general objective of litigation (and the courts), from a state perspective, is dispute resolution through the authoritative application of state law. This principle is general enough to apply to any particular area of law. For our purposes, however, we must consider the more specific and substantive objective of environmental litigation, especially when viewed from the perspective of the environmental litigant who seeks redress for or amelioration of environmental damage or pollution. The broad objective of litigation in this respect may be termed 'environmental justice', defined as the objective and accurate application of procedural and substantive environmental law through which an environmental litigant may enforce environmental rights and/or achieve redress for environmental damage or pollution. For our purposes the specific defining parameters and criteria of environmental justice are defined by the surrounding legal framework, which will be discussed in more detail in Chapter II. Environmental justice is thus defined in a narrower legal sense in the present context, when compared to its wider usage in numerous international instruments and agreements such as the Rio Declaration and Agenda 21, where it is used in a more general (and trans-jurisdictional) sense in recognition of ecological interdependence and the need for environmental sustainability (Robinson 1998:349).

From a private litigant's perspective, environmental justice implies the vindication of key individual rights such as the right to a 'good and healthy environment', as guaranteed by article 5 of Indonesia's Environmental Management Act 1987, or the right to adequate compensation and restoration where environmental damage or pollution has occurred. Other rights may be more procedurally defined, such as the right to access accurate environmental management or the right to participate in environmental management. In this manner, the judicial process plays a crucial role in 'making rights effective' and facilitating access to justice through bridging the gap between formal legal rights and the actual inability of many people to recognize such rights and realize them satisfactorily (Cappelletti and Garth 1978:6-10). Litigation may thus provide a concrete link between formal environmental rights and entitlements and actual social realities. Such a link is especially important given the growing interconnection between environmental principles and human rights in both theory and practice.[11] It is increasingly common to find environmental principles couched in terms of 'rights', such as the right to a pollution-free or healthy environment. Whilst a rights approach to environmental matters is not without its drawbacks, it also has great potential for facilitating environmental protection (Anderson 1996:21).

From a public interest perspective, environmental justice also may imply protection of the public interest in environmental sustainability. The specific manner in which this public interest is realized in practice will again depend on the specific features of the prevailing legal framework. Environmental justice from a public interest perspective, for instance, might encompass compliance with regulatory standards on the discharge of industrial waste, rehabilitation or restoration of areas where environmental damage or pollution had occurred, or the prevention of potential environmental harm through mechanisms such as environmental impact assessment. In the wider political context, environmental litigation may also act as a 'catalyst' for policy or political change on particular issues and thus facilitate environmental justice in a broader extra-legal sense.[12] The primary focus in this book, however, is the realization of environmental justice through effective enforcement of the laws designed to protect the public interest in environmental sustainability.

Environmental litigation; Evaluative criteria

Our discussion above has highlighted several salient aspects of environmental litigation, which will be relevant to our analysis in subsequent chapters. As we have seen, dispute resolution is achieved through litigation by the objective and impartial application of state law. The court's decision provides

11 For a discussion of the indivisibility of environmental and human rights, see Simpson and Jackson 1997:268-81.

12 Nonetheless, some writers have questioned the political or social 'value' of public interest litigation. For example, Hutchinson and Monahan refer to the desegregation cases in America, which, they claim, had little or no impact on social practices of segregation: Hutchinson and Monahan 1987:167. Furthermore, some critics have argued that pursuing such a process is actually counterproductive, as it has the effect of legalising political issues and removing such issues out of the public domain into the rarefied and elitist world of legal 'experts'. It may thus be a moot point whether public interest litigation exposes or 'simply paper[s] over the abyss, which separates formal legal promises from [...] social reality'. See Cassels 1989:495.

an authoritative determination of the rights and remedies of the disputing parties. From an environmental claimant's perspective, litigation provides an important mechanism to enforce rights, such as the right to a healthy environment, redress damage done and resolve disputes. From an environmental public interest perspective, litigation is another important mechanism through which the public interest in environmental sustainability may be protected. From these functions of environmental litigation, we may distil several relevant criteria, in the form of questions, which will be used to assess and evaluate environmental litigation in subsequent chapters:

1 To what extent have environmental claimants had access to the legal process to enforce environmental rights and obtain justice in environmental matters?
2 To what extent has litigation enabled private litigants to achieve environmental justice in practice, including the enforcement of environmental rights and the compensation of environmentally related damage?
3 To what extent has litigation facilitated protection of the public interest in environmental preservation through the application of relevant environmental legal provisions?
4 To what extent has environmental law been applied in an objective, impartial and accurate manner by courts?

Conditions for environmental litigation

In the previous section we considered the objectives of environmental litigation, from both a state and a claimant or disputant's perspective, and endeavoured to distil from these objectives a number of evaluative criteria to apply to our consideration of environmental litigation in subsequent chapters. A review of the literature relating to environmental litigation, and litigation more generally, indicates that the manner and extent to which environmental law is applied through the process of litigation and the extent to which environmental litigation is likely to fulfil the objectives discussed above, is contingent upon a complex range of legal, political, social and economic conditions, which are discussed in some detail below.[13] This section is intended to provide a theoretical starting point for the consideration in later chapters of the legal and non-legal factors that influence the outcome and effectiveness of environmental litigation in Indonesia.

13 This section draws upon the discussion of conditions for effective environmental public interest law in Robinson 1995a:294-326.

Condition 1: procedural access to justice

The term 'access to justice' was popularized in the late 1970s by, amongst other things, the seminal Florence Access to Justice Project, which undertook an extensive comparative study of access to justice in 23 nations. According to Mauro Cappelletti, the editor of the study, 'access to justice' encompassed a number of elements including procedural representation for 'diffuse' interests, such as environmental protection. Procedural representation of environmental interests was a problem in many jurisdictions, because traditional standing rules only recognized interests of a private, personal nature. A person could thus only initiate a legal action if his or her personal interests had been directly compromised by the action in question. Environmental issues, being matters of public interest, fell outside the scope of such 'private' interests and thus remained unrepresented within the legal system.

Reformation of traditional 'standing' rules to facilitate representation of environmental interests became the subject of considerable academic debate following Donald Stone's influential treatise entitled *Should trees have standing?* (Stone 1974:102). Whilst the notion of environmental standing has on occasion been criticized by some jurists as ambiguous, unrealistic and potentially wasteful or counterproductive (Bowden 1995; Kramer 1996:1-18), broader rights of standing 'caught on' in the context of a growing global environmental movement and have now been established in a diverse range of jurisdictions.

In the United States, for instance, citizen suit provisions in both federal and state law have enabled a considerable number of environmental organizations to utilize the courts for the protection of environmental interests (Robbins 1995:5-37). In Australia, judicial precedent provided some limited scope for 'special interest' litigants, although the grounds for environmental public interest suits have now been more significantly expanded by legislative reform at the federal and state level.[14] Within the European Union, environmental organizations, and in some cases private citizens, already enjoy access to the courts in environmentally related proceedings in a number of member states.[15] Following the Aarhus Convention on Access to Information, Public Participation in Decision-Making and Access to Justice in Environmental Matters, which was signed by the European Union in 1998, the Union is currently considering a proposed directive on Access to Justice in Environmental Matters, which would facilitate access of citizens and organizations to environmental proceedings.[16]

14 In New South Wales, for instance, 'any person' has the right to apply to the land and environment court to remedy a breach of the Environmental Planning and Assessment Act 1979. See discussion in Barker 1996:186-208.

15 See the detailed discussion of the law in individual member states in Fuhr et al. 1995:77.

16 Directives on Access to Information and Public Participation in Decision-Making in

India is another notable example of a country where traditional standing rules were radically reformed, in this instance by the Supreme Court in the early 1980s, a move that greatly facilitated public interest litigation in a number of spheres including environmental (Du Bois 1995:144-6). The broadening of standing provisions has also facilitated environmental public interest litigation in a number of other developing countries including Sri Lanka, Brazil and the Philippines.[17] In some cases reform of traditional standing rules has been a result of judicial activism, whilst in other cases reform has been legislative in nature. It is thus apparent that procedural access to the courts for environmental litigants, based on broadly defined rights of standing, is a basic or threshold condition for successful environmental public interest litigation.[18]

In certain circumstances procedural access may also be an issue for private litigants, who have suffered personal loss as a result of environmental pollution or damage. It is not uncommon in the environmental context for environmentally harmful activities to negatively affect hundreds or even thousands of people. In such a situation, the practicalities and expense of each individual victim bringing a separate legal action may be prohibitive and certainly inefficient. As a result of situations such as these, a number of jurisdictions have reformed procedural law to permit class or representative actions, through which 'classes' or groups of people suffering loss of a similar nature may be represented in a single legal suit.[19] Provision for representative actions in the environmental context is also thus an important condition for effective environmental litigation (Cappelleti and Garth 1978:3-124).

Condition 2: 'strong' environmental law

In addition to flexible rules on environmental standing, the broader, substantive legal framework should ideally be rule oriented, giving expression to environmental principles in specific, enforceable procedures, rules or objectives. Legislation of this nature has been termed 'strong' environmental law (Robinson 1995b:40-69). This has generally the case in the United States, where civil environmental suits have often resulted in the enforcement of environ-

---

Environmental Matters have already been issued.

17 In Sri Lanka the Environmental Foundation Limited, a non-profit environmental organization, has been successful in utilising rights of environmental standing to try and compel state agencies to carry out statutory functions relating to environmental protection. In Brazil environmental organizations can undertake civil public action suits pursuant to federal law to protect environmental interests. See Fernandes 1995:118.

18 Robinson makes this point in his analysis of conditions for successful environmental public interest law. See Robinson 1995a:294-326.

19 For a historical account of the political-legal evolution of the modern class action, see Yeazell 1987:306.

mental regulation through judicial decision. Where, however, environmental legislation is non-specific, vague and creates a wide scope for administrative discretion, then enforcement through the courts will be much more difficult. This has largely been the case in the UK, where the wide discretion accorded to enforcement agencies by environmental legislation in the UK has been cited as one factor contributing to the weak state of environmental public interest law in that country (Robinson 1995a:294-326).

Condition 3: institutional resources

The first wave of 'access to justice' reforms in the 1970s focused on providing legal aid to those unable to afford legal services. Such reforms were undertaken because the high cost of legal services was perceived to be one of the greatest obstacles to access to justice in many countries (Cappelletti and Garth 1978:6-10). For example, even where a satisfactory legal framework is in place, potential litigants may only initiate public interest suits where they possess the necessary institutional and financial resources, which are lacking more often than not in the majority of countries. Legal aid programs in Western countries such as Australia and the UK are usually directed towards areas of private law, and any support for environmental public interest suits has been the exception rather than the rule. Not surprisingly, governments have been generally reluctant to fund such legal actions, given they are often directed against their own regulatory agencies (Robinson 1995a:294-326). In the United States environmental public interest law firms have been funded largely by membership organizations including the Conservation Law Firm, the Environmental Defense Fund, the Sierra Club Legal Defense Fund and the Natural Resources Defense Council. Most of these membership-based organizations started out as fledgling volunteer groups, but by the 1990s had evolved into influential national organizations with considerable membership bases and organizational incomes.[20] In developing countries, the necessary political and economic conditions for such organizations generally do not exist, yet in many instances environmental public interest groups in such countries have been able to obtain funding from foreign aid agencies, in addition to using volunteer assistance.

The issue of institutional resources is also relevant to the ability of the judiciary to perform the functions discussed above. In the institution build-

20 For example, in 1992 the National Resources Defense Council had an income of US$18 million and a membership base of 170,000. A significant role has also been played by smaller public interest law firms, including environmental law 'clinics' associated with universities which research and run public interest cases as part of students training. In addition to income derived from membership dues and donations, such organizations have also benefited from special rules as to legal fees for public interest litigants; see Robinson 1995b:40-69.

ing model developed by Esman and Blase and applied by Jan Otto to judicial institutions, the internal resources of an institution are a significant determinant of its ability to perform its respective tasks and functions (Otto 1991:10). Whilst judicial institutions are typically well-resourced, or at least sufficiently resourced in developed countries, this is certainly not always the case in developing countries such as Indonesia. Both Sebastiaan Pompe's study of the Supreme Court and Adriaan Bedner's study of the administrative courts in Indonesia have demonstrated how a lack of financial, human and organizational resources has contributed to serious problems with the quality of judicial administration in Indonesia (Bedner 2000; Pompe 1996).

A lack of institutional human and financial resources may also be an obstacle to the continuing education of judges. This is an issue of particular importance in the area of environmental law, which remains a relatively new area of law, containing numerous legal principles (such as environmental standing or strict liability) that may even contradict traditional legal doctrine. Effective interpretation and application of modern environmental law requires a judiciary that is adequately educated and informed about the laws and the principles underlying them before their promulgation. For this end to be achieved it is necessary that sufficient resources be applied to implementation of continuing education of judges and other legal officers in environmental law.

Condition 4: legal and environmental activism

In his commentary and analysis on environmental public interest law, David Robinson also identifies 'alliances of reformist lawyers with legally informed activists' as an important precondition to the further development of environmental public interest law (Robinson 1995b:40-69). In this respect Robinson suggests that environmental lawyers need to take a broader approach beyond mere client representation and technical compliance with the letter of the law. Rather, environmental lawyers should seek to represent the environmental public interest, and to this end play a direct role in opinion-shaping and lobbying toward the further and substantive improvement of environmental law.

Condition 5: judicial independence and impartiality

For courts to apply the law and resolve disputes effectively and authoritatively, a basic condition is that the court be impartial and independent in the dispute before it. Becker identified this ideal of judicial impartiality and independence as a defining characteristic of the judicial process across different societies (Becker 1970:26). Without impartiality or independence the legitimacy of the court as an adjudicating institution is undermined, as one or other of the disputing parties may perceive themselves to be disadvantaged.

On a broader societal level, the consistent and objective application of state law by courts is essential to the creation of 'real legal certainty', which Otto has described as a 'systemic' objective of law (Otto 2002:23-34).

How is judicial independence defined? The comparative legal scholar Theodore L. Becker (1970:26) offered the following definition.

> Judicial independence is a. the degree to which judges believe they can decide and do decide consistent with their own personal attitudes, values, and conceptions of judicial role (in their interpretation of the law), b. in opposition to what others, who have or are believed to have political or judicial power, think about or desire in like matters, and c. particularly when a decision adverse to the beliefs or desires of those with political or judicial power may bring some retribution on the judges personally or on the power of the court.

As this definition illustrates, judicial independence implies that judges adjudicate the cases before them without any intimidation, control or influence from the executive branch of government. Freedom from executive influence is also central to transnational standards such as the International Bar Association (IBA) Code of Minimum Standards of Judicial Independence. Article A.2 of the Code states: 'The judiciary as a whole should enjoy autonomy and collective independence vis-a-vis the Executive'. Article A.5 reiterates this point stating: 'The Executive shall not have control over judicial functions'. Accordingly, individual judges should enjoy 'personal independence and substantive independence' (Article A.1) in that the terms and conditions of judicial service are adequately secured, to ensure judges are not subject to executive control and that 'in the discharge of his judicial function, a judge is subject to nothing but the law and the commands of his conscience'.[21]

A related concept is that of judicial impartiality, which requires that the judge not have any bias, personal interest or stake in the dispute before her. Article G.45 of the IBA Code addresses this issue, stating: 'A judge shall not sit in a case where there is a reasonable suspicion of bias or potential bias'. Similarly, article G.46 states: 'A judge shall avoid any course of conduct which might give rise to an appearance of partiality'.

Where judicial impartiality or independence is lacking then the litigation process will not provide access to 'justice' in any meaningful sense of the word, as the decision may be the result of either external influence or personal interest rather than an independent exercise of judgment.

21 See International Bar Association Code of Minimum Standards of Judicial Independence: Shetreet and Deschênes 1985:388-92.

Condition 6: political character of the judiciary
The basic concept of judicial independence as explained above should not be confused with the traditional, juristic conception of judicial decision-making as a purely value-neutral and deductive process by which general legal principles are applied to specific factual situations. This latter notion has come under considerable and legitimate academic criticism from a number of quarters. For instance, the influential Australian academic professor Julius Stone was an early critic of traditional juridical explanations of legal reasoning. His analysis of precedent and judicial decision-making argued that legal doctrine and logic did not in themselves compel particular decisions in appellate cases, but rather provided so-called 'illusory categories of reference', which justified decisions ultimately based on a policy choice (Stone 1974:102). Other critics of traditional, 'objective' notions of judicial decision making have argued that it is the personal attitudes and values of judges, not legal principles, that are a primary, or at least a significant, factor influencing judicial decision-making. Critics such as J.A.G. Griffith have thus sought to debunk the 'traditional view' that depicts the judge as a kind of 'political, economic and social eunuch, [with] no interest in the world outside his court' (Griffith 1985:193-8). Griffith's analysis of the English appeal courts highlighted how English judges were guided by a particular, homogenous view of the 'public interest' rooted in their professional training and socio-economic background (Griffith 1985:193-8). In America, judicial behaviouralists, such as Glendon Schubert, endeavoured to quantitatively analyse the correlation between empirically ascertainable elements of a judge's background, including age, sex, race, social-economic class, attitudes and values, with actual pattern of judicial decision-making (Schubert 1975:347). Other critics, however, have criticized the 'psychologising' of judicial behaviouralism as both over-simplistic and unconvincing, in part due to the looseness of the concept of 'attitude', which theorists have sought to correlate with judicial behaviour (Cotterrell 1992:219; Tomasic 1985:81).

Despite the critics, behaviouralism, like legal realism before it, has at least succeeded in questioning traditional notions of judicial 'neutrality' and re-contextualising understandings of the judicial process within its political and social context. In this vein, Griffith challenged the notion of the judiciary as a 'check and balance' on government power, instead arguing that judicial opposition to the government (in Britain) was 'an aberration' and that the judiciary was synonomous with 'established authority' and was thus 'necessarily conservative and illiberal' (Griffith 1985:223). Other theorists have also recognized the important role of the judiciary in preserving the status quo. For instance, in Shapiro's comparative, functionalist analysis of courts he argues that courts, in addition to their dispute processing function, serve as a 'social controller' and an extension of the administration and in doing so play an important part in the maintenance of political regimes (Tate 1987:1-28).

Nonetheless, oversimplified 'elitist' accounts of judicial power do not serve to explain examples of liberal judicial activism, including judicial review of state decisions and the promotion of minority rights. According to Roger Cotterrell, such contrasting judicial functions reflect the contrasting values of order and justice, both of which are the foundation of law's legitimacy (Cotterrell 1992:235). Whilst the judiciary helps maintain the stability of the social and political order by providing legal frameworks and legal legitimacy for government and government acts, it also strives to preserve the integrity of the legal order itself. This is achieved by both upholding professional standards of doctrinal rationalization and judicial impartiality, and meeting the wider demands of justice, part of which relates to the effective administration of the 'dispute resolution' function of courts (Cotterrell 1992:234). Clearly how the demands of 'order' and 'justice' will be interpreted will vary widely amongst individual judges, let alone amongst the varying social-legal contexts of different jurisdictions.

What these various theoretical perspectives do illustrate is the considerable discretion exercised by any judge who applies or interprets a legal framework. The bare fact that an exercise of judicial judgment is free from executive interference or personal interest (as judicial independence would require) does not inform us as to what other, legitimate, forms of influence have bearing upon the judicial judgment. Judicial discretion may be influenced by a range of factors highlighted in the literature, ranging from personally held values or notions of the 'public interest', to wider, indirect pressures of an institutional, social or political nature. As the influential social-legal scholar Donald Black observed, legal doctrine alone cannot adequately predict or explain how cases are handled (Black 1989:6). Judicial decision-making thus can not be comprehended solely as the logical extrapolation of legal principles, but must be understood and analysed within the broader social-legal context within which it occurs.

Therefore, although legal rhetoric depicts litigation as a purely objective process determined by the letter of the law itself, in reality the subjective interpretation of the judge plays a large role. As discussed above, the values and political views of judges have been recognized as an important influence on the manner in which they interpret and apply legislation (Cotterrell 1992:230-4). In this respect, a more rigorous approach to environmental law enforcement is likely to be taken where judges value environmental sustainability as a matter of public interest comparable with economic growth or national security. Such an approach was taken by US courts in the 1970s, when 'activist judges interpreted provisions of the National Environmental Policy Act in order to require rigorous environmental assessment' (Robinson 1995a:294-326). An activist judiciary, moreover, is prepared to go beyond the adjudication of individual, legal conflicts and address more far-reaching issues of social or political policy (Holland 1991:1-55). However, where judges regard environmentalism as merely a 'partisan' cause, or where they are unwilling to stray into the realm of judicial law or policy making, then they may be more reluctant to adopt a rigorous approach to the interpretation of environmental law. In the United Kingdom, for instance, judges have for the most part shunned the activist mantle, stressing the liberal, individualist view that judges should remain independent of supposedly 'partisan' interests (Robinson 1995a:294-326).

In this respect, Robinson has distinguished between communitarian and Diceyan, individualist attitudes to environmental public interest law (Robinson 1995a:294-326). A communitarian attitude sanctions environmental public interest actions, regarding them as a legitimate means of political participation and a check or balance to the authority of parliaments and bureaucrats. Such a view supports a more radical, political role for the judiciary. In contrast, a Diceyan, liberal attitude, such as that adopted by the judicial majority in the UK, sees the role of the court in a solely legalistic light – as an independent, neutral arbiter of disputes and means for impartial application of the law (Robinson 1995a:294-326). Such a view allows little scope for a judiciary seeking to respond in a creative legal fashion to society's values with regard to the environment.

The political character of a judiciary, and the extent to which it is prepared to be activist, is a function of a number of political and intellectual conditions. Activist judiciaries are more common in federal polities, such as the United States, Canada, Australia and India, where parliamentary and executive power is more diffused (Holland 1991:1-55). The absence of a career judiciary has also been identified as a factor contributing to more activist judiciaries in common law countries such as the United States and Australia, although this has not been the case in England (Holland 1991:1-55). Judicial independence is a necessary precondition for judicial activism, although in itself it will not necessitate an activist judiciary (Holland 1991:1-55). In the United Kingdom, for instance, appellate courts have displayed little tendency toward activism despite a long history of judicial independence. The available scope for judicial activism will also depend upon the predominant political and legal doctrines. Generally the scope for judicial law making in the common law tradition appears greater than in the civil law tradition (Holland 1991:1-55).

Condition 7: effective implementation

Legal certainty and effective environmental litigation require not only an independent and impartial application of law but also actual implementation of the eventual decision made by the court (Otto 2002:23-34). Without an effective process of implementation, legal certainty and the integrity of the judicial process are undermined. The efficacy of the implementation process depends, once again, on the integrity of the government officials charged with the task and the adequacy of the resources at their disposal.

Condition 8: societal context

According to the institution building model, applied by Otto to judicial institutions, the ability of an institution to perform certain tasks depends upon a number of factors, namely a) institutional factors (such as internal structure, resources and leadership), b) linkages with the target group (access of disputants to court), and c) the wider social, economic and political context or 'environment' (Otto 1991:10). In a separate study, Otto elaborated on the nature of contextual 'countervailing forces', which may undermine legal certainty, as encompassing cultural mores, political power structures, economic interests and the capacity of state institutions (Otto 2002:23-34). Ideally, cultural mores or values should support both compliance with state laws and an awareness of legal rights and a willingness to enforce them. From a political perspective the rule of law should not only be embraced ideologically but be reflected in the structural separation of legislative, executive and judicial functions in government. The economic interests of key groups in society should also support legal certainty and a functioning legal system. Finally, key institutions within the legal system should have sufficient resources and linkages to their target group and wider environment so as to function effectively (Otto 2002:23-34).

Kanishka Jayasuriya has also argued that our understanding of the rule of law and legal institutions needs to be grounded in the specific political-economic context within which they are located (Kanishka Jayasuriya 1999:173-204). In East Asia, Jayasuriya argues, law and legal institutions have been utilized to consolidate state power rather than limit it, in contrast to the historical development of law and judicial power in Western liberal democracies, where they became a check or balance to legislative and executive power.[22] In this sense, East Asian countries have experienced 'rule by law', rather than 'rule of law'. Jayasuriya describes the relationship between judicial and executive arms of government as 'corporatist', based upon close consultation and collaboration and exercised within a broader ideological concept of an 'integral' state. This is in contrast with the relationship between judiciary and executive in Western liberal democracies, which is based on a very different liberal conception of the state and the separation of powers doctrine. In each case, the development and role of legal institutions have been influenced

22 Although authors such as Griffith (1985) or Shapiro (1981)would tend to suggest that even in Western liberal democracies, law has been strongly oriented toward the consolidation and strengthening of state power and the maintenance of social control.

by very different political and economic contexts. In East Asia, Jayasuriya argues, the presence of a regulated economy, strong state structures and a managed civil society has tended to engender legal institutions which reflect and seek to implement state objectives. On this basis he argues that Western notions of 'rule of law' have only limited application or relevance in the East Asian context.

In this respect, Jayasuriya's argument is similar to earlier arguments by social-legal scholars such as Trubek and Galanter, who questioned the 'ethnocentric and naive' application of the liberal rule of law model, which they labelled 'liberal legalism', to the developing world (Tamanaha 1995:470-3). Whilst the arguments of Trubek and Galanter helped stymie the growth of law and development studies in the Western world, the practical work of legal institution building continued apace in the developing world notwithstanding such 'ecletic' critique (Tamanaha 1995:470-3). In support of such efforts, Brian Tamanaha has persuasively argued the case for a more 'constructive' approach to legal institution building in developing countries. As Tamanaha points out, the gap between the liberal legal model and the reality in Third World countries was well-known and acknowledged even by those who espoused its application (Tamanaha 1995:470-3). The mere fact that such a gap exists, or that there are difficulties in application, is not a reason to reject the 'liberal legal' model as irrelevant. On the contrary, 'liberal-legal' principles such as the rule of law may be particularly relevant in developing countries as a check on the untrammeled power of authoritarian governments. On this account alone, argues Tamanaha, law-and-development theorists 'should be striving to devise ways in which the rule-of-law model can be adapted to local circumstances and nurtured into maturity, rather than expending the bulk of their efforts in tearing this model down' (Tamanaha 1995:470-3). To this end, Tamanaha contends that the 'basic elements are compatible with many socio-cultural arrangements and, notwithstanding the potential conflicts, they have much to offer to developing countries' (Tamanaha 1995:470-3).

For our purposes the common ground of the different theoretical approaches discussed above is that an understanding of the wider social, political and economic context is vital in our comprehension of the process of environmental litigation and the institutions upon which it depends. The effectiveness of environmental litigation will depend to some extent upon the wider social-legal context, including the relationship between the executive and the judiciary and the extent to which the rule of law has been established. Our discussion of environmental litigation in subsequent chapters will accordingly examine, in the constructive manner proposed by Tamanaha, the influence of these wider societal conditions upon the process, outcome and effectiveness of environmental litigation.

Environmental mediation

Definition of mediation

Mediation may be defined as a form of dispute resolution in which negotiations between the disputing parties are facilitated by a third party (the mediator) who assists the parties in resolving their differences (Boulle 1996:7). Mediation processes, whilst in practice varying widely according to context and circumstance, usually share a number of features:

- Third party facilitation. As already stated above, mediation is facilitated by a third party 'mediator', distinguishing it from negotiation where the disputing parties negotiate directly with each other. In most cases the mediator is chosen by the parties, however, this may not always be the case.
- Voluntary. The choice to commence mediation, continue and eventually conclude an agreement is usually a voluntary one made by the parties to the dispute. However, in certain circumstances legislation or court regulation may require disputing parties to at least attempt mediation prior to, for instance, the furtherance of a legal suit.
- Neutrality of mediator. The third party mediator is ideally neutral, although the extent to which this is the case may vary in practice. Mediation may thus be distinguished from conciliation, which involves the intervention of a third party acting as a representative of one of the parties, rather than a neutral facilitator.
- Consensual decision-making. The outcome in mediation is determined consensually by the parties and is not imposed by the mediator. Mediation thus differs from arbitration or litigation where a decision is imposed upon the disputing parties by an authorized third party.
- Post-dispute. Mediation usually commences at 'point of impasse' when discussions between parties degenerate into conflict and neither party can unilaterally achieve their objectives. In this respect mediation may be distinguished from 'conflict anticipation', 'joint problem-solving' and 'policy dialogue', which involve consensus-based deliberations facilitated by a third party, yet are aimed at conflict prevention rather than resolution and hence commenced at an earlier stage.
- Informal. Mediation is usually characterized by less formal or rigid rules and procedures, especially when compared to litigation.
- Private/confidential. Mediation is essentially a private process of dispute resolution in that settlement is determined in accordance with each party's private or personal interests rather than in reference to a public legal or societal standard. In most cases, mediation is also conducted in private

between disputing parties and the content of negotiation is the subject of confidentiality.

Besides these most common features of mediation processes, there are many other factors that will vary considerably from one mediation process to another, including the nature, type and extent of the mediator's interventions, the manner in which negotiations are structured and the legal status of any negotiated settlement.[23]

Comparison of mediation and litigation as approaches to dispute resolution

Mediation, as defined above, is thus a process in which disputing parties negotiate with the assistance of a third party mediator in an attempt to resolve their differences and create a mutually acceptable settlement. In most cases the objective of mediation is the resolution of the dispute, which is signified by both parties accepting that the dispute has ended (Brown and Marriott 1999:130). From our discussion above, it is evident that litigation and mediation approach the task of dispute resolution in quite different ways. As we have seen, dispute resolution is achieved in litigation through a court's authoritative determination of the rights, remedies and relationship of disputing parties, by reference to legal norms. In mediation, however, resolution is a consensual process of facilitated negotiation, which is based on the interests of the disputing parties, rather than legal or societal norms. In litigation, decision making control is held by a third party authority, some parties may be coerced by law to participate and the parties exercise little control over the outcome. By contrast, mediation is a voluntary and consensual dispute resolution process, over which the parties have much greater control.[24] Furthermore, the adversarial character of litigation usually necessitates an outcome of a binary nature, that is a party will either win or lose. In contrast, mediation endeavours to accommodate and reconcile the interests of both parties, thus obtaining (in theory at least) a 'win-win' outcome (Boulle 1996:74-6).

In the literature on mediation and alternative dispute resolution (ADR), there are extensive references to the purported advantages of these approaches to dispute resolution when compared to 'traditional' or court-based dispute resolution through litigation. Whilst we will not undertake an exhaustive review of this debate, we will at least review the main criticisms of litigation as a process of dispute resolution, and the advantages which mediation sup-

23 For a more detailed discussion of different models and approaches to mediation, see Menkel-Meadow 1995:217-42.

24 For a more detailed discussion of the differences between mediation and litigation, see Boulle 1996:74-6.

posedly offers as an alternative. The main faults of litigation as detailed by its critics include:[25]

- the high cost of legal representation;
- the frequently protracted nature of litigation, which is often subject to delays before a case is heard;
- the formality of the court process, which is usually beyond the comprehension of the layman;
- the adversarial character of litigation, which tends to further damage rather than restore human relationships;
- the tendency of litigation to focus on and turn on legal technicalities, rather than issues of substance to the parties;
- the lack of control that disputants have over the course and outcome of the litigation process;
- the inflexibility and restricted scope of legal claims and remedies.

Studies on access to justice have proposed mediation (and other approaches to ADR) as one response to overcoming these and other problems identified in the litigation process, thus streamlining the adjudiciation of disputes in cases where the parties were willing to undertake mediation. Mediation and ADR were advocated by their proponents as a solution to many of the problems associated with litigation. Meditation has been claimed to be (Astor and Chinkin 1992:30-58; Boulle 1996:54-66):

- more affordable and hence accessible to the average disputant;
- more time efficient when compared to the delays in the litigation process;
- less confrontational and adversarial, thus tending to restore rather than destroy relationships between disputants;
- directed and controlled by the disputants themselves;
- focused on issues of substance and import to the disputants rather than revolving around legal technicalities;
- flexible in its process and outcome and responsive to the needs and wishes of the parties;
- conducive to 'win-win' outcomes where the outcome benefits both parties to the optimal degree.

Certainly some of the claimed advantages of mediation have been verified by experience and research, contributing to its widespread acceptance in many countries as an alternative to litigation and in many cases its insti-

25 This summary is based on the discussion in Astor and Chinkin 1992:30-58.

tutionalization as a 'court-connected' adjunct to litigation. Yet a number of authors have questioned the basis for some of the more strident claims of mediation and ADR's superiority. Rosemary O'Leary, for instance, notes that the frequent claims of environmental mediation's 'success' in the literature were not adequately supported by empirical evidence (O'Leary 1995:17-36). Hilary Astor and Christine Chinkin also emphasize the need to separate the rhetoric around ADR from the reality of its application and note that many of the more strident claims for ADR have been presented by those with a direct stake in its wider acceptance, often without sufficient empirical support (Astor and Chinkin 1992:30-58). Those authors also cite a number of studies, which demonstrate that ADR does not always prove to be more affordable, efficient or consensual in practice, and further question the basis upon which high 'success rates' of ADR have been calculated.[26] Laurence Boulle also refers to a number of studies where unsuccessful mediations had an increased cost in time and expense compared to similar cases that went to trial.[27]

Criticism of litigation has also certainly not remained unanswered. In an early broadside against advocates of 'settlement', Owen Fiss argued that litigation is better equipped than mediation to protect parties in a powerless position. Settlement, he contended, 'is also a function of the resources available to each party to finance the litigation, and these resources are frequently distributed unevenly'. Where an imbalance of power influences the bargaining process then 'settlement will be at odds with a conception of justice that seeks to make the wealth of the parties irrelevant' (Fiss 1984:1073-90). Fiss' account of litigation, however, is somewhat idealized. As Marc Galanter has demonstrated, the litigation process is also far from a 'level playing field', and frequent litigants (whom Galanter terms 'repeat players') are at a significant advantage over one-off litigants (Galanter 1974:95). Nonetheless, litigation does offer procedural safeguards which mediation lacks, including principles of due process, rights of appeal and rules on the collection and evaluation of evidence (Astor and Chinkin 1992:30-58).

The litigation-mediation (ADR) debate has also focused on the broader philosophical and social-political differences between these two approaches to dispute resolution. One important point of distinction and contention in this respect is the public character of litigation and the private character of mediation. Dispute resolution through litigation is achieved by the application of public legal norms. The actual process of litigation is also usually

26 For instance, the authors cite one study of divorce mediation in which the parties with the highest costs where those who had tried mediation and failed, see *Report Lord Chancellor* 1989, cited in Astor and Chinkin 1992:30-58.

27 Boulle 1996:63-4. Although he also cites numerous studies in support of mediation's claims to greater efficiency.

open and may be viewed by members of the public. In contrast, dispute resolution through mediation is largely a private matter between the disputing parties, which attempts to reconcile their private, subjective interests. As such, the relationship of mediation and mediated agreements to law and the public domain may be ambiguous. In his influential article 'Against settlement (1984)', Fiss criticized this aspect of mediation, arguing that 'parties might settle while leaving justice undone'. According to Fiss the purpose of adjudication should be understood in broader, more publicly defined terms. Adjudication was not simply about resolving individual conflicts, but rather concerned the interpretation and application of values embodied in laws and national constitutions, and the effort to bring reality to accord with those values (Fiss 1984:1073-90).

Menkel-Meadow (2001:12-33) has also elaborated on this point, describing mediation as going

> beyond the law, 'legislating', as it were, for the particular and not for the general population. Solutions to mediated problems may be 'beyond' or 'outside' the law (or located in interstices) when the parties choose remedies, solutions or outcomes that are not specifically identified in more general legal pronouncements.

The private, 'extra-legal' nature of mediation has prompted criticism from some scholars who have argued that legal standards should serve to define justice and that matters of public significance should not be 'privatized' through mediation processes (Boulle 1996:73; Menkel-Meadow 2001:12-33). It has also been argued that the widespread practice of private settlement could make litigation less efficient by reducing the stock of available legal precedents.[28] Certainly the private and subjective character of mediation is potentially problematic in the environmental context, where the public interest in environmental preservation is often at stake in what otherwise might be regarded as 'private interest' disputes. Environmental mediation therefore aims, at least in theory, to create a 'holistic' solution, in which environmental interests are accommodated along with the private interests of the disputants. Where this does not occur, conflict related to continuing environmental externalities is more likely to recur. From a state or legal perspective, accommodation of environmental interests would entail compliance with environmental legislation, so that mediated agreements would further rather than undermine legal certainty in the environmental field.

Whilst litigation, as 'rights-based' dispute resolution, and mediation, as 'interest-based' dispute resolution, are distinct approaches they are nonethe-

28 Galanter and Lande 1992:398, cited in Boulle 1996:73.

less closely related in many respects. Both mediation and litigation adopt the basic 'logic of the triad in conflict resolution', namely that 'whenever two persons come into a conflict that they cannot themselves solve, one solution appealing to common sense is to call upon a third for assistance in achieving a resolution' (Shapiro 1981:1-10). Litigation and mediation thus share a common goal, that of dispute resolution, and a common means, the use of a 'triad structure' to resolve conflict. It is in the actual role of the third party that litigation and mediation differ. In litigation, the role of the third party (the court) is that of the authoritative decision-maker, whose decision the disputants must abide. In mediation, the role of the third party (the mediator) is facilitative, assisting a consensual resolution between the parties themselves. Yet even this distinction is not absolute. Whilst courts are the least consensual and most coercive on the continuum of dispute resolution, in many cases judicial systems still retain strong elements of mediation, for example through the use of court annexed mediation (Shapiro 1981:1-10). Similarly, a mediator may play a highly directive role in the mediation process in a manner not dissimilar to some types of litigation.

In the framework of this book our comparison of litigation and mediation is also based on a common subject matter, namely environmental disputes. The claimants in an environmental dispute share the same objective of environmental justice, whether they choose litigation or mediation as a means to this end. Both litigation and mediation, as different approaches to environmental dispute resolution, in practice share the following objectives:

- Compensation of personal loss related to environmental damage or pollution.
- Restoration or rehabilitation of environmental damage or pollution.
- Resolution of the dispute, whether through a rights-based (litigation) or interest-based (mediation) approach.
- Adequate implementation of the judicial decision or mediated agreement.

The precise emphasis of these goals may vary according to the private or public interest nature of the dispute. For example, a dispute between an environmental organization, government agencies and a polluter may focus more on the issue of environmental restoration than compensation. Conversely, a dispute arising out of personal loss caused by environmental damage or pollution may be more focused on the issue of compensation for that personal loss. As discussed above, private or public interest perspectives often overlap and either or both may be pursued through litigation or mediation.

Objectives of environmental mediation and evaluative criteria

As we have seen, the objectives of environmental mediation are distinct, but certainly comparable to those of environmental litigation. The objective application of public norms is not ostensibly a function of mediation, which instead seeks first and foremost a harmonious resolution of the disputing parties' interests. Nonetheless, environmental legal norms are likely to be of considerable relevance in defining the substantive objectives of environmental claimants in a mediation process, which in practice may be quite similar to objectives of environmental claimants in a litigation process. Accordingly, the following evaluative criteria may be elaborated:

1 To what extent have the disputing parties been able to arrive at a mutually beneficial resolution of the dispute?
2 Has this resolution adequately compensated personal loss relating to environmental damage or pollution?
3 Does the mediated agreement provide a holistic solution to the dispute, incorporating environmental interests?
4 Has the agreed resolution to the dispute been implemented and do the parties thus consider the dispute to have ended?

Conditions for effective environmental mediation

A review of the literature indicates that a range of conditions may influence the outcome and ability of mediation to fulfil the objectives discussed in the previous section. These conditions are examined in more detail below and are intended as a theoretical framework and starting point for the consideration and analysis of environmental mediation in Indonesia undertaken in subsequent chapters. Whilst it may not be possible to comprehensively stipulate the conditions sufficient for effective mediation, it is at least possible to identify a number of conditions that will make mediation more likely to succeed (Boulle 1996:77). The following section discusses some of these conditions, drawing upon the growing body of literature relating to mediation and the practice of environmental mediation in particular.[29]

29 The summary draws upon the 'Electic theory of environmental mediation' presented by Blackburn 1995:267-80, and Laurence Boulle's leading text on mediation: Boulle 1996, in addition to other sources where noted.

Condition 1: skilled and impartial mediator

In most cases the selection and appointment of a mediator is a matter determined by the parties to a dispute.[30] A mediator should firstly possess the appropriate skills, experience and/or qualifications to undertake this task and maintain the confidence of the disputing parties.[31] The majority of commentators also recommend that the mediator be accepted by all parties as an impartial and neutral figure and not possess any personal stake in the dispute. Personal bias on the part of the mediator is likely to undermine the commitment of one or other disputing party to the dispute resolution process, which is voluntary in nature. There will be little incentive for a disputant to voluntarily remain in a mediation process in which the mediator is biased against their interests. Impartiality is thus essential and is described in Boulle's leading text on mediation (Boulle 1996:14) as 'a core requirement in mediation, in the sense that its absence would fundamentally undermine the nature of the process'.

Nonetheless, impartiality does not necessarily imply complete independence from the disputing parties. As Boulle notes, impartiality, which is essential, may be distinguished from neutrality, which may be a question of degree. Mediation may be conducted effectively by a mediator who has some pre-existing relationship with the disputing parties or someone who is interested, as opposed to disinterested, in the outcome of the dispute (Boulle 1996:14). In Indonesia, for example, consensus-based dispute resolution termed *musyawarah* was traditionally conducted by a respected village elder (see Chapter IV). The social authority of such a mediator may allow she or he to more actively direct the parties toward resolution.[32] As long as the parties accept the position and authority of the mediator, and he or she is still perceived as sufficiently impartial, then mediation may still be effectively conducted in this manner. Where a related mediator is not acceptable to either party, then it is preferable if the mediator operates from an institutional base that is also independent from any of the parties. Finally, the mediator must also be prepared to maintain the confidentiality of all communications made pursuant to mediation, and have the confidence of the parties that this requirement will be carried out.

30 Exceptions to this include court assisted mediation where the mediator is appointed by the court.

31 These qualifications may vary in practice and include prior experience in mediation, training in mediation skills and/or a history of experience in environmentally related matters. A moderate level of technical expertise in the subject of the dispute may be of assistance, although some commentators have thought it advisable that the mediator does not have great technical expertise in the specific subject of the dispute as this may result in a technical over-emphasis at the expense of relationship building. See Blackburn 1995:267-80.

32 Of course if it is the mediator who ultimately makes the decision then the process is no longer one of mediation.

A comprehensive discussion of the specific skills and techniques employed by mediators is beyond the scope of this chapter. However, several of the more important basic tasks which must be performed by a successful mediator bear mentioning here. Given the complexity of environmental disputes, an initial task of the mediator is to clearly define the problem at hand and reach agreement between the parties on the specific issues that will be addressed in the mediation process. It may also be necessary for the parties to agree on the geographical boundaries and time horizons of the issues in dispute (Baldwin 1978:1-28). Once the relevant issues have been identified, these may be broken down into smaller steps and addressed systematically. In this way, a mediator can help clarify the problem situation and achieve an initial consensus between the parties as to the parameters of the dispute and the specific issues requiring resolution (Boulle 1996:9).

Another general task of the mediator is to facilitate better communication between the disputing parties. Miscommunication or unfounded inferences about a disputing party's statements or claims can be a major contributing factor in the origin and escalation of a dispute (Moore 1996:62). A mediator should endeavour to correct such misperceptions, enabling each party to comprehend more clearly what the other actually means, wants and feels. The mediator may also encourage parties to attack the problem rather than the people, thus assisting disputants to shift from personal recrimination to finding mutually acceptable solutions to the specific issues at hand.

Misunderstandings may also arise over factual matters, especially in the context of environmental disputes where the subject matter of the dispute may be scientifically or technically complex. The mediator should thus also endeavour to ensure that all representatives have an adequate understanding of the facts relevant to the dispute (Blackburn 1995:267-80). It may be useful for the participants to reach agreement over the facts and data relevant to the dispute, even if agreement cannot be reached over the consequences of those facts, although this will not be possible in all cases (Blackburn 1995:267-80). To this extent, the mediator has an obligation to bring the best and most complete substantive environmental information into the discussions, thereby ensuring that all important issues will be confronted and any decision will reflect sound environmental data (Baldwin 1978:1-28). To achieve this aim, it may be necessary to arrange information sharing by all participants and also for third party experts to participate in the mediation process.

Condition 2: feasibility of compromise

As noted above, mediation is a voluntary and consensual process and so dispute settlement in mediation inevitably involves a 'search for compromise' (Baldwin 1978:1-28). A mediator aims to facilitate the process of compromise by encouraging the parties to distinguish between their respective positions and interests, thus facilitating compromise. A position may be defined as a specific outcome or action, which a party perceives as meeting its immediate needs.[33] It is typically concrete in nature and as a result, minimally negotiable. In contrast, a party's 'interest' refers to their desires, fears, values and concerns that they hope to advance. An interest is a broad concept rather than a specific action or outcome, which fosters discussion and enables compromise as it may be satisfied by a range of potential outcomes. By assisting the parties to distinguish between their positions and interests, a mediator may identify potential areas for compromise that were not apparent before.

Given that mediation is premised upon mutual compromise, one condition necessary for successful mediation is that some compromise is actually possible between the disputing parties. Consequently, one category of disputes typically not able to be mediated is that where no common ground exists between the disputing parties. Such disputes, which may involve conflicts of fundamental values, have also been described as 'either-or' disputes, a common example being the construction of a nuclear reactor. Disputes concerning broad matters of policy, or cases where one or both parties seek to set an important legal precedent, would also be less amenable to mediation (Boulle 1996:80-1). The possibility of compromise may also be reduced where a history of contentious or intensely hostile relationships between the opposing parties exists (Blackburn 1995:267-80). Thus a dispute may be considered mediable only where some common interest exists between the disputing parties, even though initially confrontational positioning may obscure this common ground (Baldwin 1978:1-28). Initially intransigent parties may become willing to negotiate where a skilled mediator is able to highlight common interests, the mutual benefits of a 'win-win' solution to both parties and the costs of not pursuing the mediation process. Compromise may also be more feasible in cases where there is more than a single issue in dispute, as multiple issues provide more scope for creative bargaining arrangements involving tradeoffs and linkages between issues (Boulle 1996:79).

The existence of appropriate measures to mitigate the adverse impact of a proposed development will also increase the potential for compromise. Such measures must satisfactorily resolve the objections of opponents, and the appropriate party should be willing and fiscally able to undertake the mitigation measures (Baldwin 1978:12-3). Where satisfactory measures cannot be realistically undertaken to mitigate the adverse impact of a project then the likelihood of compromise is slim.

33 For a more detailed discussion of the distinction between positions and interests, see Fisher and Ury 1991:200.

Condition 3: absence of a better alternative to a negotiated agreement (BATNA)
The willingness of parties to reach compromise will also be more likely where a stalemate or impasse has been reached between the parties (Blackburn 1995:267-80). An impasse implies that neither party is likely to have the ability to unilaterally achieve their objectives through alternative channels, whether they be power-based (political, repressive, demonstrations) or rights-based (litigation). If a party believes that a 'Better Alternative to a Negotiated Agreement' (BATNA) exists then they will possess little incentive to compromise. In this respect there should be, at the least, uncertainty about the outcome of pursuing resolution of the dispute through other judicial or administrative channels (Blackburn 1995:276). Where, moreover, parties stand to suffer adverse consequences if a stalemate or impasse continues, then the requisite motivation to undertake mediation will most likely be present. Of course, the possibility of adverse consequences is dependent to a large extent on the existence of a functional system of administrative and judicial environmental law enforcement. The threat or prospect of litigation often provides the most direct incentive to mediate; a phenomenon termed 'bargaining in the shadow of the law'. Where law enforcement is fickle, and the law casts little 'shadow', the more powerful disputant may not be compelled to undertake mediation.

Condition 4: commitment to a negotiated settlement
Given the voluntary nature of the mediation process, the extent to which compromise is possible will ultimately depend upon the willingness of each party to compromise and their commitment to pursue the mediation process until an agreement is reached. As discussed above, the presence or absence of a 'better alternative to a negotiated settlement' may influence this commitment. However, the perceived presence or absence of alternatives will not necessarily be sufficient to ensure a personal commitment to a negotiated settlement, which ultimately must come from each party themselves (Boulle 1996:79). Where either party lacks this commitment, a negotiated settlement is less likely and an adjudicative process of dispute resolution, such as litigation, may be a more appropriate choice.

Condition 5: balance of power between disputing parties
One of the criticisms of mediation discussed above was that less powerful parties may be more vulnerable in the mediation process than they might be in litigation. Certainly, the issue of power disparities between disputants in mediation has generated much comment in the mediation literature. A number of mediators and writers on the subject have also emphasized the need for a perceived balance of power between the disputing parties, for mediation to be successful. As one practioner put it in relation to environ-

mental disputes, 'the "public interest" side must be able to offset the "deep pocket" of business or government' (Golten 1980:2-3). Nonetheless, mediation has been used successfully in disputes where power disparities existed. Some mediators justify this by reference to mediation's voluntary character, pointing out that participation in and agreement reached through mediation is a matter of voluntary choice. Other authors have even argued that the mediation process may be particularly suited to addressing and redressing power disparities between disputants (Davis and Salem 1984:6-17).

Power disparities are frequently a problem in environmental disputes, where economically and politically powerful government agencies or companies are sometimes at loggerheads with often under-resourced environmental or citizen organizations. Whether or not an adequate balance of power can be achieved between disputing parties will depend upon a diversity of factors, including the strength of civil society, the influence of the media or the political influence held by industry lobby groups. If a party is in a position sufficiently powerful to achieve its aims unilaterally, then may lack motivation to undertake mediation in the first place.

The difficulty inherent in this requirement or precondition for a balance of power, is its ambiguity and somewhat subjective nature. Clear criteria have not yet been identified which could be used to assess the so-called 'balance of power', and indeed such criteria would be difficult to formulate due to the diversity of variables affecting a party's 'power' in relation to others. Although ambiguous, the power balance is nonetheless a consideration borne in mind by many environmental mediators. Moreover, whilst mediation is not precluded by an 'imbalance' of power, the eventual outcome may be less equitable, tending to favour the more powerful party. A mediator may therefore seek to ensure that parties participating in mediation at least maintain parity in their access to information, resources and representation.

Condition 6: continuing relationship between the parties

As discussed above, the conciliatory style, in Black's styles of social control, is most suited to situations where the social distance between parties is close. Research has also indicated that mediation may be a suitable choice where the parties in dispute have a continuing relationship (Boulle 1996:93). The continuing relationship may be a matter of necessity, as in the case of parents in a matrimonial dispute or neighbours, or a matter of choice, as in the case of commercial entities that wish to maintain future relations. A continuing relationship is not only an incentive to seek a harmonious resolution to the conflict, but enables parties to integrate future interests into the bargaining process.

Condition 7: inclusion of all stakeholders

Environmental disputes are usually characterized by a diversity of stakeholders, which may include industry, local resident groups, regional or national environmental organizations and government agencies at the national, regional or local level. A generally accepted principle in the literature on environmental mediation is that all stakeholders in a dispute should be included in the mediation process. A stakeholder is defined generally as a person or institution with a direct interest in the outcome of the resolution process. The term 'stakeholders' usually includes government agencies with jurisdiction over the subject of the dispute, any party that would be affected by the decision, and any party that has the capacity to intervene in the decision-making process, or block implementation of an agreement (Shrybman 1983:32). All such parties should ideally be included in the mediation process as the failure to do so may subsequently compromise the implementation of an agreement. Besides the practical reasons for comprehensive stakeholder inclusion, several commentators have additionally argued that it is ethically incumbent upon the mediator to ensure, or at least encourage, sufficient representation of all affected interests. Of particular concern in environmental disputes are interests of an environmental nature, which may not have sufficient representation for a variety of reasons.

A successful mediation process should not only ensure adequate participation of all interested parties but also adequate representation. Each party involved in the mediation process should have a clearly identified constituency, which they are representing. Other commentators have emphasized the need for representatives to have sufficient understanding and competency in the concept of representative bargaining in order to ensure that their constituencies stay properly informed through the process and the authority of the representative remains effective (Baldwin 1978:17-8). This is an important consideration as where representation is not properly negotiated, an alienated constituency may subsequently undermine an agreement concluded by a representative. Representatives should also possess full decision making authority on the issues at hand, so that the process of negotiation will not be unduly obstructed or delayed. For such authority to be effective, constituencies must remain informed and representation must remain current.

Condition 8: effective mechanisms for implementation of agreement

The outcome of an effective mediation process should be a comprehensive written agreement acceptable to both parties, that encompasses all disputed issues. Satisfactory implementation of this agreement is essential to the success of the mediation process as a whole. Consequently, the issue of implementation should be addressed early on in the mediation process and mediation should only be attempted where implementation will be possible. Where a government agency or other third party will be responsible for monitoring or implementation of an agreement, such party should ideally participate in the mediation process as a stakeholder. The solutions specified in the agreement, and the means by which they will be implemented, should be politically, technically and financially feasible (Baldwin 1978:17-8). The agreement itself should clearly establish legal mechanisms to bind the parties to its terms and provide sufficient detail as to what steps will be undertaken to implement the agreement, by whom and when. There are various legal mechanisms to achieve enforceability. These include formalising the agreement as a binding contract enforceable through the courts, adoption of the agreement as a decision by a government agency enforceable through administrative sanction, ratification of the agreement by judicial order, or enactment of an agreement by government regulation/legislation; thus providing the agreement with the force of law (Blackburn 1995:267-80). Finally, provision in the agreement should be made to deal with further disagreement between the parties over the matter of implementation. Such disagreement may be referred to further mediation, arbitration or an administrative/legal forum depending on the legal enforcement mechanisms employed in the agreement.

Condition 9: supportive social-political context

Like litigation, the effectiveness of mediation as an approach to dispute resolution will be influenced by and contingent upon the wider societal context, including the nature of prevailing cultural mores, the distribution of political power, economic interests and the capacity of key institutions.[34] The wider social-political context may influence several of the conditions discussed above. For instance, the balance of power between disputing parties will be directly affected by social-political context. The social, political and economic resources of each disputant will be determined by this context, as will the role played by other influential actors, such as state agencies. Where, for instance, protests against polluting activities are regularly repressed by the state, or where civil society is weak and disorganized, it may be difficult to achieve an equitable balance of power. Similarly, the presence or absence of a better alternative to a negotiated agreement (BATNA) may be largely determined by the wider social-political context. For instance, the potential sanction of judicial or administrative enforcement of environmental law will only exist where the administrative apparatus to support such enforcement is functioning effectively. Thus our analysis of environmental mediation in subsequent chapters must be cognizant of the impact of this wider social-political context on the process and outcome of mediation.

[34] This process is comparable to the influence this range of factors has upon the implementation of law, see Otto 2002:23-34.

Environmental dispute resolution in Indonesia; An overview

Legal framework

In Indonesia 'environmental dispute' is defined by article 1(19) of the Indonesian Environmental Management Act 1997 (EMA 1997) as 'a disagreement between two or more parties which arises as a result of the existence or suspected existence of environmental pollution and/or damage'. As with the definitions drawn from the literature and discussed above, a dispute must be characterized by a tangible disagreement between identifiable parties, which usually means that the stages of 'naming, blaming and claiming' will have been passed through. Thus an environmental problem, such as deforestation or water pollution, which one party might identify, highlight or discuss, is not in itself a dispute. An environmental problem becomes a dispute when distinct parties make incompatible claims over it, concerning, for instance, responsibility for and remedying of the problem.

Absent from the EMA 1997 definition and also from the scope of this research are 'environmentally related' disputes, which may concern an aspect of the natural environment, but do not specifically concern environmental pollution or damage – for example, land tenure disputes. There are also certain limited categories of disputes not covered by the EMA definition, which I have included within the scope of my analysis. The EMA definition refers only to the 'existence or suspected existence' of environmental pollution and/or damage, and so seemingly excludes disagreements over prospective environmental pollution or damage which may involve attempts to prevent certain actions or policies that are expected to result in environmental damage or pollution. I have included such environmental disputes concerning prospective environmental damage, which appear rare in Indonesia in any case, within the scope of my analysis.

Chapter VII of the EMA 1997 concerns Environmental Dispute Settlement (Penyelesaian Sengketa Lingkungan Hidup). Article 30(1) in Part One of that chapter makes a distinction between court-based and non-court based dispute settlement, stating: 'Environmental dispute settlement can be reached through the court or out of court based on the voluntary choice of the parties in dispute'. The two formal, legally prescribed channels of environmental dispute resolution are thus litigation (through the court) and mediation (out of court).[35] Pursuant to article 30(2) these two choices do not apply to dispu-

35 As noted below, a range of approaches for out-of-court settlement may be undertaken pursuant to article 30, including (besides mediation): negotiation, conciliation or arbitration. However, mediation is the most commonly adopted ADR approach and the main focus of the present research.

tants whose actions would attract criminal liability, which is separately regulated in Chapter IX of the EMA. Part Two of Chapter VII of the EMA makes more detailed provision for environmental dispute settlement outside of the court. According to article 31 the object of this process is reaching agreement between the disputing parties concerning the form and size of compensation (for environmental damage or pollution) and/or the carrying out of certain actions to prevent further environmental damage or pollution. Article 32 clarifies that out of court settlement may involve the use of a third party, who may or may not have final decision-making authority to bind the disputing parties. Thus, a range of ADR techniques may be utilized as 'out-of-court dispute settlement' for the purposes of the EMA 1997, including negotiation, mediation, conciliation or arbitration. Whatever the particular approach, the choice to pursue out-of-court dispute settlement itself is a voluntary one made by the parties (EMA 1997 article 30[1]). However, where out-of-court settlement has been undertaken, then court-based settlement (litigation) may only be commenced where one of the parties has declared the out-of-court settlement to have failed (EMA 1997 article 30[3]). The legal framework pertaining to environmental mediation, and its application, is examined in more detail in Chapter V of this book.

Part Three of Chapter VII EMA 1997 stipulates a number of principles relevant to environmental litigation. Article 34 requires compensation for environmentally polluting or damaging actions contrary to law, which cause damage to other persons or the environment. Article 35 enacts the principle of strict or 'no-fault' liability for industries that produce a significant impact on the environment, use hazardous materials or produce hazardous waste. Article 37 allows a community that has suffered environmental damage or pollution to bring a representative action to court or report such damage or pollution to administrative enforcement bodies. Pursuant to article 38 an environmental organization may also bring a legal action on behalf of environmental interests, although the organization must meet certain criteria, and the available remedies do not include compensation. The legal framework for environmental litigation, and its application, is examined in more detail in Chapter II of this book.

Environmental disputes by sector

An exhaustive inventory of environmental disputes in Indonesia is certainly beyond the scope of this chapter, as is a comprehensive discussion of the political, economic and social antecedents of such disputes. Nonetheless, in this section we will pursue the more limited objective of outlining the nature, context and types of environmental disputes in several different industry sectors in Indonesia. The discussion is intended to further illustrate the private interest/

public interest distinction introduced above and to contextualize the discussion of specific environmental disputes that follows in subsequent chapters.

Industry sector

After 1965, under President Suharto's leadership, Indonesia embarked on an intensive process of industrialization. The subsequent expansion of manufacturing and the industrial sector contributed greatly to economic growth, with manufacturing's share of GDP tripling from 10% in 1967-1973 to 29% in 1987-1992 (Hill 2000:21). Yet the rapid expansion of industrial plants in Java and Sumatra also resulted in the dumping of (often untreated) industrial effluent into the waterways of Java, Sumatra and other islands. Whilst assessing the extent of industrial pollution in Indonesia is difficult given the paucity of data, what information there is indicates the problem to be extremely serious, particularly in the areas mentioned above where industry is concentrated.[36] The problem of industrial waste disposal has been compounded by a number of factors.[37] Despite the enactment of environmental legislation and regulations for pollution control, poor law enforcement has allowed many industries to operate without a waste management unit, contrary to their legal obligations. In several cases larger, more heavily polluting factories have been protected by their considerable economic and political influence.[38] Bribery of government officials overseeing factories is also common, as is intimidation of regional officials seeking to enforce environmental regulations (Lucas and Arief Djati 2008:16-7). Even where an industry has installed a waste management unit, such units are frequently incomplete, not maintained adequately or simply not used due to high operating costs (Lucas 1998:229-61). As a result, discharged industrial waste is frequently in excess of stipulated regulatory limits and thus a grave danger to the environment and human inhabitants. In islands such as Java and Sumatra, a combination of high population density and poor spatial planning has also contributed to the location of most factories in close proximity to both agricultural and residential areas. The same rivers used for agricultural and human use are utilized by factories as waste dumping grounds, with both pollution and serious conflict the inevitable result. It is not surprising, therefore, that industry related environmental disputes are among the most common types of envi-

36 In a 1994 report by the Australian International Development Assistance Bureau (AIDAB), testing carried out in all four provinces in Java showed the level of pollutants in rivers to significantly exceed government standards. See Lucas and Arief Djati 2000:8.

37 See also useful discussion of river pollution in Indonesia in Lucas 1998:229-61.

38 For example PT Barito Pacific, one of the more infamous 'environmental vandals' in Indonesia due to its illegal logging and discharge of large volumes of untreated waste from wood processing factories, is owned by Projo Pangestu, a business partner of two of President Suharto's children during the New Order period. See Hidayat Hibani 1994 and Lucas 1998:184, 97.

ronmental disputes (Hidayat Hibani 1994) and account for almost half of the total number of civil environmental court cases to date.[39]

In the case of industry, the most common category of dispute is 'private interest' disputes involving local communities afflicted by pollution from nearby factories. A significant number of the environmental court cases discussed in Chapter II, 'Environmental litigation in Indonesia; Legal framework and overview of cases', where local communities had initiated legal suits for compensation and environmental restoration, fall within this category. For instance, in the PT Pupuk Iskandar Muda case a poisonous gas leak from a factory in North Sumatra caused symptoms ranging from unconsciousness to nausea in over six hundred nearby residents. In the PT Sarana Surya Sakti case, zinc and chromium waste from a tyre factory polluted residents' wells in a village in East Java. Similarly in the Sari Morawa case, effluent from PT Sari Morawa, a pulp and paper mill in Kalimantan, had allegedly polluted the Belumai River upon which the 260 plaintiffs in that case depended for their daily needs and agriculture. The two disputes that form the basis of the litigation case studies examined in Chapter III also fall within the category of 'private interest', industry related environmental disputes. In the Banger River case, industrial effluent from three textile factories in Pekalongan, Central Java, polluted river and ground water used by the village community of Dekoro. In the Babon River case, the dispute arose due to pollution from industrial effluent from a group of six factories. The factories' effluent had been disposed, untreated, into the Babon River, the waters of which were also used to flush the ponds of a small group of prawn farmers. The high level of pollutants in the water caused a significant decline in the farmers' prawn catch, to the point of threatening their livelihood.

Private interest, industry related disputes also account for the majority of environmental mediation cases considered in Chapter IV, 'Environmental mediation in Indonesia' and Chapter V 'Case studies of environmental mediation'. In these cases, communities that have suffered the effects of industrial pollution sought recourse through a mediation process. In the 1991 Tapak River dispute, for instance, the disposal of untreated effluent by a number of factories into the Tapak River in Central Java had caused severe and ongoing pollution. The pollution caused considerable damage to local residents' health, agricultural yields and the surrounding environment. Similarly, in the more recent (2000) Kanasritex dispute the disposal of industrial effluent by a textile factory near Semarang caused pollution of surrounding fields and the consequent failure of rice harvests. The same recurrent and increasingly common pattern of industry related water pollution and resultant conflict between

39 See Appendix I: Table of cases.

factory owners and local residents is also found in the Sambong River, Siak River, Sibalec, Ciujung River and Naga Mas disputes discussed in Chapter IV. The two environmental mediation case studies examined in Chapter V are further examples of predominantly private interest, industry related environmental disputes. In the Palur Raya case study, the Ngringo community situated in Solo (Central Java) was severely afflicted by ground, water and air pollution from a local mono-sodium glutamate (MSG) factory, PT Palur Raya. With the assistance of local NGOs, the community commenced a mediation process in an attempt to obtain compensation and improvement in the factory's environmental performance. In the second case study of environmental mediation, the Kayu Lapis Indonesia case, land owned by a traditional prawn farming community in Mangunharjo (Central Java) was flooded due to development work carried out by the Kayu Lapis Indonesia wood-processing factory. In conjunction with several NGOs and related government agencies, the afflicted community commenced a structured mediation process aimed at resolving issues of compensation and environmental restoration.

Pollution from industrial sources has also been the background to several public interest environmental cases. One of the earliest environmental cases in Indonesia, the PT Inti Indorayon Utama (PT IIU) case, was brought by Wahana Lingkungan Hidup Indonesia (WALHI), a national environmental organization. The case concerned the Indorayon pulp and paper factory in North Sumatra, whose operation had caused severe environmental damage in the surrounding area. WALHI sought to represent the public 'environmental interest' and contended that issuance of operating permits to PT IIU was contrary to environmental law. The principle of standing for environmental organizations was ultimately accepted by the court, paving the way for other environmental public interest suits such as the Surabaya River case. In that case WALHI brought an environmental action against three paper processing factories accused of polluting the Surabaya River, the main source of drinking water for the two million residents of Java's second largest city, Surabaya (see Chapter II).

Forestry sector

Exploitation of Indonesia's rainforests, approximately 10% of the world's remaining rainforest, intensified in the late 1960s as the New Order government endeavoured to service the increasing foreign debt and reduce spiralling inflation (Dauvergne 1994:497-518). Since that time commercial logging of rainforests, and the consequent deforestation, has continued to increase. By the late 1980s Indonesia was estimated to be losing approximately 900,000 hectares of forest every year (Dauvergne 1994:497). Large forest concessions were rewarded to favoured military and business cronies of the Suharto family, the operation of which was often financed by foreign multinationals who benefited from investor friendly laws granting extensive tax breaks (Poffenberger 1997:453-5). Foreign earnings from timber rose 2800% from 1969 to 1974, allowing the national government to fund five-year development programs through foreign revenue from unprocessed log exports (Dauvergne 1994:513).

The economic and political crisis that marked the end of the New Order does not seem to have slowed the rate of deforestation. On the contrary, any remaining forest was seen by regional governments and illegal loggers alike as a valuable source of revenue in a time of economic crisis. As the remaining areas of timber have become scarcer, the level of illegal logging has increased dramatically, to the point where it is now estimated to outstrip the output of logging from legal concessions.[40] Due at least in part to the diminishing area available for forest concessions, illegal logging activities have spread even into national parks. Currently illegal logging is the prime contributing factor to Indonesia's annual deforestation rate of around two-three million hectares per year (Hartanto 2001). As both legal and illegal logging continue apace, most commentators now predict the extinction of Indonesia's primary forests to occur within the next five-ten years.[41]

Rapid deforestation in Indonesia has resulted in a devastating loss of biodiversity, and serious land degradation leading to increased soil erosion and flooding.[42] Widespread logging has also contributed to higher temperatures, drought and the outbreak of uncontrollable forest fires in 1997, 1998 and most recently in late 2006. In 1997 and 1998 alone the devastating fires consumed more than five million hectares of forestland, contributed to the deaths of more than a thousand people and carried an economic toll to Indonesia estimated at over US$9 billion (Mayell 2001). International environmental groups described the fires, which resulted in extraordinary amounts of carbon emissions, as a 'planetary disaster'.

Intensive logging has also had serious social consequences for the indigenous communities who lived within the forests and whose livelihoods depended upon them. The mapping of forest concessions, usually ranging from 100,000 to several million hectares, was not based on any consideration

40 According to a recent statement by WALHI, Indonesia's annual timber consumption was around 100 million cubic meters a year, of which only 43 million cubic meters originated from legal sources. Thus the majority of the timber supply, some 57 million cubic meters, is the product of illegal logging. See Bambang Nurbianto and Fitri Wulandari 2001.

41 World Bank predictions estimate the disappearance of Kalimantan's forests within nine years, whilst Sumatra's lowland forests are predicted to last for only another four years: Hartanto 2001. See also Bambang Nurbianto and Fitri Wulandari 2001.

42 Over a decade ago the Indonesian government had classified 8.6 million hectares as 'critical land' defined as 'unable to fulfil any of the normal soil functions, including water absorption or the production of even a meagre subsistence crop'. A further 12 million hectares was classified at that time as suffering from serious erosion. See Hurst 1990, quoted in Dauvergne 1994:497-518.

of the use of forest tracts by indigenous communities for hunting, gathering or swidden agriculture (Poffenberger 1997:453-5). In Kalimantan alone some 2.5 million indigenous Dayak peoples were displaced or resettled due to development activities such as logging and related resettlement projects (Poffenberger 1997:453-5). Indigenous forest-dwelling communities such as these have had no legal recourse, given the lack of legal recognition afforded to *adat*, or traditional community rights over forests.

Given the environmental damage and social dislocation that have accompanied logging activities, it is not surprising that one of the most common types of forestry related disputes is private interest disputes involving local, indigenous communities long dependent on forest resources, whose livelihood and very survival have been threatened by commercial logging interests. During the New Order period, such communities were generally displaced from their land or resettled, thus severing their traditional (*adat*) rights over their land. Any protests or resistance were routinely suppressed by the military, which itself developed extensive interests in the forestry sector during the New Order (Lynch and Harwell 2002:60-5).

Following the collapse of the New Order regime in 1998 and the corresponding contraction of military control, many of these suppressed conflicts have re-emerged. In March 2000 for instance, the Association of Indonesian Forest Concessionaires (Assosiasi Pengusaha Hutan Indonesia, APHI) reported that at least fifty companies with concessions totalling around ten million hectares of forests in West Papua, Kalimantan and Sulawesi had stopped logging because of conflicts with local communities.[43] In East Kalimantan itself 77 logging companies threatened to close in the event authorities failed to resolve disputes, where local people have seized logging equipment and demanded compensation.[44] Illegal logging operations have also resulted in disputes with local communities opposed to the further destruction of forestland. As indigenous communities have resorted to direct action to assert their rights, logging companies have been forced to negotiate or, alternatively, face the closure of their operations.[45] In one case, in February 2000, negotiations resulted in fourteen cooperatives and four indigenous councils receiving a 20% share in profits worth Rp 100 to Rp 200 million each.[46]

Several of the private interest environmental court cases discussed in Chapter II are also forestry related. For example, in the Laguna Mandiri case

43 'Communities confront loggers', *Down to Earth* 45 (May) 2000. Newsletter of the International Campaign for Ecological Justice in Indonesia. http://dte.gn.apc.org/45Log.htm.

44 'Communities confront loggers', *Down to Earth* 45 (May) 2000. Newsletter of the International Campaign for Ecological Justice in Indonesia. http://dte.gn.apc.org/45Log.htm.

45 See also 'Dana reboisasa Rp 1.6 trilyun diselewengkan', *Kompas*, 15-10-1999.

46 'Communities confront loggers', *Down to Earth* 45 (May) 2000. Newsletter of the International Campaign for Ecological Justice in Indonesia. http://dte.gn.apc.org/45Log.htm.

members of the Dayak Samihim community in the regency of Kota Baru, Kalimantan, brought a legal action for compensation against several companies, including PT Laguna Mandiri, which owned coconut plantation estates adjoining the plaintiffs' villages. The community claimed that fires intentionally lit by the companies to clear forestland between July and November 1997 had spread out of control, destroying large areas of the plaintiff community's crops and housing (see Chapter II).

Several prominent environmental public interest cases have also arisen in the forestry sector. These cases have emerged out of a growing debate over Indonesian forest policy, fuelled by increasing opposition to the continued destruction of Indonesia's unique forest ecosystems amongst a range of non-government organizations both within Indonesia and internationally. The Eksponen 66 case, which arose out of the devastating forest fires in 1997 and 1998, blended elements of both public and private interest. In that dispute a group of environmentally minded community organizations launched a class action against the Indonesian Forestry Entrepreneurs Association (APHI), headed at the time by timber tycoon Bob Hasan, together with five other timber industry associations. The organizations demanded compensation for the social, economic and environmental damage caused by the forest fires and resultant thick haze which blanketed much of Indonesia in the latter half of 1997. The environmental organization WALHI also brought an environmental public interest suit relating to the forest fires in South Sumatra in the same year.[47] In that case, WALHI claimed Rp two trillion for environmental restoration from a number of plantation and logging companies whose operations had allegedly contributed to the outbreak of fires. Other forestry related public interest cases have been more policy related than site specific in nature. For example, in the Reafforestation Fund (IPTN) case a group of environmental NGOs mounted a legal challenge to the transfer of money from a fund for the reforestation of logged-over land to a state company involved in aircraft manufacture. The Reafforestation Fund in question was something of a 'cash-cow' during the New Order period for a range of state projects other than reafforestation, and became symbolic of the corruption that pervaded the entire sector.[48] In another case related to the Fund, PT

47 WALHI v. PT Pakerin, Decision No. 8/Pdt.G/1998/PN.Plg.

48 Illegal pay-outs from the Reafforestation Fund included: a loan of Rp 80 billion to Suharto's grandson Ari Sigit for a urea tablet fertiliser project; a Rp 500 billion loan for Suharto's pet Kalimantan Peat Land project (discussed further in Chapter II); Rp 35 billion was given to the Consortium financing the 1997 Southeast Asian Games (chaired by Suharto's son Bambang); in 1996 over Rp 400 billion was used to finance construction of the N2130 jet by state-owned aircraft manufacturer IPTN, a project coordinated by Suharto crony B J Habibie. See 'Bob Hasan's fall from favour', *Down to Earth* 38 (August) 1998 International campaign for ecological justice in Indonesia.

Kiani Kertas, environmental organizations challenged the transfer of funds from the State Reafforestation Fund to a company funding the development of a pulp and paper factory located in East Kalimantan.

Mining sector

The Indonesian archipelago is home to a diverse wealth of minerals, including significant deposits of diamonds, copper, gold, nickel, coal, tin, mineral sands, chromite, uranium and bauxite (Marr 1993:9-11). Since 1967, when the Suharto government signed a contract allowing Freeport to establish the giant Grasberg mine in West Papua, mining in Indonesia has been a drawcard for foreign investment and the Indonesian government's largest source of revenue.[49] Yet whilst the wealth of Indonesia's minerals has enriched both foreign investors and the domestic (mostly Jakartan) political elite, it has in many cases brought little benefit to local, indigenous communities, which have instead borne the brunt of mining's environmental and social fallout (Marr 1993:3). In Indonesia the environmental impact of large-scale mining operations, whilst inadequately documented, is known to include water pollution (surface and subsurface) from the disposal of mining wastes, erosion, deforestation, large-scale land excavation and air pollution from smelting and refining activities (Lynch and Harwell 2002:65; Marr 1993:19). Serious environmental effects such as these have had a severe impact on communities living in close proximity to mine sites.

Mining operations have also caused the displacement and relocation of indigenous communities, resulting in the breakdown of cultural traditions, social cohesion and the loss of food self-sufficiency and economic autonomy. Not surprisingly, disputes between local, usually indigenous, communities and mining companies are common in this sector. Disputes usually centre on issues of land ownership and compensation, and the environmental impact of mining operations. State agencies responsible for issuing or administering mining law, regulations and particular licences, and the security forces responsible for mine security, are also key players in such mining disputes.

One of the most prominent and long running disputes between a mining company and local communities in Indonesia has centred on the operations of the giant Grasberg copper-gold-silver mine in West Papua, owned by Freeport McMoran. Freeport was the first major foreign investor in Indonesia following General Suharto's take-over in 1965. The company's investment was initially made on the most lucrative terms, including an extended tax holiday, concessions on normal levies, an exemption from royalties and an

49 The Freeport contract was signed before the UN sponsored 'Act of free choice' in West Papua, which was to transfer sovereignty over that area to Indonesia, was completed in 1969. See Marr 1993:73.

exemption from the requirement for Indonesian equity.[50] Operation of the Grasberg mine resulted in the displacement of two indigenous tribes, the Amungme and Komoro, from their traditional lands. Human rights abuses of local residents, including torture and killings, were also alleged to have been committed by security and company personnel.[51] Currently, a legal action claiming damages from Freeport has been initiated by community representatives in the United States (Budiardjo and Liong 1988:151).

In the Freeport case, the issue of the mine's environmental impact has been pursued by several environmental NGOs through political and legal channels. The mine's operations, which produce nearly 300,000 tonnes of waste daily, have resulted in the regular dumping of unprocessed tailings, widespread deforestation and the destruction of entire landscapes through open cut mining.[52] For the first two decades environmental monitoring of the mine's operations was lax or non-existent. The first environmental impact assessment was done more than a decade after the mine commenced operation and the results of this were never made public (Budiardjo and Liong 1988:151). The environmental impact of the mine is likely to worsen with the increased scale of Freeport's operations, following an expansion in the company's concession area from 10,000 to 2.5 million hectares covering much of the West Papuan central mountains (Marr 1993:71).

Conflict over Freeport's environmental impact has provided the backdrop for at least two environmental public interest actions in Indonesia. In 1995 the national environmental organization WALHI mounted a legal challenge against the approval granted by the Department of Mining and Energy to Freeport's environmental management plan. WALHI cited widespread environmental damage and social dislocation caused by Freeport's operations, arguing that the Department should have withheld environmental approval. A further legal suit was filed by WALHI following an incident in May 2000 when a dam holding overburden waste burst, flooding the lands of nearby villagers and claiming the lives of four workers.[53] In its highly publicized case WALHI argued that the mining company had provided misleading information in relation to the dispute and deliberately misled the public.

Besides the several court cases relating to Freeport's operations, there has only been one other reported civil mining related case concerning environ-

50 Subsequent renegotiation of the contract in 1976 led to cancellation of the remaining 18 months of tax exemption and purchase by the government of an 8.5% stake in the company's operations. See Marr 1993:15.

51 'Court orders Freeport to clean up its act', *Down to Earth* 51 (November) 2001. Newsletter of the International Campaign for Ecological Justice in Indonesia. http://dte.gn.apc.org/51Frp.htm.

52 'Rio Tinto under pressure', *Down to Earth* 38 (August) 1998. Newsletter of the International Campaign for Ecological Justice in Indonesia. http://dte.gn.apc.org/38min.htm.

53 See further discussion of this case, Chapter II: WALHI v. PT Freeport, 2001.

mental issues, the Muara Jaya case. In that case, a community suffered environmental damage from the installation of an oil pipe in West Kalimantan. After several appeals the community was ultimately successful in obtaining compensation in the Supreme Court. In most cases, the legal or practical obstacles associated with litigation appear to be sufficient to compel communities to adopt a more 'direct action' approach in disputes with mining companies, employing tactics such as blockades and occasionally violence or damage to property. For example, in May, June and July 2000, local Dayak villagers blockaded a gold mine operated by PT Kelian Equatorial Mining (PT KEM) in Kalimantan, a subsidiary of international mining giant Rio Tinto, for almost one month. The blockade, which forced a suspension of mining operations, signalled the breakdown of an agreement reached in June 1998 between PT KEM, a community organization (LKMTL), Rio Tinto and environmental NGO WALHI to address issues of land compensation, human rights abuses and environmental pollution.[54] According to local NGOs, PT KEM had refused to pay fair compensation for requisitioned land and had endeavoured to divide the local community by negotiating with local government heads rather than community appointed representatives.[55] A mediation process was subsequently resumed and is discussed in more detail in Chapter IV.

The proliferation of illegal or unlicensed mining, much like illegal logging in the forestry sector, has also contributed to the rise in the number of environmentally related disputes in the mining sector. Unlicenced mining first became prominent in the mid-1980s, and by 1990 the production of unlicenced gold mining was estimated at 10-14 tonne per annum compared to the 2-4 tonnes of licenced gold mines (Marr 1993:50). Unlicensed mining has further spread in the wake of economic instability and political crisis following the collapse of the New Order. In November 2000, illegal mining was estimated to be occurring in over seven hundred locations throughout the archipelago and to be costing the state in lost revenue around Rp 315.1 billion per year (Marr 1993:52). As illegal mining has spread, disputes have frequently emerged between unlicensed and licenced miners over rights to resource extraction. In the vast majority of disputes the position of the larger mining companies is supported by both the legal framework and govern-

54 Environmental pollution at the KEM mine in Kalimantan has included hazardous levels of manganese and cyanide in water discharged from the mine and excessive levels of suspended solids discharged into the Kelian River. See 'Rio Tinto under pressure', *Down to Earth* 38 (August) 1998. Newsletter of the International Campaign for Ecological Justice in Indonesia. http://dte.gn.apc.org/47Rio.htm.

55 'Rio Tinto; Blockades and strikes hit Kalimantan mines', *Down to Earth* 47 (November) 2000:13-5. Newsletter of the International Campaign for Ecological Justice in Indonesia. http://dte.gn.apc.org/47Rio.htm.

ment agencies.[56] Nonetheless, government agencies have struggled to control unlicenced miners, prompting several mining companies to threaten closure of mining operations due to unregulated illegal mining. Yet the matter of so-called 'illegal' mining is a complex one. Advocates for the rights of indigeneous communities have argued that traditional mining carried out by local communities should be protected and allowed by the law (Lynch and Harwell 2002:66). In response to such criticisms, the government has directed that only unlicenced miners using sophisticated equipment in large scale operations would be considered 'illegal', whilst local residents using traditional methods would not.[57] Unlicenced mining on a larger scale is often coordinated by profiteering middlemen who employ unsafe and environmentally hazardous methods. For example, the widespread use of mercury in unlicenced mining in Central Kalimantan has had a grave environmental impact, with some ten tonnes of mercury being released into the major tributary Kapus River annually.[58] The spread of illegal mining is likely to cause further environmental pollution and related disputes. Already in Western Kalimantan a NGO called the Community Forum for the Victims of Unlicenced Mining has been formed to oppose such environmentally damaging methods of mining and seek compensation for victims who have suffered its effects.[59]

Agriculture sector

The modernization of agriculture through the Green Revolution was another much lauded achievement of the New Order. Whilst agricultural modernization greatly increased productivity, enabling Indonesia to briefly achieve 'self-sufficiency' in rice production, the limitations of modern, industrial approaches to agricultural production have become more evident in recent years. The environmental impact of the Green Revolution has included the loss of genetic diversity in rice strains and the widespread use of environmentally damaging artificial fertilizers, pesticides and herbicides. More recently, grandiose 'Green Revolution' approaches have been applied to some of the outer islands in an attempt to dramatically increase agricultural productivity. One of the last 'mega-projects' of the Suharto era was the Kalimantan Peat Land Project, which aimed to convert some one million hectares of peat land

56 Article 26 of the Basic Mining Law requires local communities to surrender their traditional property rights to mining concessionaires, see Lynch and Harwell 2002:66.

57 In practice, however, traditional miners have continued to be displaced and prosecuted by enforcement agencies, see Marr 1993:9-11.

58 'Kalimantan rivers highly contaminated by mercury', *Indonesian Observer*, 13-9-2000.

59 'Wilayah pertambangan tanpa izin mencapai 713 lokasi', *Bisnis Indonesia*, 24-11-2000; 'Tim Terpadu PETI Tak Mampu Atasi Maraknya Penambangan Liar', www.MinergyNews.Com (accessed 24-11-2000).

into productive rice fields. The project was commenced in 1995 and bypassed many of the usual environmental assessment procedures due to personal backing from the President (Longgena Ginting 1998:2-3). The environmental impact of the grandiose project was severe and included widespread deforestation and destruction of a vast area of fragile wetlands. This environmental devastation, together with the displacement of local indigenous communities, failed to bring the expected benefits in agricultural yield, as the land ultimately proved unsuitable for agriculture purposes. The vast area of land had been devastated environmentally, and local indigeneous communities displaced. The agricultural debacle resulted in two legal suits to obtain environmental compensation and restoration. In the Kalimantan Peat Land case, WALHI sued a number of government agencies allegedly responsible for the project and its environmentally damaging outcome. In a separate case, a group of local farmers whose livelihood had been undermined by the project's devastating environmental impact sued the government for compensation.[60]

The purpose of the last section of this chapter was to provide some introduction to environmental disputes and the legal framework for their resolution in Indonesia. As already outlined in the Introduction, it is the purpose of this book to examine environmental dispute resolution from an empirical and normative standpoint, thus analysing its effectiveness and making appropriate recommendations for its further development. We commence this examination and analysis in the next chapter with a detailed study of environmental litigation in Indonesia, centring on the legal framework and its application by courts in environmental cases to date.

60 See details of these cases in Chapter II.

CHAPTER II

Environmental litigation in Indonesia
Legal framework and overview of cases

The ability of citizens or environmental organizations to utilize law and the legal process to prevent, ameliorate or compensate environmentally related damage has become increasingly relevant over the last several decades in Indonesia, which have been characterized by rapid industrialization, intensive exploitation of natural resources and a proliferation of environmental disputes, as discussed in the previous chapter. For concerned citizens affected in some way by environmental pollution or damage, environmental litigation represents one possible response and avenue of dispute resolution. This chapter firstly examines the legal framework governing the process of environmental litigation, focusing in particular on a number of key provisions relevant to environmental litigation from Part Three, Chapter VII of the Environmental Management Act (EMA) 1997 which governs 'Environmental Dispute Settlement through the Court'. The legal issues provided for within that chapter include environmental standing (article 38), representative actions in environmental disputes (article 37), compensation for environmental damage (article 34), strict liability (article 35) and environmental public interest suits (article 38). Reference is also made to other relevant provisions in the EMA, notably the community rights and obligations stipulated in Chapter III, such as the right to a good and healthy environment and the right to environmental information, both of which, as enforceable legal rights, hold particular relevance to the process of environmental litigation. Each of these issues is considered in detail below, with attention given to the legal provisions in question and how these provisions have been implemented in practice through the courts.

Other laws of direct relevance to environmental litigation include the Administrative Judicature Act (AJA) No. 5 of 1986, which governs legal suits against the state in the administrative courts.[1] Public state agencies have a direct stake in most environmental disputes as both the grantors of licences for industrial development or natural resource exploitation and as the authority for environmental protection and/or conservation. On several occasions to date, state agencies that have allegedly improperly performed their duties have become the subject of environmental public interest suits in Indonesia. In most cases of this nature, the AJA provides the legal framework for environmental litigation, although in some cases the act may not be applicable and general principles of public administrative law will apply. This chapter thus also discusses provisions of the AJA and principles of public administrative law of particular relevance to environmental litigation and examines how these have been implemented in cases to date in Indonesia.

As stated above, this chapter endeavours to not only document and analyse the legal framework for environmental litigation, but particularly to examine its interpretation by Indonesian courts in environmental cases to date. The discussion of pertinent legal principles or provisions is therefore accompanied by a summary and analysis of cases where those provisions have been applied by Indonesian courts. The concluding discussion in this chapter considers overall trends in judicial interpretation of Indonesian environmental law with reference to the theoretical framework elaborated in Chapter I. The cases examined in this chapter are environmental civil and administrative cases that relate in some way to the Environmental Management Act of 1982 and 1997. Cases involving criminal prosecution for environmental offences under the EMA are thus not represented. Due to the lack of an organized judicial reporting system, the data on environmental cases have been gathered from a range of sources including judicial decisions, newspaper reports, NGO reports and interviews. Given the limitations of judicial reporting in Indonesia, the overview in this chapter cannot claim to be an exhaustive overview of all civil and administrative environmental cases from 1982-2002. Nonetheless, the chapter endeavours to present the most comprehensive summary of civil environmental cases possible, given the information available.

Standing

Standing or *locus standi,* which refers to a right of audience before a court or tribunal, is a necessary prerequisite to most forms of litigation (Geddes 1992:29-39). The conventional approach to the issue of standing in both

[1] Actually, the AJA does not necessarily govern all such actions but rather has a specific jurisdiction defined in the act itself. See further discussion on this point later in this chapter.

civil and common law jurisdictions requires a potential litigant to possess a personal, typically proprietary, interest in the subject matter of the dispute. This principle was confirmed by the Indonesian Supreme Court (Mahkamah Agung) in its decision of 7 July 1971 No. 294/K/SIP/1974 (Mas Achmad Santosa 1998:100). In Indonesia, as in other jurisdictions, the requirement of standing has been a significant procedural obstacle to the public interest litigant seeking to enforce a public, often non-pecuniary, interest.[2] Consequently the common interest in environmental sustainability has remained, until recently, largely unrepresented in judicial forum due to its non-private nature. However, in many modern jurisdictions, courts have taken the lead in revising the traditionally restrictive doctrine of standing.[3] They have done so within a social context of growing environmental concern and within a developing legal context of environmental laws and regulations. As will be described below, Indonesia has proved to be no exception to this global trend.

PT Inti Indorayon Utama case, 1989

A more liberalized approach to standing in relation to environmental matters was first adopted by an Indonesian court in the now well known PT Inti Indorayon Utama (PT IIU) case.[4] The Indorayon factory, located on the Asahan River near Lake Toba in North Sumatra, commenced operations within a 150 000 hectares concession area at the beginning of 1984. Severe environmental damage has been attributed to the factory's operations ever since by local residents and environmental organizations, including deforestation of the surrounding area identified as a contributing factor to floods and a landslide that claimed the lives of nine villagers. The factory has also caused heavy pollution of the Asahan River, which local people had previously relied on for their day-to-day living needs (*Environesia* 1988:1). Pollution of the river reached a height when an artificial lagoon built by the company to hold toxic waste burst, releasing some 400,000 cubic metres of toxic waste into the Asahan River near Lake Toba (Heroepoetri Arimbi 1994b:1). The case

2 For example, standing was an obstacle in a celebrated public interest action concerning cigarette advertising and its impact on youth by R.O. Tambunan against the cigarette company P.T. Bentoel: see Mas Achmad Santosa 1988:100. Note, however, in the case of persons directly and materially affected by environmentally damaging activities the requirement of standing would be fulfilled.

3 Liberalized approaches to environmental standing have been adopted in many jurisdictions around the world. For example, in the Netherlands a liberalized approach to standing was judicially adopted in the Nieuwe Meer and Kuunders cases. In Australia the traditional doctrine of standing was modified in Onus v. Alcoa (1981) 36 ALR 425, and further modified by legislation.

4 Decision No. 820/Pdt./G/1988/PN.

was brought before the Central Jakarta district court by WALHI, a national environmental organization. WALHI argued that it should be allowed to represent the public 'environmental interest' and contended that issuance of operating permits to PT IIU was contrary to environmental law.[5]

In its decision, the court granted WALHI standing to bring its suit against five government agencies as well as the Indorayon Company. The court justified its decision, notwithstanding the lack of a material interest on WALHI's part, on a number of grounds. Firstly, the court described the environment as 'common property' and emphasized the public interest in environmental preservation.[6] It also emphasized the environment was a legal subject itself with an intrinsic right to be sustained. The 'environmental interest' in question could be legitimately represented by WALHI, a national environmental interest group, in court. Such a representative capacity was legally justified, given the right and obligation of every person to participate in environmental management[7] and the specific endorsement given to the participatory function of NGOs by article 19 of the EMA 1982, which recognizes self-reliant community institutions as performing 'a supporting role in the management of the living environment'.

Legislative standing for environmental organizations

The PT IIU decision was significant in that it helped surmount the procedural obstacle of environmental standing, thus paving the way for future legal actions protecting 'environmental interests'. The judicial precedent on this issue furthermore acted as an impetus for subsequent legislative reform through the EMA 1997. Article 38(1) of that EMA grants environmental organizations the right to bring a legal action 'in the interest of preserving environmental functions'. This provision thus marks the legislative adoption of the liberalized approach to standing taken by Indonesian courts in the cases discussed in the previous section. The elucidation confirms that standing according to the stipulated criteria is available in respect of actions in both the general courts and the administrative courts.[8]

5 In the Samidun Sitorus et al. v. PT Inti Indorayon case a number of local families also sought compensation for environmental damage attributed to PT IIU through a case in the Medan district court. This case is discussed later in this chapter.

6 The court justified its view in this respect by reference to the 1973 Broad Outline of the Nation's Direction (GBHN) and statements made in front of the national parliament (Dewan Perwakilan Rakyat) on 23-1-1982 prior to the enactment of the EMA 1982.

7 Article 6(1) of the EMA 1982.

8 An 'Elucidation' in Indonesian law is an explanatory appendix commonly included in Indonesian legislation. Whilst not formally a part of the Law, it is nonetheless a primary reference point for its interpretation.

As defined in article 38(3), an environmental organization must be a legal body or foundation, the articles of association of which clearly state environmental preservation to be one of the founding goals of the organization. The organization must also have undertaken activities in pursuit of this aim. The requirements stipulated in article 38(3) were largely an adoption of criteria enunciated in the IPTN (Reafforestation Funds) case (1994), where the Jakarta state administrative court granted standing to four of six environmental organizations who challenged Presidential Decree No. 42 of 1994, concerning a transfer of funds from a reafforestation fund to PT Industri Pesawat Terbang Nusantara (IPTN).[9] The court justified its decision, stating

> the contended decision afflicted the interest that could be induced from the well-defined goals they pursued according to their statutes. Moreover, they had a clear organisational structure, and could prove that they had actively sought to realize their goals.[10]

The IPTN case confirms the precedent of Indorayon in accepting the principle of environmental standing, but stipulates further criteria to restrict the scope of the doctrine. Some NGO workers have questioned the need for such restrictive criteria, fearing they might exclude a number of potential public interest litigants whose articles do not state their founding goal to be preservation of the environment.[11] In the IPTN case, two of the six plaintiff organizations were in fact excluded by the court, yet this was on the grounds that their purported representatives had not been correctly appointed in accordance with procedural requirements, rather than the requirements in article 38(3).

Representative actions

Whilst legal claims of a purely public interest nature have been excluded in the past due to a lack of standing, another procedural obstacle is raised where a large number of litigants seek to bring a joint claim grounded in similar legal and factual circumstances. In environmental cases, pollution from a single source may affect hundreds or even thousands of people. Processing numerous claims arising out of similar factual circumstances on an individual basis is inefficient, time consuming and expensive. The legal doctrine of a 'class action' evolved in common law jurisdictions in the 1800s to facilitate the

9 Note that the court in this case actually stipulated a fourth criteria, that an organization should be 'sufficiently representative', however this was not incorporated in article 38(3). Decision No. 088/G/1994/Piutang/PTUN.Jkt.

10 *Forum Keadilan* 5-1-1995 quoted in Bedner 2000:91.

11 Nur Amalia, interview at LBHS seminar, Jakarta, 24-11-1999.

efficient adjudication of such cases. In a class action, a large number of plaintiffs whose claims are grounded in common factual and legal circumstances, are legally represented by a smaller, representative group drawn from their number. Whilst the doctrine of class actions originated in the common law world, it has also been introduced more recently to a number of civil law jurisdictions.

Representative actions in Indonesia; Pre-EMA 1997

Unlike common law jurisdictions such as England or America, there was no specific legal basis in the Indonesian Civil Codes for a representative action. Yet, whilst class actions in the common law sense were unknown, it was not uncommon for multiple plaintiffs or defendants to be joined in a single action.[12] Traditional civil procedure thus provided some scope for common claims to be grouped together, although the practicality of this approach was limited by the requirement of each plaintiff to individually issue an authority for representation (*surat kuasa*).[13] Whilst the matter of class actions was not specifically regulated in the first EMA of 1982, a number of more general principles enunciated within that act held considerable relevance to the issue of class or representative actions. For instance, article 5(1) confirmed the right of every person to 'a good and healthy living environment'. The elucidation defined 'person' as 'an individual person, a group of persons, or a legal body'. Thus the EMA 1982 explicitly recognized the possibility that the right referred to in article 5 be vested in, and hence was exercisable by, a group of persons. Similarly, the act envisaged both an individual and collective vesting of the obligation contained within clause 2 of article 5, which recognizes the obligation on every person 'to maintain the living environment and to prevent and abate environmental damage and pollution'. The elucidation to the act stipulated that this obligation 'is not separated from [a person's] position as a member of the community, which reflects the value of man as an individual and as a social being'. Thus the EMA 1982, whilst failing to make explicit provision in relation to class actions, did nonetheless provide statutory grounds for at least the consideration of group compensation claims due to pollution or environmental damage.

Legislative scope for the introduction of representative actions was also found in the Judicial Authority Act No. 14 of 1970. Article 4(2) of that act

12 See for instance the Sari Morawa case where 260 individual plaintiffs in a common claim sued PT Sari Morawa for pollution of the Belumai River. Whilst the claim was rejected on substantive grounds, the joinder of the individual claims was allowed by the court. See further discussion of the case later in this chapter.

13 Individual authorities for representation are not required in a representative action.

requires justice to be administered in an 'efficient, swift and economical' manner.[14] Article 5(2) of the same act states courts shall 'assist justice seekers and make the utmost effort to overcome all obstacles and distractions so as to achieve justice which is efficient, swift and economical'. The act thus affords some discretion to courts and, particularly, emphasizes the important of efficiency, speed and economy in the administration of justice, all of which are greatly facilitated in cases involving numerous plaintiffs by a representative mechanism.

Pre-EMA representative action 1: PT Pupuk Iskandar Muda, 1989

The Pupuk Iskandar Muda (PT PIM) case was the first environmental case where a large number of plaintiffs who had suffered pollution attempted to sue a common defendant.[15] The case involved 602 plaintiffs, yet was not a 'class action' in the strict sense, as each plaintiff had provided legal authority and was identified in the claim. The defendant in this case, PT PIM, owned a liquid gas-processing factory in northern Aceh, from which, in 1988 and subsequently on several occasions, poisonous gas leaked out and spread through several villages in the near vicinity. A large number of residents who inhaled the fumes experienced symptoms ranging from unconsciousness to nausea (Hutapea 1993:15-48). In the case that followed, 602 local residents, represented by the Medan Legal Aid Institute, sued PT PIM claiming compensation for damages (Sundari 1999:12). The claim for compensation failed, both at the first instance and in a subsequent appeal to the high court of Aceh. In rejecting the legal suit, both courts stated that the individual claims of respective victims could not be contained in one, single claim. According to the court, no legal connection existed between the respective claims, and consequently each claim should be advanced individually on its own grounds.

Contrary to the court's opinion, it is actually arguable in this case that the plaintiffs' claim did comply with existing civil procedure. Each of the 602 claimants had provided legal authority to sue and were identified respectively in the formal claim.[16] There are many cases where courts have entertained in practice claims involving either multiple plaintiffs or multiple defendants. Indonesian civil procedure does not limit civil cases to single defendants or plaintiffs necessarily (Sundari 1999:12). There were, furthermore, obvious factual circumstances that connected the claims in this instance. Nonetheless, the number of plaintiffs in this case (602) was arguably so large as to make

14 Peradilan dilakukan dengan sederhana, cepat dan biaya ringan.

15 Decision No. 45/Pdt.G.1989/PN.Lsm. This account draws upon the comprehensive discussion of this case in Hutapea 1993:15-48.

16 Compared to a class action proper where individual claimants need not be identified.

a joined claim impractical for the court to adjudicate. A more appropriate response on this point would have been the separation of the claim into several, more adjudicable claims, rather than its outright rejection on the grounds that no connection existed between the claims. Furthermore, the environmental nature of this case clearly fell within the scope of the EMA 1982, which arguably supports a broader vesting of environmental rights in both groups and individuals (Hutapea 1993:15-48).

Pre-EMA representative action 2: Ciujung River, West Java 1995

In this case, liquid waste which was discharged from a group of five factories on the Ciujung River in West Java had severely affected several villages since September 1992.[17] The approximately five thousand residents of the villages depended on the river for fishing, irrigation, prawn farming and other daily needs. Residents' claims of pollution had been confirmed by research conducted by the national Environmental Impact Agency and the Centre for Fisheries Research and Development.[18] After several attempts at mediation had failed,[19] a number of community representatives conveyed their legal authority to the Legal Aid Institute of Jakarta. A representative action was subsequently registered with the district court of North Jakarta. In the pioneering class action a group of seventeen residents acted as class representatives for a class membership of some five thousand residents who had been affected by pollution from the five factories the subject of the claim. The plaintiffs argued that both the EMA 1982 and the Law on Judicial Authority No. 14 of 1970 provided a legislative basis for a representative action in this case, in which a large number of people had allegedly suffered damage as a result of pollution from the same source.[20]

However, the procedural issue of a representative action and the substantive liability of the defendants were never addressed by the court. The plaintiffs' claim in this case proceeded no further than the issue of jurisdiction, upon which it foundered. The plaintiffs had lodged the claim in the North

17 This account is based on the following sources: *District court North Jakarta* 1995; Indonesian Centre for Environmental Law, Legal Aid Institute of Jakarta and Association of Ciujung Water Users 1995:35; Prihartono 1995:1-4; Mas Achmad Santosa and Yazid 1998:5-15; Yazid 1995:5, and a compilation of newspaper clippings. The five factories were PT Indah Kiat Pulp and Paper, PT Cipta Paperia, PT Onward Paper Utama, PT Sekawan Maju Pesat and PT Picon Jaya all of which produced paper except the last which produced leather: See *District court North Jakarta* 1995.

18 District court North Jakarta 1995; Indonesian Centre for Environmental Law, Legal Aid Institute of Jakarta and Association of Ciujung Water Users 1995:35; Prihartono 1995:1-4.

19 The residents' attempts at mediation are discussed further in Chapter IV.

20 See the discussion of the specific provisions pertaining to representative actions from these two Acts above.

> from the fires and was ready to resign although not due to the result of any of his own actions, so as associations, communication forums, consulting and coordinating bodies for their members the entrepreneurs, who until this time have profited greatly from the forests now burning, it is morally appropriate and legally justified for [the defendant associations] to bear compensation (*Eksponen 66 v. APHI* 1998:41-5).

The decision in this case also illustrates the confusion that surrounded the procedural application of article 37, at least before enactment of the Supreme Court Regulation No. 1 of 2002 on Procedure for Class Action. Neither the plaintiffs' claim, nor the court's decision, clearly specified the usual elements of a class action, particularly the defining factual and legal characteristics of the class in question. The manner in which class members were to be notified of the action was not addressed, nor was the distribution of compensation. On the latter point, the court's decision only directed that compensation be paid in coordination with relevant agencies. Clearly, the payment of such a large sum to the community of an entire province requires more specific direction and management if it is to be effective (Mas Achmad Santosa and Indro Sugianto 2002:3).

Yet, despite its particular flaws, the district court of Medan's decision in this case stands out as a rare example of judicial activism in the environmental context. Given the absence of procedural law supporting article 37, and the extremely wide ambit of the plaintiffs' claim, it would have been certainly possible for the court to refuse this claim on a number of legal grounds. Yet, notwithstanding these factors, the court was willing to hear the claim and attempt to apply article 37 to the circumstances of the case. The court's reasoning demonstrated a clear recognition of the public interest in environmental preservation rarely apparent in prior environmental cases. The court's more activist stance in this case appears from the decision to have been influenced by the extent of the disaster, which caused widespread social disruption, health complaints and significant economic loss. The court's view of the impact of the fires and the resultant public sentiment was apparent in their judgment.

> It would seem there is not a single person from the community of North Sumatra who would not complain of this recent national disaster of smog [...]. School children were sent home, people were warned to reduce their activities outside the home and use masks for fear of suffering breathing disorders.

The court also appeared to justify, or at least frame, its decision by reference to statements and actions taken by senior government figures in the response to the fires. For instance, the judges' decision referred to a statement by a senior official describing the fires as 'a threat to national development and a state emergency in eight provinces', as well as to the Forestry Minister's offer of resignation and pending adminstrative sanctions being taken against forest concession holders (*Eksponen 66 v. APHI* 1998:41-5). The activist stance adopted by the district court of Medan in this case was not followed by the high court of North Sumatra when the decision was subsequently appealed. The appellate court subsequently overturned the decision by the district court, thus denying the claim for compensation.

Article 37 action 2: way Seputih River, 2000

In the Way Seputih River case a representative legal action was initiated on behalf of 1,145 family heads (*kepala keluarga*) drawn from eleven villages who had suffered loss due to pollution of the Way Seputih River in the Lampung region of southern Sumatra.[31] The large group of plaintiffs, all fishermen by trade, was represented by a smaller group of 27 consisting of community leaders who had also suffered loss of the same nature. The plaintiffs alleged that three industries: PT Venong Budi Indonesia, an MSG factory; PT Sinar Bambu Mas, a paper factory; and PT Budi Acid Jaya, a tapioca chip factory, had polluted the Way Seputih River from 26 April until 2 May 1999. Residents reported the waters of the river turning red and foul-smelling, causing the deaths of fishes in the river. The river's pollution caused the deprivation of the plaintiffs' livelihood as fishermen and rendered the waters unusable for daily needs by the adjoining villages.

Following a report by the plaintiffs to the regional government of Central Lampung, an administrative warning was issued to the three industries, requesting the industries' waste management units be improved. Following this, a further investigation into the incident was launched by a Prokasih[32] team, which was to examine the condition of the waste management units and quality of the discharged effluent. The results of inquiry showed the rudimentary units to be inadequate,[33] with the discharged effluent from all factories clearly exceeding stipulated standards.[34] The team's findings

[31] In fact 13 villages had been adversely affected by the river's pollution, however two villages chose to withdraw from the action and were not represented. See Decision No. 04/Pdt.G/2000/PNM.

[32] 'Prokasih' stands for Program Kali Bersih, 'the Clean Rivers Program', a major environmental law enforcement initiative undertaken by national and provincial environmental impact agencies to improve the management of industrial waste discharged into rivers.

[33] All three factories lacked an instrument to measure the volume of discharged water, contrary to Ministerial Decision KLH No. 51/MENLH/10/1995, as well as a permanent tank for storage of waste.

[34] As an illustration of variance in 'scientific' investigations, the results of this investigation may be contrasted with that of an investigation carried out in the same month by a Prokasih team from the provincial (Level I) government. The latter investigation did not find evidence to indicate that PT Ve-Wong had polluted the river, and concluded that the factory's waste management unit was in functioning order and that the company had not in fact disposed of waste into the river since commencing production.

prompted the district regent to issue a final warning (*peringatan keras*) to the industries to improve waste management. Despite subsequent assurances by industry to resolve the matter by negotiation, industry representatives failed to attend several meetings convened by regional government officials and denied any culpability in the pollution.[35]

The subsequent legal claim of the plaintiffs referred firstly to article 37 of the EMA 1997, which granted the communities 'a right to bring a class action to court [...] concerning various environmental problems which inflict losses on the life of the community'. The plaintiffs' claim emphasized that the losses suffered by the 'class members' and the 'class representatives' were identical in nature, namely the pollution of the Way Seputih River, which had deprived all the plaintiffs of a livelihood and source of clean water.[36] On the substantive matter of liability, the plaintiffs alleged that the pollution of Way Seputih River was contrary to the companies' obligation 'to preserve the continuity of environmental functions and protect and combat environmental pollution and damage' (article 6, EMA 1997). The actions of the three industries had thus 'given rise to adverse impacts on other people or the environment' (article 34, EMA 1997) resulting in an obligation to pay compensation and stop the discharge of any further waste pursuant to article 34. The plaintiffs also argued that, as the defendant industries had caused a 'large impact on the environment', the defendants were consequently strictly liable for any losses arisen, with the result that the plaintiffs were absolved of the burden of proving fault as would usually be the case. In any case, the unambiguous results of the investigation into the pollution by the Prokasih team were sufficient, in the plaintiffs' opinion, to establish the fact that the companies had in fact polluted.

In comparison to the Eksponen 66 case, the representative claim in this case complied more closely to the typical elements of a class action. The plaintiffs' claim clearly specified the class members, class representatives and the common circumstances out of which the claim had arisen. The representative nature of the claim was accepted by the district court of Metro notwithstanding the absence of a specific procedure for representative actions. The court rejected procedural objections by the defendants concerning the legal authority of the plaintiffs and the adequacy of representation, and recognized that the 27 plaintiffs 'had the right to represent the interests of the class members' (Lukman 2000:1-5). The argument of the defendants that as only eleven of the thirteen communities affected by pollution were represented (two communi-

35 Whilst denying culpability, two of the three defendants did offer 'voluntary assistance' in the form of construction of a place of worship, and assistance in reestablishing fish stocks in the river.

36 To the credit of the legal representatives of the plaintiffs, the claim also provided a useful summary of the legal history, nature and elements of the class action mechanism, which until recently has been unknown in Indonesian law.

ties had withdrawn from the action) the class representation was inadequate and therefore inadmissible was also rejected by the court. On this point, the court ruled that the eleven villages were entitled to bring an action themselves and did not require representation from the remaining two villages as they were not puporting to act on their behalf.

Ultimately, however, the plaintiffs' suit was defeated on procedural grounds of a different nature. In a surprising decision, the court held that the plaintiffs' application was procedurally defective, as it had failed to include the regional government, represented by the provincial and regency level environmental impact agencies, as defendants in its claim. The court referred to several provisions in concluding that it was these agencies which held legal responsibility for environmental monitoring and so should properly be included in any legal action relating to environmental matters. The conclusion of the Metro district court on this point may be criticized on several grounds. The legal suit in this case did not address the issue of environmental monitoring generally, but rather the specific, private law matter of the damage caused to the plaintiffs by the defendants' alleged actions contrary to law. The issue was, therefore, a matter of private rather than public law, notwithstanding the use of the class action mechanism. There thus seems to be no legal basis for compelling the plaintiffs to sue public agencies when they are simply seeking to enforce their private interests. It should not have been incumbent upon on the plaintiffs, as private citizens, to take the time consuming and expensive step of suing public agencies and compelling performance of their public duties. Whilst the latter action would be open to the plaintiffs, it should properly be a matter of choice and not a prerequisite for the enforcement of private rights. There are also numerous precedents where communities have brought legal actions against polluting companies without involvement of government agencies as defendants.[37] In any event, the reasoning adopted by the court seems inadequate grounds upon which to defeat an entire action. If the court was of such an opinion, it is difficult to fathom why it did not instruct the plaintiffs at an earlier stage, inviting appropriate revision of the plaintiffs' claim.

Article 37 action 3: Pekanbaru smog case, 2000

Like the Eksponen 66 case, this case arose out of forest fires caused by land clearing activities on the island of Sumatra.[38] In this representative action the plaintiff, the Legal Aid Institute of Riau, sought to represent the 600,000

37 See for example the Babon River case discussed in detail in Chapter IV. In that case, the plaintiffs were actually pressured by the district government to drop the mayor of Semarang as a co-defendant in the legal suit. Eventually the mayor was excluded as a party and the plaintiffs' suit proceeded solely against the accused polluting companies.

38 Decision No. 32/PDT/G/2000/PN-PBR.

residents of Pekanbaru in a claim relating to smog that had blanketed the city from 1 February until 10 March 2000. The severe smog had caused a range of health complaints in the populace of Pekanbaru and deprived the plaintiffs of a clean and healthy environment during that period. In its claim, the Riau Legal Aid Institute argued that the land clearing activities carried out by the four defendant companies, in which existing forest was burnt down, was the cause of the smog covering Pekanbaru during this period. The 'class members' in this case were the 600,000 residents of Pekanbaru, whilst the 'class representative' was the Legal Aid Institute of Riau, described in the claim as a group of people from the community of Pekanbaru.

One of the objections raised by the defendants was that as the plaintiff was a legal foundation and not a natural person it could not be described as a member of the group of persons, which it sought to represent. On this point, however, the Pekanbaru district court disagreed, stating that whilst a foundation, the plaintiff was nonetheless a group of persons within the community that was represented in this case. The issue that ultimately became a legal obstacle for the plaintiff in this case, was that of notification. The court emphasized both during the hearings and in its decision that the plaintiff in a representative action was required to notify potential class members of the pending claim. Notification would allow potential members to opt-out if necessary and would enable a more exact determination of the number of plaintiffs. The court informed the Riau Legal Aid Institute of the necessity of carrying out notification during the course of the hearing. Notification, however, was not carried out by the plaintiff due to a lack of funds. As a result, the district court of Pekanbaru refused the plaintiff's claim because it did not fulfil the stipulated requirements in article 37.

In the decision, the district court of Pekanbaru appeared willing to adjudicate a representative action despite ambiguity regarding the correct procedure with which to do so. The court was conversant with the elements of a representative action and correct in requiring notification of potential class members to the claim. In the absence of regulation governing the matter of notification, the court adopted a flexible approach, stating that notification could be carried at the commencement or during the course of proceedings. The class representative in this matter was a legal foundation, the Legal Aid Institute of Riau, rather than a natural person as was also the case in the Eksponen 66 claim. The defendants' objections on this point were ultimately disallowed by the court, which accepted the plaintiff as a legitimate representative of the class. Nonetheless, the use of organizations in representative actions does point to a tendency amongst Indonesian jurists to confuse the causes of action available to environmental organizations pursuant to article 38 with representative actions pursuant to article 37 of the EMA 1997, which actually have quite distinct requirements (Mas Achmad Santosa and Indro

Sugianto 2002:2). A class or representative action is of a personal or private nature and requires a class representative to have suffered the same loss as the other class members he or she seeks to represent. The use of an environmental organization, rather than an individual or group of individuals, as class representative will in most cases only confuse the issue and compound the task of establishing commonality in fact and law.

Compensation for environmental damage

Overcoming the procedural hurdles discussed, whilst crucial to the success of any environmental public interest action, does not guarantee success in any substantive sense. Whilst environmental litigation may be initiated in pursuit of political objectives, legally speaking the primary objective is to obtain an appropriate remedy for the loss in question. The cause of action and remedy sought in environmental suits may vary from case to case. A common legal remedy, especially where the litigant has suffered direct loss because of environmentally damaging activities, is that of compensation. In this section of the chapter, the different statutory grounds for claiming compensation in civil environmental cases and their application in recent cases are considered in some detail.

Article 1365 of the Civil Code

Article 1365 of the Civil Code states that: 'Every action contrary to law, which causes loss to another person, obliges the person by whose fault the loss has resulted, to compensate that loss' (Koesnadi Hardjasoemantri 1993:358). To establish that an action contrary to law (*perbuatan melawan hukum*) has been committed, four elements must thus be established:

- The action in question must be contrary to law.
- The person committing the action must be at fault.
- There must be damage or loss.
- There must be a sufficient causal connection between the action and the damage in question (Nusatara 1989:57).

An act (or omission) 'contrary to law' may be contrary to legislation, imply transgression of a personal right, or constitute a failure to exercise reasonable care in particular circumstances (Lotulung 1993b:19-27). Fault is generally understood to encompass both a subjective and objective element. Subjectively, a person must have understood the meaning and nature of the action which he or she undertook. The person must also have acted with deliberate intention or negligence in carrying out an action or omission contrary to law (Andri 1999:1-13). Objectively, a reasonable person in the same circumstances would have foreseen the potential damage that resulted and acted differently. To establish fault both elements must be fulfilled. Damage or loss may refer to both material and immaterial loss. Examples of the latter include damage to one's health or enjoyment of life. Causation implies the action in question was the most proximate and actual cause of the loss in question.

The burden of proof in respect of article 1365 lies upon the plaintiff, who seeks compensation for damage.[39] In environmental disputes, the elements of fault and causation may be particularly difficult for a plaintiff prove. Personal loss resulting from pollution involves a complex chain of causality, most stages of which are not apparent to the human eye. Expert scientific testimony is a necessity in such cases to establish a chain of causation for legal purposes. Pollution also often originates from multiple sources, and it may therefore be difficult to establish that the actions of a particular defendant caused the loss in question. Moreover, incriminating evidence may be withheld or deliberately concealed by polluting companies.[40] The complexities of discharging the plaintiff's burden of proof in environmental suits can result in protracted and expensive legal proceedings with only a small chance of success. Victims of pollution or environmental damage, who in the majority of cases originate from the socially and economically weak sectors of society, are seldom in a position to afford the expenses associated with such proceedings. The legal structure of 'fault liability', as contained in article 1365, acts as a deterrent to environmental victims to seek redress and on the other hand does little to deter potential polluters.[41]

A reversed burden of proof has been suggested as a possible solution to the difficulties mentioned above (Siti Sundari Rangkuti 1995:52-4). It is, however, established law that the burden of proof in respect of article 1365 is borne by the party claiming compensation. The Civil Code only provides for a reversed burden of proof in certain prescribed circumstances. For instance, section 1367(2) and 1367(5) establishes a reversed burden of proof in cases concerning the responsibility of animal owners.[42] Whilst the court may not apply a reversed burden of proof in environmental disputes based on the Civil Code, it may nonetheless limit the burden placed upon the plaintiff by making a balanced apportionment of the evidential burden, according to the

39 Whilst the burden of proof does lie upon the plaintiff, the judge retains a general discretion to vary the distribution of the burden of proof in the requirements of justice in each case.

40 See for instance WALHI 1991:6.

41 On this point see discussion in Andri 1999:1-13.

42 As per article 1865 BW; article 163 HIR; article 283 R.Bg.

discretion of the court (Siti Sundari Rangkuti 1995:52-4). However, this does not seem to have actually occurred in practice.

Article 20 EMA 1982

In addition to containing a number of important legislative principles that provided the basis for a judicial reconsideration of standing, the EMA 1982 also explicitly provided for a right of compensation for victims of environmental damage. Article 20(1) of the EMA 1982 stated: 'Whosoever damages and/or pollutes the living environment is liable for payment of compensation to victims whose right to a good and healthy living environment has been violated'. Article 20(1) does not explicitly refer to the notion of 'fault' as does article 1365. Nonetheless, Indonesian jurists have generally regarded the article as a particularized (*lex specialis*) restatement of article 1365 in the environmental context, thus implicitly encompassing the elements of fault and causation.[43] Article 20 clause 2 further provides for the investigation of complaints and determination of damages by a tripartite team including representatives of the respective parties, government and expert opinion as required. Where conciliation via the tripartite team fails to produce agreement then the matter may be taken to court.[44]

Article 20 EMA 1982 case 1: Samidun Sitorus et al. v. PT Inti Indorayon, 1989
The necessity of a prior government investigation into pollution pursuant to article 20(2) was a legal bar to an environmental suit arising out of the Indorayon dispute discussed in relation to standing above.[45] In this action a claim was made by residents adjoining the Asahan River who had suffered loss due to the pollution from the Indorayon factory. The claim was dismissed on the basis of article 20 which required, according to the court, prior investigation by a team into the type and extent of damages and the procedures for seeking compensation and restoration. Only where unanimous agreement could not be reached within a certain time, should the matter be taken to court.

Given the general reluctance of regional government agencies to investigate pollution claims, the procedural requirement for a tripartite investigation prior to lodging a legal claim for compensation in practice obstructed, rather than facilitated, claimants' access to justice. Another legal obstacle was

43 Fault based liability on the basis of article 1365 Civil Code and article 20 EMA 1982 is distinguished from the system of strict liability (based on risk rather than fault) enacted in article 21 EMA 1982 and article 35 EMA 1997.

44 Elucidation article 20(2).

45 Decision No. 154/Pdt.G/1989/PN.Mdn. Account adapted from Heroepoetri Arimbi 1994a:1.

the absence of implementing regulations referred to in article 20(2), which contributed to a general judicial reluctance to apply the provision.

Article 20 EMA 1982 case 2: PT Sarana Surya Sakti case, 1991
The issue of mediation pursuant to article 20(2) was considered in the decision of the Surabaya district court in the PT Sarana Surya Sakti (PT SSS) case.[46] In that case, a claim for compensation was made by the residents of village Tembok Dukuh who claimed zinc and chromium waste from the PT SSS factory had resulted in pollution of groundwater and village wells. The claim was rejected by the Surabaya district court on the grounds that article 20(2) required a claim for compensation to the court be preceded by mediation via a tripartite team. Siti Sundari Rangkuti (1995:38) has criticized the decision in this case, arguing that article 20 did not require that mediation precede any claim for compensation but rather presented mediation as an alternative course of action. According to Siti Sundari Rangkuti (1995:37), article 20 presented two possible and separate courses of action: a claim for compensation in court based on article 20(1) read in conjunction with article 1365 of the Civil Code and secondly a process of mediation via a tripartite team to agree on a sum of compensation as stipulated in article 20(2). Paulus Lotulung (1991:66), on the other hand, has suggested that the terms of the elucidation required all claims for compensation to be preceded by mediation.[47] Certainly, the language of the article itself, when read in conjunction with the elucidation, seems to explicitly link the two clauses together and thus require any claim for compensation to be preceded by the stipulated process of mediation.

In any case the reasoning of the court in PT SSS case seems hard to justify even on the facts, as extensive government facilitated mediation had in fact taken place both prior to the claim being advanced to the court and subsequently, at the request of the court (see Hutapea 1993:6). Furthermore, the community's allegations of pollution had been substantiated by the investigation of an official government technical team, the outcome of which the parties had agreed to accept.[48] However, the attempts at mediation and the results of the official investigation were apparently not given consideration in the decision of the court. A subsequent statement by the presiding judge in that case indicated that it was the absence of implementing legislation

46 Sarana Surya Sakti 1993. Decision No. 373/Pdt.G/1991/PN. Sby.

47 Lotulung does maintain, however, that article 1365, as a general provision (*lex generalis*), presented an alternative course of action to article 20, as a specific provision. Thus in practice the two views are not that different, as litigation could still be undertaken even if it were not preceded by mediation. See discussion in Lotulung 1995.

48 Letter from Walikotamadya Kepala Daerah Tingkat II to Director PT SSS dated 25-10-1990.

referred to in article 20(2) that contributed to the reluctance to interpret or apply the provision.[49]

Article 20 EMA 1982 case 3: Muara Jaya, 1991

The Muara Jaya case is the sole example of a successful claim for compensation relating to environmental damage under the EMA 1982.[50] In this case, installation of an oil pipe in West Kalimantan by PT Santan Mas DRC, a subcontractor of Total Indonesia Inc., caused significant damage to the environment of local residents of a housing estate.[51] Following the protests of local residents the Samarinda mayor had ordered PT Santan Mas to cease its activities, as it did not hold the required regional mining permit. The environmental damage was subsequently confirmed, and payment of compensation recommended, by a government investigation carried out pursuant to article 20. A claim for compensation for environmental damage totalling Rp 977,433,500 was then advanced by the affected community to the Balikpapan district court, but was rejected.[52] The plaintiffs were, however, successful on an appeal to the high court of Samarinda, where compensation of Rp 677,433,500 was awarded.[53] A final appeal by PT Santan Mas DRC to the Supreme Court failed. In its decision dated 17 March 1993, the Supreme Court stated that nothing in the previous high court's decision conflicted with existing law, and that as a result the decision was valid.[54] It is interesting that the Supreme Court did not see fit to reject the suit due to the lack of implementing regulations in respect of article 20, and yet few lower courts have followed this precedent.

The discussion above illustrates the inadequacies of the legal framework for compensation of environmental damage under the EMA 1982. The cases discussed also demonstrate the markedly conservative approach of the Indonesian courts to this matter. The fact that implementing regulations in respect of article 20 had not been enacted should not have been sufficient

[49] Toha 1993:83. This issue is discussed in relation to the Surabaya River case. Whether this was actually the reason for the court's decision in this case is difficult to say. In any case, the absence of implementing regulations certainly provided a reason for the court to avoid applying the provision.

[50] Decision No. 2727K/Pdt/1991.

[51] Damage included entry of mud and sand into the residential area of the plaintiffs, as well as closure of irrigation channels and water pipes, and damage to the plaintiffs' crops, local roads and drinking wells. See *Muara Jawa* 1991.

[52] Decision No. 18/Pdt/Cl/1989/PN.BPP.

[53] Decision No. 03/Perd/1991/PT KT SMDA.

[54] See *Buletin informasi hukum dan advokasi lingkungan*, No. 02/1993, Indonesian Centre for Environmental Law.

to preclude plaintiffs from enforcing their rights. Certainly, courts have the option of exercising judicial discretion in applying legal provisions, even in the absence of more specific implementing regulation. In any case, even where compensation claims could not be received based on article 20 due to a lack of implementing regulations, there is no reason why such claims could not have proceeded based on article 1365.[55] Similarly, the requirement in article 20(2) for mediation by a tripartite team was interpreted in a formalistic manner by courts to preclude claims, even where mediation had in fact taken place as in the PT SSS case. Conservatism also characterized judicial evaluation of evidence, as in the Sari Morawa case, where strong evidence of pollution was discounted by the court. Overall, article 20 thus only facilitated access to justice for citizens suffering the effects of environmental damage or pollution in one out of five reported cases: Muara Jaya.

Article 20 EMA 1982 case 4: Singosari SUTET case, 1994

This case arose when a high voltage power line was constructed in Singosari in Gresik regency, East Java.[56] The power lines crossed over a number of residences in the Singosari and Indro villages. Whilst the project commenced in November 1989, residents were only informed of the planned power lines in January 1991. By August 1992 construction was complete and operation of the high voltage lines commenced. The claim for compensation was brought by 92 residents of Singosari and Indro villages whose residences were located under the power lines. The majority of these residents had voluntarily relocated into makeshift accommodation once the power lines had been made operational. The plaintiffs claimed that the high voltage cables posed a threat to human health due to the effects of electro-magnetic radiation. Lawyers for the plaintiff cited six different international scientific studies, which had concluded that electro-magnetic fields from high voltage power lines did pose a threat to human health. According to the studies, possible effects included a higher incidence of childhood leukemia and cancer.

The plaintiffs sued the State Electricity Industry, the Department of Mining and Energy and the East Java regional government claiming material damages of Rp 70,025,000 (relating to their relocation and land devaluation) and immaterial damages of Rp 4,000,000,000 (relating to the anxiety and emotional suffering caused by the project) in addition to the relocation of the power lines. The plaintiffs also argued that the high voltage power line project was contrary to law, as it transgressed their right to a good and healthy environment (article 5 EMA 1982), contravened a statutory obligation for the State

55 For a more detailed discussion of this point, see Lotulung 1991:8.

56 Decision No. 35/Pdt.G/1994/PN.Jkt.Pst.

Electricity Industry to show consideration for public health (article 15[1], Law No. 15 of 1985 on Electricity), and furthermore contravened Government Regulation No. 29 of 1986 on Environmental Impact Assessment, as an environmental evaluation had only been approved in March 1993, subsequent to the project's commencement.

The case was heard by the Central Jakarta district court, which rejected the plaintiffs' claim for compensation. The court accepted the defendants' argument that the high voltage power lines complied with standards stipulated by the International Radiation Protection Association (IRPA) and the World Health Organization. The court discounted the substantial body of scientific evidence presented by the plaintiffs, on the grounds that the research was not carried out in Indonesia and hence could not be considered relevant in this case. On these grounds the court concluded that the high voltage power lines did not in fact pose a threat to the health of residents living under them and so did not give rise to an obligation to pay compensation. Whilst the effects of electro-magnetic radiation from power lines are obviously a matter of some controversy the court's decision in this case to simply discount a large body of international scientific opinion on the grounds that it was not Indonesia-based seems difficult to support.

Article 20 EMA 1982 case 5: Sari Morawa case, 1996

A narrow and rather blinkered approach to the evaluation of scientific evidence was also taken in the Sari Morawa case.[57] In this case, a group of some 260 plaintiffs who resided next to the Belumai River sued PT Sari Morawa, the owner of a pulp and paper mill adjoining the same river upstream from the villages of the plaintiffs. The villagers alleged that since July 1992 the Belumai River had been severely polluted by untreated waste discharged from the PT Sari Morawa factory into the river. Convincing evidence of the pollution was presented by the plaintiffs to the Lubuk Pakam district court, including research carried out in 1994 by PT Sucofindo, which indicated that hazardous waste was being discharged from the factory greatly in excess of stipulated limits. Further data compiled by the Central Environmental Impact Agency (Bapedal), confirmed that waste discharged from the Sari Morawa factory failed to comply with applicable regulations. The continuing discharge of untreated waste from the factory, and the company's failure to install appropriate waste management facilities, prompted Bapedal to give the factory a 'black' rating, the worst pollution rating available.[58]

57 Decision No. 24/PDT/G./1996/PN-LP.

58 The rating was part of an environmental enforcement initiative (PROPER) carried out by the national Environmental Impact Agency, where industries were publicly rated according to their compliance with environmental regulations.

The district court of Lubuk Pakam consented to hear the plaintiffs' claim based on article 20(1) of the EMA 1982 and article 1365 of the Civil Code, notwithstanding the lack of implementing regulations for the former provision. Yet, on the substantive issue of compensation, the court rejected the plaintiffs' claim. In its decision, the court concluded that the evidence presented to it did not establish that the action of the defendant in discharging waste into the River Belumai had resulted in pollution and thus caused the plaintiffs' loss.[59] Such proof, the presiding judges stated, would require samples to be taken from the river and examined in laboratories especially designed for testing environmental pollution. Strangely, in coming to this conclusion the court did not discuss the main evidence upon which the plaintiffs' case was based – laboratory research carried out by PT Sucofindo demonstrating that waste discharged from the Sari Morawa factory was greatly in excess of regulatory standards, and in fact constituted hazardous waste.[60] According to the plaintiffs, PT Sucofindo was also authorized to carry out and publish laboratory examinations in relation to pollution,[61] a fact not commented upon by the court.

Article 34 EMA 1997

The right of compensation in relation to environmentally damaging activities was revised in the new Environmental Management Act 1997, article 34 of which reads

> Each action contrary to law in the form of pollution and/or environmental damage causing loss to another person or the environment, obligates the party responsible for the enterprise and/or activity to pay compensation and/or carry out certain actions.

In contrast to the EMA 1982, a claim pursuant to article 34 need not be preceded by any process of mediation. The drafters of the new law made a clear distinction between resolution of environmental disputes within and outside of courts, in order to avoid the confusion that had arisen in relation to article

59 As discussed above, article 1365 of the Civil Code requires proof of causation, that is that the defendant's action caused the loss of the plaintiff.

60 The PT Sufocindo data presented a laboratory analysis of waste discharged from the PT Sari Morawa factory. The data were as follows (regulatory limits are in parantheses for comparison): pH 10.77 (6-9); Biological Oxygen Demand (BOD) 1,045.46 mg/L (150 mg/L); Chemical Oxygen Demand (COD) 1,712.18 mg/L (350 mg/L); suspended matter 1,568 ppm (200 ppm). The court's decision was also contrary to testimony from expert and eye witness testimony confirming pollution from the factory.

61 In accordance with Governor's Decision No. 660.3/1776/K/1993.

20 EMA 1982.[62] Whilst parties may choose to opt for mediation in environmental disputes, the choice is voluntary and if declared to have failed by one or both parties, then the matter may proceed to court. Article 34 also has a wider scope of application when read in conjunction with article 37, which enables a community to bring a representative action in respect of environmentally-related damage, as already discussed.

The wording of article 34, unlike article 1365 of the Civil Code, does not make explicit reference to the element of fault. Nonetheless in practice article 34, like article 20 of the EMA 1982, has been treated as a particularized restatement (*lex specialis*) of article 1365 of the Civil Code, thus encompassing the element of fault. In addition to compensation, the court may order 'certain actions' (*tindakan tertentu*) be carried out by the defendant pursuant to article 34. This category of actions is not limited by the terms of the article, although examples of certain actions are provided in the elucidation, including:

- Install or repair a waste treatment facility such that the waste complies with environmental quality standards which have been applied.
- Restore environmental functions.
- Remove or destroy the cause of the arising of environmental pollution and/or damage.

Article 34 thus affords courts with considerable discretion to not only compensate victims of environmental damage but also to order appropriate action to remedy the causes of the environmental damage or pollution and prevent their recurrence. Article 34 has been the basis for several environmental claims since the enactment of the EMA 1997, which are considered below.

Article 34 EMA 1997 case 1: Babon River case, 1998

In the Babon River case, a community of prawn farmers sued a group of industries for damage attributed to water pollution from the factories.[63] The farmers practiced a traditional method of prawn and fish farming in which their ponds were flushed by the tidal flow from the mouth of the nearby Babon River and the ocean. The six industries that were the subjects of the claim were located further upstream on the Babon River, into which they regularly discharged their waste effluent. Prior to 1995, when none of the industries had owned or operated a waste management unit, the effluent was untreated. In September 1994, the prawn harvest of the fishpond farmers failed for a period of four months and subsequent to this resumed but at a

62 Mas Achmad Santosa, personal communication, May 1999 Leiden University.

63 Decision No.42/Pdt.G/1998/PN.Smg. The Babon River case is the subject of a detailed case study in Chapter IV.

much-depleted level. The group of prawn farmers attributed the loss to the six industries located on the Babon River and sued them in the district court for compensation of environmental damage. The plaintiff farmers were partially successful at the district court level, obtaining an award for compensation in respect of environmental damage of Rp 4,400,000, although this was well short of their claimed amount of Rp 51,645,000. Upon appeal to the high court of Central Java, however, the claim was rejected on the grounds that a previous payment to the community from the industries in fact constituted compensation and so absolved the defendants of further liability. The factual circumstances, legal issues and conditions influencing the final outcome in this case are analysed in further detail in Chapter IV.

Article 34 EMA 1997 case 2: Laguna Mandiri, 1998

Another case where claimants succeeded at the district court (*pengadilan negeri*) level yet failed at the high court (*pengadilan tinggi*) level was the Laguna Mandiri case, which arose out of the devastating fires that swept much of the Indonesian archipelago in 1997.[64] The fires consumed an estimated 1.5 million hectares of forest and blanketed much of the Southeast Asian region in a thick haze.[65] In this case a number of members of the Dayak Samihim community in the regency of Kota Baru, Kalimantan, brought a legal action for compensation against several companies, including PT Laguna Mandiri, that owned coconut plantation estates adjoining the plaintiffs' villages.[66] The plaintiffs claimed that fires intentionally lit by the defendants for the purpose of land clearing between July and November 1997 had spread out of control, destroying large areas of the plaintiff community's crops and housing. By way of compensation for their loss, the plaintiffs sought payment of a sum of Rp 406,813,788,780 from the defendants[67] and in addition requested that the court order the defendants to undertake environmental rehabilitation (*District court Kọta Baru* 1998:18-39; Toha 1993:83).

64 Decision No. 09/Pdt.G/1998/PN.KTB.

65 Whilst the Indonesian government initially sought to attribute the fires to natural phenomena, independent analyses of the destruction and subsequent statements by Indonesian authorities themselves identified illegal man-made fires as the primary cause. See Vayda 1999.

66 The defendants to the claim were PT Laguna Mandiri I, II and III, PT Langgeng Muaramakmur III and PT Swadaya Andika. All the companies subject of the claim were part of the Salim Group, one of the largest corporate conglomerates in Indonesia, owned by Liem Sioe Liong. The environmental dispute in this case was not the first dispute between the plantations and the adjoining communities, who had already been at loggerheads regarding the companys' appropropriation of traditional lands owned by the communities without proper compensation.

67 Rp 813,788,780 was in respect of material loss, including the loss of crops, housing, and income (due to time spent fighting the constant fires); Rp 300 billion for environmental restoration and Rp106 billion for immaterial loss.

The plaintiffs alleged that the defendants' act of land clearing by fire and their failure to implement a system of fire prevention and control constituted acts or omissions contrary to law, contravening a number of legal provisions or regulations including the following:[68]

- Article 5(1) EMA 1997 – The right of the plaintiffs to a good and healthy environment.
- Decision of the Director General of Agriculture No.38/KB.110/SK/DJ.BUN/05.95 concerning Land Clearing without Burn offs which, according to the plaintiff, in effect prohibited the use of fire for land clearing (*District court Kota Baru* 1998:18-39).
- Decisions of the Director General of Forestry (PHPA) No. 243/Kpts/DJ-VI/1994 and No. 248/Kpts/DJ-VI/1994 concerning the prevention and control of forest fires, which requires the installation of fire barriers and monitoring of potential fire outbreaks which the defendants had allegedly failed to do.

The plaintiffs' case was actually pleaded based on article 35, which applies the principle of strict liability.[69] Strangely, the district court of Kota Baru did not refer to this article in their decision, or to the equally applicable article 34, but rather considered the case as an action contrary to law based on article 1365 of the Civil Code.[70] The court considered that the documentary and witness evidence submitted by the plaintiff was sufficient to establish that the fires which had destroyed the crops and housing of the plaintiffs during the period from July to November 1997 had in fact originated from fires deliberately lit for the purpose of land clearing in the plantation areas of the defendants. It was found that whilst the rapid spread of the fire beyond the defendants' control to the plaintiffs' land was related to the unusually long dry season at the time, the loss caused to the plaintiffs was nonetheless a result of the negligence of the defendants and constituted an action contrary to law (*District court Kota Baru* 1998:18-39). Accordingly, the defendants were held liable to pay compensation Rp 150,000,000 to the plaintiffs, and further-

[68] The plaintiffs further argued that article 35 EMA 1997, concerning strict liability, applied in this case with the effect that it was not necessary to prove the fault of the defendants in this case. This issue was considered by the appellate court and is discussed in more detail below.

[69] Strict liability, and the application of article 35 in the Laguna Mandiri case, are discussed further below.

[70] This is a good illustration of the propensity of most Indonesian judges to rely on 'traditional' legal provisions, such as those in the Civil Code, rather than more novel environmental legislation with which they evidently have less understanding or familiarity. Instances such as these demonstrate the need for further judicial education in environmental law, a subject considered further in Chapter VI.

more the court ordered the defendants to implement systems of fire control on their properties as a preventative measure.

The district court's decision was greeted with elation by the plaintiffs, with a spokesperson for the environmental organization WALHI describing the decision as

> an important moment for environmental law enforcement, and a precedent for the judiciary to handle cases of intentional environmental damage seriously, whether such cases were brought by a government agency, NGO or community. [...] Whilst the district court of KotaBaru did not accept all the community's claims, the decision legally and politically proves that large scale commercial industries had a close connection with the devastating forest fires that occurred [in 1998] in Indonesia.[71]

The decision of the district court of Kota Baru in the Laguna Mandiri case was appealed by both the plaintiffs and the defendants, and subsequently heard by the high court of Banjarmasin. The high court reversed the legal finding of the district court, rejecting the compensation claim of the plaintiffs. The court did not consider article 35 applicable, for reasons discussed below,[72] and furthermore did not discuss the potential applicability of article 34. In considering the claim for compensation based on article 1365 of the Civil Code, the court was of the opinion that the evidence presented was insufficient to prove that the fires causing the loss to the plaintiff had resulted from the fault of the defendants. Items of evidence evaluated by the court included a letter from the Director of Forestry Protection naming the defendants as among a list of companies under suspicion of causing forest fires through land clearing by fire. The judges also referred to the fact that there had not been any subsequent investigation or prosecution in a criminal court concluding that the fires had been caused by an action of the plaintiffs. Finally, the court concluded that none of the nine witnesses who testified on behalf of the plaintiffs 'knew for certain that the cause of the crops fire was the fault of the defendants'.

The high court decision in this case illustrates the difficulty of establishing causation and 'fault' and, implicitly, the need for legal provision for environmental compensation that excludes the 'fault element'. The failure of the court to even refer to article 34 of the EMA 1997 in this respect is unfortunate, whilst the court's decision and evaluation of the evidence based on article 1365 of the Civil Code appears seriously flawed. The fact that no successful prosecu-

71 This connection also was seemingly confirmed in the WALHI v. PT Pakerin case and the Eksponen 66 v. APHI case relating to the 1997/1998 fires, both of which were at least partially successful. See WALHI 1999.

72 See section on strict liability in this chapter.

tion of the defendants had been made was, in legal terms, entirely irrelevant to the present proceedings. The lack of a successful prosecution may imply more about the inadequacy of prosecutorial agencies than it does about the faultlessness of the defendants. It is also difficult to justify the court's discounting of the rather convincing testimonial evidence in this case.[73] All of the seven witnesses testified that they had seen fire on the defendants' estate that subsequently spread on to the property of the plaintiffs, causing damage to crops and houses. Two of the witnesses (witness two and witness nine) not only had seen the fire spread from the defendants' property to the plaintiffs' property, but had also witnessed employees of the defendants burning off piles of wood, the fire from which had subsequently spread. The appellate court in this respect took an opposite view to the court at first instance, which concluded that the witness evidence 'proved that the fire originated from the area of the coconut plantation of the defendants'. Thus, from an objective evaluation of the witness evidence, it is clear that the fires were intentionally lit by the defendant companies, which in itself satisfies the element of fault. It is also clear that the use of fire for land clearing per se was contrary to law and that certainly the defendant's failure to maintain an adequate system of fire control was similarly illegal. The fact that the defendant knowingly used fire without proper precautions should thus have been sufficient to establish fault. The Laguna Mandiri decision at the appellate level is thus difficult to justify on either legal or factual grounds.

Article 34 EMA 1997 case 3: Banger River case, 1999

A claim for compensation based on article 34 was also brought in the Banger River case,[74] which is the subject of a more detailed analysis in Chapter IV. In this case, three large textile factories located near Pekalongan in Central Java disposed of their waste effluent into the Banger River, which by 1992 had become visibly polluted. The pollution also had a severe impact on the residents of Dekoro village, who lived a short distance downstream from the three factories. Drinking wells became polluted, small livestock drinking from the river perished and residents were no longer able to use the river

[73] The majority of the witnesses who testified in this case gave eye witness accounts of fires deliberately lit within the properties of the defendants and then spreading to the village of the plaintiff community. In some cases the witnesses were actually past employees of the defendant companies. For example the following excerpt from Dedi Suprianus bin Kumuj, who at the time was working as a work supervisor for the defendant company: 'Around 2pm the witness saw fire on the industry's property from a distance of 30 metres. The witness knew and saw himself Arpani (industry foreman) lighting a pile of wood. Upon being asked Arpani said that the burn-off was an order from above [...] after being lit the fire slowly got bigger and burnt coffee, rattan and coconut plantations owned by the community.' See *District court Kota Baru* 1998:56.

[74] Decision No. 50/Pdt.G/1998.PN.Pkl. See also Chapter IV.

water for any domestic use. The Dekoro community sued the three factories for compensation and environmental restoration based on article 34. At the district court level the community was successful in its claim, obtaining an award for compensation of Rp 49,184,000. In its decision, the court demonstrated a clear understanding of environmental legal principles, noting the legal responsibility of each person 'to protect environmental sustainability' and emphasising that 'industrial development must be sustainable for the safety of humankind'.[75] Notably, and in contrast to the Babon River and Laguna Mandiri cases, the decision was upheld on appeal to the high court of Semarang. In fact, the court not only upheld the district court's previous decision but also increased the award of compensation for environmental damage to Rp 165,523,000 (US22,000) and ordered the industries to ensure optimal operation of their waste management unit. The decision of both the district and high courts in this case is an important demonstration of the growing familiarity of Indonesian courts with environmental law and a corresponding willingness to apply it.

Article 34 EMA 1997 case 4: Kalimantan peat land case, 1999

This claim arose out of the controversial and ultimately unsuccessful attempt of the Suharto government to convert some one million hectares of peat land in Kalimantan into productive rice fields.[76] The project had a devastating environmental and social impact, disrupting the fragile ecology of this unique wetlands area and undermining the subsistence agriculture practiced successfully by many indigenous Dayak communities (Hanni Adiati 1998:14-8). In this particular case, a group of 49 traditional fish farmers from the regency of Kapuas sued a number of national and regional government agencies for compensation relating to environmental damage caused by the Peat Land Project.[77] Land clearing and construction of a network of irrigation canals had resulted in the destruction of traditional fishponds (*beje*) used by the farmers for generations.

The farmers' compensation claim was upheld at first instance by the district court of Kuala Kapuas on 30 November 1998. The court calculated material damage on an individual basis according to the number of fishponds owned by each farmer. The total amount of compensation awarded, which related

75 Banger River case: Indra Prasetya, PT Bintang Triputratex, PT Kesmatex, CV Ezri. district court of Pekalongan: No. 50/Pdt.G/1998.PN.Pkl. 1999:36-40.

76 Decision No. 06/Pdt.G/1998/PN.K.Kp; Decision No. 03/PDT/1999/PT.PR (appeal). The project is discussed further below, in relation to a public interest action brought by WALHI.

77 The defendants to the action were the Coordinating Minister for Economy, Finance and Industry; the Minister of Public Works; the Minister for Finance; Environment Minister; PLG project director; the Governor of Central Kalimantan.

to material damage of the fishponds, was Rp 625.6 million. The court also awarded compensation totalling Rp 23.4 million for the farmers' lost income since July 1996. The defendants appealed to the high court of Palangka Raya. Before the hearing at the appellate level, both parties indicated their willingness to attempt to settle the matter. The court then adjudicated to a pre-trial settlement conference at which an agreement was reached between the parties. Pursuant to the agreement, compensation was granted at a slightly lower rate totalling Rp 383 million.[78] The agreement was adopted as a decision of the court.

Strict liability

Concern over the difficulties associated with establishing fault-based liability in environmental disputes has contributed to the enactment of 'strict liability' for environmentally dangerous activities in a number of jurisdictions. Pursuant to the principle of strict liability, the element of 'fault' is excluded. Thus, a defendant may not be absolved of responsibility because he or she did not intentionally or negligently commit the act in question. It is sufficient rather that the plaintiff establishes the defendant committed the action in question and that the action caused loss to the plaintiff. The subjective or objective 'fault' of the defendant is, for the purposes of strict liability, irrelevant. Given the inherent difficulty in establishing the element of fault, and the corresponding reduced burden of proof on the plaintiff when fault is excluded, strict liability thus has a significant potential to greatly increase access to justice.

The first Environmental Management Act 1982 introduced the principle of strict liability in the environmental sphere, yet its application required the enactment of further implementing regulations which never occurred (Eko Nuryanto 1995:7-9). Unsurprisingly, the article was never applied by courts as a result. Article 35 of the new EMA 1997 has made more specific provision for strict liability.

> The party responsible for a business and/or activity which gives rise to a large and significant impact (*dampak besar dan penting*) on the environment, which uses hazardous and toxic materials, and/or produces hazardous and toxic waste, is

[78] In the original district court decision the court awarded compensation of Rp 10 million for a larger fishpond (*tatah ikan*) and Rp 200,000 for a smaller fishpond (*beje ikan*). In the court adjudicated agreement the compensation rates were Rp 5 million for a larger fishpond and Rp 1 million for a smaller fishpond.

> stricktly liable for any resulting losses, with the obligation to pay compensation directly and immediately upon occurrence of environmental pollution and/or damage.[79]

Article 35 thus applies strict liability to three situations:

1 Where a business or activity gives rise to a large and significant impact on the environment.
2 Where a business or activity uses hazardous and toxic materials.
3 Where a business or activity produces hazardous and toxic waste.

Whilst 'large and significant impact' is not defined in the EMA 1997 the term is also used in article 15(1) of the act which states that every business or activity plan which may 'give rise to a large and significant impact on the environment, must possess an environmental impact analysis'.[80] Implicitly then, every business or activity obliged to undertake an environmental impact assessment would also be subject to strict liability in the event of resulting pollution or environmental damage – a wide scope of application indeed.[81] Whilst 'large and significant impact' is not defined by the EMA, the elucidation to article 15(1) states a number of criteria to be used in measuring the potential environmental impact of an activity. These criteria include:

- the number of people who will be affected by the impact of the business and/or activity plan;
- the extent of the area affected;
- the intensity and duration of the impact;
- the amount of other environmental components which will be affected;
- the cumulative nature of the impact;
- reversibility or non-reversibility of the impact.

79 Article 35(2) also stipulates several exceptions to the application of strict liability. Strict liability will not apply where it can be proved that the pollution or environmental damage resulted from a natural disaster, war, an extraordinary situation beyond human control or the actions of a third party. In the latter case strict liability will apply to the third party responsible for the environmental damage.

80 The elucidation to article 15(1) states a number of criteria which may be used in assessing the impact of an environmental activity: the number of people affected, the extent of the area affected, the intensity and duration of the impact, the amount of other environmental components which will be affected, the cumulative nature of the impact, and the reversibility or non-reversibility of the impact.

81 A more restrictive interpretation of the article was made by the high court in the Laguna Mandiri case discussed below.

As discussed above the principle of strict liability excludes the element of fault and thus lightens the burden of proof on the plaintiff. Only limited defences are available to the defendant who wishes to relieve himself of strict liability. If the defendant can prove, or the plaintiff fails to establish, that the defendant's business or activity caused the loss in question, then strict liability will clearly not apply.[82] Further defences are stipulated in article 35(2) of the EMA 1997 and include natural disaster or war, forced circumstance beyond human control or actions of a third party that cause environmental pollution or damage.[83] Given the wide scope of article 35, and its potential impact in facilitating access to justice, it is surprising that the article has been considered in so few cases. Two cases are discussed below where the issue of strict liability was at least raised, although ultimately not applied in either case. As in the case of representative actions, the failure of the courts to apply strict liability may at least partially be attributed to a lack of familiarity and understanding of the doctrine.

Laguna Mandiri, 1998

The Laguna Mandiri case was discussed earlier in relation to the issue of compensation for environmental damage.[84] It may be recalled that in that case it was claimed by the plaintiffs that the fires intentionally lit by the defendants for the purpose of land-clearing between July and November 1997 had spread out of control, destroying large areas of the plaintiff community's crops and housing. The plaintiffs argued, amongst other things, that the burning off carried out by the defendants had resulted in a large and significant impact on the environment, including the loss of crops that represented the livelihood of the plaintiffs and, moreover, far-reaching ecological damage. Accordingly, based on article 35(1) of the EMA 1997, it was argued that the defendants were strictly liable for loss caused by their actions and obliged to pay compensation.

The claim for compensation was accepted, in part, by the district court of Kota Baru on the basis of article 1365 of the Civil Code, without reference to the doctrine of strict liability. The court ordered the defendants to pay Rp 150 million in compensation and implement a fire control management system as a preventive measure. On appeal, however, the plaintiffs' claim was rejected by the high court of Banjarmasin, which nonetheless did consider the issue of strict liability. The court adopted a more restrictive interpretation of article 35, stating that the clause applied only to industries producing a large and signifi-

82 Causation is not stated as an explicit defence in article 35(2) but is implicit in the wording of article 35(1).

83 The elucidation defines action of a third party in this clause as 'an action of unfair competition or a Government fault'.

84 Decision No. 09/Pdt.G/1998/PN.KTB.

cant impact on the environment, which used hazardous and toxic materials and/or produced hazardous and toxic waste. Article 35 was thus interpreted as applying to only two rather than three categories of circumstances. As the defendants in the Laguna Mandiri case did not use such materials in the course of their activities, given that they were a plantation company rather than an industrial company, strict liability could not apply. The language of the article itself does not, on the face of it, seem to support such a restrictive interpretation. If it had been the intention of the drafters to restrict application of strict liability to two rather than three categories of circumstances, then the article presumably would have been drafted differently.[85] Furthermore, the phrase 'large and significant impact' is also used in the EMA in relation to environmental impact assessment and is defined in a manner that supports a broader interpretation of this article. Legal commentary concerning article 35 to date has also adopted the wider interpretation, applying strict liability to three distinct situations as discussed above (Koesnadi Hardjasoemantri 1998:7; Suparto Wijoyo 1999:32-3).

WALHI v. PT Pakerin et al., 1998

The issue of strict liability was also raised in the WALHI v. PT Pakerin case, in which WALHI claimed an amount of Rp 2 trillion for the purpose of environmental restoration from eleven forestry companies whom they alleged were responsible for catastrophic environmental damage caused by the 1997 forest fires.[86] The eleven companies operated extensive forest concessions located in the region of southern Sumatra, one of several regions devastated by uncontrollable forest fires between September and November 1997. Besides widespread devastation of flora and fauna, the thick smoke from the fires caused record levels of air pollution and an outbreak of serious breathing disorders among the general populace.[87]

85 The restrictive interpretation of article 35 adopted by the high court of Banjarmasin would be justified only if the article read as follows: 'The party responsible for a business and/or activity which gives rise to a large impact on the environment and which uses hazardous and toxic materials, and/or produces hazardous and toxic waste, is strictly liable for losses which are given rise to, with the obligation to pay compensation directly and immediately upon occurrence of environmental pollution and/or damage'. However, the absence of the conjunction 'and' and the inclusion of the conjunction 'and/or' suggests the three categories contained in article 35 should be separately applicable.

86 See *WALHI v. PT Pakerin* et al. 1998. The companies the subject of WALHI's claim were: PT Pakerin, PT Sentosa Jaya, PT Inhutani V, PT Sukses Sumatera Timber, PT Inti Remaja Concern, PT Nindita Bagaskari, PT Musi Hutan Persada, PT Sinar Belanti Jaya, PT Sri Bunian Trading and Co, PT Daya Penca, PT Family Jaya Group.

87 Data from the Palembang Department of Health stated that on 7-10-1997 dust levels measured 2.7762 mg/m^3, compared with a regulatory limit of 0.26 mg/m^3. See *WALHI v. PT Pakerin* et al. 1998.

The defendant companies were included in a list compiled by the Department of Forestry of 176 companies suspected of the illegal yet common practice of land clearing through burn-offs. Detailed satellite photos, cross-referenced with maps of forest concessions, also confirmed the location of 'hot-spots', or fire epicentres on concessions operated by the defendant companies.[88] Further testimonial or eye-witness evidence presented by WALHI related to only two of the eleven defendants: defendant VII (PT Musi Hutan Persada) and defendant III (PT Inhutani), two forestry companies which were originally amalgamated within a larger company, PT Enim Musi Lestari.

In its decision, the court only evaluated the testimonial evidence, which, as discussed above, related to defendant III and defendant VII. In the case of defendant III, PT Inhutani, a further witness called by the defence had stated that the fire burning within the PT Inhutani's property had actually originated outside the area of land owned by the company. The court considered this account sufficient evidence that the fire in question had not been caused by PT Inhutani and the company therefore could not be held liable. The latter defendant VII, PT Musi Hutan Persada, however, had failed to advance evidence contrary to the plaintiff's claims.[89] The court therefore held that the plaintiff's claims against PT Musi Hutan Persada were established. Defendant V, PT Inti Remaja Concern, had failed to file a defence or attend the court hearings despite being properly served notice of the proceedings. Consequently, the court concluded that this particular defendant had no objection or defence to the claim in question, which was held established.

The court made only passing reference to the other documentary and expert witness evidence advanced by the plaintiff, and considered that it did not specifically establish the claim in respect of the other eight defendants. The judges' decision in this respect was disappointing, as in doing so they failed to explicitly discuss the main grounds of WALHI's claim: the analysis of satellite pictures which depicted with a high level of precision the location of fires during the period September to December 1997 within the forest concessions operated by the thirteen defendants within southern Sumatra. Certainly, the main limitation of such evidence was that it could not prove conclusively that the companies themselves had intentionally lit the fires. Yet, if the doctrine of strict liability were to be applied, this should not have been

88 Satellite photoes from the American satellite NOAA illustrated the hottest points of the fires, which corresponded with their sources, or points of origin. These data were overlayed with Department of Forestry maps detailing the concessions held by particular companies, to determine from which specific areas the fires had originated.

89 Actually five witnesses were called by defendant VII, who provided not so much eye witness accounts of the fires but rather general assertions, including that the PT Musi Hutan Persada had not cleared land with slash and burn methods since 1994, and that the company made efforts to assist the local community with fire control. See *WALHI v. PT Pakerin* et al. 1998:30.

sufficient to defeat WALHI's claim. WALHI (*WALHI v. PT Pakerin* 1998:7-9) argued on this point:

- That the defendants should be held strictly liable on the basis of article 35 EMA 1997 for such 'a large impact on the environment [and] losses given rise to', in which case fault or intention would not be relevant.
- That the negligence of the plaintiffs in failing to maintain an adequate system of fire control on their properties was in any case contrary to environmental law and obliged the companies to carry out environmental restoration and pay compensation for resulting damage.

Taken in the context of the above legal arguments, the documentary evidence produced by WALHI, particularly the satellite photos the accuracy of which could not be disputed, constituted a strong case for the culpability of the defendants. This case was not seemingly negated by the argument that the fires were a natural disaster and the result of an exceptionally long dry season and the 'El Nino' weather phenomena. Expert witnesses for both the plaintiff and defendant VII confirmed that whilst the El Nino pattern might have increased dryness, it would not in itself have caused the outbreak of fires (*WALHI v. PT Pakerin* et al. 1998:26). In any case, if the fires constituted a 'large and significant impact on the environment', then the burden of proof should have been borne by the defendants not the plaintiff, through application of the strict liability doctrine.

The stipulation of strict liability for such a wide range of environmentally damaging acts by article 35 is one of the most far reaching legal provisions enacted in the Environmental Management Act 1997. By excluding the element of fault in certain situations the doctrine of strict liability is a legal means of implementing the important environmental principle that the polluter must pay. However, despite the legislative basis provided in article 35 and several opportunities to apply the article in the cases discussed above, the potential of this important legislative principle has yet to be realized in the course of environmental litigation.

Environmental restoration

The two previous sections have discussed the grounds upon which persons directly affected by environmental damage may claim compensation from those responsible. Yet, as explained in the Introduction to this chapter, environmental litigation encompasses both private pecuniary interests as well as public, environmentally related interests. An issue of particular significance in environmental litigation then is the legal grounds upon which a polluting party may be obligated to compensate for or restore public environmental damage.

Article 20(3) EMA 1982

An obligation to pay environmental restoration costs was first introduced by the EMA 1982, article 20(3) of which provided that: 'Whosoever damages and/or pollutes the living environment is liable for payment to the State of the restoration costs of the living environment.' According to the elucidation to the EMA, evaluation of environmental restoration costs was to be undertaken by the same government investigation team established under article 20(2) for the determination of compensation levels. From the article itself it was unclear whether environmental organizations could bring an action to compel payment of restoration costs to the State.[90]

Surabaya River case, 1995

In the Surabaya River case, the environmental organization WALHI brought an environmental public interest suit against three paper mills accused of polluting the Surabaya River – the source of drinking water for the residents of Java's second largest city, Surabaya.[91] During the proceedings, WALHI produced laboratory tests taken over a period of some 22 months to support its allegation that the three defendant industries had discharged liquid waste exceeding stipulated pollutant limits into the Surabaya and Tengah Rivers. The laboratory results demonstrated considerable ecological damage and pollution caused by the discharged waste which had, in addition, rendered the water in the Surabaya River unfit for use as drinking water.[92]

The plaintiff WALHI argued that the defendant factories had acted contrary to a number of environmental laws:

- Decision of the Governor of East Java No. 414 of 1987, concerning Waste Standards, which stipulated maximum BOD (30mg/L) and COD (80mg/L) levels.
- Article 13(1) of Government Regulation No. 22 of 1982, concerning Water Management, which states that where water is utilized for drinking (as the

[90] The article was cited, and compensation claimed for environmental restoration by WALHI in the Surabaya River case, however the suit was rejected due to the lack of implementing regulations both in respect of article 20(1) and (3).

[91] Decision No. 116/PDT.G/1995/PN.SBY. The three factories were PT Surabaya Mekabox, PT Surabaya Agung Industri Pulp dan Kertas and PT Suparma.

[92] Tests of waste discharged from PT Surabaya Mekabox over a 22 month period indicated an average BOD (Biological Oxygen Demand) level of 680, approximately 22 times the maximum legal level of 30, and an average COD (Chemical Oxygen Demand) level of 1408, appoximately 17 times the maximum level of 80. In the same period, waste from PT Surabaya Agung Industri Pulp dan Kertas showed an average BOD level of 417 and COD level of 870 whilst effluent from PT Suparma tested at an average of 197 BOD and 352 COD.

Surabaya River was in this case) this need takes priority above all others.
- Article 33 of Government Regulation No. 22 of 1982, concerning Water Management, which states that the community is obligated to assist in controlling and preventing water pollution which could compromise water use and/or the environment.
- Article 5(2) EMA 1982, obligating 'each person' to protect the environment and prevent environmental damage or pollution.
- Article 21(1) Law No. 5 of 1984, concerning Industry, requiring industries to prevent environmental damage or pollution resulting from industry activities.
- Article 17(1) Government Regulation No. 20 of 1990, concerning Control of Water Pollution, which requires each person disposing of liquid waste to comply with regulatory standards.

On the basis of article 19 of the EMA 1982, which recognizes the 'supporting role' of community institutions in environmental management, WALHI had researched water consumer complaints over a period of one month and undertaken testing of the Surabaya River for water quality. The environmental organization claimed the reimbursement of these expenses from the defendant industries. The organization's second claim related to environmental restoration. Article 20(3) of the EMA 1982 required any person responsible for environmental pollution or damage to pay the costs of environmental restoration to the State. Similarly, article 36(1) of Government Regulation No. 20 of 1990 stated that the costs of controlling and restoring water pollution resulting from an activity were to be borne by the person or company responsible for that activity. To ensure environmental restoration and prevention of further pollution, WALHI requested that the court order an interim cessation of the factories' operations, an open environmental audit, installation of waste management units, environmental rehabilitation, and continuing monitoring of environmental compliance with local community participation (WALHI 1995a).

In an interim decision, the Surabaya district court rejected one of the plaintiff's witnesses, the assistant governor, because he possessed an interest in environmental matters. This particular senior official had developed a reputation for responding firmly to polluting industries, upon which he often launched surprise examinations. Ultimately, information was received from the official in question, but on a private basis (Eko Nuryanto 1995:7-9). In relation to the substantive claim the Surabaya district court at first instance rejected it, because implementing regulations for article 20(1) and 20(3), concerning payment of compensation for environmental damage and restoration of the environment respectively, had not yet been enacted. As a result, the court held that the claim could not be further considered. The court also criticized the compensatory sums claimed by WALHI, stating that the basis for such amounts was not clear and that, pursuant to article 20, a team should be established to determine the form, type and amount of compensation. The district court's decision was upheld on appeal to the high court of East Java.

Article 38(2) EMA 1997

The legal rights of environmental organizations to bring a public interest suit have been more clearly stipulated in article 38 of the Environmental Management Act 1997. As discussed above article 38(1) acknowledges that: 'In the scheme of implementing responsibility for environmental management consistent with a partnership principle, environmental organisations have the right to bring a legal action in the interest of environmental functions'.

Article 38(2) makes further stipulation as to the exact nature of the legal action that environmental organizations may initiate. That clause states that the right of an environmental organization to bring a legal action is limited to 'a claim for the right to carry out certain measures excluding any claim for compensation, with the exception of expenses or real outlays'.

The elucidation to the EMA 1997 describes three sub-categories of 'certain measures' which may be legitimately claimed by an environmental organization pursuant to article 38:

1 Application to the court for an order that a person undertake certain legal actions connected with the preservation of environmental functions.
2 A declaration that a person has carried out an action contrary to law due to pollution or damage to the environment.
3 An order that a person carrying out a business and/or activity install or repair a waste treatment unit.

Pursuant to article 38(2), an environmental organization may thus initiate a legal suit to compel restoration of environmental damage. The elucidation further states that 'expenses or real outlays' which an environmental organization may claim are 'expenses which can in fact be proven to have been outlaid by an environmental organisation'. Although the elucidation does not explicitly present the list of remedies as exhaustive, the language used suggests that this is indeed the case.[93] Notably absent from the list of potential remedies provided in the Elucidation is an order of an injunctive nature, that a person refrain from carrying out actions which cause pollution to or damage of the environment. This could, however, conceivably be included within the scope of sub-category 1, if cessation of an ongoing activity could

93 Note that whilst the elucidation is not formally a part of the law, it is nonetheless the primary reference point for its interpretation.

be described as a 'legal action', which might be the case if compliance with a regulatory standard were required and a legal consequence thus intended. The absence of an expedited procedure to cease polluting activities is a further deficiency of the remedies presented above. A possible alternative in this respect would be a tort action encompassing a provisional claim for the cessation of unlawful polluting activities, based on the *Wetboek van burgerlijke rechtsvordering*.[94]

The exclusion of claims for compensation of environmental damage by environmental organizations on behalf of environmental interests significantly diminishes the potential deterrent effect of public interest suits towards potential polluters. Such exclusion also seems somewhat inconsistent with the right of environmental compensation created by article 34(1). That article states: 'Every illegal action of pollution and/or damage to the environment, which has an adverse impact on other people, or the environment, obliges the party responsible for the business and/or activity to pay compensation and/or to carry out certain actions'. The article thus explicitly creates an obligation on the part of a polluting party to pay compensation, amongst other things, where the environment is damaged or polluted as a result of their activities. It is unclear why environmental organizations should be excluded from claiming compensation for environmental damage when an obligation for polluters to pay compensation is created by article 34(1). Moreover, there has been to date no administrative or regulatory initiative to stipulate which government should claim and/or administer such compensation. In the absence of a reliable government mechanism, it is difficult to see how such an obligation is to be enforced if environmental organizations are prevented from claiming such compensation through legal action on behalf of environment interests. The existing scope allowed by article 38(2) to enable an environmental organization to claim restitution of expenses outlaid in cleaning up the environment is insufficient in this respect, as this will only occur where such an organization has the required funds in the first place. Clearly, this will not always be the case. On both logical and practical grounds, then, the exclusion of compensation as a remedy available to environmental organizations seems inconsistent with both the legal obligation in article 34 and the recognition of environmental organizations as representatives of environmental interests in article 38(1).[95]

94 Adriaan Bedner, personal communication, 7-12-1999.

95 See Mas Achmad Santosa and Sembiring 1997:36. It is notable also that compensation is excluded as a potential remedy in articles 3:305a and 3:305b of the Dutch Civil Code, which possibly provided a model in the drafting of the above provision.

WALHI v. PT Pakerin and others

The issue of what 'measures' an environmental organization might apply for pursuant to article 38(2) was raised in the case of WALHI v. PT Pakerin,[96] discussed above in relation to the issue of strict liability. In its claim, WALHI had described the amount of Rp 2 trillion claimed by it as costs of environmental restoration (*pemulihan*), rather than compensation. The presiding judges, however, ruled that the amount claimed by WALHI, whilst described as restoration costs, in fact constituted compensation (*penggantian rugi*) and was thus disallowed by the terms of article 38(1). Nonetheless, two of the defendants were found to have committed actions contrary to law in polluting and damaging the environment, and were accordingly ordered to implement a forest fire management system in their respective areas.[97]

Thus, whilst the procedural obstacles to environmental public interest suits are to some extent overcome by the recognition of standing in article 38(1), much of the potential impact of such suits is undermined by the exclusion of compensation as a possible remedy. The possibility of environmental organizations claiming 'real expenses' is not a sufficient answer to this problem. Clearly, the damage caused by the catastrophic forest fires in the WALHI v. PT Pakerin case was beyond the capacity of an NGO like WALHI to clean up itself. There is thus little prospect that environmental restoration could be first carried out and then such 'real expenses' claimed against the companies responsible. Yet the restrictions of article 38(2) prevent a concerned environmental NGO such as WALHI from claiming compensation against those parties responsible. Given the widely acknowledged failure of prosecutorial agencies to deal with those responsible for the forest fires, it is unfortunate that such a claim is denied by the restrictive terms of article 38(2).

Right to environmental information

The need for public access to accurate information concerning environmental management has been widely recognized as essential to community participation in environmental management and effective environmental law enforcement.[98] This principle finds legislative expression in the EMA 1997; article 5(2) of which recognizes the right of each person 'to environmental

96 *WALHI v. PT Pakerin* et al. 1998.

97 Decision No. 8/Pdt.G/1998/PN.Plg.

98 For example, international standard ISO 14001 requires industry to communicate all aspects of environmental management to the community in its vicinity. See Effendi Sumardja 1999:6.

information which is related to environmental management roles'. The right contained in article 5(2) is complemented by an obligation stipulated in article 6(2) on 'every person carrying out a business or other activity [to] provide true and accurate information regarding environmental management'.

At the institutional level, the Central Environmental Impact Agency (Bapedal Pusat) formed an Environmental Monitoring and Information Centre (Pusat Pengembangan Informasi dan Panaatan Lingkungan, PPIPL), charged with the task of developing a system for the dissemination of environmental information.[99] One of the problems confronted by the PPIPL at the institutional level has been a lack of coordination and consistency between government agencies. Thus, multiple investigations by different agencies into the same incident of pollution have often produced wildly different results and conclusions. Moreover, at the community level, access to environmental information remains extremely problematic with access often denied by industries or government agencies or, not infrequently, with deliberately misleading information being provided. To date the issue of environmental information has only been raised in one case, that of WALHI v. PT Freeport.

WALHI v. PT Freeport, 2001

On May 4, 2000, a breach in an upholding wall of Lake Wanagon, which was used as a receptacle for overburden waste by PT Freeport Indonesia, caused the overflow of a vast quantity of water, sludge and overburden waste. The burst in the dam wall tragically claimed the lives of four workers and flooded the land of the nearby Banti village. Subsequent government investigations into the tragedy attributed it largely to Freeport's negligence – an unsurprising conclusion given similar breaches of the lake's walls had occurred twice before.[100] The company's questionable handling of this human and environmental tragedy, and its previous history of environmental controversy, prompted WALHI to file its second legal suit against Freeport in the Central Jakarta district court. The suit accused Freeport of deliberately misleading the public and providing false information in relation to the incident. This, asserted WALHI, was contrary to article 6 of the EMA 1997 which states that: 'Every person carrying out a business or other activity must provide true

99 One initiative taken by Bapedal to increase access to environmental information is publicising of a daily Air Pollution Standard Index for five major cities via Bapedal's web site and local radio. See Yunun Sudarsono 1999:4.

100 An investigation by a team from the Environmental Impact Agency was launched into a similar incident in 1998, with this team's report criticising inadequate construction and waste disposal carried out by Freeport, as well as the incapacity of Lake Wanagon to receive overburden waste, especially given the susceptibility of the area to seismic activity.

and accurate information regarding environmental management'. WALHI argued that public statements issued by Freeport had misrepresented the extensive environmental pollution and damage caused by its mining operations, including the discharge of heavy metals and hazardous waste into Lake Wanagon and the Wanagon River, and thus contravened article 6.[101] In contrast to previous claims, the outspoken environmental watchdog did not make any monetary claim, but rather demanded Freeport publicly apologize, via a range of media, for its alleged misdeeds. An order was also sought for the company to immediately reduce its production level, to avoid further unsustainable levels of overburden and tailing waste.

In a decision issued on 28 August 2001, the South Jakarta district court concluded that the mining giant had acted illegally in polluting the environment in the vicinity of the factory, and in making factually incorrect statements at the time of the Lake Wanagon incident regarding the impact of tailing. The presiding judges stated that Freeport was incorrect in stating that the company's mining activities did not pose a threat to either human health or the environment in the long term. Contrary to such statements, evidence indicated that hazardous tailing waste had indeed had a negative impact on the environment. Whilst the court did not order a public apology by Freeport, as requested by the plaintiff, the company was ordered to improve waste management of tailings containing hazardous waste and ensure that stipulated water quality standards were met in respect of Lake Wanagon and Wanagon River.[102]

The Freeport case is one of the few public interest environmental cases in which the claimant has been at least partially successful. The decision of the district court in this case was in line with and may have been partially influenced by the government's response to the Wanagon incident, which had attracted significant national and international publicity. In a cabinet meeting on the issue, the then Environment Minister Sonny Keraf had ordered the mining company to stop dumping overburden waste into Wanagon Dam and devise a new plan, subject to government approval, for the processing of such waste. In any case, the decision of the South Jakarta district court was at least a partial victory for WALHI's efforts to 'implement' key environmental law provisions through public interest cases and its sustained political campaign against Freeport's mining operations in Irian Jaya. The court's decision has potentially opened another 'door' for environmental public interest litigants and is the first indication that the right to environmental information stipulated in article 6 may have more than a purely symbolic value.

101 'Walhi akan ajukan Freeport ke pengadilan', *Kompas*, 22-5-2000.

102 WALHI 2001. The decision was immediately appealed by Freeport and later also by WALHI.

Administrative environmental litigation

Community-initiated enforcement of environmental laws via the courts in Indonesia may also occur in the context of public administrative law, where the subject of litigation is typically a decision or action of the state, which permits or condones environmentally damaging activities. Decisions of the state in the environmental context usually take the form of state-issued licences, a number of which are required for almost all forms of development in Indonesia.[103] Where it is believed that an administrative decision to grant or withhold an operating licence is erroneous, that decision may be challenged in the state administrative court (*pengadilan tata usaha negara*).[104] The process of challenging state administrative decisions is governed by the Administrative Judicature Act No. 5 of 1986 (AJA), which stipulates a number of conditions for contesting a state decision.

Standing in the administrative courts

Firstly, the applicant must have suffered a loss as a result of the contested decision (article 53[1], Administrative Judicature Act 1986). Material damage to person or property caused by polluting activities would certainly constitute a 'loss' under article 53(1), justifying challenge of the operating licences facilitating such activities. Moreover, the scope of administrative standing was extended in the case of environmental public interest actions in the 1994 Reafforestation Funds (IPTN) case.

Standing in the administrative courts: Reafforestation Fund (IPTN) case, 1994

In this case a group of environmental NGOs lodged a legal suit with the state administrative court in Jakarta requesting that Presidential Decree No. 42 of 1994, concerning a transfer of funds from a reafforestation fund to PT Industri Pesawat Terbang Nusantara (IPTN), be declared invalid.[105] The Reafforestation Fund was created by Presidential Decree No. 29 of 1990 and comprised of levies upon forest concessionaries. The use of proceeds from the

103 Typical licences include the industry enterprise permit (*izin usaha industri*), the location permit (*izin lokasi*), the building permit (*izin mendirikan bangunan*) and the mining authority (*kuasa pertambangan*). The hinderordonnantie (*ordonansi gangguan nuisance ordinance*) also requires permits to be obtained for a wide range of development activities, including most forms of industrial development.

104 Pursuant to the Administrative Judicature Act No. 5 of 1986. A state administrative action, as distinct from a written decision, may not be challenged in the state administrative court. In certain circumstances, however, it may be challenged as an 'action contrary to law' (*perbuatan melawan hukum*) in the general or civil courts, which is discussed further below.

105 Decision No. 088/G/1994/Piutang/PTUN.Jkt.

levies was restricted to reafforestation, commercial plantation development and land rehabilitation. In practice, however, the fund was used to bankroll a wide range of projects outside these legally sanctioned purposes. In a statement on 15 October 1999 the then Forestry Minister, Muslimin Nasution, estimated that between 1993/1994 and 1997/1998 financial years Rp 1.6 trillion had been misappropriated from the fund for unauthorized purposes.[106]

In its decision the court endorsed the principle of 'environmental standing', whereby an environmental organization may bring a legal action in defence of the public interest of environmental preservation.[107] The court emphasized, however, that only environmental organizations fulfilling certain criteria would be qualified to bring such an action. The court set out four such criteria:

- That the aim of an organization must be environmental protection or preservation and stipulated as such in its Constitution.
- That the organization must be a Legal Body or Foundation.
- That the organization must demonstrate a concern for the environment in its actual activities.
- That the organization must be sufficiently representative.

The court found that four out of the six plaintiffs fulfilled these criteria and they were thus allowed legal standing. In the case of the second plaintiff, The Indonesian Foundation for Tropical Nature (Yayasan Alam Tropika Indonesia) the court found that the foundation's Articles of Association were not properly executed by a notary as legally required. Similarly, a letter appointing the representative of the foundation did not fulfil the necessary legal requirements. In the case of the sixth plaintiff, the Indonesian Rainbow Foundation (Yayasan Pelangi Indonesia), the purported representatives had not been appointed in a way that satisfied stipulated legal requirements. The criteria enunciated by the Jakarta state administrative court in this case were given legislative force by article 38(2) of the EMA 1997, the elucidation to which specifically extends that provision to the administrative courts. Note,

106 See 'Dana reboisasa Rp 1.6 trilyun diselewengkan', *Kompas*, 15-10-1999. Non forestry projects to which funds were applied included Minister Habibie's aeroplane (IPTN) project (Rp 400 billion), the Kalimantan peat swamp project (Rp 527 billion), an enterprise credit program (Rp 100 billion), loan deposit for PT Ario Seto Wibowo (Rp 80 billion), converting foreign currency for PT Mapindo Parama (Rp 186,279 billion) and the 1997 Sea Games Consortium (Rp 35 billion). See 'DR dan IHH bocur Rp 15,025 triliun', *Bisnis Indonesia*, 15-10-1999.

107 The court referred to literature published by jurists on this subject (Lotulung 1993a:1) and the previous decision of the Jakarta District in the PT Inti Indorayon Utama case (Chapter II) to justify its position in this respect. See WALHI 1995b:35.

however, that the fourth requirement, that the organization be sufficiently representative, was omitted from article 38(1).[108]

Administrative court jurisdiction

The extent of the administrative courts' jurisdiction is defined by a number of provisions in the Administrative Judicature Act. The border of jurisdiction between the administrative and general courts has been the subject of considerable confusion and even conflict on a number of points. The AJA begins with article 47 which conveys upon administrative courts 'the duty and jurisdiction to examine, decide, and solve administrative law disputes'. The latter phrase 'administrative law disputes' is further defined in article 1(4) as 'disputes that arise in the field of administration between a person or civil legal body with a (central or regional) administrative body or official, as a consequence of an administrative decision being issued'. A jurisdictionable dispute must thus have arisen due to the issuance of an administrative decision, a term which is further defined by article 1(3) as

> a written determination issued by an administrative body or official containing an administrative act in law based on prevailing legislation, that is of a concrete, individual and final nature, which has given rise to legal consequences for a person or civil legal body (Bedner 2000:60).

This provision encompasses a considerable number of specific criteria which must be fulfilled for an administrative decision to be within the administrative courts' jurisdiction. Some of the criteria, such as 'written',[109] are reasonably well defined in both law and application. Other elements of the definition, such as 'administrative act in law', 'final' or 'giving rise to legal consequences' have been less consistently defined by the courts and the source of considerable confusion as a result.[110]

Administrative court jurisdiction: Reafforestation Fund (IPTN) case, 1994

The issue of jurisdiction was raised in the Reafforestation (IPTN) case discussed above, which was the first environmental public interest suit brought in the administrative courts. Whilst the plaintiffs in that case won the procedural victory of environmental standing (discussed above), the substan-

108 See discussion of article 38(1) above, earlier in this chapter.

109 'Written' does not require that the decision be in an official form, but rather that it be evidenced by, at the least, some written note or memorandum, see Bedner 2000:60-1.

110 For a detailed discussion of all of these criteria, which is outside the scope of this chapter, see Bedner 2000:60.

tive application was, unsurprisingly, defeated.[111] In their application, the plaintiffs had argued that the contested Presidential Decree, authorising the transfer of Rp 400 billion to PT IPTN from the Reafforestation Fund, was a reviewable administrative decision, according to the provisions of the Administrative Judicature Act.[112] It was submitted by the plaintiffs that the decision in question was inconsistent with, amongst other things, the provisions of the EMA 1982 concerning the government's role in sustainable development, Presidential Decision No. 29 of 1990 and Presidential Instruction No. 6 of 1986 which stipulated the use of Reafforestation Fund money was to be solely for reafforestation and rehabilitation.

In reply, legal counsel for the president argued that any Presidential Decree possesses the same legal force and standing as laws (*undang-undang*) enacted by the Indonesian Legislative Assembly (Dewan Perwakilan Rakyat) and thus is not subject to judicial review. It may be noted here that the term 'judicial review', in contrast to common law jurisdictions, has a restricted meaning in Indonesian law, being limited to reviewing the validity of regulations and similar instruments made pursuant to legislation. Legal counsel for the president also asserted that Presidential Decree No. 42 of 1994 fell outside the jurisdiction of the state administrative court as it was not yet a decision of a 'final' nature.[113] In support of this assertion counsel for the defence cited article 5 of the Decree, which stated that the loan which was the subject of the Decree, and the manner of its repayment, would be further implemented by both the Minister of Forestry and the director of IPTN. As the terms of the decree had yet to be fully implemented, and as further regulation on a ministerial level was required in this respect, the decree could not be said to be a decision of a 'final' nature.[114]

In its decision the Jakarta state administrative court concurred with this latter opinion, concluding that the Presidential Decision in question did not constitute an administrative decision as defined in the Administrative Judicature Act, as it was not final in nature. As a result, it was not within the authority of the court to review the Presidential Decision in question. The court's decision in this respect was justified on the facts, given that the

111 In the political context at that time, it was considered a victory that the administrative court would even entertain a legal action against the president in the first place. See Nicholson 1994:54.

112 The Presidential Decree in question was No. 42 of 1994 regarding Loan Funds to PT IPTN.

113 Article 1(3) of the Administrative Judicature Act of 1986 states that a state administrative decision which may become the subject of a state administrative court's jurisdiction, may be defined as a 'written determination issued by a state administrative body or official containing administrative action based on valid regulations or legislation, of a concrete, individual and final nature'.

114 *Harian Umum Republika*, 1-11-1994.

transfer of money to IPTN was indeed in the form of a loan requiring further implementation via an official contract,[115] and serves to illustrate the limitations of the administrative court jurisdiction. Significantly, whilst the court ruled the contested Presidential Decree was not 'final' and thus not reviewable, the judges did not state that Presidential Decrees were, by their very nature, not subject to judicial review as had been argued by counsel for the president. The potential for future judicial review of this highly important form of executive decision-making thus remained, at least in theory.[116]

Administrative court jurisdiction: Reafforestation Fund (Kiani Kertas) case, 1997

The Reafforestation Fund was the subject of a further suit in the administrative courts, initiated by environmental public interest groups challenging the validity of Presidential Decree No. 93 of 1996, which authorized the loan of Rp 250 billion from the Reafforestation Fund to PT Kiani Kertas for the development of a pulp and paper factory located in East Kalimantan.[117] This apparent misappropriation of public funds earmarked for reafforestation attracted the ire of several environmental groups, who sought to utilize the courts as a avenue to stymie the loan or, at the least, embarrass the government.

The case that followed was heard by the Jakarta administrative court. The plaintiffs argued that the Decree authorising the loan was contrary to previous Presidential Decrees (No. 29 of 1990 and No. 40 of 1993), which had stipulated the nature and purpose of the Reafforestation Fund. The Decree was also allegedly contrary to a Ministerial Decision[118] concerning Mechanisms for Utilisation of the Reafforestation Fund, and various provisions of the EMA 1982, which stipulated the obligation of each person to protect the environment and prevent environmental damage and the role of the government in ensuring the sustainability of development for present and future generations (*Jakarta state administrative court* 1997).

In its decision dated 31 July 1997, the Jakarta state administrative court rejected the public interest suit, citing grounds almost identical to those used by the court in the Reafforestation (IPTN) case of 1994. The court accepted the defendant's submission that the Presidential Decree 'still required further implementation by an act of civil law, such as a cooperative agreement

115 Perjanjian no. 928/Menhut/II/RHS/1994. Note that the decision in this case was appealed to the high administrative court. The judges at appellate level endorsed the decision and reasoning of the first instance court without any further alterations.

116 The decision of the state administrative court was upheld on appeal to the Jakarta administrative high court without any further substantive judicial comment. See IPTN 1995.

117 Decision No. 037/G.TUN/1997/PTUN-JKT.

118 Decision of Forestry and Financial Ministers No. 169/Kpts-II/90; No. 456/KMK.013/90 concerning Mechanisms for Use of Reafforestation Fund. See *Jakarta state administrative court* 1997.

between the Forestry Minister/Funding Bank with PT Kiani Kertas [...] which would stipulate the length of the loan, level of interest, provisions etcetera' (*Jakarta state administrative court* 1997). As the Decree required further implementation by act of civil law to be effective, it had not given rise to a legal consequence for a person or legal body and could not be said to be 'final'. Accordingly, surmised the court, it was not an administrative decision as defined by the Administrative Judicature Act and thus was not within the authority of the court to review (*Jakarta state administrative court* 1997). The decision was subsequently upheld on appeal to the Jakarta administrative high court without further substantive judicial comment.[119]

General court jurisdiction

Both the cases discussed above illustrate the problems of jurisdiction in the administrative context. As discussed, administrative court jurisdiction is limited to administrative legal disputes arising because of the issuance or non-issuance of a state administrative decision, which must be final, individual and concrete in nature. A state action which does not constitute a 'state administrative decision', and thus is outside the jurisdiction of the state administrative courts, may nonetheless in certain circumstances be litigated as an 'action contrary to law' (*perbuatan melawan hukum*) within the jurisdiction of the general courts, pursuant to article 1365 of the Civil Code. The elucidation to the AJA confirms that 'administrative disputes which according to this Law are not within the competence of the Administrative Court shall be resolved by the General Courts'. The general courts thus retain an important residual jurisdiction in the field of administrative law, in respect of disputes not falling within the specific field of jurisdiction held by the administrative courts. Several criteria have been adopted by the Indonesian courts in determining whether a particular action constitutes an administrative 'action contrary to law'. Firstly, inconsistency with valid regulations, legislation or even community norms or general principles of good governance would provide grounds for the court to conclude a particular action was 'contrary to law'. However, in making its determination the court must also consider the appropriateness of the government action in the circumstances.[120] In evaluating such 'appropriateness', the court should weigh the need to protect individual rights against the interest of the wider community as represented by the state (Hadjon 1993:306). It is usually only in instances where a government agency or official has acted arbitrarily and in disregard of the public

119 *Kiani Kertas – Appeal* 1997. Jakarta Administrative High Court: No. 113/B/1997/PT.TUN JKT.
120 *Kepatutan yang harus diperhatikan oleh penguasa*. See Hadjon 1993:306.

interest that this particular cause of action would be established (Indroharto 1993). Finally, the Indonesian Supreme Court has clearly stated that acts of the state constituting policy do not fall within the scope of the court's powers of review. Based on the principle of executive policy discretion (*kebebasan kebijaksanaan*),[121] areas of state policy that may not be evaluated by the courts include: military and policing matters, foreign affairs, public interest matters, and emergency actions (Hadjon 1993:306).

General court jurisdiction: PT Inti Indorayon Utama case, 1989

The Inti Indorayon Utama case, discussed above in relation to the issue of standing, is an illustration of an environmental public interest suit based upon the administrative jurisdiction of the general court, in this case the Central Jakarta district court.[122] In this case WALHI argued that the government agencies, the subject of the claim, had acted contrary to law in issuing their respective operating permits to PT IIU, and accordingly sought nullification of PT IIU's operating permits and the payment of environmental rehabilitation costs by the defendants. WALHI contended that the issuance of the permits conflicted with existing legislation, including the obligation of the government as outlined in article 8(1) of the EMA 1982 to 'sustain the capability of the living environment to support continued development'. WALHI also argued that the issuance and renewal of PT IIU's operating licences conflicted with article 16 of the EMA 1982 and Government Regulation No. 29 of 1986, which required any plan 'likely to have a significant impact upon the environment [...] to be accompanied with an analysis of environmental impact'. Whilst the Government Regulation No. 29 of 1986 had been enacted subsequent to PT IIU commencing operation, the company was still required by article 39 to complete a Presentation of Environmental Information (Penyajian Informasi Lingkungan, PIL) which it had not done.

In its decision the Central Jakarta district court denied all the claims of the plaintiff.[123] The court considered that as the implementing regulations referred to in clause (2) of article 8 of the EMA 1982 had yet to be implemented the article conferred an unlimited authority (*kewewenang bebas*) upon the government in terms of its implementation. The court made a similar interpretation of article 16, noting that at the time PT IIU's operating licences were issued, the implementing regulations in respect of article 16 had not been enacted. Thus, as in the case of article 8, the government enjoyed an unrestrict-

121 Being a translation of the Dutch term *beleidsvrijheid*.

122 Decision No. 820/Pdt./G/1988/PN.Jkt.Pst.

123 Interestingly, the district court decision in this case was never appealed by the plaintiffs who, during the course of the case, had already been subject to intense government pressure and branded 'anti-development' - Isna Hertati (WAHLI), interview, 4-1-2001.

ed authority in its implementation of the provision at the time the licences were issued. According to the court, where there is an unrestricted government authority to implement a particular provision, then only two grounds are available for judicial review of an executive action or decision. Neither of these two grounds, being abuse of power[124] or arbitrary action (*tindakan kesewenang-wenangan* or *willekeur*), were in the court's view established by the plaintiff WALHI. Furthermore, given that Government Regulation No. 29 of 1986, concerning environmental impact analysis, had not been enacted at the time the first through fifth defendants issued operating licences to PT IIU, the defendants could not be held negligent for failing to take those Government Regulations into consideration when issuing the licences in question.

Certainly, the court was correct in concluding that the government agencies had not acted contrary to law at the time of the original issuing of the licence, as this date had preceded the enactment of the environmental provisions in question. Nonetheless, it is difficult to see why the agencies were not required to amend or reissue their licences to bring them into line with current environmental legislation. As discussed above, article 39 at the minimum requires companies who have already commenced activities at the time the law takes effect to complete a Presentation of Environmental Information, which PT IIU had not done. In any case, the plaintiff argued that PT IIU should have been legally obliged to comply with the requirements of the regulations once enacted and upon renewal of their licences.[125] This argument appears convincing and it is unfortunate it was not given proper consideration by the court, which instead applied a narrow interpretation of the environmental impact analysis regulations, excluding all previously licensed activities from its scope.

General court jurisdiction: Sulae case, 1992

In this case, eight community representatives from the Tana Toraja area in Sulawesi challenged a government decision to grant PT Bina Produksi Melosia a permit to develop a coffee plantation in the Tana Toraja area of southern Sulawesi.[126] A large area of forest within the planned plantation had been used by the local indigenous communities, both as a source of livelihood and as a site for important cultural rituals. Part of the forest also served as a water catchment area for two nearby villages. The plaintiffs argued that the company's proposal was likely to have a large and significant impact on the environment, given the planned size of the plantation at 1500 hectares. Accordingly, it was required by article 16 EMA 1982 and Government

124 *Penyalahgunaan wewenang* or *détournement de pouvoir.*

125 Article 38 of Government Regulation 29 of 1986 applies an implicit obligation in this respect.

126 Decision No. 20/Pdt.G/1992/PN. Mkl.

Regulation No. 29 of 1986 to carry out an environmental impact assessment. This requirement, however, was not fulfilled prior to the governor of South Sulawesi (first defendant) issuing a permit for the planned development. Other government agencies, including the Forestry Department, the Coordinative Agency for Investments, the regent of Tana Toraja and the Tana Toraja Department of Public Works had similarly issued permits or letters of recommendation to support the proposed development without the completion of an environmental impact assessment. The plaintiffs had therefore had no opportunity to voice their objections to the proposed development prior to its approval by government agencies. Subsequent to the granting of government approvals, the development commenced; resulting in the destruction of forest, the exclusion of local communities from lands traditionally used by them, and the disruption of water catchment and a large water course used for agricultural purposes. The plaintiffs requested that the court nullify the government decisions approving the development and, in addition, order an investigation by a government team into the payment of compensation for environmental damage pursuant to article 20 EMA 1982.

The plaintiffs' suit was ultimately rejected by the district court of Makale. The court found that the purported decisions challenged by the plaintiffs were in fact only recommendations, as the final operating permit for the land in question had not actually been granted by the regional government at the time of the case. The court also found that the seventh defendant, PT Bina Produksi Melosia, was currently undertaking an Environmental Evaluation Study, Environmental Management Plan and Environmental Monitoring Plan in accordance with Government Regulation No. 29 of 1986. The court also found, on the basis of testimony from the defendants' witnesses and contrary to community reports, that environmental damage had not in fact occurred in the area in question, which still remained largely uncleared.

General court jurisdiction: Kalimantan Peat Land case, 1999

The Kalimantan Peat Land case arose subsequent to the enactment of the AJA and raised a number of issues of administrative law, but was nonetheless brought to the district court of Central Jakarta.[127] The well publicized claim by WALHI against the president, nine ministers and ten senior government figures related to the highly controversial plan of the Suharto government to convert some one million hectares of peat land into productive rice fields. Conceived in 1995, the mega-project's lauded objective was regaining Indonesia's self sufficiency in rice production, although, like most large resource development projects, it also produced lucrative opportunities for the enrichment of the president's personal network of family and cronies. Due to its presidential

127 Decision No. 27/Pdt.G/1999/PN.Jkt.Pusat.

backing the project was fast tracked, bypassing many of the usual planning procedures, including environmental impact assessment, to enable implementation to commence immediately (Akhmad Supriyatna 1998). The environmental consequences of these initial stages of the project were immense. Wood extraction permits (*izin pemanfaatan kayu*) were granted to a number of companies who commenced intensive clearing of the one million hectares. Land clearing and construction of a network of irrigation canals extracted a devastating toll on the biodiversity, local climate and land of this fragile wetlands area. The indigenous population, displaced from their traditional lands and deprived of their former subsistence livelihoods, fared little better.[128] The extensive land clearing was also subsequently identified as a contributing factor to destructive forest fires that burned unchecked for six months.

Serious problems soon emerged in the implementation of the ambitious but poorly designed project. An expert team, which reviewed the project in 1998, concluded that the cleared peat land was largely unsuitable for intensive rice cultivation. Moreover, peat land comprised only some 40-50% of the land cleared, the remainder being wetlands of great ecological significance but little agricultural value. The team harshly criticized the 'implementation first, planning later' approach that the project's architects had adopted. The National Research Council (Dewan Riset Nasional) also concluded that the cleared land was unfertile and hence unsuitable for agriculture, recommending that the project be stopped (Akhmad Supriyatna 1998). Ultimately, as financial and political upheaval gripped Indonesia and mounting environmental and agricultural problems proved insurmountable, the government was forced to abandon the project around mid-1999, leaving behind an ecological and social disaster of gigantic proportions.

The legal suit lodged by WALHI in the Central Jakarta district court was an attempt to hold the government accountable for the environmental and social damage wrought by the failed project and nullify the Presidential Decree upon which the project had been based. WALHI's claim probed a string of alleged illegalities which had been committed in the efforts to fast-track the project in accordance with the president's wishes. These included:

- failure to provide adequate information regarding the project and facilitate community input contrary to spatial planning laws;[129]

128 Land clearing destroyed the tropical forest from which local communities had harvested forest products to sell at local markets. Plantations of rattan and other crops owned by local communities were also destroyed by the rampant forest fires triggered by the frenzy of intensive clearing accompanying the project's commencement. See Hanni Adiati 1998:14-8.

129 Article 4 of the Spatial Planning Act No. 24 of 1994 states: 'Each person is endowed with a right to be informed of a spatial plan and participate in formulating the spatial plan, utilizing

- appropriation of monies from a Reafforestation Fund;[130]
- failure to complete an Environmental Impact Assessment prior to the project's commencement;[131]
- ministerial approval of the eventual Environmental Impact Assessment despite it containing serious factual discrepancies;
- displacement of the indigenous populace from their traditional lands and destruction of their source of livelihood;
- irreversible ecological damage through intensive land clearing, uncontrolled forest fires, canal and rice paddy construction contrary to environmental legislation.[132]

WALHI thus argued that the actions of the defendants in implementing the Peat Land project were contrary to law and general principles of good governance. The plaintiff requested that the court order:

- the annulment of Presidential Decrees No. 82 of 1995, 74 of 1998 and 83 of 1995;[133]
- the closure of primary canals already constructed in the project area;

---

space and controlling space utilization in addition to obtaining fair compensation for conditions experienced as a result of implementing development activities in accordance with a spatial plan'. See WALHI and President 1999:14. Article 12(1) states: 'Spatial Planning is to be carried out by the government with community participation. Community participation is a matter of great importance in spatial planning because ultimately space is for the interests of all parts of the community.'

130 The provisions relating to which required monies from the fund to be allocated towards reafforestation and land rehabilitation, as discussed above in relation to the IPTN and PT Kiani Kertas cases.

131 Intensive land clearing and construction of canals over 1923 km in length were completed in the first stage of the project, prior to completion of the Environmental Impact Assessment process.

132 Particular provisions of the EMA 1997 referred to by WALHI included article 5, which guarantees the right of each person to a 'clean and healthy environment' and to 'participate in the framework of environmental management', and article 6, which guarantees access to information relating to participation in environmental management. WALHI also argued that as the project resulted in a 'large and significant' impact on the environment then, according to the terms of article 35, the government should be held strictly liable for any resulting losses. Environmental damage resulting from the project was also alleged to have contravened the terms of other legislation, including Law No. 5 of 1990 on Conservation of Biodiversity, Law No. 10 of 1992 on Population and Family Welfare, Law No. 5 of 1994 on Biodiversity, and Presidential Decision No. 48 of 1991 ratifying the International Convention on Wetlands.

133 Decree No. 82 of 1995 concerning 'Development of Peat Land for Agricultural Food Crops in Central Kalimantan' was the original decree initiating the project. Decree No. 83 of 1995 concerning 'Formation of a Presidential Assistance Fund for Development of Peat Land in Central Kalimantan' provided for the appropriation of monies from the Reafforestation Fund toward the Peat Land project. Decree No. 74 of 1998 made minor changes to Decree No. 82 of 1995.

- rehabilitation of damaged land based on ecological principles appropriate to tropical peat swamp areas;
- creation of a biodiversity rehabilitation centre;
- protection of traditional community patterns of natural resource management;
- withdrawal of wood cutting permits.

As one of the most disastrous environmental policies carried out by the New Order government, the Kalimantan Peat Land project was a predictable target for an environmental public interest suit. The hasty and unplanned execution of the project was blatantly contrary to basic provisions in environmental and spatial planning legislation, as WALHI's lengthy claim pointed out. Critics also suspected more serious improprieties and corruption associated with the project, given the number of Suharto's closest associates who benefited from the lucrative tenders handed out in the early stage of the project. However, such illegalities were not brought to light in the courtroom, as the claim was rejected in a summary fashion on jurisdictional grounds by the Central Jakarta district court. The court referred to article 10 of Law No. 14 of 1970 on the Judiciary which stipulates that judicial authority is to be divided amongst: general courts, religious courts, military courts, and administrative courts.

The court then referred to various provisions of the Administrative Judicature Act No. 55 of 1986, defining the jurisdiction of the administrative courts as a dispute concerning the issuance of a state administrative decision by a state agency or official.[134] In the present case the claim by WALHI, a legal body, was directed against a number of state officials including the president, ministers and subordinate officials. The claim also was directed toward the withdrawal of decrees or decisions issued by those officials or agencies. Consequently, the presiding judges concluded that the dispute in this case fell within the jurisdiction of the administrative courts rather than the general courts, to which it had been brought by the plaintiff.

The court's analysis of the jurisdictional issue in this case is disappointingly superficial, going so far as to note only that the plaintiffs' claim was directed against a number of state officials, requested the withdrawal of certain state decisions and as a result fell within the jurisdiction of the administrative courts. Further analysis leads one to question this conclusion, as the two main decisions raised in the plaintiffs' claim, Presidential Decrees No. 82 and 83 of 1995, could not accurately be said to be either 'final' or 'individual' as required by article 1(3) of the AJA. Both decrees, like all Presidential

[134] Article 1(3) defines state administrative decision (see discussion above) as 'a written stipulation issued by a state agency or official based on valid legislation of a concrete, individual and final nature which results in a legal consequence for a person or legal body'.

Decrees in most cases, required further implementation in the same way as did the decrees in the IPTN and Kiani Kertas cases – which the administrative courts had rejected jurisdiction over. Furthermore, both decrees were arguably general in nature and not directed toward specific, named individuals. It is therefore likely that if WALHI's claim were taken to the administrative courts, jurisdiction also would have been refused – no doubt the reason it was advanced to the general courts in the first place. If this was indeed the case, then the district court should have legitimately exercised jurisdiction over this matter, and was incorrect to refuse to do so.

Substantive grounds

Besides satisfying requirements of standing and jurisdiction, an application contesting an administrative decision must also establish one or more of three substantive grounds stipulated in article 53(2) of the Administrative Judicature Act. The first ground is inconsistency with regulations or legislation, of either a procedural or substantive nature. One regulatory restriction of considerable relevance in environmental matters is the requirement to undertake an environmental impact analysis (EIA). An EIA is required where a business and/or activity may give rise to a large and significant impact on the environment. In this case the business concerned must prepare an environmental impact analysis as a prerequisite to obtaining the necessary operating licence.[135] Once granted, the operating licence also includes conditions and obligations to carry out environmental control efforts stipulated in article 18(3) of the EMA 1997. Where an EIA is required, but not undertaken, prior to the issue of an operating licence, then the decision to issue the licence may be contested as inconsistent with existing legislation.[136]

A second ground that may invalidate a state administrative decision is the use of an administrative decision maker's authority for a purpose other than that authorized by statute. This ground, also termed 'abuse of power' (*penyalahgunaan wewenang*), is usually difficult to prove and as a result holds little practical significance in administrative court practice (Bedner 2000:96). The third and final ground stipulated in the Administrative Judicature Law is that, on a consideration of interests relevant to the decision, the government agency concerned should not have issued a particular decision or should not have issued a decision at all. This ground further restricts the scope of the administrative discretion by necessitating a consideration of relevant interests in the decision making process. Relevant interests are usually defined

135 Article 18 of the EMA 1997; Regulation No. 27 of 1999 regarding Environmental Impact Assessment now sets out the requirements for environmental impact analysis.
136 This occurred in the Transgenic Cotton case, discussed below.

by the immediate legislative framework under which the decision is made. The potential environmental impact of a project may constitute such a 'relevant interest', especially where that impact may be of a significant nature. Finally, a fourth substantive ground, not stipulated in article 53(2) of the Administrative Judicature Act, the ground of principles of proper administration, is in practice becoming increasingly accepted in administrative court procedure (Bedner 2000:97). These substantive grounds were considered in WALHI's first public interest suit against Freeport Indonesia in 1995.

Substantive grounds: Freeport case, 1995

In this case, WALHI challenged an administrative decision by the secretary-general of the Department of Mining and Energy to approve the environmental management and monitoring plans proposed by PT Freeport Indonesia. WALHI argued that the Department had failed to take into account the evaluation and recommendations of the environmental impact analysis commission, of which WALHI was a non-permanent member.[137] At a hearing of the commission held on 22 December 1994, WALHI had recommended that the environmental management and monitoring plans proposed by Freeport should be rejected. One of the most vocal critics of Freeport Indonesia, WALHI maintained that the mining company's operations had caused widespread environmental damage including the dumping of unprocessed tailings into local rivers over a period of twenty years, flooding, widespread deforestation, and irreversible damage to the mountainous landscape through open-cut mining. Socially, the impact of mining operations was also said to be severe, causing the removal of two indigenous tribes – the mountain dwelling Amungme, and the Komoro who inhabited the lower coastal regions – from their traditional lands. The commission itself had recommended that Freeport's environmental management plans be revised in accordance with its evaluations, including those submitted by WALHI, and subsequently resubmitted to the commission for further evaluation. A field visit to Freeport's mine was subsequently conducted and revisions to the plans carried out. The secretary of the environmental impact analysis commission later approved the revisions, before the formal decision by the Department for Mining and Energy approved the plans on 17 February 1995.

WALHI challenged the decision of the department firstly on procedural grounds, arguing that only the commission, not the secretary, had the authority to re-evaluate and approve the plans, and that it had not done so. WALHI

[137] According to article 9(3) of Government Regulation No. 51 of 1993 regarding Environmental Impact Assessment, the decision of an authorised agency (in this case the Department of Mining and Energy) regarding an environmental impact assessment should be based upon the evaluation of that assessment carried out by the Commission for Environmental Impact Assessment.

further argued on substantive grounds that the revised plans did not satisfactorily meet the concerns and objections raised in WALHI's original submission, including consultation with the local Amungme and Komoro communities. In response, the defendant in this case, the Department for Mining and Energy, contended that WALHI had in fact been afforded an opportunity to present its own opinion and evaluation of the plans in question, at the original hearing on 22 December 1994 and during a field visit in January 1995.

In its decision dated 9 November 1995 the Jakarta state administrative court concluded that the commission had in fact discharged its duty of evaluating the environmental management plans in question, as required by legislation.[138] The final decision of the Department of Mining and Energy approving the plans was thus, in the opinion of the court, in accordance with regulatory procedures. In relation to the substantive grounds argued by WALHI, the court concluded that whilst the commission was bound to consider WALHI's submissions on a proposal before it, it was not bound to decide in accordance with such a submission. The ultimate decision lay within the discretionary power of the commission, which in this case was exercised to recommend approval of Freeport's proposal. Accordingly, the court concluded that the decision subsequently made by the Department to approve Freeport's proposal was also within its proper authority and in accordance with established procedures. Thus, the application of WALHI to nullify the decision was dismissed.

Substantive grounds: Transgenic cotton case, 2001

This case concerned the controversial test planting of genetically modified (GM) cotton in South Sulawesi.[139] The test crop of GM cotton, over an area of 465 hectares, was to be planted by PT Monagro Kimia, a joint venture between the US company Monsanto and the Indonesian-Chinese conglomerate the Salim Group (Rino Subagyo 2002a:5). Environmentalists argued that the 'test crop' was actually an attempt to by-pass environmental regulations and introduce GM cotton to Indonesia on a commercial basis.[140] On 29 September 2000, the Environment Minister formally notified the Minister for Agriculture, who held authority in the matter, that the proposal had been introduced without an environmental impact assessment.[141] Despite this notification the Minister for Agriculture proceeded to approval the proposal

138 In reaching this conclusion, they did not appear to consider WALHI's argument that the re-evaluation of the environmental management plans had been carried out by the secretary to the commission, rather than the commission proper.

139 Decision No. 71/G.TUN/2001/PTUN-Jkt.

140 Rino Subagyo, ICEL, interview, 6-6-2003.

141 Letter No. 1882/MENLH/09/2000.

on 7 February 2001, authorising the restricted planting of transgenic cotton in seven regencies in South Sulawesi.[142]

On 4 May 2001 an environmental public interest suit was lodged by six environmental organizations in the Jakarta administrative court, challenging the decision of the Agriculture Minister.[143] The plaintiffs argued that the decision was contrary to environmental regulations as it had not been preceded by an environmental impact assessment and thus was invalid pursuant to article 53(2)(a) of the Administrative Judicature Act. Particular provisions cited by the plaintiffs included (*Jakarta state administrative court* 2001):

1 Article 15(1) EMA 1997: 'every enterprise or activity which may cause a large or significant impact on the environment is required to undertake an environmental impact assessment'.
2 Government Regulation No. 27 of 1999 concerning Environmental Impact Assessment.
3 Article 3(1) 'enterprises and/or activities which may cause a large or significant impact on the environment include: [...] (f) the introduction of plant types, animal types and microorganisms'.
4 Article 7(1): 'environmental impact assessment is a requirement that must be fulfilled to obtain a permit to carry out an enterprise or activity from an authorized official'.

The plaintiffs argued that the introduction of transgenic cotton to South Sulawesi was an activity which could cause a large and significant impact upon the environment and thus should have been preceded by an environmental impact assessment. Further grounds presented for the plaintiffs' claim were that after considering all relevant interests the Minister for Agriculture should not have made the decision he did, or that the Minister acted arbitrarily in coming to the decision he did (article 53[2c] Administrative Judicature Act 1986). Relevant considerations allegedly ignored by the Agriculture Minister in his decision to approve Monsanto's project without an environmental impact analysis (EIA) included requests from both the Environment Minister and the legislature of southern Sulawesi that a environmental impact assessment be carried out. According to the plaintiffs, the Minister also failed to apply the precautionary principle, as stipulated in Act No. 5 of 1994 on Ratification of the UN Convention on Biological Diversity and associated

142 Decision No. 107/Kpts/KB.430/2/2001.

143 The six environmental organizations were the Indonesian Centre for Environmental Law, the Indonesia Institute of Consumers, the National Consortium for the Nature and Forests Conservation, the Foundation for Biodynamic Agriculture, the Southern Sulawesi Consumers Foundation and the Community Research and Capacity-Building Institute.

international protocols to which Indonesia was a signatory.[144] The plaintiffs also argued that the minister had failed to consider legal violations by PT Monagro Kimia, who had already carried out planting of transgenic planting before the minister's decision and in fact intended the planting to be carried out at a commercial rather than experimental level (*Jakarta state administrative court* 2001).

The Jakarta administrative court handed down its decision on 27 September 2001, after hearings over a period of four months, refusing the plaintiffs' claim. The court held that in this case the Minister of Agriculture's decision was not part of the process of 'obtaining a permit' referred to in article 7, Government Regulation No. 27 of 1999, for which an EIA was mandatory. The minister's decision did not constitute the issuance of a permit but rather was an administrative action within the scope of his legal authority. The other basis upon which an EIA could have been required was article 15 of the EMA 1997, which required that in the case of all activities causing a large and significant impact on the environment, an environmental impact assessment be completed. Activities of this nature are defined in article 3 Government Regulation No. 27 of 1999, which, as the plaintiff had pointed out, included in sub clause (f) the introduction of plant types, animal types and micro-organisms. Nonetheless, the court maintained that as such activities were not specifically stipulated in the Environment Minister's Decision No. 3 of 2000, the Minister for Agriculture was not obligated to complete an EIA. The court also considered that as the proposed activity was an 'experimental' planting, if any serious or negative effects were exposed these could be reviewed in a subsequent EIA process.

On the question of the precautionary principle, the court concluded it was sufficient that several measures had been carried out before the Minister for Agriculture's decision. These included a community announcement and a review of the recommendation of a team of biotechnology experts and various laboratory tests, which apparently demonstrated that the cotton strain would be safe to introduce to the environment (*Jakarta state administrative court* 2001). On these grounds, the plaintiffs' application to invalidate the decision of the Minister for Agriculture was refused. Both grounds for the court's decision appear questionable. Given the planting of transgenic cotton fell within the scope of article 15 of the EMA 1997 and article 3 Government Regulation No. 27 of 1999 on EIA, it is difficult to justify the court's position that an EIA was not required. Furthermore, the Environment Minister had informed the Minister for Agriculture in writing that an EIA would be required. The court's interpretation of the precautionary principle also appears to be very narrow

144 Including the Rio Declaration – see article 15.

in this case. Given the controversy and uncertainty surrounding the impact of biotechnology, one would expect a proper application of the precautionary principle would have at least required that an environmental impact assessment be completed.

Remedies

Challenges to state administrative decisions are heard by the state administrative court, although in certain circumstances disputes must undergo administrative review prior to the process of judicial review. Upon evaluating the legality of an administrative decision, the court decides whether an invalidation of the decision is appropriate in the circumstances. The court does not itself possess authority to re-decide the issue on its merits, but may invalidate a decision and submit it to the administrative decision-maker for re-decision. The administrator must take into account the decision of the court but is not obliged to arrive at a decision substantively different from that originally made. Of some significance in the environmental context is the court's authority to award compensation and rehabilitation where the applicant has suffered loss as a result of the administrative decision (article 97[10] Administrative Judicature Act 1986).

One limitation on the efficacy of this process is the court's lack of authority to directly implement its own decision. Rather, an obligation rests with the government agency responsible for issuing a decision subsequently invalidated by the court, to cancel and/or issue a new decision after considering the judgement of the court (Hadjon 1993:309). Nonetheless, where a defendant refuses or otherwise fails to rescind a decision pursuant to court order, it will become void in four months (article 116[2]). One limitation on the applicability of this process in the environmental context is the stipulation that any challenge to a state administrative decision must be brought within ninety days of the decision being issued.[145] The position in respect of interested third parties adversely affected by the decision is not clearly defined under the Administrative Judicature Act.[146] This distinction is of particular importance in environmental matters, as the effects of pollution or other environmental damage caused by a particular industry or enterprise upon third parties may only be felt a number of months, or years, after the industry begins operation (Niniek Suparni 1992:107).

145 Article 55: In respect of a third party the limitation period runs from the date at which he/she knew of the decision.

146 However, the Supreme Court has issued a guideline on this subject in its Circular Letter no. 2/1991 (at V-3), advising judges to determine the date upon which the third party first became aware of her loss and commence the period from that day. See Bedner 2002.

Conclusion

This chapter has discussed the legislative framework for environmental litigation, and its judicial interpretation, in Indonesia. This legislative framework proscribes several important rights and remedies connected with the compensation and restoration of environmental damage and pollution. Firstly, article 38(3) of the EMA has provided legislative endorsement of environmental standing, thus enabling environmental groups to initiate legal actions in relation to environmental disputes, despite the absence of a personal or material interest. The procedurally important principle of environmental standing was, as discussed, introduced eight years prior to the EMA 1997, by the Central Jakarta district court in the Inti Indorayon Utama case of 1989. This significant procedural reform is notable as an example of judicial 'law-making' and activism in the environmental field. Other Indonesian courts have been consistent in following the precedent of Indorayon and recognizing this procedural right despite frequent arguments to the contrary by defendants.

The procedural scope for environmental litigation was further widened by article 37 of the EMA 1997, which introduced a right for a community to bring a representative action in respect of environmental damage. Attempts to bring representative actions previous to the enactment of article 37 had failed in the PT Pupuk Iskandar Muda (1989) and the Ciujung River (1995) cases. Since the enactment of article 37, there have been several attempted environmental representative actions. In the Eksponen 66 case (1998) a poorly defined representative action succeeded at the district court level, yet was overturned by the high court of North Sumatra on appeal. The decision by the district court of Medan in that case demonstrated the court's concern for the far-reaching environmental damage caused by the fire, yet the requisite legal elements of factual and legal commonality and causation were not properly established in this case. In the Way Seputih case (2000) a class action pursuant to article 37 was procedurally accepted, yet was unsuccessful subsequently on substantive grounds. In the Pekanbaru Smog case (2000) a representative action was heard by the court but ultimately failed due to the failure of the plaintiff to undertake notification as ordered by the court. Certainly an early obstacle to effective utilization of this provision was the confusion amongst Indonesian jurists over the proper procedure accompanying a representative action. This confusion, however, appears to have been resolved by the enacted Supreme Court Regulation No. 1 of 2000 on Procedure for Class Action, which has stipulated a detailed guide to the procedure requirements relating to class actions.

Another significant feature of the Indonesian legal framework for environmental litigation is the right to claim compensation for environmental damage or pollution. A right to compensation for environmental damage or pollution was first introduced in the environmental context in article 20 of the EMA 1982. Application of this article was apparently obstructed, however, by two major obstacles: the requirement for a government facilitated investigation before a claim and the lack of implementing regulations. In four of the five cases concerning this article, courts rejected claims for compensation of environmental damage on either of these grounds. These two legal impediments were resolved with the introduction of article 34 of the EMA 1997, which removed the necessity of prior government investigation or conciliation and did not depend upon subsequent regulations for its implementation. Claims for compensation of environmental damage or pollution pursuant to article 34 have apparently been more successful. In the four cases reviewed above all claimants were at least partially successful in winning compensation at the district court level. Interestingly, in two of these four cases – Laguna Mandiri (1998) and Babon River (1998) – the decisions awarding compensation were reversed upon appeal to the respective high courts, a trend also evident in the Eksponen 66 case concerning representative actions. However, in the Banger River case (1999) the high court upheld, and actually increased, the award of compensation, whilst in the Kalimantan Peat Land (Farmers Compensation) case (1999) a compensatory settlement was adjudicated and endorsed as a decision of the high court.

The difficulties experienced by victims of environmental damage or pollution in obtaining compensation pursuant to article 20 (EMA 1982) and article 34 (EMA 1997) illustrate the pitfalls of a fault-based liability regime where claimants are required to prove causation and fault. It is precisely such difficulties, experienced in a range of jurisdictions, that have led many environmental jurists to advocate shifting to a risk-based system of strict liability in order to provide a more accessible, effective and fair system of compensating environmental damage or pollution. As we have seen strict liability was first introduced in Indonesia by article 21 of the EMA 1982. The implementing regulations for that article were never enacted, however, and as a result the article was not applied in practice. The situation was definitely improved by article 35 of the EMA 1997, which provided a more detailed application of the strict liability principle without the need for further implementing regulations. The terms of article 35 stipulate strict liability in situations causing a large and significant impact upon the environment, where hazardous materials are used, and/or hazardous waste produced. Given the wide scope of application of article 35 and its significant effect in excluding the element of fault, this article has perhaps the greatest potential to facilitate access to justice in environmental suits. Yet, whilst strict liability has been pleaded as the basis for several environmental suits, the majority of courts have avoided discussion of this issue and have proceeded to deal with disputes on a fault liability basis only. Where the article has been considered, as in the Laguna

Mandiri case, its application has been restrictive and legally incorrect.

As discussed above, the ability of environmental organizations to represent environmental interests in court has been greatly facilitated by the legal doctrine of environmental standing first recognized in the Inti Indorayon Utama case. Yet standing for environmental organizations in itself is not sufficient to achieve environmental justice in a more substantive sense. Upon gaining access to the courts, the remedies available to environmental organizations are equally as important as their procedural access. Under the EMA 1982 the role of environmental organizations in environmental management was recognized by article 19.[147] The EMA 1982, however, did not specifically stipulate either procedural standing nor substantive remedies for environmental organizations. Nonetheless, article 20(3) of the EMA 1982 did create an obligation for those polluting or damaging the environment to pay restoration costs to the state. Utilising the judicially recognized principle of environmental standing, WALHI brought a public interest action to compel environmental restoration in the Surabaya River case (1995). The case failed, however, largely due to the absence of implementing regulations for article 20. Access to remedies for environmental organizations has been improved by article 38(3) of the EMA 1997, which enables environmental organizations to sue for a range of measures to be carried out in support of environmental functions. Yet in practice the impact of environmental public interest suits has been limited by the exclusion of compensation from the scope of article 38(1). As discussed above, the broadening of public interest remedies to include compensation for environmental damage would increase the deterrent effect of public interest suits on potential polluters and facilitate enforcement of the obligation in article 34(1) to compensate for damage to the environment.

In this chapter we have also explored other legal grounds for environmental public interest suits. One such ground, utilized in the Freeport case (1995), was article 6, which requires the provision of 'true and accurate information regarding environmental management'. In the political context of *reformasi* in the post-Suharto era, transparency and provision of information have become issues of fundamental import.[148] WALHI's partially successful claim in this case establishes article 6 as a valuable mechanism to increase transparency in the provision of environmental information. Environmental public interest suits have also been advanced pursuant to the Administrative Judicature Act in the administrative courts. In the first environmental public interest suit in

147 Article 19 states: 'Self-reliant community institutions shall perform a supporting role in the management of the living environment'.

148 Much attention has focused, for instance, on the drafting and enactment of Freedom of Information legislation, which is currently being considered by a Special Committee of the national legislature.

the administrative courts, the IPTN case (1994), the principle of environmental standing was endorsed by the court. However, as in the general courts, this procedural success has not always been matched by substantive legal results. In both the IPTN and Kiani Kertas cases (1997), environmental public interest suits failed on jurisdictional grounds, demonstrating the significant jurisdictional obstacles confronting environmental claimants in the administrative courts. In a subsequent environmental dispute, the Kalimantan Peat Land case (1999), environmental organizations tried to sidestep this jurisdictional obstacle by taking their challenge to several Presidential Decrees to the general courts, rather than administrative courts. As we have seen, this attempt failed, as the Central Jakarta district court also refused jurisdiction. The court stated that the matter fell within the ambit of the administrative courts, despite the fact that the Presidential Decrees that were the subject of the suit were likely to be neither 'final' nor 'individual'. Between the administrative and general courts, environmental public interest suits have thus fallen into something of a jurisdictional black hole. This jurisdictional failure is not a necessary result of the legal framework, however. As discussed above, the jurisdiction of the general courts, correctly applied, would encompass administrative cases that fell outside the specific scope of the administrative court's jurisdiction.

Even where a contested administrative decision falls within the jurisdiction of the administrative court, establishing its illegality on the limited grounds available again presents a difficult task for the potential environmental litigant. As the court noted in the PT Freeport case, an agency's discretion may be procedurally limited – in that case requiring it to hear WALHI's submission – but the agency may still possess considerable discretion in coming to an ultimate decision itself on the substance of the matter. In a country with a history of executive dominance such as Indonesia, moreover, it is not uncommon for judges to display considerable reluctance to review administrative discretion, particularly that exercised at a senior level on issues of considerable political and economic significance as in the Freeport case. Similarly, in the Transgenic Cotton case (2001), jurisdiction was not an obstacle to the public interest suit, yet the court declined to invalidate the Minister for Agriculture's decision despite the fact an environmental impact assessment had not been carried out. Furthermore, even where a challenge to an administrative decision is successful, its implementation may be undermined by an entrenched administrative patrimonialism and resistance to judicial review (Bedner 2000:322).

Whilst the majority of environmental public interest claims in the general and administrative courts may not have achieved their substantive legal claims, such suits have often helped in achieving the broader political or policy objectives of environmental organizations. Public interest litigants such as WALHI have endeavoured to use the courts as a mechanism not only for the application of environmental law, but as another strategy to increase community and political pressure to change environmental policy on particular issues. As a member of WALHI's legal team commented

> On a substantive level we don't expect much from these court cases. But the cases do serve as a stage for our campaigns. In most cases we target particular policies and aim to change that policy on the national level. The Kalimantan Peat Land case was an example of this strategy. The court case failed but was part of a broader campaign to halt the project which was ultimately successful.[149]

In a similar vein, the bold legal action of several environmental NGOs in challenging President Suharto himself in the IPTN case was successful in capturing considerable media attention, although it did not achieve its legal objective. Politically, that legal action, together with the PT Kiani Kertas case that followed it, were significant elements in a concerted campaign by NGOs to expose government and industry corruption connected with the Reafforestation Fund. Ultimately this campaign appears to have been successful, as in the changed political circumstances of *reformasi* – after the fall of Suharto – the government successfully convicted several influential figures involved in the embezzlement of considerable sums of money from the Reafforestation Fund.[150]

Whilst the political context may provide an important motivation for some environmental public interest claims, it may equally influence the process and outcome of both private and public interest environmental litigation. The discussion in this chapter has focused primarily on the legal framework for environmental litigation and its interpretation by Indonesian courts in environmental cases to date. Yet the process and outcome of environmental litigation cannot be separated from the social, political and institutional context within which it occurs. This chapter has examined cases since the enactment of the EMA 1982 until 2001. The most dramatic political change to occur during this period was the forced resignation of President Suharto on 21 May 1998, caused by severe economic crisis and political upheaval. The dissolution of Suharto's system of authoritarian control has certainly increased political openness and pluralism, but also apparently contributed to widespread

149 Isna Hertati, Bidang Hukum Lingkungan, WALHI pusat, interview, 4-1-2001.

150 For example Bob Hasan, who as chairman of APKINDO and close friend of Suharto was at one time the most influential individual in the forestry industry, is now serving a six year jail term for misappropriation of reforestation funds and a fraudulent aerial mapping project carried out by one of his companies. See 'Forests, people and rights: *Down to Earth special report* (June) 2002:22. Newsletter of the International Campaign for Ecological Justice in Indonesia. http://dte.gn.apc.org/srf1.htm.

lawlessness and social disorder. There is a striking contrast in the outcome of environmental suits in the period before 1998 and in the period subsequent to it. Prior to 1998 all of the twelve environmental claims brought to the district courts were defeated on substantive issues. However, during and subsequent to 1998, of the nine cases surveyed seven were at least partially successful on substantive issues at the district court level – a striking contrast. On the whole, Indonesian courts have appeared more willing to uphold environmental claims for compensation or restoration of environmental damage/pollution in the period subsequent to 1998. This holds true more for the district level courts than for appellate (high) courts. Subsequent to 1998, appellate courts have played a noticeably more conservative role, with only one of four decided cases being successful on substantive grounds.

CHAPTER III

Case studies of environmental litigation

In the previous chapter, we have discussed the noticeable change in the outcome of environmental cases subsequent to 1998. Between 1982 and 1997, only one environmental claim out of thirteen reported claims was successful. In contrast, in the period between 1998 and 2001, seven out of eleven claims were at least partially successful at the district court level. As we have discussed, the important legal milestone separating these two periods was the enactment of the EMA 1997. This revised Environmental Management Act improved the enforceability of several key provisions relating to the compensation or restoration of environmental damage or pollution. The most significant political event separating these two periods is the dissolution of President Suharto's New Order regime. It has been suggested that the far-reaching political and institutional ramifications of this event may have also had an important influence on the outcome of environmental cases. In this chapter, we explore the influence of these, and other legal, institutional and political conditions through two case studies of these recent 'successful' environmental claims, the Banger River case and the Babon River case. Each case study provides a detailed discussion of the history of the environmental disputes that preceded litigation. The discussion then closely considers the legal and evidential issues raised during the course of each case and undertakes a critical examination of the interpretation and application of environmental law by the respective courts. Finally, the scope of the case studies is extended beyond the legal and evidential issues raised in the course of litigation to the wider social and political context in which the dispute resolution process occurs.

Banger River case, 1999

History of the dispute

The Banger River is a river of some twenty metres in width, which traverses the eastern section of the bustling city of Pekalongan, in Central Java.[1] Like most rivers it has traditionally been a source of water for the everyday needs of residents in its vicinity and has also provided some with a livelihood, through fishing and small scale sand mining (YAPHI 2000). Pekalongan, renowned as a centre of 'batik' in Java, is also the location for a number of textile factories. The majority of these are located adjacent to the Banger River, which provides both a source of water for production and a means of waste disposal. In 1988, three of the largest textile factories, PT Kesamtex, PT Bintang Triputratez and CV Enzritek, were established. From 1989, when the factories commenced operations, their untreated liquid waste was disposed of directly into the waters of the Banger River. By 1992, as the factory operations increased, the resulting pollution had become severe and most evident in the dramatic changes in colour and odour of the water, and in the deaths of fishes and small livestock drinking from the river.[2] Among those most directly affected by the pollution were the residents of Dekoro village, located a short distance downstream from the three textile factories. Residents were unable to use the water for washing or cooking, whilst livestock that grazed near the river or drank its water perished. Local fishermen were also no longer able to earn their livelihood from the river. Acute conditions associated with severe water pollution, such as skin rashes and vomiting, became common within the community. Pollution of residents' wells through contamination of ground water also occurred, to the point where residents could no longer use their wells as a source of potable water.

In 1990, in response to the pollution, the community of Dekoro formed an action group: the Association of Banger River Waste Victims (Kerukunan Korban Limbah Kali Banger, KKLB). Following the 1992 increase in pollution levels, this group made a number of direct and written representations concerning the pollution and its effects; initially to administrative agencies and subsequently to legislatures at the district (Pekalongan) and provincial (Central Java) levels. Representations were also made by the community

1 Decision No. 50/Pdt.G/1998.PN.Pkl.

2 The three industries that were the subject of this dispute were not the only factories disposing of waste into the Banger River. In a statement to the press on 8-3-1997 a representative of the Dekoro community stated: '16 factories along the Banger River have been dumping their toxic waste into the river for the past 10 years'. See 'Pollution haunts villagers' livelihood', *The Jakarta Post*, 8-3-1997.

directly to the three industries, in an unsuccessful attempt to resolve the problem via negotiation.[3]

The advocacy efforts of KKLB, facilitated by a network of environmental organizations, successfully raised the public profile of the Banger River pollution and increased community pressure on the regional government to take action. In August 1995, the three industries were prosecuted in the district court of Pekalongan and ultimately convicted of contravening article 12 of Regional Government Regulation 2 of 1993, concerning 'Cleanliness, beauty, tidiness and order'. The regulation under which the three polluting factories were prosecuted, however, carried a penalty of only Rp 45,000.[4] According to community sources, the prosecution was actually suggested by the industries themselves, who saw this as a way of pacifying the local community whilst paying only a minimal fine.[5] No prosecution was commenced under the Environmental Management Act, which carries more weighty sanctions.[6]

Subsequent to this apparently symbolic prosecution, the three industries undertook to install a common waste management unit in 1996. The unit, however, failed to function adequately, and waste discharged from the factories continued to exceed stipulated levels. In frustration at the lack of progress, community representatives took their complaints to the national level. In July 1996 a delegation met with the second deputy of the National Environmental Agency, Nabiel Makarim, to report the severe and ongoing pollution levels. In March 1997, following no apparent progress towards resolution of the dispute, KKLB petitioned the National Environmental Agency a second time. Community representatives also filed a complaint with the National Human Rights Commission, citing intimidation by local security forces acting on behalf of the industries.[7]

The community complaints of pollution at the national level were widely reported in the mass media, prompting an examination of the factories' waste management unit by the National Environmental Agency on 6 May 1997 (Trias Purwadi and Syam Dakrita 1999). The examination revealed that the industries had failed to install the necessary equipment to measure the volume of liquid waste discharged, contrary to government regula-

3 Ismar (Dekoro), interview, 5-3-2001.

4 'Ketua majelis merasa terganggu demo', *Suara Merdeka*, 1999.

5 'Ketua majelis merasa terganggu demo', *Suara Merdeka*, 1999.

6 For example, article 41(1) carries a maximum imprisonment of 10 years and a maximum fine of Rp 500 million for 'any person who in contravention of the law intentionally carries out an action which results in environmental pollution and/or damage'.

7 The visit produced at least some result, in the form of a letter signed by a commission member, Asmara Nababan, requesting relevant government agencies to resolve the complaints of the Dekoro community. See 'Pollution haunts villagers' livelihood', *The Jakarta Post*, 8-3-1997.

tion.[8] An administrative warning was subsequently sent from the National Environmental Agency on 26 May 1997 to the three factories, requesting the unit be altered in compliance with regulatory standards (Trias Purwadi and Syam Dakrita 1999). Despite this high level administrative warning, the factories' waste management performance did not appear to improve. In June 1997 an inspection by a regional government official confirmed community reports of untreated liquid and solid waste being dumped into local irrigation channels, and the factories were subsequently ordered to discontinue the illegal dumping (Trias Purwadi and Syam Dakrita 1999). The continuing regulatory breaches finally prompted the regional government to take the more severe administrative sanction of rescinding the three industries' operating permits (*izin tempat usaha*); the industries, however, continued their operations regardless.[9] The pollution of the Banger River continued unabated, as confirmed in an analysis conducted in July 1998 by Gita Pertiwi, an environmental NGO, which concluded that the waste management unit required further improvement before discharged waste would comply with stipulated levels (Adi Nugroho 1998). A certain amount of liquid and solid waste was also being discharged from the factories without any processing.[10]

By late 1998 the Banger River was still polluted and its water remained unusable for domestic and agricultural purposes. The community's attempts to resolve the dispute through environmental advocacy and direct negotiation had failed. Furthermore, the administrative and criminal sanctions applied by regional and national government agencies had also failed to ensure ongoing compliance with environmental standards. Litigation thus presented itself as an avenue of last resort to the Dekoro community. To this end the villagers requested the Indonesian Foundation for Legal Service (Yayasan Pengabdian Hukum Indonesia, YAPHI), based in Solo and Kudus, in conjunction with several concerned local legal advocates, to represent the community in a claim for compensation and environmental restoration.[11] Legal representatives from YAPHI were keen to use the case as an opportunity to test the new provisions

8 Such an instrument is required by article 6(e), Decision of the Environment Minister No. 51/MENLH/10/1995.

9 The companies later argued that the permits could only be legally withdrawn by the Minister, who had granted them. See 'Penggugat yakin terjada pencemaran', *Suara Merdeka*, 30-6-1999.

10 Adi Nugroho 1998. The failure of the unit to function properly was attributed by some to a rise in the price of neutralising solution due to the monetary crisis and the consequent unwillingness of the three industries to actually use the unit: Ismar (Dekoro), interview, 5-3-2001.

11 The community had in fact previously engaged the Legal Aid Institute of Semarang (Lembaga Bantuan Hukum Semarang, LBHS), who had initiated the attempt at negotiation with the industries. However, the failure of this attempt and the lack of any other substantive progress prompted community representatives to seek assistance from alternative sources: Yusuf and Haryati (YAPHI), Solo, interview, 12-10-2000.

relating to environmental compensation in the recently enacted EMA 1997. On 16 November 1998, almost ten years after pollution of the Banger River commenced, 79 villagers from the Dekoro community provided their legal authority (*kuasa hukum*) to carry out the action on behalf of the community.

District court of Pekalongan case

During the court case the plaintiffs – the community of Dekoro – argued that since 1989, when the three factories commenced operations, untreated waste from the factories had been discharged into the Banger River. Although, under community pressure, the factories had installed a waste management unit in 1996, the unit did not function effectively and pollution had continued. As a result of the pollution, the Dekoro community claimed to have suffered a range of damages, including:[12]

- residents were no longer able to use river water for everyday needs, such as washing and cooking;
- death of livestock (chickens, ducks and goats) that had grazed near the river;
- death of fish in the Banger River and consequent loss of livelihood for local fishermen;
- skin disorders and health complaints experienced by residents due to contaminated water;
- failure of rice harvests in fields where river water had been used for irrigation;
- pollution of residents' wells to the point where well water could no longer be utilized for everyday consumption;
- fear and apprehension experienced by residents for years due to the ongoing hazard of pollution.

The plaintiffs argued that the action of the defendants in discharging polluting waste into the Banger River was contrary to a number of laws and regulations. Firstly, the defendants' actions had violated the residents' 'right to a good and healthy environment'; a right enshrined in the EMA No. 23 of 1997. Article 34 of that EMA further states that

> every action which infringes the law in the form of environmental pollution and/or damage which gives rise to adverse impacts on other people or the environment, obliges the party responsible for the business and/or activity to pay compensation and/or to carry out certain actions.

12 Banger River case: Indra Prasetya, PT Bintang Triputratex, PT Kesmatex, CV Ezri. District court of Pekalongan: No. 50/Pdt.G/1998.PN.Pkl. 1999:5; Adi Nugroho 1998.

Lawyers for the Dekoro community thus argued that the environmentally damaging actions of the three industries obliged them to pay compensation to victims of the pollution and to carry out environmental restoration. The right of the Dekoro community to compensation was also based on article 1365 of the Civil Code, which stipulates that where an action contrary to law (*perbuatan melawan hukum*) causes loss to another person, then the person responsible for that action is obliged to pay compensation to the person sustaining such loss. The discharge of polluting effluent by PT Kesamtex, PT Bintang Triputratez and CV Enzritek was furthermore said to contravene legal obligations and standards stipulated in Law No. 5/1984 concerning Industry, Government Regulation No. 20/1990 concerning 'Control of Water Pollution', Decision of the Minister of Population and Environment No. MNKLH/02/1991 concerning Stipulated Waste Standards, and the Decision of the Minister of Population and Environment No. 35/MNKLH/07/1991 regarding the Clean Rivers Program (Prokasih).

On the basis of these provisions, the plaintiffs claimed compensation for material and immaterial loss as a result of the pollution caused by the defendants' actions. Compensation claimed for material loss amounted to a total of Rp 1,322,303,500 in respect of failed crops, fishermen's loss of livelihood, death of livestock, and pollution of residents' well water. The plaintiffs also claimed compensation for immaterial loss, described as 'the feeling of fear and apprehension suffered by those living alongside the Banger River due to the danger caused by the pollution'. The sum claimed in respect of immaterial loss was Rp 1,500,000,000. On the basis of article 34 of the EMA 1997, the plaintiffs also requested the defendants be ordered to carry out environmental restoration by improving the waste management unit so as to ensure that discharged waste satisfied stipulated standards.

The plaintiffs' claim was supported by a range of testimonial and documentary evidence, including first hand witness testimony from nine local residents and one NGO worker. According to witnesses, the liquid waste discharged daily from the factories via open water channels was described as alternately brown, violet, black, yellow and red. Residents reported that the discharge was foul-smelling and would burn and blister the skin on contact. Accounts were also given of villagers' ducks, chickens and goats which had died when grazing near the Banger River. According to one account, a Dekoro resident suffered the loss of two hundred ducks in 1993 subsequent to their foraging on the banks of the river.[13] One hundred wells adjoining the river in Dekoro village were reported to have become 'black and smelly' and unusable follow-

[13] Banger River case: Indra Prasetya, PT Bintang Triputratex, PT Kesmatex, CV Ezri. District court of Pekalongan: No. 50/Pdt.G/1998.PN.Pkl. 1999:19.

ing the pollution; another witness reported the failure of rice harvests in some 43 hectares of village land. Prior to the river's contamination, local fisherman had been able to catch up to 10 kg of fish per day; subsequently (from 1988 onwards) no fish were to be found in the river.[14] To further support their case, lawyers for the plaintiffs also submitted records of the abovementioned decision of the Pekalongan district court, in which the defendants were held criminally liable for illegally discharging waste which polluted public water and the environment, contrary to article 12(2) of Regional Government Regulation No. 2 of 1993. As discussed above, the conviction was largely symbolic in nature, carrying a penalty of only Rp 45,000. Nonetheless, it was technically a criminal conviction and it was, in the words of a community representative, a 'weapon' of some significance during the course of the trial.[15] Lawyers for the Dekoro community also drew attention to administrative sanctions applied by the Regional Pekalongan Government to the defendant companies, due to the companies' failure to implement measures to control pollution measures. Initially the mayor of Pekalongan had made a written recommendation to the governor of Central Java that administrative action be taken against the defendant companies, due to their pollution of the Banger River. Subsequently the regional government of Pekalongan, through its mayor, had allegedly withdrawn the three factories' operating permits, although this was contested by the industries themselves.

Considerable evidence of a scientific nature was also presented in support of the Dekoro community's legal suit. Amongst these, laboratory tests conducted by Badan Penelitian dan Pengembangan Industri (BPPI, Industry Research and Development Institute) on 29 April 1998 demonstrated that liquid waste discharged from the factory subsequent to waste management processing still did not fulfil stipulated standards.[16] Earlier examinations conducted by the National Environmental Impact Agency had also concluded that waste discharged from the factories exceeded stipulated limits. Finally, the testimony of two expert witnesses further supported the plaintiffs' assertion that the waste discharged from the factory had caused pollution and environmental damage to the surrounding community.[17]

The three industries the subject of the claim raised a number of procedural and substantive defences in the case before the district court of Pekalongan. Firstly, the three industries argued that the plaintiffs possessed no legal

14 Ismar (Dekoro), interview, 5-3-2001.

15 Yusuf and Haryati (YAPHI), Solo, interview and mediation comments, 12-10-2000.

16 Banger River case: Indra Prasetya, PT Bintang Triputratex, PT Kesmatex, CV Ezri. District court of Pekalongan: No. 50/Pdt.G/1998.PN.Pkl. 1999:8.

17 The expert witnesses were Professor Ruchayat and Dr Norma Afiati.

interest connecting them with the Banger River and therefore had no legal 'standing' to bring the case in question. Given the principles enunciated in the EMA 1997 and the acceptance of environmental standing in the PT IIU case (1989), this was a defence that was unlikely to succeed. In an even more tenuous defence, from the perspective of environmental law at least, the co-defendants claimed that their waste management consultant, PT Sarana Tirta Kutolestari, was legally responsible for management of industry's waste and thus liable for any resulting damage. It was this company, in the defendants' opinion, together with the Environmental Impact Agency – as supervisor of waste management – that should have been made the subject of this claim.

On a substantive level, the defendant industries further argued that even if pollution had occurred it should not give rise to any claim, as the Banger River was not legally categorized as a source of agricultural or drinking water. It was therefore, at least in the industries' eyes, legitimate for it to be utilized as a means for disposal of industrial waste. In any case, argued the lawyer for the defendants, waste discharged from the three factories was processed via a waste management unit, operational since 1996 with a monthly operating cost between Rp 25-60 million. Contrary to the plaintiffs' assertion otherwise, the waste management unit did function effectively and its effluent was examined on a monthly basis. Tests carried out by the Institute for Industrial Research and Development on 7 December 1998 demonstrated that effluent from the factory fulfilled regulatory standards.[18] Whilst other factories along the Banger River dispose of untreated waste directly into the river, waste from the three defendant factories was processed prior to disposal. It was thus a central tenet of the defence that other factories disposing of waste into the Banger River should also have rightly been made a subject of the claim in question.

Interestingly, the defendants pointed to a lack of administrative sanction as evidence contradicting the plaintiffs' claims. If the defendant factories had in fact contravened the legal standards relating to effluent, then their permit for disposal of liquid waste would have been revoked in accordance with article 33 of Government Regulation No. 20 of 1990, whereas this had not occurred. The defendants denied the plaintiffs' allegation that their operating permits had been withdrawn by the regional government of Pekalongan, arguing that the permits could only be legally revoked by the Minister who had originally granted them.[19]

18 Banger River case: Indra Prasetya, PT Bintang Triputratex, PT Kesmatex, CV Ezri. District court of Pekalongan: No. 50/Pdt.G/1998.PN.Pkl. 1999:16.

19 According to evidence produced by the plaintiff it seems the case that the Pekalongan Regional Government did at least attempt to revoke the industries' operating permit. The defendants' position was based on their argument that only the Minister, who had issued the permits, could revoke them. In any case the administrative action in question seems to have had no impact

Court hearings

The hearing of the Banger River case at the Pekalongan district court was attended by a large number of residents of Dekoro village bearing banners demanding a fair trial. The ensuing session was reported in a local newspaper as 'coloured by the protests of the residents' lawyers and numerous visitors who nearly destroyed a dividing wall in the session hall'.[20] Considerable anger was triggered by the apparent intimidation of a witness by the sitting judge, and contained only by the appeals for calm by the residents' lawyers and representatives.[21] Subsequent sittings of the district court were equally well attended by residents of the Dekoro community, prompting the Head Justice to complain: 'if there is a demonstration at each sitting, the sitting cannot go smoothly. For the sake of a smooth hearing, the case should be entrusted to the legal representatives'.[22] Despite the Chief Justice's protestations, no attempt was made to restrict access to the sittings and the Dekoro community showed no decline in interest in the matter before the court. In the words of one community member: 'We are allowed to watch the hearing, because it's open for the public. And as this case involves a lot of people, what's wrong if a lot of people attend?'[23] The disorder experienced in the first hearing was repeated in a subsequent session, when around two hundred visitors 'pounded their chairs in disappointment' when the decision of the court was postponed to a subsequent date. After the group was pacified by community and NGO representatives, the presiding judge conceded that he would 'in principle [...] defend the people's interests'.[24]

The visible and vocal presence of the Dekoro community during court hearings was notable. Legal representatives for the community considered this a key influence on the judges in both the district and high court hearings.[25] The pressure on the presiding judges to return a 'fair' verdict was tangible and made explicit at several points during the trial when community members threatened to destroy a partition and throw objects into the courtroom.[26] Legal representatives for the community realized that behaviour of

on the operations of the three industries which continued regardless as discussed above. This issue was specifically discussed in the decision of the high court – see later in this chapter.

20 'Sidang pencemaran Kali Banger: Pengacara dan pengunjung protes pada majelis', *Suara Merdeka*, 7-4-1999.

21 'Soal Kali Banger, warga datangi polres', *Suara Merdeka*, 20-4-1999.

22 'Ketua majelis merasa tenganggu demo', *Suara Merdeka*, 1999.

23 'Ketua majelis merasa tenganggu demo', *Suara Merdeka*, 1999.

24 'Pengunjung sidang gebrak kursi', *Suara Merdeka*, 29-6-1999.

25 Bambang, Lala and Yusuf, interviews at YAPHI, Kudus, 3-11-2000 and 4-11-2000.

26 'Sidang pencemaran Kali Banger; Pengacara dan pengunjung protes pada majelis', *Suara Merdeka*, 7-4-1999.

this nature was unacceptable in a court setting and were successful in pacifying the community members present, enabling the trial to proceed.

Decision of Pekalongan district court

The decision of the district court of Pekalongan in this case stands out from most previous judicial decisions in environmental cases in that the court appeared to be relatively well informed about environmental legal principles, rights and responsibilities. The judges first recognized that the dispute before them was of an environmental nature and that according to the EMA 1997 each person 'has a responsibility to protect environmental sustainability [and] to participate in efforts toward that end'.[27] The efforts of the Dekoro community in contacting government agencies and finally in bringing a legal suit for compensation and environmental restoration clearly fell within this category. As individuals within a living environment, the court recognized that the plaintiffs 'held an interest in their environment's preservation'.[28] The panel of three judges thus rejected the defendants' argument that the plaintiffs held no standing in the matter. The dispute before them was 'connected with the environment, and so must be differentiated from interests connected only with civil law'. The judges also rejected the defendants' procedural exception that its third party waste management contractor, PT Sarana Tirta Kutolestari, bore the legal responsibility for the pollution. According to the court, 'legal responsibility for waste pollution is held fully by the owner of the industry that produces the waste'.[29]

On the substantive issues before it the court concluded that the three defendant industries 'had disposed of liquid waste into the Banger River [...] causing pollution to the environment and damage to the defendants [by] polluting sources of water used by humans, animals and plants'.[30] The affirmative decision of the court in this respect caused great elation among the members of the Dekoro community observing the trial, a number of whom exclaimed: 'These are what you call reformist judges!'[31] The fact that the Banger River was not legally categorized as a source of drinking water did not, in the court's opinion, justify or excuse the pollution carried out by the

27 Banger River case: Indra Prasetya, PT Bintang Triputratex, PT Kesmatex, CV Ezri. District court of Pekalongan: No. 50/Pdt.G/1998.PN.Pkl. 1999:36-40.

28 Banger River case: Indra Prasetya, PT Bintang Triputratex, PT Kesmatex, CV Ezri. District court of Pekalongan: No. 50/Pdt.G/1998.PN.Pkl. 1999:36-40.

29 Banger River case: Indra Prasetya, PT Bintang Triputratex, PT Kesmatex, CV Ezri. District court of Pekalongan: No. 50/Pdt.G/1998.PN.Pkl. 1999:36-40.

30 Banger River case: Indra Prasetya, PT Bintang Triputratex, PT Kesmatex, CV Ezri. District court of Pekalongan: No. 50/Pdt.G/1998.PN.Pkl. 1999:36-40.

31 'Tiga pencemar Kali Banger dihukum Rp 48.69 juta', *Suara Merdeka*, 20-7-1999.

defendants. On the contrary, the three justices emphasized that

> industrial development must be sustainable (*berwawasan lingkungan*), for the safety of humankind. Thus, regardless of whether the Banger River was stipulated as a source of drinking water or not, environmental preservation must still be observed.[32]

On the evidence before it the court concluded that pollution had at least occurred between 1992 and 1996, as it was only at that point that the waste management unit became operational.[33] Evidence of tests carried out by BPPI, presented by the defendants, only demonstrated that the factories' effluent satisfied regulatory standards from December 1998 onwards. The court thus determined that pollution had occurred between 1992 and 1997. For this period it was thus 'proven that the defendants had contravened article 34 of the EMA 1997 and committed an action contrary to law as per article 1365 of the Civil Code'.[34] The defendants were consequently legally obliged to pay compensation to the victims of the pollution, in this case certain members of the Dekoro community.

Whilst upholding the plaintiffs' claim for compensation based on article 34 EMA 1997 and article 1365 Civil Code, the court chose to make its own assessment of the level of damages to be awarded and did not award immaterial damages. The total amount of damages awarded was Rp 49,184,000 calculated by reference to the loss each particular claimant had suffered. Furthermore, the order requested by the plaintiffs that the defendants improve their waste management unit to an adequate level was declined by the court. In the court's opinion, the unit was already functioning at an adequate level, and further restoration was not needed. In arriving at this conclusion the justices noted the expenditures made on the unit by the three industries, some Rp 2.5 billion for installation and between Rp 25-60 million for monthly operating costs. The court considered the amount of money spent monthly by the defendants to date on the waste management unit and also the fact that tests had been taken on 7 December 1998 which demonstrated that the waste output satisfied stipulated levels of pollutants.[35] Accordingly, the court concluded that it was not necessary to make any further orders in this respect.

32 Banger River case: Indra Prasetya, PT Bintang Triputratex, PT Kesmatex, CV Ezri. District court of Pekalongan: No. 50/Pdt.G/1998.PN.Pkl. 1999:36-40.

33 This was a conservative estimate as most witnesses for the plaintiffs referred to pollution dating from around 1988 when the factories commenced operations.

34 Banger River case: Indra Prasetya, PT Bintang Triputratex, PT Kesmatex, CV Ezri. District court of Pekalongan: No. 50/Pdt.G/1998.PN.Pkl. 1999:42.

35 Banger River case: Indra Prasetya, PT Bintang Triputratex, PT Kesmatex, CV Ezri. District court of Pekalongan: No. 50/Pdt.G/1998.PN.Pkl. 1999:16.

Appeal and decision high court of Central Java

On 2 August 1999, the legal representative of the Dekoro community lodged an appeal against the decision of the district court of Pekalongan. Whilst the decision was a victory for the community, there was nonetheless disappointment at the level of compensation awarded, which was considerably less than the community had claimed.[36] A spokesman for the Dekoro community stated at the time

> The appeal was made because the decision of the district court absolutely failed to satisfy the claims of the community concerning compensation for pollution from factory waste. The compensation awarded was only Rp 49 million whereas we asked for Rp 2,82 billion.[37]

The legal representative for the community also strongly criticized the failure of the court to adequately address the issue of environmental restoration, emphasising that the Dekoro community were not only concerned with matters of material compensation.[38]

The appeal was subsequently adjudicated by the high court of Semarang which, in a decision dated 8 December 1999, reaffirmed the decision of the district court and the grounds upon which it had been made. In particular, the high court emphasized that several letters of administrative sanction sent by the regional government to the defendant industries provided sufficient evidence that the industries had in fact polluted. The letters in question, dated 15 October 1997, related to the withdrawal of the operating permit (*izin tempat usaha*) of the three industries due to their failure to implement pollution control measure. The high court's decision in this case illustrates the common tendency of Indonesian courts to elevate evidence of prior administrative sanction above other evidence that may also present, including eyewitness testimony, expert evidence, and laboratory research. From an evidential perspective this is questionable, as prior administrative sanction, or the lack of it, can only really provide secondary evidence of actual pollution or environmental damage, when compared to 'first-hand' evidence such as witness testimony or laboratory tests. In this case, however, the high court considered that the letters of administrative sanction issued by the regional government to the companies established 'that the defendants committed actions contrary

36 As discussed above, the court awarded Rp 49,184,000 whereas the Dekoro community had claimed compensation of Rp 1,322,303,500 for material damage and Rp 1,500,000,000 for immaterial damage, a total of almost Rp 3 billion – approximately 60 times the amount actually awarded by the court.

37 'Korban Kali Banger naik banding ke PTi', *Suara Merdeka*, 9-10-1999.

38 'Tiga pencemar Kali Banger dihukum Rp 48.69 Juta', *Suara Merdeka*, 20-7-1999.

to law'. It is unfortunate that the high court chose to base its decision solely upon the prior administrative sanction by the regional government, without reference to the range of other evidence presented in the case.

The court went on to reassess the amount of compensation awarded on an individual basis, arriving at a total amount of Rp 165,523,000 an amount which accounted for perished livestock, failed rice harvests, the costs of cleaning polluted wells and the loss of fishermen's livelihood. However, the three judges in this case felt that the amount so calculated could not accurately reflect the full extent of the damage suffered by the plaintiff community, as the loss in question was not just a loss of property, but a loss of capital. When this loss of capital was considered over a period of seven years – from 1992 to 1999[39] – the three justices considered it appropriate to treble the calculated amount of compensation to arrive at a rounded figure of Rp 500,000,000 a more than ten-fold increase on the sum awarded by the district court. In addition, the high court acknowledged that the pollution caused by PT Kesamtex, PT Bintang Triputratez and CV Enzritek had resulted in pain and suffering experienced by the local community over a period of seven years. Accordingly, the plaintiffs, as a part of the community whose environment had suffered pollution, were legally entitled to receive compensation for the immaterial damage suffered by them. The court thus awarded an amount of Rp 250 million to account for this damage, bringing the total compensation amount to Rp 750 million.

The high court finally addressed the issue of environmental restoration, which had been raised in the plaintiffs' claim, emphasising that payment of compensation did not alleviate the defendant industries from preventing further environmental damage. The defendant industries were thus obliged to ensure the optimal operation of their waste management unit to prevent any further environmental pollution and ensure compliance with regulatory standards. For each day the three industries failed to do this, they would be liable to pay an additional fine of Rp 50,000.

Appeal to Supreme Court

The Banger River case has yet to be finally resolved as an appeal, lodged by both parties, is currently pending to the Supreme Court of Indonesia. From the Dekoro community's perspective, the decision of the high court came much closer to satisfying their claim than the previous decision of the district court. Indeed, it is surprising, given the scarcity of successful

39 The appellate court did not seem to adopt the view of the district court that the pollution only continued until the end of 1997, but it did not expressly address this matter.

claims for environmental compensation or restoration in Indonesia, that the plaintiffs chose to lodge a further appeal to the Supreme Court. The decision of the high court, in significantly increasing the award of compensation for environmental damage, seems unlikely to be endorsed by the Supreme Court, which in the past has been noted for its political conservatism and deference to executive will.[40] A further appeal will also result in more delays in an already lengthy dispute resolution process dating back twelve years. Nonetheless, not all members of the community representative group, KKLB, were satisfied with the decision of the high court. In a vote subsequent to the high court's decision, 75% chose to lodge a further appeal to the Supreme Court.[41] Representatives of the Dekoro community felt the decision, whilst it did require optimalization of the waste management unit, did not adequately address the issue of environmental restoration. The community had hoped, for instance, that measures such as dredging toxic solid waste from the river would be implemented to ensure proper restoration of the environment to its original condition.[42] In the plaintiffs' view, it would have been appropriate therefore if the defendants had been obliged to pay compensation toward such restoration.[43]

As in the previous hearings in the district and high courts, the Dekoro community has attempted to pursue a strategy of political advocacy alongside the ongoing legal proceedings. Representatives of the community have made several trips to Jakarta and attempted to meet with the judges adjudicating the case as well as senior political figures from the Environmental Impact Agency and the Ministry of the Environment. Whilst the representatives were successful in communicating their views to officials at the latter two government agencies, they were unable to communicate with the judges presiding over the case and were advised that resolution of the case was in process.[44]

Conclusion

The Dekoro community's struggle for environmental justice has been a prolonged one, and still, at the time of writing, had not been resolved.[45] The community first felt the effects of pollution around 1990, shortly after the

40 See, for instance, the discussion of Supreme Court decision making in Pompe 1996.
41 Ismar, interview, 5-3-2001.
42 Ismar (Dekoro), interview, 5-3-2001.
43 '3 Pabrik harus bayar ganti rugi Rp 750 juta', *Suara Merdeka*, 31-3-2000.
44 Ismar, interview, 5-3-2001.
45 At the time of writing, November 2003, the appeal was still pending to the Supreme Court: Lusila Anjela Bodroani, interview, 18-11-2003.

three factories commenced operations. In the ensuing eight years, a process of advocacy and lobbying was undertaken by representatives of the community, assisted by NGOs based in Pekalongan and the nearby regional capital, Semarang. The community's claims were taken to administrative agencies and parliaments at the district, provincial and national levels. Partly because of this sustained and often publicized campaign, and partly because of regional government pressure, the three factories agreed to install waste management units in 1996. Yet this did not end the pollution. The intransigence of the industries involved in this case undermined subsequent attempts that were made to resolve the dispute through mediation. The Dekoro community chose to pursue litigation as an option of last resort. In this case, access to the courts was not an obstacle, given the willingness of a non-government legal aid agency (YAPHI) to act as representatives for the community. The willingness of the legal agency to bring the case was bolstered by the new EMA 1997, which stipulated a clear right to compensation for environmental damage that was not dependent upon prior investigation by a government team or the promulgation of implementing regulations, as had been the case with the EMA 1982.

The decisions of the Pekalongan district court and the high court of Central Java in the Banger River case provide some evidence of an increasing familiarity with environmental legal principles amongst Indonesian judges. The decisions also demonstrate a hitherto rare willingness to award significant amounts of compensation for environmental damage against industry defendants on the basis of such legal principles. In line with a number of decisions since the PT IIU case, the district court in this case had no hesitation in discounting the defendants' contention that the Dekoro community lacked a legal connection with the Banger River, emphasising instead the broad right and interest of the community to participate in environmental preservation. The court was also clear in its emphasis of the non-delegable responsibility of the industries to ensure proper waste management, rejecting their attempt to shift liability onto a third party contractor. Moreover, in marked contrast to the more formalistic approach of Indonesian courts in earlier cases, the court based its decision upon the broad concept of sustainable development as enshrined in the Environmental Management Act.[46]

Yet probably the most notable feature of the Banger River case, beyond the courts' comparatively adept discussion of environmental legal principles, is the outcome at both district and high court level. Whilst several past environmental cases have obtained only procedural concessions, the plain-

46 Banger River case: Indra Prasetya, PT Bintang Triputratex, PT Kesmatex, CV Ezri. district court of Pekalongan: No. 50/Pdt.G/1998.PN.Pkl. 1999:36-40.

tiffs' victory in this case has been more than procedural, extending to the substantive remedies of compensation and, to a lesser extent, environmental restoration. As the discussion in the previous chapter demonstrates, this is, in the context of Indonesian environmental litigation, a rarity. In particular, the Banger River case is an exception to the pattern found in a number of other cases, where the plaintiffs win at the district court level only to lose later on appeal at the high court level.[47] The high court decision in this case was also conspicuous in its award of compensation fifteen times higher than that awarded by the district court. Moreover, the high court issued orders to optimise the companies' waste management unit, whereas the district court before it had not done so.

Several factors may be identified as contributing directly to the legal outcome in this dispute. The pollution of the Banger River was severe and renowned in the area in which it occurred. Furthermore, the allegations of the plaintiffs were supported not only by local knowledge but also by research from several government agencies. The fact that the industries in question did not even possess a waste management unit before 1996 made it extremely difficult for the pollution, at least during the period prior to this, to be discounted. The allegations of pollution were also supported by expert witnesses, whose testimony proved influential during the case.[48] The plaintiffs' case was thus bolstered by strong evidence from a number of sources.

Further weight was added to the claims of the plaintiffs by the previous criminal conviction and administrative sanction that had been applied by the government. In the words of the legal counsel for the plaintiffs

> In this case it was clear the companies had polluted. The administrative sanctions and the criminal conviction were evidence of this. Although the criminal conviction was a minor one, with a fine of just Rp 45,000, it was still a conviction. So we were able to use this as a weapon.[49]

Whilst the administrative and criminal sanctions that were applied to the three industries were not given particular emphasis in the district court decision, the high court made a point of doing so, stating: 'the withdrawal of the operating permits due to the Industries' failure to implement measures to control waste pollution in the Banger River [...] proves that the defendants committed an action contrary to law which damaged the plaintiffs'. As discussed above, the logic employed by the high court in this instance appears questionable. The fact that the regional government chose to withdraw operating permits on certain grounds does not establish that the factual and

47 This for instance happened in the Babon River case discussed in detail below.
48 Isna Hertati, WALHI, interview, 4-1-2001.
49 Bambang, Lala and Yusuf, interviews at YAPHI, Kudus, 3-11-2000 and 4-11-2000.

legal elements of an action contrary to (environmental) law have been made out. This latter determination is one for the court to make, rather than a government agency. In any case, the court's statement serves as an indication of the weight given in this case to the previous administrative and criminal sanctions applied by the government. Prior executive and criminal sanction of the polluting companies in this case seemed to strongly influence the court in deciding upon compensation and restoration for environmental damage.

Another notable feature of the Banger River case was the strong and sustained community pressure both before and during the litigation process. The vocal presence maintained by the Dekoro community during the court hearings expressed a strong public sentiment to the presiding judges. Several of the lawyers who had represented the community considered this a likely influence on the eventual decision of the courts.[50] The influence of community pressure in this case may certainly have been amplified by the political circumstances of that particular time. The Pekalongan district court hearing and the high court of Central Java hearing were held in a period of economic and political turmoil following the fall of President Suharto's New Order government. The transition to the post-Suharto era was accompanied by massive student demonstrations and waves of urban rioting in several cities in Java. Neither the military nor police were able to contain the explosion of civil discontent which acted as a catalyst for the eventual resignation of Suharto as president. In the ensuing era of *reformasi*, the continuing dissolution of the rigid political and military control that had characterized the New Order created new opportunities for the expression of civil and political discontent, yet also brought a lingering fear of social anarchy. Security could no longer be guaranteed, and government decision makers, such as judges, were seemingly in a much more vulnerable position than had been the case previously. In the more politically open and vulnerable environment of post-Suharto Indonesia, it may be the case that the community presence and pressure maintained during the court hearings had an increased influence on the Pekalongan district court and the high court of Central Java. This is less likely to be an influence on appeal to the Supreme Court, however, given the reduced proximity and accessibility of the Supreme Court to the community.

50 Yusuf and Haryati (YAPHI), Solo, interview (Babon and Banger River cases) and mediation comments, 12-10-2000.

Babon River case, 1998

History of the dispute

The Babon River is located on the outskirts of the sprawling city of Semarang, capital of Central Java.[51] Like the Banger River, the Babon River provides a source of water for the everyday needs of residents in its vicinity, including in this case the villagers of Sriwulan and Bedono, numbering some four thousand people. Traditionally the river's waters have been used for cooking, washing, livestock and irrigation. In particular, the villagers of Sriwulan and Bedono are renowned as traditional fishpond farmers, practicing a small-scale method of prawn farming whereby prawns (and small fish) are flushed into the ponds with the rising tide and then trapped and raised within the ponds. The villagers' ponds are located near the mouth of the Babon River and rely on the tidal flow of water from the river and ocean (YAPHI 1998).

Like many rivers in Java, the Babon River has also been utilized by a diverse collection of industries for production needs and the disposal of waste effluent in more recent years. The dispute in question involved six industries operating adjacent to the river, all but one of which are still in operation today. The six industries were PT Condro Purnomo Cipto (leather processing), PT Puspita Abadi (leather processing), PT Rodeo (clothing manufacture), PT Bintang Buana (leather processing), CV Sumber Baru (paper), and Puskud Mina Buana (cold storage). Before 1995, none of the industries had installed or operated a waste management unit. Waste effluent had as a result been disposed, untreated, into the Babon River. Unsurprisingly, the impact of this waste was soon felt by the nearby villagers of Sriwulan and Bedono. Beginning in September 1994, the prawn harvest of the fishpond farmers of Sriwulan and Bedono failed for a period of four months. This was at a time when the pollution levels in the Babon River had reached a peak. Whilst the level of pollution decreased after January 1995, the prawn catch of the farmers remained significantly diminished, forcing many prawn farmers to seek employment as factory workers (Gita Pertiwi 2000b:1).

Initially, prawn farmers in Bedono and Sriwulan did not suspect that industrial effluent had caused the sudden death of their prawns and fish. Their suspicions were raised, however, by newspaper reports of unusually high pollution levels in the Babon River and the subsequent inclusion of the Babon River in the Clean Rivers Program.[52] While the Babon River was

[51] Decision No.42/Pdt.G/1998/PN.Smg. The river is actually in the western part of Demak Regency 18 km from the city of Demak, and bordering on Semarang municipality.

[52] Program Kali Bersih, an environmental law enforcement initiative spearheaded by the

located some 4-5 km from the prawn and fishponds, its waters nonetheless routinely entered the ponds via the river's mouth, when the ponds were opened to the rising tide in order to trap prawns and fish. In the period of September-December 1994, when the most severe losses of prawns and fish occurred, the water entering the ponds was noticeably discoloured, similar to the waters of the heavily polluted Babon River.

On 21 December 1994, community representatives took their complaints to the regional legislative assembly of Demak regency. A member of the assembly then requested that the environmental administrative section head (*kabag lingkungan hidup*), investigate the claims (Gita Pertiwi 2000b:2). Research into the pollution claims was subsequently carried out by a Jepara-based institute, Balai Budidaya Air Payau Jepara, which confirmed not only that the deaths of the farmers' prawn stock were due to pollution, but also that the water of the Babon River contained hazardous waste (*bahan beracun dan berbahaya*) (Muhaimin 1998:35). At the suggestion of Demak officials, community representatives then conveyed their complaints to the legislative assembly of Semarang in February 1995, where they were referred on to the legislative assembly at the provincial level (in this case Central Java) as this particular dispute fell into two administrative districts.[53] Ultimately, a more substantive hearing did eventuate through the Commission C of the Central Java legislature in February 1995, involving legislative members, community, industry representatives and officials from the Environmental Impact Agency of Semarang (Gita Pertiwi 2000b:1). Initially, industry representatives denied responsibility for the farmers' loss, and officials from the provincial Department of Fisheries attributed the prawns' deaths to illness. Yet when community representatives presented the research confirming pollution in a follow-up meeting three days later, industry representatives finally conceded that their operations had polluted the Babon River. At this meeting, the community also presented its claim for compensation for the environmental damage, although exact amounts at that point had not been determined. A legislative member suggested that a goodwill payment (*uang tali asih*) be made by the industries to the two villages. Community representatives initially opposed this suggestion as the payment would be unilateral in nature and would not address the ongoing problem of water quality. Subsequent to the hearing however, community members were pressured by the village heads (*lurah*) and the local government council (*muspika*) to accept the payment of Rp 15 million, which eventually was made (in June 1995) and utilized for local

National Environmental Agency designed to improve industrial waste management and water quality of rivers in Java.

53 The villages were located in Demak, whilst the factories were in Semarang municipality some seven kilometres from the city of Semarang.

road works and the payment of local government taxes (Gita Pertiwi 2000b; YAPHI 1998).

In 1995, there was a gradual lessening of pollution after the six industries were targeted in the Clean Rivers Program (Muhaimin 1998:39). Pursuant to the program, the industries were required to install a waste management unit and have waste effluent tested every three months. Yet, despite some improvements in environmental management and the goodwill payment by industries in June 1995, the fishpond farmers of Bedono and Sriwulan villages did not consider the dispute to be at an end. Pollution from the Babon River, whilst lessened, nonetheless continued to reduce the farmers' yields from the fishponds, which never returned to the levels enjoyed pre-September 1994. Tests conducted in March 1997 by NGO Gita Pertiwi and the Technical Institute of Environmental Health in Yogyakarta, confirmed that the Babon River continued to be polluted above regulatory standards by industrial effluent.[54] Furthermore, the personal loss of the farmers due to the pollution had not been compensated, despite the goodwill payments made to the villages as a whole. The farmers resolved to pursue their claim for compensation, and in 1997 a group of some three hundred farmers approached the Legal Aid Institute of Semarang providing legal authority to pursue a claim on their behalf. However, after little progress on the claim was made, the group of farmers withdrew their legal authority. Subsequently, in 1998, a smaller group of nine farmers who were not included in the original group approached the Kudus-based Indonesian Foundation for Legal Service (YAPHI) and instructed them to bring a legal suit on their behalf.[55] Initially, legal representatives considered a large 'class action' suit representing all three hundred farmers. This idea was ultimately judged premature, due to the lack of regulations governing class actions in environmental law and the considerable resources required to manage such a case. Instead the nine farmers, in conjunction with their legal representatives, decided to bring a 'test case' in which they alone would sue the polluting industries for compensation and environmental restoration. In the event this initial suit succeeded, a larger representative or class action suit would be brought at a later date.[56]

District court of Semarang case; Claim and defence

In the case subsequently filed at the district court of Semarang, the plaintiffs – the nine prawn farmers from Sriwulan village – claimed compensation for environmental damage caused by the defendants' illegal disposal of waste into

54 Balai Teknik Kesehatan Lingkungan 1997.
55 Bambang, Lala and Yusuf, interviews at YAPHI, Kudus, 3-11-2000 and 4-11-2000.
56 Bambang, Lala and Yusuf, interviews at YAPHI, Kudus, 3-11-2000 and 4-11-2000.

the Babon River. The farmers' claim was directed against the six industries PT Condro Purnomo Cipto, PT Puspita Abadi, PT Rodeo, PT Bintang Buana, CV Sumber Baru and Puskud Mina Buana. In addition, the mayor of Semarang was initially named as a co-defendant due to the alleged failure of that office to properly supervise and monitor the operation of the industries in question.[57] Subsequently, however, the mayor's office was omitted as a co-defendant by the plaintiffs in exchange for an undertaking that evidence of pollution held by it would be made available during the course of the trial.[58]

The damage suffered by the farmers included the failure of their prawn/fish harvest from September until December 1994. In the 39 months after this, the farmers claimed to have experienced a reduction in their fish/prawn catch to 70% of previous levels. The total loss of income suffered by the farmers for these two periods was calculated to be Rp 51,645,000. As in the Banger River case, the farmers' claim was based upon both article 1365 of the Civil Code and articles 34(1) and 35(1) of the Environmental Management Act of 1997. As discussed above, article 34(1) obliges a business which 'infringes the law in the form of environmental pollution and/or damage which gives rise to adverse impacts on other people or the environment [...] to pay compensation and/or to carry out certain actions'. Article 35(1), concerning strict liability, was also pleaded by the plaintiffs as a basis for the claim (Muhaimin 1998:14). That provision stipulates strict liability for resulting losses on any business 'which gives rise to a large impact on the environment, which uses hazardous and toxic materials, and/or produces hazardous and toxic waste'. Whilst the provision was named as a basis for the claim, the plaintiffs' case lacked more specific argument supporting the application of the strict liability provision.

A range of documentary and oral evidence was produced by the plaintiffs in support of their claim, including government correspondence which stipulated the six defendant industries as priority targets of the government's Clean Rivers Program. Yet despite the industries' participation in the program, described as 'pioneering' by the industries themselves, pollution had apparently continued. A newspaper report dated 13 April 1998, also tendered as evidence, reported the Semarang government's statement that pollution in the Babon River continued two years after the commencement of the Clean Rivers Program (Muhaimin 1998:33). Earlier waste analysis results from 1994, carried out by the Environmental Impact Agency of Semarang, moreover indicated

57 The Semarang district government had carried out a 'Clean Rivers Program' (Prokasih) and even named the 6 defendant industries as priority targets within this program. However, according to the plaintiffs, this attempt to monitor the industries' operations had failed as the pollution of the Babon River had continued regardless. See Muhaimin 1998:6.

58 The evidence in question was data collected by the regional Environmental Impact Agency in Semarang: Bambang, Lala and Yusuf, interviews at YAPHI, Kudus, 3-11-2000 and 4-11-2000.

that effluent from the six factories had greatly exceeded stipulated levels. Further test results from the Technical Institute for Environmental Health (Balai Tehnik Kesehatan Lingkungan) dated 22 April 1997 provided additional evidence of effluent levels in excess of stipulated government standards.[59]

According to several fishpond farmers called as witnesses during the course of the trial, all of their prawn-catch perished during the months of September-December 1994. Whereas the farmers typically received between Rp 5000-30,000 per day from 1 ha of ponds, during this four month period no marketable catch was made. From January 1995 onwards the situation improved, but the level and quality of the farmers' catch never returned to normal (Muhaimin 1998:6). Testimony from the Head of the Semarang Environmental Impact Agency, also called as a witness, confirmed 'the waters of the Babon River were polluted and had polluted the farmers' fishponds'. The environmental official nonetheless emphasized the regional government's efforts to monitor and control the pollution via the Clean Rivers Program (Muhaimin 1998:38). According to this official, whilst pollution levels were very high in 1995, by 1995/1996 the majority of the industries had brought their waste within stipulated limits, contrary to some of the other evidence presented by the plaintiffs.[60]

Whilst several of the defendants lodged separate defences, in general the procedural and substantive arguments presented by the respective defendant industries were similar in nature (Muhaimin 1998:15). An initial procedural objection made to the plaintiffs' application was that the claims of the plaintiffs should have been advanced individually, rather than as a common claim. The industries also argued that there was no legal interest connecting them and that as a result they could not be held collectively liable for the damage suffered by the plaintiffs. Moreover, the defendant industries contended that other industries located on the Babon River, of which a number purportedly operated without waste management units, should also have been included in the plaintiffs' claim. In the defendants' opinion, evidence that the waters of the Babon River were polluted did not necessarily prove that the six industries that were the subject of this claim were responsible. In any case, it was submitted, the industries had fulfilled the requirements of the Clean Rivers Program since 1995, including three-monthly testing of waste effluent with satisfactory results.[61]

59 Balai Teknik Kesehatan Lingkungan 1997.

60 This statement was, however, contrary to the test results from Balai Teknik Kesehatan Lingkungan and the statement of the regional government as reported in the *Suara Merdeka* article on 13-4-1998.

61 As discussed above, evidence presented by the plaintiff contradicted this claim.

The industries also challenged the factual basis of the farmers' claim, emphasising the distance of 6 km between the Babon River and the ponds of the plaintiffs. Furthermore, no tributaries of the river flowed adjacent to nor fed into the ponds. Given that the Babon flowed straight to the sea it was unlikely, in the defendants' opinion, that the waters of the Babon could have polluted the farmers' ponds. This seeming incongruity had, however, been addressed in evidence presented by the farmers themselves. The waters of the Babon were channelled by a natural sand embankment adjoining the mouth of the river in the easterly direction of the fishponds, and then directed into small intake rivulets which fed into the farmers' ponds (Muhaimin 1998:35).

Finally, the defendants drew the court's attention to the fact that the farmers operating the fishponds in Bedono and Sriwulan did not have the necessary permits to do so. The fishpond operations were thus technically illegal and, as a result, should not be afforded the protection of the law. In what then appeared to be an attempted deterrent to further claims of this nature, all the industries counter-sued the farmers for damage to their credibility and reputation. The second defendant claimed one billion rupiah in damages on this basis, whilst the third through sixth defendants demanded a public apology and retraction of the pollution claims.[62] Evidence presented by the defendants included a number of tests results from the Semarang Environmental Impact Agency and the Institute for Industrial Research and Development (Muhaimin 1998:41). The tests, most of which were carried out in late 1996 and 1997, showed effluent levels mostly within government stipulated standards. The six companies also presented evidence of the good-will payment made to the villages of Sriwulan and Bedono in September 1995.

Several witnesses were also called by the defendants, the first of which was a technical environmental consultant responsible for the installation and upkeep of waste management units for several of the defendant industries. According to this witness, following the installation and improvement of the waste management units, effluent from these industries – PT Puspita Abadi, PT Bintang Buana, PT Condro Purnomo Cipto, CV Sumber Baru and Puskud Mina Buana) – was below stipulated standards. Another waste management consultant for PT Rodeo attested that waste discharged from the factory satisfied government standards, whilst acknowledging that renovation of the waste management unit was undertaken in 1995 as it was unable to process the necessary volume of liquid waste. Interestingly, one fishpond farmer from the village of Bedono was also called as a witness by the defendant industries. This farmer, whose ponds were located one kilometre from the plaintiffs ponds, claimed that whilst his prawn catch varied, he had never found dead prawns as reported by the other farmers (Muhaimin 1998:53).

62 The first defendant in this case, PT Condro Purnomo Cipto, did not file a defence.

Evidence heard in the course of the trial was not limited to that presented by the parties themselves. The court also chose to call four witnesses to elucidate certain issues between the parties (Muhaimin 1998:53). One such issue was the payment made in September 1995 by the industries to the communities of Bedono and Sriwulan, which was addressed in the testimony of two witnesses called by the court. The matter of the payment was of some contention as the defendants argued it was specifically directed to the farmers (as compensation), whilst the plaintiffs maintained the payment did not constitute compensation and was a unilateral payment applied to road improvement for the general welfare of the two villages. The first witness called by the court was the Village Head (*kepala desa*) of Bedono who verified that the farmers in that village had received a payment of Rp 10,000,000.[63] The witness did not know for certain whether the payment had been directed to all fishpond farmers or only those affected by pollution. Following a village meeting, it had been agreed that the money would be used to pay taxes of all villagers and to fund road improvement (Muhaimin 1998:53-4). A second witness, who had previously represented the farmers in their petition to the provincial legislature, stated that the money was paid on behalf of farmers whose fishponds had been polluted, yet was used to pay the taxes of all villagers and fund road improvement work. He also confirmed that the farmers had not previously been invited to negotiate the amount of the payment with industry or government representatives (Muhaimin 1998:54).

Greatest clarification on this issue was found in the testimony of a third witness, an official of the Environmental Impact Agency of Central Java who had participated in attempts to resolve this environmental dispute in 1995 (Muhaimin 1998:55). According to the testimony of this official, an agreement was reached between the agency and the industries that each industry would make a payment of Rp 2,500,000, totalling Rp 15,000,000. The money was to be divided between the residents of Bedono village (Rp 10,000,000) and Sriwulan village (Rp 5 million) and was handed over on 18 September 1995. Most significantly, representatives of the two communities had not been present at this meeting and the money paid was not, in the witness' opinion, compensation but rather made as a goodwill payment (*uang tali asih)*. Finally, an expert witness from the Environmental Research Centre of Diponegoro University was called by the court (Muhaimin 1998:57). The expert witness considered that the distance between the fishponds and the factories did not preclude the possibility of pollution. It was further attested by this witness that laboratory evidence presented by the plaintiffs did confirm that the factories' effluent would have polluted the waters of the Babon River. Even some

63 The remaining Rp 5 million was directed to Sriwulan village.

of the laboratory evidence presented by the defendants, from samples taken at a later date, demonstrated a significant degree of pollution; although to a lesser extent than the earlier samples.

Decision of the district court of Semarang

In its decision dated 13 October 1998, the district court of Semarang first addressed the procedural propriety of the claim brought by the plaintiffs. The three judges rejected the procedural objections of the defendants, stating that the plaintiffs were justified in bringing the suit collectively given their common experience of pollution and environmental damage resulting from the defendants' actions (Muhaimin 1998:59). Similarly, the common liability of the defendants in this case was justified as all had caused pollution in the Babon River. Thus, from the perspective of civil procedure, the closely related interests of the co-defendants and co-plaintiffs respectively justified their joinder in this case.

On the issue of substantive liability, the court concluded that the second through fifth defendant had in fact discharged industrial waste into the Babon River, contrary to applicable laws and regulations, causing pollution and environmental damage.[64] On the evidence presented to it, the court determined that the water from the polluted Babon River had entered the sea, from where it was diverted into the prawn ponds of the plaintiff farmers, causing the deaths of the prawns and consequent loss to the plaintiffs. In support of its decision, the court relied upon documents prepared by the regional government before implementation of the Clean Rivers Program (Prokasih) in 1995. These documents, submitted by the plaintiffs as evidence, demonstrated the Babon River was polluted from liquid waste discharged from the industries. The documents also indicated the six defendant industries had been targeted as potentially the most serious sources of pollution adjoining the Babon River, due to the excessive levels of pollutants detected

64 The claim was rejected against the first defendant, PT Condro Purnomo Cipto, who failed to appear or present any legal representative at any sitting of the court. According to two witnesses, the first defendant was continuing operations but had changed its name to PT Tri Mulyo Kencono Mas. According to the court bailiff, the office of the first defendant had been long closed. The court thus concluded that defendant I was no longer in existence and thus the claim against defendant I failed. The court's decision in this respect seems highly formalistic and open to criticism, given the factory was continuing its operations albeit under a different name. If a change of name and office location is sufficient to relieve an industry of corporate liability for environmental damage, then a dangerous legal precedent has been set. The claim against defendant VI also failed, as the factory that was the subject of the claim had been sold to another company and further rented to a third party. By the time of the trial the factory had ceased operations.

in their waste discharge (Muhaimin 1998:61). In further confirmation of this conclusion, the court referred to the numerous records of the Semarang Environmental Impact Agency, which recorded effluent levels above stipulated levels during 1994.[65] Other evidence considered significant by the court included the testimony of several of the plaintiffs who had suffered devastating losses to their prawn and fish catch during the period September-December 1994 (Muhaimin 1998:63).

Based on this documentary and supporting witness testimony, the court found that from September to December 1994 the second through fifth defendants had discharged waste in excess of stipulated limits into the Babon River, causing both pollution and loss to the plaintiffs. Given that the plaintiffs had suffered loss as a result of the defendants' illegal actions, the court held that defendants in question were obligated to pay compensation on the basis of article 1365 of the Civil Code and article 34(1) of the EMA 1997. Each of the second through fifth defendants were ordered to pay an amount of Rp 1,100,000 to the plaintiff farmers. In awarding compensation for this period, the court rejected the argument of the defendants that the previous payment of Rp 15 million to Bedono and Sri Wulan villages had exonerated them of any further obligation to compensate loss due to pollution. On this issue the court ruled on the side of the plaintiffs, stating the payment concerned did not constitute compensation (*ganti rugi*) that was agreed upon by the plaintiffs and defendants in accordance with article 30 of the EMA 1997. The fact that the payment was made without consultation with the two communities seems to have been most relevant in this respect. Thus, whilst the payment of Rp 15 million had been made by the defendants it was more in the nature of a good will payment and did not discharge the obligation of the defendants to pay actual compensation for the environmental damage experienced by the plaintiffs.

Whilst the plaintiffs were successful in obtaining compensation for the period September to December 1994, when their total prawn stock perished, their further claim for revenue lost since the commencement of the Prokasih (Clean Rivers Program) in 1995 was rejected by the court. The plaintiffs alleged that during this period of 39 months prior to their claim being lodged, their prawn stock levels remained 30% below normal. Accordingly, they sought compensation from the defendants of Rp 45,045,000. The court rejected the claim in respect of this period, justifying its decision by referring to statements by the plaintiffs' witnesses indicating that pollution levels had decreased after 1994, and that by 1995/1996 all but one of the defendant

[65] The date of such laboratory examinations is not specified in the court decision but is presumably some time in 1994.

industries had complied with waste discharge standards (Muhaimin 1998:77). The court further considered the fact that the defendant industries had all installed waste management facilities in accordance with the Prokasih, the implementation of which had commenced in January 1995. The payment of Rp 15 million already made by the defendants also indicated their good will towards the communities in their vicinity. Given these circumstances, the court concluded that the second claim of compensation was excessive and therefore should be refused.

The court's decision on this point is open to some criticism. Certainly some evidence of pollution during this latter period (January 1995 onward) was presented and, moreover, accepted by the court. The Technical Institute for Environmental Health (Balai Tehnik Kesehatan Lingkungan) Yogyakarta tests in March 1997, for instance, demonstrated that pollution from factory effluent continued in the Babon River – a fact that was accepted by the court (Muhaimin 1998:62). Further documentary evidence included reported statements of government officials that pollution in the river was continuing after two years of the Clean Rivers Program's operation. This particular evidence was disallowed on procedural grounds as a reported statement of a third party without verification. Moreover, whilst emphasizing the plaintiff witness statements acknowledging a decline in pollution levels from 1995, the court neglected their further statements that the prawn/fish catch never returned to the pre-September 1994 levels. In the case of defendant II (PT Puspita Abadi), tests undertaken in 1996 still indicated polluting levels of waste discharge. In the case of the other defendants, tests only indicated that effluent fulfilled stipulated standards from around April/May 1996 onwards. It was therefore not conclusively established that the defendant industries had not polluted during 1995 at least, and perhaps after that, given the conflicting evidence presented to the court. Furthermore, the fact that the defendants had installed waste management units in accordance with the Prokasih did not constitute evidence per se that those units were successful in reducing pollution below regulatory standards. Similarly, the unilateral payment of Rp 15 million by the industries to the two communities was an indication of goodwill that should not have discharged the legal obligation of the industries to properly compensate for environmental damage.

The counter claim of the defendants II, III, IV and V for compensation due to damage to their reputation by the plaintiffs' claim was rejected by the court. The court was correct in emphasising that the fact that a party brings an action against another to defend his/her legal rights cannot be characterized in itself as an action which damages the reputation of another, nor as an action contrary to law (Muhaimin 1998:79). This aspect of the court's decision is to be commended both on legal and policy grounds, as an important endorsement of the rights of environmental claimants. The court's decision in the Babon River case offers a valuable precedent against the proliferation of so called 'SLAPP' suits (Strategic Law Suits Against Public Participation), which have been used by companies in a number of jurisdictions to intimidate potential environmental litigants from enforcing their rights.[66]

Appeal to high court of Central Java

Both the six defendant industries and the plaintiff farmers subsequently lodged an appeal against the district court's decision to the high court of Central Java. Over a year passed following the lodgement of the appeal, before the decision of the appellate court was revealed in somewhat unusual circumstances. On 9 August 2000 a group of the affected farmers, together with NGO workers and legal representatives, had decided to protest directly to the high court concerning the protracted delay of the court's decision. After an angry exchange between a court representative and the demonstrators, court officials agreed to search for the case's file. Upon locating the file, it transpired that the case had actually been decided a year earlier on 26 August 1999, yet had not been announced and was only returned to the district court on 5 July 2000.[67]

In its decision dated 26 August 1999, but belatedly revealed a year later, the high court reversed the prior decision of the district court, thus rejecting the plaintiffs' claim for compensation.[68] The crux of the court's decision was that the payment of Rp 15 million made by the industries to the farmers on 18 September 1995 in fact constituted compensation even though it was not called such. Therefore, the farmers had in fact been compensated for damage up until that date, including the four-month period from September-December 1994 when the pollution was at its height. The three appellate judges also rejected the plaintiffs' further claim for compensation subsequent to this date. In respect of this period, the court concluded that the plaintiffs had failed to establish that their reduced catch was a result of the defendant industries' actions. In coming to this conclusion the court cited the fact that 'the defendants had already become participants in the Clean Rivers Program (Prokasih) and thus were not polluting the Babon River nor, as a consequence, the ocean'. Furthermore, the court stated that

66 For example in a dispute in Bali over development near the Tanah Lot temple three Balinese farmers lost their legal suit against the Bali Nirwana Resort in the Tabanan court. The farmers were ordered to pay Rp 75 million to cover legal costs as well as damages to 'restore the company's good reputation'. *Bali Post*, 30-12-1995 cited in Warren 1998:229-61. The issue of protection against 'SLAPP' suits is discussed further in Chapter VI.

67 'Warga Demak demo ke pengadilan tinggi Jateng', *Solo Post*, 10-8-2000.

68 Babon River Appeal, high court of Central Java, No. 329/Pdt/1999/PT.Smg.

> the ocean on the north coast could be polluted by other rivers or by other industries on the Babon River that were not members of the Clean Rivers Program, thus the loss of productivity of the plaintiffs' prawn farmers could not be proven to be a result of the defendants' actions.[69]

The high court's decision was disappointingly superficial in its analysis and flawed in several respects. The judges' characterization of the Rp 15 million payment as compensation is legally incorrect given the fact that the payment was made without direct consultation with the farmers themselves. According to article 31 of the EMA 1997: 'Out of court environmental dispute settlement is held to reach agreement on the form and size of compensation and/or on certain actions to ensure that negative impacts on the environment will not occur or be repeated.' The elucidation to article 31 provides further clarification of out of court settlement: 'Settlement of environmental cases through out of court discussions is carried out voluntarily by the parties which have an interest, namely the parties which have experienced losses and caused losses.'

Yet, from the evidence presented at the district court level, it was clear that the decision to make the Rp 15 million payment involved only government officials and the industries themselves. The farmers, as the party that 'have experienced losses', were notably absent from this negotiation process and the decision to make such a payment. Given the unilateral nature of the payment it is impossible to legally characterize the payment as compensation. Furthermore the payment was administered by the respective village heads and applied to village projects, including road improvement, and did not redress the individual losses of the nine farmers that brought this legal suit.

The court's decision to reject compensation for the period subsequent to September 1995 was also made on questionable grounds. The fact that the industries were 'participants' in the Clean Rivers Program could not be sufficient proof that they had not polluted, although the court seemed to think this was the case. No consideration was given to evidence that contradicted this conclusion, such as the Technical Institute for Environmental Health laboratory tests which indicated pollution was still occurring in March 1997. The failure of the court to substantively reappraise the evidence in this case was also very apparent. The appellate judges instead relied on generalities such as the fact the defendant industries were participants in the Prokasih, or that other industries may also have caused pollution. Noticeably lacking was a specific reappraisal of the evidence that had been presented at the district court level. In this respect the high court's decision compared poorly to the

69 Babon River Appeal, high court of Central Java, No. 329/Pdt/1999/PT.Smg.:12.

more thorough decision at the district court level.

A further defect of this appellate judgement was its outright dismissal of the plaintiffs' claim. The court's reasoning was based on its characterization of the September 1995 payment as compensation. Implicitly, the court was thus acknowledging that an action contrary to law had been committed, yet that the party suffering loss – the farmers – had already been properly compensated. Logically, the court should at least have received the plaintiffs' claim that an action contrary to law had been committed, even whilst refusing to provide further remedy.[70] Instead the court dismissed the claim outright, thus burdening the plaintiffs with the court costs accrued to date.

The judgement of the high court, upon its delayed announcement by a court official, caused much disappointment and anger in the demonstrating farmers and NGO workers. The group immediately departed for the provincial legislature to continue their protest and communicate their disapproval at the decision. An appeal to the Supreme Court was subsequently lodged, and at the time of writing a decision was still pending. Community and legal representatives have also publicly mooted the possibility of bringing a larger, representative action of seven hundred farmers against the industries, although at the time of writing this had not commenced.[71]

Conclusion

The Babon River dispute commenced in late 1994, when the prawns of fishpond farmers in Sri Wulan and Bedono villages perished due to pollution originating from the Babon River. As in the Banger River dispute, the farmers of the two villages took their complaints concerning the pollution to district and provincial parliaments and environmental agencies. The farmers' efforts, aided by local NGOs, were at least partially successful. A good will payment of Rp 15 million was made to the two villages and increased administrative pressure on the factories resulted in the installation of waste management units and ongoing monitoring. Nonetheless, the dispute was not resolved from the farmers' perspective, as pollution continued to reduce the productivity of the fishponds and the individual farmers had not received compensation for lost income. In these circumstances, litigation presented a final option for the community in their efforts to resolve the conflict. As in the Banger River case, access to the judicial system was ensured by the presence of the Indonesian Legal Aid Foundation (YAPHI) in nearby Kudus, which acted as legal representatives for the group of farmers for a nominal fee.

70 Bambang, Lala and Yusuf, interviews at YAPHI, Kudus, 3-11-2000 and 4-11-2000.
71 'Warga bisa menempuh jalur mediasi', *Suara Merdeka*, 12-8-2000.

The factual circumstances of the Babon River dispute gave rise to markedly different judicial decisions at the district court and high court levels respectively. The district court decision provides a notably detailed analysis of the evidence presented in this case, based on a clear comprehension of environmental legal principles. Whilst the decision of the court in respect of the post 1995 period is, in the opinion of the author, questionable, it was at least defensible on the evidence presented to it. In the words of one commentator, the decision was 'like a breath of fresh air for environmental cases'.[72] In contrast, the high court decision was based on a superficial and perfunctory analysis of the evidence before it. The court's characterization of a previous payment as compensation seems unsustainable on both legal and factual grounds. In any case this issue had already been addressed in some detail at the district court level. The superficial nature of the decision, its summary rejection of the plaintiffs' claims and the furtive nature of its release immediately gave rise to suspicions amongst the farming communities of Bedono and Sri Wulan that the judges had been bribed by the defendant industries. When interviewed, the farmers' legal representative referred to the prevalence of corruption in the courts; a fact that has been well documented by independent research (Bedner 2000:289). However, whilst the circumstances and nature of the high court decision caused considerable community suspicion of corruption, no direct evidence of corruption was available.[73]

The discussion of the Banger River case considered the possible influence of direct community pressure upon the judicial decisions at the district court and high court levels. In the Babon River case, a similar community presence and pressure were also present, but only during the district court hearing; no community representatives attended the hearing of the high court, which eventually decided against the community. One of the lawyers for the Bedono and Sri Wulan communities saw the failure to maintain community pressure as a factor contributing to the outcome at the high court level.

> In the Babon River case the community came to the district court hearing. The people were visible and we won at that level. But the farmers didn't come for the high court appeal. We had a problem with organization at the community level. So the judges felt no pressure from the people.[74]

Another of the community's lawyers also regretted not maintaining more frequent contact with the court before its decision, which may have placed the judges under greater scrutiny and minimized the possibility of bribery

72 Dr Sudharto P. Hadi, quoted in 'Warga bisa menempuh jalur mediasi', *Suara Merdeka*, 12-8-2000.

73 Bambang, Lala and Yusuf, interviews at YAPHI, Kudus, 3-11-2000 and 4-11-2000.

74 Bambang, Lala and Yusuf, interviews at YAPHI, Kudus, 3-11-2000 and 4-11-2000.

occurring. Certainly, the judicial process was less public and open at the high court level, to the point that the community was not even aware that the court had decided the case. The court itself did not appear over-anxious to publicize its decision either, which was only returned to the district court a year after it was made.

In contrast to the process of advocacy that preceded litigation in this case, the focus of the litigation process seems to have been primarily concerned with the pecuniary issue of compensation, rather than the issue of environmental restoration. It is surprising, and certainly a defect of the plaintiffs' claim, that environmental restoration was not a remedy sought by the farmers, especially given their contention that pollution was continuing despite the Prokasih. Certainly the industries would have been potentially liable to undertake environmental restoration, as required by article 34. Environmental restoration and prevention of further pollution was also not addressed by the presiding judges at either the district court or high court level. It seems a common tendency amongst environmental cases to place more focus upon pecuniary remedies than remedies of environmental restoration. This is perhaps influenced by a juridical predilection to attempt to resolve such cases through private civil law principles, such as article 1365 of the Civil Code, which focus on remedies of a pecuniary nature. Even in cases where environmental restoration has been raised by a party, such as in the Banger River case, the presiding judges may ignore or neglect to properly address the issue. Consequently, cases such as this often fail to provide a comprehensive resolution of the dispute at hand, as the focus of the case is of a monetary rather than an environmental nature.

The Babon River case also highlights the difficulty of proving pollution in court and the ambiguity that frequently surrounds evidence of pollution in environmental cases. In this case, the court was presented with laboratory evidence that showed significant levels of pollutants in the Babon River in March 1997, whilst other data (from the Semarang Environmental Impact Agency) showed the industries' effluent to comply with regulatory standards at that time. Such inconsistencies may arise from the process of sample taking and examination, which is often bedevilled by a range of practical problems. The level of waste effluent discharged from a factory also typically varies greatly at different points in time. It is reportedly common practice for factories to intentionally dispose of waste effluent during the night or during periods of high rainfall, when the disposed waste will be least noticeable.[75] The result of any testing will therefore depend on the particular time at which it is car-

75 Adi Nugroho (Gita Pertiwi, Solo), interview regarding Babon and Banger River cases, 20-12-2000.

ried out. An accurate assessment of a factory's waste disposal is thus difficult, especially when routine tests by Environmental Impact Agencies are only carried out on a three monthly basis, thus providing at best a very partial picture of a factory's potential impact. Waste management by factories may also be conducted in a sporadic, ad hoc manner in response to agency pressure. For example, whilst many factories are forced to install waste management units by regulation, often the units are not operated, or only occasionally operated when effluent is to be tested, due to the running costs involved.[76] In some cases factories may also utilize concealed by-pass pipes, through which untreated effluent bypasses the waste management system and is disposed of directly into the environment.[77] Thus, whilst the legal process demands conclusive scientific proof of environmental pollution or damage, in practice the scientific evidence available may be partial, ambiguous, contradictory or, in the worst cases, simply incorrect.

76 Adi Nugroho (Gita Pertiwi, Solo), interview regarding Babon and Banger River cases, 20-12-2000.

77 See for instance the Sambong River dispute, Siak River dispute (Chapter IV) and Palur Raya mediation (Chapter V) cases.

CHAPTER IV

Environmental mediation in Indonesia

According to article 30 of the EMA 1997, a person aggrieved by environmental damage or pollution may choose to pursue environmental dispute resolution in court, through litigation, or outside of court through 'informal' methods of dispute resolution such as mediation or negotiation. In this chapter, we provide an overview of the practice of environmental mediation in Indonesia, considering its cultural basis, legal and institutional framework and its reported success to date.

Cultural basis for mediation

Mediation can hardly be described as a new practice in Indonesia, where a range of approaches to consensus-based decision-making and dispute resolution, referred to loosely as *musyawarah,* have been utilized widely by a diversity of ethnic groups.[1] Indeed *musyawarah untuk mufakat* ('group deliberation toward consensus') is enshrined as one of the five basic principles (Pancasila) of the Indonesian Republic, reflecting the high priority afforded to values of compromise, consensus and harmony within Indonesian culture.[2] In contrast, litigation, appropriate to its Western origins, is predicated upon individuality and emphasizes rights rather than obligation, competition rather than compromise. The widespread practice of *musyawarah,* and the broader value base upon which such practices are based, have been regarded by some commentators and policy makers as a favourable precedent for the introduction of modern forms of mediation to environmental and other disputes.[3] Certainly

1 See for instance the study of traditional mediation practices in Achmad Romsan 1998:43-7 (South Sumatra) and Takdir Rachmadi 1998:34-6 (West Sumatra).

2 The high cultural value attached to compromise and consensus is particularly evident in Javanese culture but is not necessarily found throughout the archipalego. In contrast, the Batak people in North Sumatra demonstrate a more combative and argumentative tendency in their culture. See Lev 1990 cited in Mas Achmad Santosa and Hutapea 1992:8.

3 Hamacher 1996:25-40; Moore and Mas Achmad Santosa 1995:23-9; Takdir Rachmadi 1998:34-6; Achmad Romsan 1998:43-7.

the process of *musyawarah,* as it is usually practiced at a village level, bears at least some resemblance to modern mediation. The *musyawarah* process is premised upon compromise, whether it is used to resolve an individual dispute or to make a decision affecting the whole community. The process aims to restore social harmony, rather than declaring one party right and another party wrong (Mas Achmad Santosa and Hutapea 1992:9). As in modern mediation, consensus can only be achieved and social harmony restored if individuals are prepared to be flexible and accommodating. Also as in modern mediation, a third party, usually a respected community elder, facilitates the dispute resolution or decision making process. The specific form of the group dialogue varies according to the particular culture, although it is most often relatively unstructured. A key function of the 'mediator' or community leader is usually to identify common interests that may encourage compromise and consensus. Consensus may emerge from a solution proposed by one or several participants, which is then commonly endorsed (Moore and Mas Achmad Santosa 1995:23-9).

The practice of *musyawarah untuk mufakat* thus shares some important similarities with modern approaches to mediation as practiced in Western countries. Nonetheless, important differences between *musyawarah* in its traditional form and modern approaches to mediation also exist. For example, the community leader who facilitates the *musyawarah* process is not necessarily neutral in the dispute. Depending on the social position of the facilitator, he or she may play a more directive or interventionist role than would usually or ideally be the case in a modern mediation process (Moore and Mas Achmad Santosa 1995:23-9). Furthermore, the political context and dynamics of modern environmental disputes differ significantly from the more circumscribed social context of the village community within which *musyawarah* has traditionally occurred. In the traditional context of *musyawarah,* disputants were closely related by social ties and thus had a strong mutual incentive to resolve their dispute and so preserve the cohesion of their community. In modern environmental disputes, however, disputants are more typically strangers with no social bonds and may consequently have much less social or cultural incentive to compromise and preserve their relationship (Takdir Rachmadi 1998:34-6). In the traditional context, *musyawarah* was carried out 'horizontally', between disputants with a common social context and comparable economic and political resources. In contrast, modern environmental disputes usually involve 'vertical' conflict between disputants from different social contexts and with vastly disparate economic and political resources. The disparity between disputants in 'vertical' conflicts tends to be exacerbated by both political and cultural factors in Indonesia. Indonesia has largely retained a patrimonial and elitist political culture since pre-colonial times, in which political power is exercised by competing factions of an economically privileged elite over the politically passive and quiescent masses.[4] During the New Order era particularly, the political quiescence of the masses was ensured by the violent elimination of popular support for the Indonesian communist party and the banning of political activity at a grassroots level (Crouch 1979:571-87). The political disparity between the political elite and the more disenfranchised sections of the population has been further accentuated in Indonesia by the hierarchical character of Indonesian, and notably Javanese, culture. In this highly stratified culture gradations of social status are of great import, with the accompanying deference ensuring that 'leaders are reluctant to give citizens equal standing in a deliberatory process because of their subordinate position' (Moore and Mas Achmad Santosa 1995:23-9). People from a village environment are usually equally reluctant to assert their rights or interests when confronted with their cultural 'superiors'. Political, economic and cultural factors may thus accentuate disparities in the balance of power between disputing parties and so influence the process and outcome of consensually-based dispute resolution processes. In this very different social and political context, some commentators have criticized the concept of *musyawarah* as providing a cultural justification for stifling dissent and resolving disputes through power-based approaches. For example Andik Hardiyanto (1999:3) claims that

> the true cultural meaning of *musyawarah* has been lost due to the intervention of the politics of development [...] *musyawarah* has become a political arena for strong developers and capitalists, who ultimately oppress communities in a more vulnerable position.

The political context of contemporary environmental disputes thus presents unique challenges to the mediation process, which may differ significantly from the traditional social context of *musyawarah*. The traditions of *musyawarah* are certainly relevant as a cultural precedent for modern forms of mediation. The *musyawarah* model, however, may imply a more directive consensus building process and thus tend to exacerbate rather than mitigate power disparities between disputing parties.

Legislation

Notwithstanding political or cultural obstacles, alternative dispute resolution (ADR) was introduced into the environmental field in legislative form by the Environmental Management Act No. 4 of 1982.[5] As discussed in Chapter II,

4 See the discussion of patrimonialism in relation to Indonesia in Crouch 1979:571-87.
5 Other legislation has also recognized or prescribed ADR in other fields including labor (Act

article 20 of that EMA stated that compensation and rehabilitation in relation to environmental damage could be determined through negotiation by a tripartite team representing the aggrieved parties, polluter(s) and relevant government agencies. Whilst the article did not explicitly state negotiation to be compulsory, it was interpreted as such in several cases.[6] The provision produced a 'catch-22' situation: on one hand, mediation of environmental disputes was seldom undertaken due to a lack of procedure or a lack of initiative on the part of government agencies; on the other hand, article 20 also barred the path of litigation, as courts deemed mediation to be a compulsory precondition to a legal suit for compensation of environmental damage.

Fortunately, this legal stalemate was resolved at the legislative level by the revised article 30 of the EMA 1997, which states that environmental dispute settlement may occur within the court or outside of the court. The choice in this respect is voluntary and thus made by the parties to the dispute. The new EMA emphasized this point to ensure that mediation would constitute an alternative, rather than an obstacle to litigation as had been the case under the old law; and that the civil rights of parties to litigate would remain intact. Nonetheless some ambiguity remains, as it is unclear from the terms of the article what course parties should take where they do not agree on the choice between litigation and mediation. Presumably, if the parties were divided as to whether to pursue dispute settlement inside or outside of court, then the matter would proceed to court by default. This view is supported by article 30(3), which stipulates that where the parties have chosen out of court settlement, then a legal action may only be commenced if one or more parties declare such settlement to have failed. Thus, where a party declares out of court settlement has failed the matter may proceed by legal action to court. The fact that legal proceedings may only be undertaken where mediation has failed also prevents the possibility of judicial and non-judicial settlement proceedings running concurrently and causing unnecessary expense in time and money, as was the case in the PT SSS case discussed below (Andik Hardiyanto 1999:3).

Further provisions within Chapter VII of the EMA 1997 stipulate the objectives of out of court settlement proceedings, being agreement on the form and size of compensation and/or certain actions to ensure that negative impacts on the environment will not occur or be repeated (article 31). Article 32 also explicitly sanctions intervention of a third party, in the form of a mediator

No. 22 of 1957), marriage counselling, commercial arbitration and court procedure. In relation to the latter, article 130 of the Indonesian Civil Procedure Law requires a judge to attempt to reconcile the disputants before legal proceedings commence. See Mas Achmad Santosa 1995:3.

6 As discussed earlier, in these cases the legal claims for compensation for environmental damage were barred on the grounds that they had not been preceded by negotiation/mediation as stipulated in article 20.

(whose decisions are not binding) or an arbitrator (whose decisions are binding). Notably, the elucidation to this article stipulates a number of conditions with which a mediator or arbitrator must comply as a 'neutral third party'. The article states that the neutral third party must:

- be agreed to by the parties in dispute;
- not have familial relations and/or work relations with one of the parties in dispute;
- possess skills to carry out discussion or mediation;
- not have an interest in the process of discussion or its outcome.

This provision is of considerable significance as, if enforced, it may serve to mitigate the tendency evident in traditional consensus-based dispute resolution, *musyawarah,* where the resolution process becomes dominated by an influential figure(s) who may have some stake in the dispute at hand. Yet the practical obstacles of finding a 'neutral third party' who does 'not have an interest in the process of discussion or its outcome' may prove an obstacle to implementation of this article. Article 33, which authorizes the creation of an environmental dispute settlement service by the government or community, is designed to overcome this problem. Government Regulation No. 54 of 2000, concerning 'Service Providers of Environmental Dispute Resolution outside of Court', has provided for the further implementation of article 33 of the EMA 1997. Environmental dispute resolution service providers may be formed by the central (Environmental Minister) or regional governments (governor, regent or mayor) by the appropriate authority or by the community via a notary. Those appointed as mediators or arbitrators must fulfil certain criteria, and be acceptable to the community.[7] Payment for the services of a mediator or arbitrator may be borne by both or one of the parties, or in some cases a third party or the government.

Implementation and institutionalization of mediation is likely to be further facilitated by proposed judicial regulations implementing court connected alternative dispute resolution. The draft Supreme Court regulations[8] are intended to integrate mediation into the court system and help overcome long delays in case processing.[9] Pursuant to the proposed regulations, litigants would be required to attempt mediation for a specified period of

7 A mediator must be at least 30 years of age and possess experience in the environmental field of at least 5 years. An arbitrator must be at least 35 years of age and hold experience in the environmental field of 15 years or more. Both must also possess the skills necessary to carry out mediation or arbitration.

8 This regulation has been issued since the time of writing - Supreme Court Regulation (PerMA) No. 1/2008 on Mediation Procedures in Courts.

9 Siti Megadiaty Adam, interview Mbak Gege ICEL, 6-6-2003.

approximately three weeks. If the parties are successful in resolving the dispute, the resultant agreement may be registered with the court. If mediation fails, the court is notified and the parties resume the process of litigation.[10]

Institutionalization of environmental mediation

Besides an adequate legal framework, the successful implementation of environmental mediation in Indonesia will require sufficient institutional backing from both government agencies and non-government organizations. Institutional support to date has included the creation of national policy relating to alternative dispute resolution (ADR) by a number of government agencies. Policy initiatives have included the formulation of a national policy paper on ADR by the National Development Planning Agency (Badan Perencanaan dan Pembangunan Nasional, BAPPENAS); formulation of draft legislation for the general use of ADR in Indonesia by the Cabinet Secretary's Office; development of court annexed ADR by the Supreme Court, and the integration of ADR into the training of public prosecutors by the Attorney General's Office (Mas Achmad Santosa 1995:1). More specific to the environmental field, the Ministry of the Environment was involved in the drafting of the ADR provisions contained within the EMA 1997 discussed above. Yet most of these initiatives have taken place at policy level only, with few reaching the level of implementation.

The government agency most actively involved in the application of mediation to environmental disputes has been the national Environmental Impact Agency (Bapedal), which received a mandate in 1993 from the Environment Minister to begin using voluntary compliance procedures, including mediation, in conjunction with command and control enforcement of environmental law (Moore and Mas Achmad Santosa 1995:23-9). Mediation was adopted by the agency as it was seen as culturally compatible with traditional decision-making practices, as well as because of its effectiveness in resolving environmental disputes in other countries, and because it provided an alternative path to the command and control approach to enforcement with which the agency had experienced some difficulty (Moore and Mas Achmad Santosa 1995:23-9). The creation of decentralized Environmental Impact Agencies (Bapedalda) at the regional levels of government has resulted in some cases in a wider application of environmental mediation, although the role of some regional agencies has been more limited due to a lack of political and economic resources.[11]

10 Draft Supreme Court Regulations on Mediation Procedure in Court 2003.

11 See, for example, the discussion concerning the role of the district environmental agency in the Palur Raya dispute in Chapter V.

At the local or regional level, other government authorities may play an active role in out of court environmental dispute settlement. Influential local figures, typically governmental authorities, often take on a facilitating or mediating role in environmental disputes where a mediation process is initiated. Depending on the scale and profile of the dispute, this may be a local sub-district head (*camat*), the head of a government agency, a mayor, regent or even a governor. The problematic aspect of government facilitation or mediation of environmental mediation is that the government itself is usually a stakeholder in the dispute and thus not a neutral party.[12]

Besides government agencies, non-government organizations have also played a very active role in the socialization and implementation of ADR approaches to environmental disputes. Well-resourced organizations such as the Indonesian National Forum for the Environment (WALHI), the Indonesian Centre for Environmental Law (ICEL) and the Indonesian Legal Aid Foundation (YLBHI) have actively sought to promote mediation as an alternative path to justice in environmental disputes. In particular, ICEL, in conjunction with its foreign donors, has concentrated its efforts on promoting ADR in environmental conflicts.[13] ICEL's initiatives have included research into environmental disputes where ADR approaches were utilized, socialization of ADR approaches to environmental disputes to government officials (including prosecutors, judges, and legal drafters), publication of literature on environmental mediation in Indonesia, participation in drafting regulatory frameworks to support the implementation of environmental mediation, conducting training and skill building workshops for potential mediators, and actual participation in mediating a wide range of environmental disputes (Mas Achmad Santosa, Takdir Rachmadi and Siti Megadianty Adam 1997:190). Besides the national NGOs discussed above, a plethora of local and regional environmental organizations have played an important role in advocacy associated with environmental dispute resolution. In nearly all of the case studies reviewed below, NGOs played a significant role in facilitating community organization before mediation and in some cases participating directly in the mediation process.

Review of environmental mediation cases

This section provides an overview and analysis of a selection of environmental mediation cases to date in Indonesia. The selection of cases is intended as a

12 The importance of an impartial or neutral mediator is discussed in Chapter I.

13 In relation to its programs to promote environmental mediation, ICEL has worked in conjunction with GTZ (a German aid agency), USAID, the Asia Foundation and the Ford Foundation. See Mas Achmad Santosa, Takdir Rachmadi and Siti Megadianty Adam 1997:190.

representative rather than comprehensive summary and was drawn from the available (predominantly Indonesian language) literature on environmental mediation in Indonesia and the author's own research in the field.[14] The cases are predominantly industry related and Java-based, although a mining dispute from Kalimantan has also been included. Each case study presented below provides a summary of the factual background of the case and mediation process together with an analysis of the variables that influenced the eventual outcome of mediation.

Tapak River, Semarang 1991

The Tapak River case is an often-cited example of successful environmental mediation in Indonesia in the period since the enactment of the first Environmental Management Act. In that dispute, a number of factories were disposing of untreated effluent into the Tapak River, the main water source for at least two hundred families living nearby.[15] The resulting damage to the surrounding land, agricultural yields and local residents' health was considerable.[16] Research from a number of sources, including the Semarang Environmental Impact Agency, the Research Institute of Diponegoro University, and the Institute of Industry Research and Development, vindicated the residents' claims of pollution (Joko Hadi Satyoga 1992:5). Samples taken from the river displayed Biological Oxygen Demand (BOD) levels nearly twenty times the Indonesian legal limit (Thorburn 1992:3).

Members of the Dukuh Tapak community had, since the late 1970s, conveyed complaints concerning the pollution to the village chief, sub-district head, officials of the Semarang district government and also to the respective industries themselves. In 1978, following protests by farmers and fishpond owners over pollution from the PT Semarang Diamond Chemical (SDC)

14 The most useful written source in this respect was Mas Achmad Santosa, Takdir Rachmadi and Siti Megadianty Adam 1997, to which frequent reference is made in the case studies that follow. Other written sources were drawn from a compilation of seminar papers, unpublished articles and newspaper clippings on particular mediation cases and environmental mediation in general.

15 The account of the Tapak River case is based on the following sources: Siti Megadiaty Adam, interview, 6-6-2003; Aditjondro 1979:66-81; Heroepoetri Arimbi 1994b:1; Lucas 1998:229-61; Takdir Rachmadi 1997b; Mas Achmad Santosa and Hutapea 1992:8; Joko Hadi Satyoga 1992; Thorburn 1992. The first industry to be established in the area was PT Semarang Diamond Chemical (SDC), which produced calcium citrate, a substance used in soft drinks. Other factories established in the early 1980s included PT Sukasari (soy sauce), PT Bukit Perak (soap), PT Kemas Tugu Industri (paper), PT Agung Perdana Tuguh Indah (clothes printing) and PT Makara Dewa Wisesa (cold storage). See Joko Hadi Satyoga 1992.

16 The devastating environmental, social and economic impact of the pollution on the residents of Dukuh Tapak is well documented in Aditjondro 1979:66-81 and Lucas 1998:229-61.

factory, some compensation was paid by the industry to the farmers whose harvest or catch had been affected by pollution.[17] There was, however, no action taken to address the problem of pollution, which increased as the district government continued to issue permits for the establishment of new industries and a public garbage dump in the area. The general view of industry and district government officials was that the area had been stipulated as an industrial estate and therefore pollution was to be expected (Joko Hadi Satyoga 1992:3).

By the mid-1980s the Dukuh Tapak community had sought the assistance of several NGOs, including WALHI and the Semarang Legal Aid Institute, in resolving their dispute over the problem of pollution. The case began to attract increasing publicity in regional, national and even international media.[18] Advocacy efforts were continued with complaints over pollution conveyed to the national Industry and Environmental Ministers. The community's complaint to the Minister for Industry attracted the ire of regional military and police, who warned community representatives to stay out of politics. However the Environment Minister, then Emil Salim, urged the Semarang district government to resolve the dispute, which was receiving increasing publicity in national newspapers (Takdir Rachmadi 1997b:6).

In January 1991, at the request of the Semarang Legal Aid Institute, the Semarang legislature arranged an initial meeting between community and industry representatives to negotiate a solution to the dispute. The Tapak residents wanted compensation (Rp 1.9 billion, an end to further pollution, and rehabilitation of the Tapak River. Industry representatives, however, denied their operations caused pollution and were only willing to undertake limited community development measures (Joko Hadi Satyoga 1992:11). Furthermore, despite promises of further meetings, the Semarang mayor appeared unwilling to take concrete steps toward resolving the dispute (Takdir Rachmadi 1997b:7).

Following the failed attempt at negotiation, the Tapak residents, together with a coalition of fifteen NGOs involved in the case, undertook in April 1991 to organize a consumer boycott of products of the seven industries responsible for the pollution.[19] The boycott was intended to increase pressure on industry and the regional government to consider the demands of the Tapak

17 A special committee appointed to address the issue of compensation recommended payment of Rp 119 million to residents. PT SDC, however, was only prepared to pay Rp 5.4 million. See Joko Hadi Satyoga 1992:7.

18 The dispute received coverage in the national Japanese newspaper *Yomiuri Shimbun* as PT Semarang Diamond Chemical was a subsidiary of the Japanese company Mitsubishi and Showa Chemical. See Joko Hadi Satyoga 1992:12.

19 The boycott was inspired by the American NGO boycott of Scott Paper, which had planned to establish a branch in Indonesia. See Joko Hadi Satyoga 1992:12.

residents.[20] The boycott action received widespread publicity and a sympathetic reception from senior Environmental Impact Agency (Bapedal) officials and the Environment Minister, who sent a suggestion to the Minister for Industry that a tripartite team be formed to resolve the dispute.[21] The boycott was successful in increasing pressure on industry and regional government to enter a mediation process, which was ultimately commenced in May 1991.

The dispute resolution process was mediated by an official of the Semarang regional government, who tended to lend greater support to the industries' position during the negotiations that followed (Takdir Rachmadi 1997b:8-9). Participants in mediation included representatives of Bapedal, the Deputy Governor of Central Java, Semarang mayor, head of the Central Java legislature, the Semarang Legal Aid Institute, two NGOs (WALHI and the Indonesia Consumer Foundation Yayasan Lembaga Konsumer Indonesia), and industry. The mediation process ultimately resulted in an undertaking by the polluting companies to install waste treatment equipment, comply with government regulations and stop the disposal of untreated effluent into the Tapak River. The companies also agreed to pay Rp 225 million compensation to local farmers and, together with the provincial government, set up a Rp 185 million fund for the rehabilitation of the Tapak village area (Mas Achmad Santosa and Hutapea 1992:37). In return, Tapak residents agreed to withdraw their threat of legal action and NGO representatives undertook to discontinue the boycott action.

Implementation of the agreement has been only partially successful. Compensation as stipulated was paid, and community members were provided with a source of clean water for their daily needs. However the agreed program of environmental rehabilitation and community development was only partially implemented. Ongoing monitoring of water quality did not occur and pollution continued to contaminate the fields and fishponds of Tapak residents.[22] Promised social and economic developments were not initiated and the social effects of the pollution continued to be felt in Tapak village, where around 60% of residents had lost their livelihoods due to pollution (Lucas 1998:195).

20 Litigation was considered as an alternative strategy but it was thought this would not have sufficient impact or pressure on industry and government and also would face considerable technical and legal obstacles. See Takdir Rachmadi 1997b:7, cited in Lucas 1998:195, who considered threats of legal action by WALHI against PT SDC to be a factor contributing to the negotiating compensation agreement.

21 In contrast the boycott was opposed by industry and the Semarang mayor. See Takdir Rachmadi 1997b:7.

22 The agreement was concluded in August 1991, but residents reported continuing indications of pollution during November and December 1991, including dead fish and prawns, discoloured and odourous river water, and skin irritation by people coming in contact with the water. See Mas Achmad Santosa and Hutapea 1992:39.

The outcome of mediation in the Tapak River dispute was at least partially successful. Compensation (actually termed 'contribution') was paid to residents of Tapak who had suffered pollution, even though it is unlikely the amount paid approached the loss actually suffered by the villagers.[23] In addition, at least limited environmental and community development measures were undertaken, even though environmental management overall did not improve and pollution continued. Given these modest successes, despite its failings, the Tapak River case was regarded by many as a milestone for environmental mediation in Indonesia. The dispute was the first high profile environmental dispute where an agreement was reached through mediation held pursuant to article 20 of the EMA 1982. The substantial compensation sum paid by industry to the Tapak villagers also set a new precedent for the compensation of environmental damage in environmental disputes.

A significant factor that contributed to the partial success of the mediation was the initiation of the NGO sponsored boycott of the Tapak industries' products. The boycott threat, widely publicized in regional, national and international media, greatly increased public pressure on the industries and the Semarang regional government to participate in a mediation process. In addition to effective public pressure, the Environment Minister and Environmental Impact Agency (Bapedal) provided strong political support for the initiation of a dispute resolution process. National level government support for the community's claims compensated for the resistance of the Semarang regional government, which tended to side with industry in this dispute. The community's success in obtaining compensation may also be attributed to the strong and well-documented evidence of pollution since 1978 that existed in this case. Whilst NGO and national government pressure facilitated the mediation process, this pressure was not maintained after the agreement during the implementation phase. The subsequent failure to prevent ongoing pollution demonstrated the need for more effective implementation mechanisms and administrative support for these at the district level.

Tembok Dukuh /PT SSS case, Surabaya 1991

In this case, already referred to in Chapter II, a group of eighteen residents from Tembok Dukuh village in East Java claimed zinc and chromium waste from the PT Sarana Surya Sakti (PT SSS) factory, which manufactured bicycle rims, had resulted in pollution of groundwater and village wells.[24] Following

23 Economic losses were calculated by a special committee of Tugu sub-district in 1978 as already at Rp 119 million. See Lucas 1998:190.

24 This account is based on the following sources: Takdir Rachmadi 1993:1-5; Mas Achmad Santosa and Moore 1997:84-7; *Sarana Surya Sakti* 1993; Surabaya Public Prosecutor 1991; Toha

complaints by the community to the local district official, government research was carried out which confirmed the pollution.[25] Subsequently, the Surabaya mayor issued an administrative warning requesting that the factory comply with waste management regulations (Mas Achmad Santosa 1996:29). Despite the warning, pollution continued, as did the protests of the Tembok Dukuh community, which were gaining increasing exposure in the mass media. Mediation was attempted on two occasions during this period, but was not successful, prompting the residents to appoint the Surabaya Legal Aid Institute as legal representatives.

Frustrated by the failure of the regional government to enforce environmental regulations and take administrative action against PT SSS, the group of eighteen Tembok Dukuh residents lodged a civil suit against the factory in the Surabaya district court.[26] Due in part to the terms of article 20(2) of the EMA 1982, which required mandatory conciliation to be undertaken prior to a legal suit, the parties agreed to adjourn proceedings while a process of court connected conciliation was undertaken. The mediation process was initially chaired by the Deputy I of the Environmental Impact Agency, Nabiel Makarim, and the parties were successful in concluding an 'agreement to mediate' and an 'agreement in principle'. The latter stages of mediation, however, were chaired by the officials from the Surabaya mayor's office, whose actions, in pressuring the Tembok Dukuh residents to compromise and emphasising the wider contribution the factory made to society by creating employment, displayed a lack of neutrality (Takdir Rachmadi 1993:1-5). The mayor had also issued a regulation rezoning the area in question to allow both residential and industrial uses, thus quashing one of the community's prior demands that PT SSS be relocated due, in part, to inconsistency with local zoning. Nonetheless, the mediation process progressed to the point where a preliminary agreement was reached on environmental restoration and the range of compensation that would be payable (Surabaya Sekretaris Kotamadya 1992). Subsequently, however, industry representatives retreated from their undertaking to pay in the range of Rp 100-150 million compensation, offering instead a much lower figure of Rp 12,960,000, which the residents rejected (Mas Achmad Santosa and Moore 1997:84-7). Ultimately, the preliminary agreement reached by the parties failed and the case returned to court on 28 July 1993.

1993 and miscellaneous correspondence and documentation of the dispute resolution process gathered during research carried out in 1993.

25 Residents of the village of Tembok Dukuh, adjoining the factory, had noticed that their well water had changed colour (to yellow-red) and started to smell. When used for washing, the water caused itching and skin irritation. The suspicions of residents were heightened when a wall between the factory and residences collapsed, causing the overflow of liquid waste into the property of two residents. See Takdir Rachmadi 1993:1-5.

26 The legal suit has already been discussed in Chapter II.

In this case, the well-publicized campaign of Tembok Dukuh residents against the pollution of PT SSS was successful in prompting some administrative action, including support for a mediation process. The commencement and early stages of the mediation process were facilitated by the national Environmental Impact Agency, resulting in both an 'agreement to mediate' and an 'agreement in principle'. In contrast, the failure of the regional Surabaya government to undertake administrative action against PT SSS ensured the company was under little pressure to come to a mediated agreement (Mas Achmad Santosa and Moore 1997:84-7). The 'soft' attitude of regional government officials toward PT SSS was also evident in the mediation process itself, where the officials of the mayor's office failed to mediate in a neutral manner, thereby contributing to the eventual failure to achieve a final agreement.

PT Tyfountex, Solo 1992

PT Tyfountex is a large textile industry, established in 1974, located near the city of Solo in the regency of Sukoharjo, Central Java.[27] The factory occupies an area of some 15 hectares and employs over 5000 workers. The environmental impact of the PT Tyfountex's operations has been felt by local residents since the mid-1970s, when residents of three villages located close to the factory reported discoloured well water and visible signs of pollution in river water. In the mid-1980s several residents of Gumpang village sent a written complaint regarding the pollution to the industry via the local village head. The complaint was unanswered, however, and the pollution continued. By the 1990s the impact of the factory's pollution had worsened and spread to several other nearby villages. Testing carried out by a local NGO, Gita Pertiwi, confirmed pollution in local residents' wells. Whilst the residents were increasingly aware of the industry's pollution, their position in response to the pollution remained passive prior to the involvement of several local NGOs.[28] With NGO assistance, a group of community representatives began to organize protest actions against the pollution from PT Tyfountex. In September 1992 a petition signed by 301 residents objecting to the pollution was sent to PT Tyfountex, as well as to the national Environment Minister, the Environmental Impact Agency, the Regent of Sukoharjo and regional press. After the protest was widely reported in the regional press, the village head of Makamhaji, one of the villages affected by the pollution, convened a meeting which included representatives from

27 This account is based on Gita Pertiwi 2000c:6.

28 Including environmentalists from the Student Association of Solo (Ikatan Mahasiswa Solo), the Foundation for Village Development (Yayasan Pengembangan Pedesaan) and local NGO Gita Pertiwi.

PT Tyfountex, sub-district heads, environmental officials from the regency of Sukoharjo, and the local community. Around two hundred villagers from three villages attended the meeting, at which PT Tyfountex acknowledged the pollution caused by its operations.[29] The industry promised to fulfil, within three to six months, the community's demands that it install a waste management unit, provide piped water to local villages, increase the height of the factory's chimney and reduce the noise levels from the factory's generator.

Later that month community members formed the Tyfountex Pollution Monitoring Group (Kelompok Pemantau Pencemaran Tyfountex, KPPT) to monitor implementation of the agreement reached with industry representatives. Several months on, Tyfountex had still not implemented any of the changes promised to the community, and the pollution had continued unabated. Residents who had played a part in organising the protest also came under pressure to sell their land to Tyfountex and leave the area. In protest, community members organized another demonstration, attended by around three hundred people in front of the factory. As a result of the protest a further process of mediation was initiated between KPPT and PT Tyfountex, facilitated by sub-district officials. One week after the protest an agreement was signed by both parties, pursuant to which an independent team was to be formed to investigate and resolve the issue of pollution. Implementation of the agreement was undermined, however, by subsequent events. In November 1992, the regent (*bupati*) of Sukoharjo held an emergency meeting with sub-district officials. At the meeting the regent directed that any future community complaints should be conveyed through 'constitutional' or official channels, that is via the local and sub-district government hierachy. Accordingly, the community group KPPT was deemed no longer necessary and was officially disbanded. The decision rendered the agreement signed between KPPT and PT Tyfountex redundant, as a result of which the independent team investigation foreshadowed by the agreement was never initiated.

In this case community pressure was instrumental in the commencement of a mediation process on two occasions. The ability of the community to successfully mobilize and convey its demands to industry and government was facilitated by the support of local NGOs and widespread coverage of the dispute in the regional press. The response of the industry Tyfountex in this case seems to have been a deliberate attempt to temporarily appease community sentiment through an apparent concession to community demands. The industry's promise of improved environmental management as reflected in the agreement with KPPT was not subsequently implemented, but rather was circumvented conveniently via the regent's direction that KPPT be disbanded.

[29] The pollution claims were subsequently verified by research conducted by an investigatory team from Sukoharjo district.

Sambong River, Batang 1993

This dispute involved three factories housed in a single complex owned by the PT Indonesia Miki Industries (IMI) company and located near the mouth of the Sambong River in Central Java.[30] Several villages located near the factories relied mostly on fishing for their livelihood, although some residents also worked as factory labourers or farmers.[31] In 1973 PT IMI began disposing its industrial effluent into the Sambong River, following a prohibition by the harbour master which prevented it from disposing the waste directly into the ocean. Whilst some of the factories' waste was processed before disposal, the factories also frequently utilized concealed outlets to dispose of untreated waste during the night (Puspo Adjie 1993:49-52). The effects of the pollution were noticeable from 1978 onwards, and included various health complaints amongst local residents and the deaths of fish in the Sambong River, which undermined the livelihood of many families (Puspo Adjie 1993:49-52).

In 1991 the community complained to the regional government of Batang, which appointed an investigative team. The ensuing investigation attributed pollution to a variety of sources, including domestic waste and smaller factories. A subsequent police investigation, following further complaints from residents, attributed the pollution to pesticide use (Takdir Rachmadi 1997a:58). The community, however, continued to maintain that the PT IMI factories were the primary source of hazardous waste and pollution of the river, and that PT IMI should bear responsibility for compensation and rehabilitation of the environmental damage that had occurred.

In October 1991, community leaders appointed the Semarang Legal Aid Institute as the community's legal representatives, and also obtained assistance from the regional Indonesian Forum for the Environment group (WALHI), while continuing a variety of advocacy initiatives including demonstrations at the factories. The continuing advocacy and involvement of a network of NGOs helped the case assume a national profile in the media by August 1991. In an attempt to increase pressure on regional officials, the case was also formally reported to the national Environmental Impact Agency. Following this report, the governor of Central Java directed the regent of Batang to obtain a formal commitment from PT IMI to install a functioning waste management

30 This account is based upon the following sources: Puspo Adjie 1993:49-52 and Takdir Rachmadi 1997a:55. PT Indonesia Miki Industries (IMI) comprises: PT Sumbertex, established in 1960, producing textile and plastic rope/nets; PT Miki Indo Industri, established in 1970, producing MSG, noodles, coffee and glucose; and PT Batang Alun, established in 1974, producing saccharin and cylcamate. See Takdir Rachmadi 1997a:55.

31 Residents subsequently affected by the pollution number around 480 families and were located in four villages (Proyonanggan, Karangasem, Klidang Wetan and Klidang Lor) in the subdistrict of Batang. See Puspo Adjie 1993:49.

unit. Shortly thereafter (in December 1991) a team from the Environmental Agency visited the factories and villages, accompanied by officials from the Department of Industry and the Batang District government. After this visit, the factory reportedly stopped disposing untreated waste directly into the river (Puspo Adjie 1993:53).

Following this renewed advocacy, a meeting was convened between the governor of Central Java, district officials, the Environmental Impact Agency of Central Java and community representatives. Agreement was reached to form a fact-finding team, which subsequently identified several sources of pollution including the PT IMI factories (Takdir Rachmadi 1997a:58). Following confirmation of the pollution by the fact-finding team, the Environmental Impact Agency and the governor's office encouraged industry and community representatives to resolve the dispute by mediation. A government appointed mediator presided over the subsequent mediation process, which for the most part consisted of separate discussion with industry and community representatives.[32] Pursuant to the final agreement, dated 13 November 1993, the regional government agreed to supply drinking water to the community and rehabilitate the eroded riverbank. The industry undertook to install a waste management unit, ensure compliance with government stipulations of water quality, and pay an amount of Rp 53 million. The company did, however, insist on describing the financial payment to the community as aid (*bantuan*) rather than compensation (*ganti rugi*) (Takdir Rachmadi 1997a:59).

Like the Tapak River dispute, the Sambong River dispute illustrates the importance of effective community organization and advocacy in the pre-mediation phase. Effective public pressure on industry and the district government was again in this case facilitated by a network of NGOs and a high level of media exposure in regional and national newspapers. The involvement of the national Environmental Impact Agency also played an important role in facilitating the dispute resolution process and prompting action toward this end from the district and provincial governments. As in the Tapak River case, the mediator in this case was a district government official who, according to community reports, tended to favour industry interests. Nonetheless, the government appointed mediator was successful in minimizing animosity between parties through 'shuttle diplomacy' and overcoming a deadlock on the matter of compensation. Subsequent reports have indicated a reasonable level of community and industry satisfaction concerning the agreement, although the regional government reportedly did not carry out rehabilitation of the riverbanks as promised (Takdir Rachmadi 1997a:60).

32 The mediator was the head of Economic Division in the Regency of Batang, who in the view community representatives tended to favour industry interests in the course of negotiations. See Takdir Rachmadi 1997a:58.

Siak River, Riau 1992

The Siak River dispute centred on water pollution originating from a pulp and paper industry, PT Indah Kiat Pulp and Paper (PT IKPP).[33] The factory, established in 1984, polluted the Siak River which was utilized by a village of around 150 families for their fishing, agriculture and daily needs.[34] Initial complaints from the local community to PT IKPP were rejected, as the industry considered that it could not be held solely responsible for pollution when other factories were also operating nearby. However, independent research from several sources confirmed that the river's pollution was caused primarily by the pulp and paper processing operated by PT IKPP.[35] The community's subsequent advocacy efforts were supported by an extensive network of local, regional and national NGOs. Several discussion groups were established between community representatives and NGO workers, and the community appointed the Indonesian Legal Aid Foundation (YLBHI) as legal representatives. Advocacy initiatives included widely reported demonstrations, threats of an organized boycott of PT IKPP's products and written complaints to a number of government agencies.

A mediation process was subsequently undertaken and facilitated by Deputy I of the Environmental Impact Agency, Nabiel Makarim. The mediation process ultimately resulted in an agreement in principle, in which the industry agreed to improve waste management, facilitate communication between industry and community and provide funds (Rp 266 million) for community development (Sunoto and Takdir Rachmadi 1997:25). Although an agreement was reached, its ensuing implementation proved to be unsatisfactory. Pollution from the factory continued, exacerbated by leaks from waste storage facilities and a hidden bypass waste outlet discovered by community members (Dadang Trisasongko 1998:28-30). Community development programs were only partially successful, and efforts to create a industry-communication forum were not successful. The implementation failure experienced in this case was the result of several factors. The agreement itself was insufficiently detailed and did not provide adequate mechanisms for implementation. Implementation

33 This account is based on the following sources: Hidayat Hibani 1994; Sunoto and Takdir Rachmadi 1997; Dadang Trisasongko 1998. At the time of this dispute, PT IKPP was a publicly listed paper and pulp industry within the Sinar Mas Group, producing between 225,000 to 234,000 ton a year for the domestic and international market. See Dadang Trisasongko 1998:28-30.

34 Whilst other smaller industries had operated in the area prior to PT IKPP, river pollution had only become apparent to residents subsequent to the start of PT IKPP's operations. See Sunoto and Takdir Rachmadi 1997:17.

35 Research confirming pollution by PT IKPP was carried out by University of Riau, Ministry of the Environment, the provincial Environmental Impact Agency and PT Sucofindo. See Dadang Trisasongko 1998:28-30.

was also undermined by the failure to involve the Riau provincial government – the level of government responsible for regional implementation of environmental regulations – in the mediation process (Sunoto and Takdir Rachmadi 1997:26). Moreover, the Environmental Impact Agency, which had played an important role in facilitating the agreement, devoted little or no attention or resources to its implementation. Similarly, the extensive network of national and regional NGOs that had provided a catalyst for the original mediation process largely dissipated subsequent to the agreement, with local NGOs playing little role in supervising implementation (Sunoto and Takdir Rachmadi 1997:26). Ultimately, continued pollution from the factory prompted the local community to initiate legal action against PT IKPP.

The Siak River dispute highlights the difficulty frequently associated with implementing negotiated agreements. Whilst community pressure or high-level government intervention may compel a polluting company to negotiate and even concede an agreement, in cases such as this it appears that such responses are intended more to appease public sentiment in the short term than resolve the dispute in the longer term. The Siak River dispute is one example of how industry and government agencies have

> viewed participation in mediation as an end in itself, regardless of outcome [...] provid[ing] an opportunity for input, but not [...] a means of direct decision making. This has led some participants to promote the process as a way of procedurally appeasing angry people, but not solving problems. (Moore and Mas Achmad Santosa 1995:23-9.)

A manipulative approach to mediation such as this leads inevitably to increased community frustration with the mediation process, prompting in this case subsequent legal action. For, as one community member commented in this case, it may seem 'better not to use negotiation when agreements are not followed' (Sunoto and Takdir Rachmadi 1997:25).

Sibalec, Yogyakarta 1994

In the Sibalec dispute, pollution from a light bulb factory in Yogyakarta had contaminated ground water and the wells of nearby residents.[36] Despite laboratory tests of ground water confirming the residents' claims of pollution, Sibalic factory denied any culpability. The Health Department, when approached by local residents, also rejected the residents' claims, dismissing the pollution as the result of domestic waste (Siti Megadianty Adam 1997:32).

[36] This account is based on Siti Megadianty Adam 1997; Endra Waluyo, Bapedalda Yogyakarta, interview, 29-11-2000; Ari Suseta, LBH, Yogya, interview, 14-9-2000.

Increasing publicity about the matter prompted the district regent (*bupati*) to organize a meeting between the company and residents, but no agreement was reached. Subsequently the government at the provincial level (Special District of Yogyakarta) formed an investigative team, which produced evidence that the pollution had in fact originated from Sibalec factory.[37] Members of the team acted as mediators in subsequent negotiations between the community and company representatives. However, members of local NGOs that had been involved in the case were not permitted to participate in the negotiations, prompting some to question the impartiality of the mediators in taking such a stance (Siti Megadianty Adam 1997:34). Ultimately an agreement was reached between the parties, which included compensation, repair of waste management facilities and monitoring of water quality. Implementation of the agreement was partially successful, with compensation being paid in full but with some community dissatisfaction remaining in relation to implementation of the water monitoring initiatives (Siti Megadianty Adam 1997:37).

Naga Mas, Central Java 1994

In this case, a dispute arose between PT Naga Mas, a textile factory located in the Batang district of Central Java, and a community of nearby residents whose wells had allegedly been polluted by liquid waste discharged from the factory.[38] The factory, despite expanding its production in the 1980s, had not installed a waste management unit, and dumped untreated liquid and solid waste in the area surrounding the factory. In 1993 pollution levels increased and a community member made a written complaint to the Batang regent (Gita Pertiwi 2000a:2). An investigation by the Batang regional government in response to the complaint confirmed pollution of ground water and the wells by the factory, and recommended that PT Naga Mas install and operate a waste management unit to prevent further pollution.[39] This clear confirmation of pollution vindicated the residents' claims, yet progress in constructing the waste management unit had still not been made by the end of 1993.

Still seeking resolution of the dispute, community representatives took their complaint to the legislative assembly of Batang district. Shortly after this visit a further investigation was carried out, which confirmed 21 wells in Petodanan

37 Endra Waluyo, Bapedalda Yogyakarta, interview, 29-11-2000.

38 This account is based on Gita Pertiwi 2000a:4 and Takdir Rachmadi 1997c. The community consisted of 21 families located in Petodanan Baru village, Batang, Central Java. Residents reported changes in the smell, taste and colour of the well water which also produced skin irritations when used for washing. See Takdir Rachmadi 1997c:65.

39 Evidence of pollutants above regulatory limits was found in tests carried out by the Semarang Institute for Industrial Research and Development. See Gita Pertiwi 2000a:2.

village were polluted by waste from PT Naga Mas (Gita Pertiwi 2000a:3). The pollution received widespread coverage in the mass media, which acted as a further catalyst for government action. District government officials, encouraged by strong support from the Batang regent, convened a meeting between community and industry representatives and urged both parties to resolve the dispute through negotiation.[40] A mediation process commenced, with various district government officials acting as mediators in a manner considered sufficiently neutral by all parties. Negotiations were nonetheless protracted, dragging out eventually over a period of a year. At one point the residents, in frustration at the lack of progress, informed the regent that they had issued their legal authority to the Semarang Legal Aid Institute. This threat of legal action seemingly acted as a catalyst for the eventual agreement achieved by the two parties (Takdir Rachmadi 1997c:69). Pursuant to the final agreement, PT Naga Mas agreed to pay for installation of piped water to those families affected by the ground water pollution, and additionally pledged to reduce its waste discharge in compliance with regulatory limits. Subsequent to the agreement, piped water had indeed been supplied to the community. On the issue of continuing pollution, the community remained apprehensive, however, as the industry's waste management was to be supervised by government agencies without any community input or supervision (Takdir Rachmadi 1997c:71).

Ciujung River, West Java 1995

In the Ciujung River case, pollution from a group of five factories[41] on the Ciujung River in West Java had severely affected several villages since September 1992, the residents of which (approximately 5000) depended on the river for fishing, irrigation, prawn farming and other daily needs.[42] The residents' claims of pollution had been confirmed by research conducted by the national Environmental Impact Agency and the Centre for Fisheries Research and Development.[43] Local residents, represented by the

40 The district government itself had an extra incentive to resolve this dispute as it had been recommended as a recipient for the environmental 'Adipura' award and thus wished the case to be swiftly resolved so as not to compromise its chances in this respect. See Takdir Rachmadi 1997c:68.

41 The five factories were PT Indah Kiat Pulp and Paper, PT Cipta Paperia, PT Onward Paper Utama, PT Sekawan Maju Pesat, and PT Picon Jaya, all of which produced paper except the last which produced leather. See *District court North Jakarta* 1995.

42 This account is based on the following sources: *District court North Jakarta* 1995; Indonesian Centre for Environmental Law et al. 1995:7; Prihartono 1995:1-4; Mas Achmad Santosa and Yazid 1997; Yazid 1995:5 and a compilation of newspaper clippings.

43 *District court North Jakarta* 1995; Indonesian Centre for Environmental Law et al. 1995:7; Prihartono 1995:1-4.

Organization of Ciujung River Users, in conjunction with the Indonesian Centre for Environmental Law (ICEL) initially approached the five industries directly as well as the Serang district government, in an attempt to initiate a cooperative dispute resolution process. Whilst some limited negotiation was carried out with the smaller three of the five industries, the district government did not respond to the community's request and the attempt at initiating a comprehensive dispute resolution process failed.

Community representatives subsequently approached the national Environmental Impact Agency in January 1995, which prioritized the case and initiated a mediation process within the month.[44] The undertaking from the Environmental Impact Agency also followed written requests by ICEL and LBHS, on behalf of the community, that a mediation process be commenced pursuant to article 20 of the EMA 1982 (Yazid 1995:3). Yet despite a reported meeting between the agency and industry representatives, a mediation process did not eventuate and the agency appeared either unwilling or unable to take further action to this end. Representations were then undertaken by community and legal representatives to the West Java provincial and Serang district government. The provincial government failed to answer the community's request, whilst the Serang district government firmly refused to initiate a mediation process and instead disputed the community's claims.[45] The only action undertaken by the Serang local government was to order the closure of PT Sekawan Maju Pesat, the smallest company amongst the suspected polluters. NGOs viewed this as an attempt to scapegoat the smaller company and thus appease public sentiment, whilst avoiding action against the large, politically well-connected companies.[46] Further approaches by community representatives to the five industries were also unsuccessful in initiating a mediation process towards resolution of the dispute. The failure of efforts to mediate the dispute prompted community representatives to initiate a class action suit on 14 August 1995, representing 5000 residents in the Ciujung River area.[47]

The lack of government support in this case appeared to be the most important factor in the failure of mediation efforts (Indonesian Centre for Environmental Law et al. 1995:2). Whilst support for a cooperative dispute resolution process was initially promised by the national Environmental Impact Agency, this did not in fact materialize in any substantive sense. The provincial government (of West Java) also took no action in response to the

44 'Perlu dibentuk Tim terpadu untuk selesaikan masalah pencemaran Sungai Ciujung', *Kompas* 17-1-1995.

45 Indonesian Centre for Environmental Law et al. 1995:35.

46 'Tak adil jika hanya PT SMP yang ditindak', *Kompas*, 23-1-1995.

47 The case is discussed in Chapter II.

community's complaints, whilst the Serang district government other than closing the smallest company contributing to the pollution, actively opposed a mediation process and challenged the community's claims of pollution. In the absence of government pressure to enforce environmental regulations or resolve the dispute, there was correspondingly little pressure or incentive for the industries responsible for the pollution to enter a mediation process.

Samitex, Yogyakarta 1995

In this case, Samitex, a large textile industry located on the outskirts of Yogyakarta, had caused noise pollution and contamination of ground water in the nearby village of Panggunghardjo, Bantul.[48] Residents affected by the pollution reported it to local officials and, via legal representatives, contacted the factory but received no reply. The pollution claims were then reported to the Yogyakarta Environmental Bureau Investigation Team and also publicized through a press conference. Research carried out by the Technical Institute of Environmental Health (Balai Tehnik Kesehatan Lingkungan) subsequently confirmed the pollution. Following the failure of early negotiation efforts initiated by district officials, the assistance of the provincial Yogyakarta Environmental Bureau Investigation Team was requested by local officials and the legal representatives of the community.[49] The Investigation Team met initially with community representatives separately to discuss the results of research into the pollution. Subsequently a series of meetings involving both industry and community representatives was commenced. Despite early denial of its culpability, the company eventually accepted responsibility for the pollution in the light of the evidence provided by the Environmental Bureau of Health. In the final agreement reached between the community and PT Samitex, the company acknowledged the pollution, undertook to repair its waste management unit and moreover agreed to pay compensation, being the cost of installing drinking water facilities for the community. For its part, the community agreed not to take issue with the matter again so long as PT Samitex continued to fulfil its obligations (Adam and Takdir Rachmadi 1997:50).

A noticeable aspect of this case was the effective support and facilitation of the mediation process by the provincial level Yogyakarta Environmental Bureau Investigation Team. Prior to the team's intervention, PT Samitex had

48 This account is based on the following sources: Adam and Takdir Rachmadi 1997; Endra Waluyo, Bapedalda Yogyakarta, interview, 29-11-2000. Complaints by farmers over water pollution from the factory previously had led to the installation of a waste management unit. See Adam and Takdir Rachmadi 1997:47.

49 Endra Waluyo, interview, 29-11-2000.

ignored approaches by the community and local district officials to enter a mediation process. The availability of scientific evidence confirming the residents' allegations of pollution was also an influential factor in the company's final decision to acknowledge its responsibility for the pollution and meet the residents' claims.

Indo acidatama, Central Java 1997

The PT Indo Acidatama Chemical Industry (PT IACI) was established in 1988 and located in Kemiri village, Karanganyar, near the city of Solo (Surakarta) in Central Java. PT IACI is one of Central Java's five largest industries; known colloquially as the five 'gods' (*dewa*) of industry due to their political and economic influence (Kritis 1999).[50] The PT IACI factory produces a number of base chemicals including ethanol, methylated spirits, *asam asetat,* and *ethyl asetat*.[51] Waste products produced daily by the factory included solid waste from the fermentation process (2.5 tonnes), distilled liquid waste (500m^3), waste water (40 tonnes), liquid condensate and CO^2 (40 tonnes). Whilst a waste management unit was operated by the PT IACI factory, the capacity of the unit was insufficient to process all waste produced by the factory.[52] Data compiled by the Environmental Impact Agency of Central Java during 1998 indicated that waste discharged from the factory was well in excess of stipulated standards. Liquid waste was often disposed into the Sroyo River, which the residents of the nearby village of Kanten also utilized as a source of water for agriculture and their daily needs.[53] In 1991 PT IACI also offered waste water from its factory to the farmers of nearby Kanten, Ngelom and Ngeldok village for use on their fields as 'liquid fertilizer'. The 'liquid fertilizer' was piped from the factory to the fields where it was used for a period of six and a half years. Initially, agricultural output from the land increased, apparently due to the high nitrogen content of the effluent. However, after only three harvests the rice crop declined until it repeatedly failed. The soil hardened to the point where other crops could also no longer be successfully planted.[54]

In 1997 the pipe which distributed the liquid effluent to the fields was cut

50 This account is based on interviews and written materials gathered during fieldwork in 2001.

51 Approximately 18,000,000 litres of ethanol, 12 million litres of *asam asetat*, 4.5 million litres of *ethyl asetat* and 1.26 million litres of methylated spirits are produced annually from the factory. See BHS 1999a.

52 This fact was acknowledged by the factory itself in one of its environmental evaluations (PEL). See LBH-Semarang 1999.

53 Farmers from Kanten village pumped water from the Sroyo River to irrigate two crops (usually rice and peanuts) in the year. See LBH-Semarang 1999.

54 Pak Bayan, interview, 9-4-2001.

and blocked by a group of farmers. As a result of wider community concern over the environmental impact of the PT IACI factory, an environmental community organization (Aksi Rakyat Peduli Lingkungan) was also formed around this time. Other environmental issues besides the impact of the waste fertilizer included the offensive odour from the factory, the disposal of liquid waste into the Sroyo River, and the dumping of solid waste in the area surrounding the factory. Due to increased community pressure a 'team of nine' was formed to resolve environmental issues connected with the factory's operation. The team initially consisted of three industry representatives, three community representatives and three government (civil and military) representatives. However, due to considerable community opposition to the composition of the team this was changed to three industry representatives, four community representatives and two additional members considered neutral by both parties. The team's mandate included resolving the problem of odour from the factory and the payment of compensation to farmers whose land had been polluted by the use of the liquid waste fertilizer. The team failed, however, to make satisfactory progress in resolving these issues. Undertakings by PT IACI to the team to reduce the odour were not met, resulting in community demonstrations and threats to blockade the factory. The team of nine also made little headway on the issue of compensation, prompting the farmers to pursue the matter independently.

The group of Kanten farmers subsequently decided to negotiate directly with PT IACI on the issue of compensation, and requested the assistance of the Legal Aid Institute of Semarang (LBHS) in doing so. In response, LBHS together with the Indonesian Centre for Environmental Law (ICEL) facilitated a training in negotiation and advocacy for the farmers (LBHS 1999a). Following the training the Kanten farmers sent a letter to PT IACI and various government agencies, criticizing the industry's failure to resolve the issue of compensation for the environmental damage caused to the farmers' land. A meeting between stakeholders including PT IACI, the farmers and the mediation 'team of nine' was held, but ended in the farmers staging a walkout due to the absence of PT IACI's director. Finally, following a further meeting and several demonstrations by community members, an agreement was reached providing for the payment of Rp 751,641,595 compensation to the farmers (*Cooperative agreement* 1999).

Whilst the final agreement was not intended to address all issues connected with the factory's operation, one visible shortcoming was its exclusive focus on the pecuniary matter of compensation and its failure to incorporate issues of environmental management or restoration. Although the agreement compensated farmers for their lost income due to failed crops, no provision was made for environmental restoration of the land. Other environmental issues connected with the factory's operation, such as air and water pollution, were also not addressed and were reported to have continued following the agreement.[55] Nonetheless, the agreement still purported to be a 'final, comprehensive resolution' and thus a potential obstacle to further claims related to unresolved environmental issues.

PT Sumber Sehat, Kudus 1999

This dispute involved a milk processing industry named Sumber Sehat ('source of health') located in Kudus, Central Java.[56] The factory was first established in 1948, at which time the area surrounding the factory was only sparsely populated. Over time, however, the factory was enveloped by the expanding city of Kudus, until it was eventually surrounded by a densely populated residential area. The dispute between the industry and residents adjoining the factory concerned waste from the industry's livestock, which had caused air and ground water pollution.[57] In 1994 negotiations were held between residents adjoining the factory and the industry. Whilst the negotiations failed to resolve the pollution issue, the industry management did undertake to install piped water to a local mosque. When, however, pollution of ground water prompted residents to attempt to utilize the piped water for their personal needs, industry management insisted they pay for the service themselves.

In 1999, legal representatives for the aggrieved neighbours of PT Sumber Sehat sent a written complaint to the regent of Kudus, requesting a mediation process be commenced to try and resolve the dispute. In response, officials from the regional government's environmental agency agreed to facilitate a mediation process between the disputing parties. After several meetings, the parties were successful in finalising a written agreement, which was signed on 21 May 1999.[58] The agreement provided for the relocation of Sumber Sehat's factory within a period of six months. Before its relocation the industry was obliged to properly manage its waste to avoid further pollution and to rehabilitate the factory site. The industry also undertook to provide two piped water outlets for local residents until the relocation had been carried out.[59]

This small scale dispute presents as a successful example of environmental mediation. The residents in this case were assisted by representation by a

55 Asianto and Waluyo, IACI, interview, 27-2-2001.

56 This account is based on fieldwork carried out in November 2000 including interviews and compilation of written materials.

57 Bambang, Lala and Yusuf, interviews at YAPHI, Kudus, 3-11-2000 and 4-11-2000.

58 *Agreement to resolve dispute between Denmaan Village* 1999.

59 Warga RT 02/VII desa Demaan, Kudus and PT Sumber Sehat 1999.

legal aid office, who conveyed the initial complaints to the regent of Kudus. The amenability of the small industry to relocation appears also to have been critical to the success of dispute resolution. The terms of the agreement were subsequently implemented with residents being provided with piped water outlets as agreed. Ultimately, the factory closed its business and thus relocation was not necessary.[60]

PT Pura, Kudus 1999

This dispute concerned pollution from PT Pura, the largest paper and printing factory in Southeast Asia, located near Kudus, Central Java.[61] Waste discharged from the factory, which commenced operations in 1990, caused pollution and environmental damage in the nearby village of Pladen from 1992-1999.[62] Liquid waste from the factory damaged large areas of rice paddies, killed livestock as well as fish in local waterways, contaminated residents' wells and resulted in a range of health complaints.[63] A statement by an official from the regional Environmental Agency confirmed that PT Pura's waste management had been inadequate during that period, and that untreated waste was frequently discharged – particularly at night.[64] Residents' protests were stifled by intimidation prior to 1998 and were first openly voiced in demonstrations in July 1998.[65] On 10 June 1999 a claim for compensation of environmental damage and environmental rehabilitation was conveyed to PT Pura on behalf of 77 residents of Pladen village.[66] Residents claimed Rp 275,625,376 for damage caused by pollution occuring between 1992 and 1999, in addition to improved environmental management. An initial meeting with industry representatives in June 1999 resulted in assurances from PT Pura that its discharged waste would satisfy regulatory standards within two months. Industry representatives also requested evidence of the pollution and resulting damage before considering the residents' claims for compensation.[67] In July 1999 the claim was extended to encompass a further 159 claimants, whilst the compensation claimed was increased to Rp 1.4 billion, an amount criticized by PT Pura as excessive and unsubstantiated.[68] After

60 Lusila Anjela Bodroani, interview, 18-11-2003.

61 This account is based on fieldwork carried out in November 2000 including interviews and compilation of written materials.

62 Bambang, Lala and Yusuf, interviews at YAPHI, Kudus, 3-11-2000 and 4-11-2000.

63 'Korban pencemaran tuntut Rp 275.6 juta', *Suara Merdeka*, 10-7-1999; 'Pabrik Uang' dituntut Rp 1,48m', *Wawasan*, 29-7-1999.

64 'Tak mungkin 24 jam awasi pencemaran', *Suara Merdeka*, 18-6-1999.

65 'Gugat PT PNP warga "ancam"', *Jakeng Pos*, 10-8-1999.

66 '77 Warga tuntut Pura Group', *Suara Merdeka*, 17-6-1999.

67 'PT Pura Jamin Limbah bebas pencemaran', *Suara Merdeka*, 26-6-1999.

68 'Pabrik Uang' dituntut Rp 1,48m', *Wawasan*, 29-7-1999.

a stalemate of several months, negotiations recommenced between PT Pura and the Pladen claimants at the industry's instigation. A series of ten meetings was held, chaired by the legal representatives for the Pladen residents.[69] Finally, in January 2000 an agreement was reached and signed by representatives of both parties. The agreement provided for payment of Rp 78 million compensation by PT Pura to the residents of Pladen village who had suffered environmental damage as a result of the pollution. The agreement also provided for a cooperative approach to environmental management, allowing for ongoing community monitoring of industry waste management practices (*Cooperative agreement* 2000). According to subsequent accounts, environmental management remained adequate and no further conflict between the local community and PT Pura was reported.[70]

Kanasritex, Semarang 1999

The dispute in this case centred on the disposal of liquid effluent from a textile factory, PT Kanasritex, located in Pringapus village near Semarang in Central Java.[71] The PT Kanasritex factory, established in 1993, produced towels for export to over fifty different countries. The estimated liquid waste produced by the factory was approximately 800/m^3 per day (LBHS 2000b). Whilst the factory owned and claimed to operate a waste management unit (Gunawan 1999:1), conflict arose in March 1999 over the lack of a permanent waste channel through which the high volumes of treated waste water could be disposed. According to the farmers, the factory's effluent had caused pollution in the surrounding fields and the consequent failure of rice harvests, in addition to damaging adjoining roads. Eddy Gunawan, the manager of PT Kanasritex, denied the factory had caused pollution and emphasized that the factory had, since its inception, operated a state-of-the-art waste management unit and complied with regulatory waste standards. He did acknowledge, however, that the channel utilized by PT Kanasritex and other factories for the disposal of waste water tended to flood into adjoining rice paddies in periods of heavy rain (Gunawan 1999:3). Mr Gunawan attributed this to the regional government's failure to provide a permanent waste channel as was required in an industrial area (Gunawan 1999:4).

Some farmers had attempted to remedy the situation by building a wall blocking the factory's waste disposal into the adjoining rice paddies. However, this attempt failed, as the effluent was then disposed into a roadside ditch, and still entered the paddy fields when it rained. The group of

69 Bambang, Lala and Yusuf, interviews at YAPHI, Kudus, 3-11-2000 and 4-11-2000.

70 Lusila Anjela Bodroani, interview, 18-11-2003.

71 Account based on LBHS 2000b and Gunawan 1999.

farmers, assisted by one of their number who had followed a environmental para-legal training course and by the Legal Aid Institute of Semarang (LBHS), then attempted to resolve the matter through a mediation process. The key demands of the farmers were that PT Kanasritex construct a permanent waste disposal channel, pay compensation for lost harvests, restore irrigation channels closed since the factory's construction, and allow community monitoring of the factory's waste management (LBHS 2000b:9).

In an initial meeting between the industry, farmers and several government agencies, PT Kanasritex attributed the environmental damage to heavy rains and effluent discharged from other factories, and refused the farmers' demands. The profile of the dispute was then raised by the farmers who appointed LBHS as legal representatives and publicized the issue in the mass media. Reports of the pollution and related conflict in two national newspapers prompted responses from several government agencies. The National Environmental Impact Agency directed its provincial counterpart in Semarang to manage the dispute. The regional police contacted the farmers and LBHS, advising that the matter would be most appropriately managed through a process of investigation and, if necessary, prosecution (LBHS 2000b:10). The farmers subsequently met with the national Environmental Impact Agency, which agreed to support the request for construction of a permanent waste channel. Subsequently, on 12 April 1999, a meeting was convened between local and district government officials, industry and community representatives to discuss the problem (LBHS 2000b:14). Somewhat unusually, the government officials present tended to support the community rather than industry position. The regional military representative stated that he had been instructed to resolve the dispute to prevent any further conflict in the volatile pre-election period. In principle, the industry then agreed to fulfil the community's demands, with the condition that compensation would only be paid if the community withdrew legal authority from the LBHS. Ultimately compensation was not paid, but the community were satisfied that their other conditions, including the construction of a permanent waste channel, had been met at the factory's expense (LBHS 2000b:15).

The successful outcome of mediation in this case may be attributed to several factors. Effective community organization, legal representation and widespread publicity of the dispute in the mass media appeared to influence the industry's response and strengthen the community's bargaining position. The community's demands for construction of a waste disposal channel were also supported in this case by government officials at both a national and regional level. The relatively limited scope of the dispute, which centred on the construction of a permanent channel for the disposal of waste water, also made it ultimately more amenable to a mediated solution.

Tawang Mas, Semarang 2000

Tawang Mas is a village located in West Semarang, Central Java.[72] The village economy was, before 1987 at least, largely based on fishing and traditional fishpond farming.[73] In 1985, the Central Java government announced the development of a large tourist park and conference centre. The project, which was to be located near Tawang Mas, was estimated to require some 108 hectares of land.[74] The land designated as a site for the project was home to a number of fishponds operated by residents of Tawang Mas. In 1985 the farmers were pressured into surrendering their land for rates well below the market value of the land. Opposition to the development resulted in physical intimidation and threats.[75] A village cemetery of 2 hectares was also resumed by the developer on the pretext of construction of a road, yet the area was in fact utilized for a private housing estate. As development of the site commenced, in 1985 all fishponds in the area were excavated regardless of whether the respective owners had in fact been compensated or not. The development works also resulted, without prior consultation with community, in the closure of the Tawang Mas River. Community leaders conveyed their complaints to the Interior Minister, and the river was reopened. However, in 1987, the river was again blocked off. This was justified as a temporary closure that was to last only three months. Access of fishermen to the sea during this time was cut off, and compensation of only Rp 7000 was given to those fishermen whose vessels were stranded at sea for this three month period.[76] The Tawang Mas River was never in fact reopened in its original course, but rather redirected to a western flood canal. Redirection of the river to the canal contributed to periodic, severe flooding in the area of Tawang Mas and the PRPP development itself. Local fishermen, numbering around 300, also lost their access to the ocean and, as a result, their livelihood.[77] The project itself enjoyed high-level political support, as the developers, PT Puri Sakti and PT Indo Perkasa Usahatama (PT IPU), were both companies owned by Ganang

72 This account is based on fieldwork carried out in November 2000 including interviews and compilation of written materials.

73 The area was reknowned in Central Java for its production of high quality *terasi,* a condiment made from pounded and fermented shrimp or small fish.

74 In fact only 10 ha of land were used for the development. The remainder of the land was sold to private developers who constructed two exclusive housing estates and a cinema complex. See Kritis 2000.

75 In 1986 one vocal community leader was jailed without trial for a period of one year. See Bagyo Nurchayo 2000b.

76 The vessels stranded at sea because of the river's temporary closure were damaged beyond repair as a result.

77 'Hak nelayan tercabut', *Kompas,* 25-3-2000.

Ismail, the son of the then governor of Central Java H.M. Ismail.[78]

Yet, whilst intimidation may have suppressed opposition temporarily, the dispute soon resurfaced following the fall of the New Order and the advent of *reformasi*. The more permissive political context served to strengthen the aspirations of the villagers to resolve the dispute. In February 2000 the residents of Tawang Mas formed a community organization – the Tawang Mas Communication Forum. This group, together with other community representatives, resolved to convey its complaints to the Semarang legislature. On 21 February 2000, a group of eight hundred Tawang Mas residents, led by representatives of the Tawang Mas Communication Forum, presented a number of demands to the Semarang legislature (Kritis 2000). Foremost amongst these was that the Tawang Mas River be returned to its original course to the sea. A group of fishermen also demanded compensation for damage to their vessels caused by closure of the river and lost income.[79] A representative member of the legislature promised to facilitate negotiations between the Tawang Mas residents and PT IPU within three weeks.[80]

In the period April-June 2000 a legislative hearing and negotiation process was facilitated by members of the Commission A, Semarang legislature. The initial meeting was held on 13 April 2000 between representatives of the Tawang Mas Communication Forum, Semarang municipality officials, members of the legislature and industry representatives. Representatives of the Tawang Mas Communication Forum were not invited to a subsequent meeting held on 4 May, at which Tawang Mas residents were formally represented by the village head. After learning of this exclusion, forum representatives protested to the legislature and were promised a meeting with legislative members on 16 May (Makmun 2000). When this meeting did not eventuate, a group of angry residents protested outside a cinema in Semarang, which had been built in the previous course of the Tawang Mas River. Protestors tore up paving outside the cinema and fought with police, resulting in the arrest of several protestors.[81] The incident was widely reported in regional newspapers, with several commentators empathising with the plight of the Tawang Mas residents, many of whom had suffered flooding and/or been

78 Bagyo Nurchayo 2000c. The project itself turned out to be something of a failure. The tourist park cum exhibition centre was constructed but rarely used. Over time it fell into disrepair due to its inability to generate sufficient income to cover maintenance costs. See Bagyo Nurchayo 2000a.

79 The compensation amounts claimed were Rp 1 million for each vessel and lost income of Rp 10,000/day/person or a total of Rp 13,746 billion. See 'Buntu kaliku, banjir kampungku', *Suara Merdeka*, 22-2-2000.

80 'Buntu kaliku, banjir kampungku', *Suara Merdeka*, 22-2-2000.

81 'Warga Tawang mas Ngamuk; Bioskop dirusak, polisi babak belur', *Kedaulatan Rakyat*, 17-5-2000.

deprived of a livelihood since the redirection of the river in 1987.[82] Shortly after the protests, following heavy rains, severe flooding was again experienced in the Tawang Mas and recreation park vicinity. Negotiations facilitated by Commission A of the Semarang legislature recommenced following the protests and renewed flooding. Industry representatives and legislative members subsequently acceded to community demands that the Tawang Mas River be returned to its original course, although this was made contingent upon a feasibility study by the Semarang Department of Public Works. Following its study, the Department recommended the installation of several pumping stations to temporarily alleviate flooding in the Tawang Mas area. It stated that redirection of the river would require further feasibility studies, considerable expense and would not necessarily solve the problems of flooding and erosion.[83] Community representatives, however, argued that the suggested measures would not solve the problem of flooding and insisted on the redirection of the Tawang Mas River to its original course. The lengthy and often volatile negotiations continued until on 14 June 2000 an agreement was finally reached between the parties.[84] According to the agreement negotiated, the river would be returned to its original course. Implementation would be carried out by an integrated team of experts comprising community, government and industry representatives. The team would address the various technical, financial, legal and social issues necessary for implementation of this task.[85] Whilst the agreement was a breakthrough in negotiations, doubt was cast on its implementation when PT IPU, the developer originally responsible for the river's redirection, reneged on its undertaking to return the river to its original course, refusing to join the expert team as agreed. A legislative member who had participated in the negotiations accused PT IPU of undermining the legislature's authority and threatened to report the company to the police.[86] Community representatives reacted with anger at the industry's refusal to implement the agreement, even threatening holy war (*jihad*) against the company should it fail to comply.[87] Finally, in the face of community and administrative pressure from the mayor of Semarang, PT IPU acceded to joining the expert team in accordance with the agreement, although it indicated it should not be responsible for financing the project.[88] By mid-July a coordinator of the expert team had been appointed, from the

82 Edi 2000; 'Mengapa mereka marah', *Radar Semarang*, 18-5-2000.
83 'DPU akan pasang tiga pompa', *Suara Merdeka*, 20-5-2000.
84 'Tawang Mas akan diluruskan', *Solo Post*, 16-6-2000.
85 'Berita acara hasil rapat komisi "A" DPRD Kota Semarang', 30-6-2000.
86 'Dewan merasa dilecehkan PT IPU', *Solo Post*, 23-6-2000.
87 'Meski alot, tim terpadu kasus Tawang Mas terbentuk', *Wawasan*, 1-6-2000.
88 'Pengembang diminta segera bentuk tim penyelesaian', *Wawasan*, 25-6-2000.

university Unika Soegijopranoto, and discussions on the team's work commenced. Yet by October 2000 no substantive progress toward implementing the proposed solution had been made. Frustrated with the lack of progress, community representatives reported the case to the National Human Rights Commission in November 2000, and in January 2001 the case was also reported to the president.

The Tawang Mas case is a complex dispute that probably could have been avoided if the original development had complied with environmental, spatial planning and consultation requirements. The mediation process in this case was unique in that it was conducted and facilitated by a commission of the regional (Semarang) legislature. The strong community pressure, large demonstrations and high media profile of this dispute certainly played an important role in initiating and expediting a mediation-based dispute resolution process. However, the tangible threat of community violence also seemingly played a role in escalating the conflict, prompting criticism from some local legal commentators who feared threats of 'mass action' could undermine the legal process.[89] The refusal of community representatives to consider any options other than redirection of the river also narrowed the potential scope of compromise in this case. Ultimately, however, agreement was reached on redirection of the river, an outcome apparently facilitated by support from the Semarang mayor for this solution. The apparently successful outcome of mediation in this case, however, has not yet been realized through implementation, illustrating a common problem in environmental mediation cases in Indonesia.

Kelian Equatorial Mining, 2001

The Kelian Equatorial Mine (PT KEM), located in Kalimantan, is 90% owned by Rio Tinto, the world's largest mining company.[90] The mine, which commenced operations in 1992, is estimated to produce 14 tonnes of gold annually. The main waste product from the 'cyanide heap-leaching' mining process is contaminated tailings, which are held in a dam before being treated in a 'polishing pond' and then discharged into the Kelian River (Lynch and Harwell 2002:67). Whilst the company claims the discharged water complies with environmental regulations, locals allege pollution from the mine has killed off fish in the river and causes various health complaints when the water is used for everyday needs.[91]

89 'Kaidah hukum perlu diperhatikan, jangan asal "pokoke"', *Wawasan*, 20-6-2000.

90 This account is based on the following sources: Endi Biaro 2000; Siti Maimunah 2002; Chalid Muhammed 2002; Kelian Equatorial Mining 2003:2; Lynch and Harwell 2002:67-9.

91 Endi Biaro 2000; Kelian Equatorial Mining 2003:2; Lynch and Harwell 2002:68; Chalid Muhammed 2002.

Local opposition to the mine began not long after operations were commenced in 1992. Conflict between the local community and the mining company centred on issues relating to traditional mining, land compensation, human rights abuses and pollution. In 1997 the dispute first attracted widespread publicity after a report providing details of human rights abuses was submitted to the National Human Rights Commission (Endi Biaro 2000). In 1998 an international campaign against PT KEM and Rio Tinto was organized by a coalition of NGOs. A local community leader and outspoken critic of PT KEM, Pius Erik Nyompe, was invited to travel to Australia and publicize the community's case, where he also met with senior management of Rio Tinto in Melbourne. After this visit, and a presentation of community demands at the annual Rio Tinto shareholder meetings in London and Melbourne in 1998, PT KEM agreed to enter into negotiations with the local community, represented by the Institution for the Welfare of Mining Community and Environment (Lembaga Kesejahteraan Masyarakat Tambang dan Lingkungan, LKMTL), a local NGO. An agreement to mediate, to which Rio Tinto and the national environmental group WALHI were also party, was signed on 25 April 1998. The parties to the agreement agreed to address through negotiation a range of issues including land compensation, alleged human rights abuses, pollution, traditional mining, and plans for the mine's closure.

Initial progress was evident after several mediation sessions. In June 1998 a preliminary agreement was reached regarding the issue of compensation for land used by PT KEM, and a timetable stipulated for the agreement's implementation. In September 1998 the industry agreed to supply electricity to Tutung village where a number of locals had been relocated. In January 1999 the parties agreed to an independent investigation to be carried out into the alleged human rights abuses, and PT KEM also undertook to seal a road leading to the mine site and so reduce the problem of air pollution caused by dust from the road (Chalid Muhammed 2002).

By early 2000, however, progress in the mediation process had apparently stalled. Differences persisted over data relating to land compensation, and the agreements relating to electricity and road improvement made in 1998 had still not been implemented. When PT KEM commenced negotiations with another group of community representatives – called the Tim Murni[92] – chosen and backed by the local district head, the first community group LKMTL accused the mining company of betraying the terms and spirit of the April 1998 agreement and attempting to divide the community.[93] According

92 This second group was called the Tim Murni ('Pure Team') apparently in reference to the allegations of corruption levelled by PT KEM at the original community group LKMTL.

93 Industry representatives accused LKTML of corruption and mismanagement. See Siti Maimunah 2002.

to LKMTL, PT KEM had originally agreed to negotiate with LKMTL as the sole community representative. On this basis LKMTL had subsequently obtained letters of authority (*surat kuasa*) from all community members who wished to claim compensation (Chalid Muhammed 2002:9). The industry also endeavoured to include the regional government in the mediation process, whilst community representatives claimed it was originally agreed not to do so. Community representatives (from LKMTL) subsequently criticized the regent (of West Kutai), who they claimed had attempted to dominate mediation proceedings. As a result, the regional government refused to participate in negotiations with LKMTL, and instead proceeded in negotiations with the newly formed Tim Murni, which had the backing of the local district head.[94]

The failure to realize the agreements reached early in the mediation process, and the escalating conflict over community representation, prompted protests and a blockade of the PT KEM mine site in April 2000. The blockade persisted for a period of three months, resulting in the temporary closure of the mine during this period. Following the intervention of mediators in June 2000 the blockade was lifted and a mediation process between the various parties was recommenced. Besides PT KEM and LKMTL, the mediation process also now involved the government of West Kutai, Rio Tinto Indonesia, the National Human Rights Commission, and an Australian federal court judge (Marcus Einfield). Despite continuing differences over the involvement of the Tim Murni,[95] a protocol was agreed upon in March 2001, and in September 2001 a Rp 60 billion compensation package was finalized by the parties (Kelian Equatorial Mining 2003:1). The compensation payment related to land utilized by PT KEM in the course of its operations, damage to land along the access road, plants and grave sites, alleged promises by the company to provide houses and livelihoods, and human rights violations (Kelian Equatorial Mining 2003:2). By May 2003, PT KEM reported having already paid Rp 34.7 billion compensation in the period 2000-2003 for claims covered in the agreement.[96] The company had also reportedly implemented its previous commitments to provide electricity to Tutung village at a cost of Rp 2.5 billion and to seal sections of the road between the minesite and Jelemeq port at a cost of 14 billion.[97] In relation to pollution, the company had imple-

[94] Representatives of LKMTL alleged the Tim Murni was financially backed by PT KEM and a deliberate tactic to undermine LKMTL's position in negotiations. See Chalid Muhammed 2002:5.

[95] These differences led to WALHI's withdrawal from the negotiation process in October 2000, in protest over the company's allegedly divisive tactics which WALHI claimed were contrary to the terms and spirit of the original agreement.

[96] The compay had also made payments of compensation prior to 2000 (relating to similar issues) that totalled Rp 7.7 billion. See Kelian Equatorial Mining 2003:2.

[97] Kelian Equatorial Mining 2003:2. However, according to community representatives, these

mented what it described as a 'stringent environmental management system to minimize the impact of its operations' (Kelian Equatorial Mining 2003:2) and there had been no further pollution related claims from local residents.

In the PT KEM dispute, the role of community and non-government organizations appears to have been significant in the dispute resolution process. Mediation was commenced after local residents' claims received national and international publicity. Representation and advocacy of residents' interests during the mediation process was coordinated by a local community organization (LKMTL). The effect of the three month blockade, which adversely affected both PT KEM and local communities, also appears to have acted as a catalyst for compromise, resulting in the final settlement package. To date, implementation of the agreement is progressing as planned, although the process is ongoing.

Conclusion

This chapter has provided a preliminary overview of environmental mediation in Indonesia. As discussed above, existing traditions of consensus-based dispute resolution, *musyawarah,* have provided a cultural foundation for the introduction and socialization of mediation in Indonesia. The relevance of these traditions is limited in practice, however, as the social and political dynamics of environmental conflict vary significantly from the more circumscribed social context of *musyawarah* at the village level. Mediation in environmental disputes now has a legislative basis, however, found in article 30-33 of the EMA 1997 and, more recently, Government Regulation No. 54 of 2000. Under this new legal framework mediation is now a voluntary choice open to disputing parties, and its implementation does not depend on either further implementing regulations or government investigation as was the case under the previous EMA of 1982.

How effective was mediation in resolving the environmental disputes surveyed in this chapter? In thirteen of the fifteen cases examined, the disputing parties were successful in concluding a written agreement as a basis for resolving the dispute. Yet whilst written agreements were reached between parties in a high percentage (87%) of cases reviewed, this did not always result in resolution of the dispute from a private or public interest perspective. In nine of the cases (60%) reviewed, compensation was paid by the polluting industry to the claimants who had suffered the effects of the pol-

two projects were both carried out several years later than was originally agreed. See Chalid Muhammed 2002:8.

lution. Mediation thus appears to have been relatively effective as a means for obtaining compensation, especially when compared to the litigation cases surveyed in Chapter II. However, even where a written agreement was concluded and compensation was paid, conflict between the disputing parties still continued in seven of the fifteen cases (47%). Similarly, mediation was not consistently effective in addressing issues of environmental management, as in seven of the fifteen cases (47%) examined, there were reports of continuing pollution or unsatisfactory environmental rehabilitation. Whilst polluting industries in a majority of cases were willing to pay compensation to end the dispute, this was not always matched by a commitment to improved environmental management or rehabilitation in the longer term. Indeed, the over-emphasis of environmental mediation on pecuniary remedies was noted by several environmentalists interviewed by the author.[98]

From this preliminary overview of environmental mediation cases, it is also possible to identify a number of key variables which influence the outcome of the mediation process. Firstly, the role of NGOs in facilitating the process of community organization, institutionalization and representation before and during the mediation process appears significant. Typically, the victims of environmental pollution and damage are communities with few social, economic or political resources. Initial responses from such communities to pollution are usually ad hoc, poorly organized and mostly unsuccessful. Commonly, as occurred in the majority of cases discussed above, environmentally related claims are met initially with indifference, denials or intimidation from industry and government agencies. If a community is to proceed further, a high degree of community solidarity, institutionalization and effective representation is necessary. Community representatives must in turn become skilled at lobbying a wide range of government agencies, negotiating with industry and utilizing the mass media to gain exposure and support for their case. In practice, most of these tasks are undertaken in conjunction with NGOs at the local, regional, national and occasionally even international level. The involvement of NGOs is thus usually of critical importance, from the community perspective, for a successful outcome to the environmental dispute resolution process. This was certainly the case in the Tapak River dispute (1991), where a national network of NGOs threatening a boycott action was a vital catalyst in the dispute resolution process. In the PT Pura (1991) and Sumber Sehat (1999) cases, residents were assisted by legal aid advocates in conveying their claims to industry and government agencies. In the Indo Acidatama case (1997), the farmers received intensive training in

[98] Adi Nugroho (Gita Pertiwi, Solo), interview regarding Babon and Banger River cases, 20-12-2000.

advocacy and negotiation before successfully negotiating an agreement with the industry. Similarly, in the Kanasritex case (1999) the advocacy and mediation process was facilitated by a farmer who had completed environmental paralegal training, in conjunction with the Legal Aid Institute of Semarang (LBHS). In the Kelian Equatorial Mining case (2001), NGO advocacy at the local, national and international levels was significant in initiating mediation and influencing its final outcome. It is through such processes of mobilization, representation and networking that the substantial power imbalance that usually exists between victim and polluter can be at least partially redressed, and the process of mediation and dispute resolution thus further facilitated.

In the mediation cases surveyed, the role of government agencies was also an important factor in influencing the outcome and success of environmental mediation. In this respect it is necessary to differentiate between government agencies at the national, provincial and district levels. At the national level the central Environmental Impact Agency provided important support for the mediation process in the Sambong (1993), Tembok Dukuh (1991), Ciujung River (1995), Siak River (1992) and Kanasritex cases. At the provincial level support for the mediation process also appeared to be an important factor in facilitating a successful outcome in the Sambong, Sibalec (1994), Naga Mas (1994), Samitex (1995) and Sumber Sehat cases. Equally, where support for mediation was lacking at the provincial government level, the mediation process appeared much less likely to succeed. In the Siak River case, for example, the failure to involve the Riau provincial government contributed to the unsatisfactory implementation of the mediated agreement. District governments also displayed a greater tendency to support industry interests and demonstrated less support for the dispute resolution process than the provincial or national level agencies. In the Ciujung River case a mediation process was not commenced due to a lack of support from the Serang district government. In the Tembok Dukuh case district officials supported a mediation process, but strongly pressured the claimants to accept settlement offers from industry. In the Samitex case district officials responded to the community's request for mediation, but were unsuccessful in convincing the industry, PT Samitex, to participate. In the Tyfountex case (1992) the regent of Sukoharjo directly undermined the outcome of a mediation process by disbanding the organization that had represented local residents. Where, however, the district government did support the dispute resolution process this was usually a significant factor in a successful outcome. For example, in the Kanasritex case the support of the district government for the community's claim was an important factor in the final agreement reached. Similarly, in the Tawang Mas case (2000) the support of the Semarang mayor for the community's claim to redirect the river was significant in bringing the industry to a final agreement.

Frequently, government authorities also acted as mediators in the dispute resolution process. In some cases, such as the Naga Mas dispute, both parties considered the government mediation satisfactory and sufficiently impartial. In certain cases the seniority and status of the government official acting as mediator appeared to have a positive influence on the mediation process. For instance, in the Tembok Dukuh case the personal intervention by a senior official of the national Environmental Impact Agency as mediator was significant in facilitating a preliminary agreement. However in other instances, such as later during the Tembok Dukuh dispute, government officials exerted strong pressure on community representatives to accept offers made by industry. In this respect, the implementation of Government Regulation No. 54 of 2000 is of considerable relevance, as the provision of independent, qualified mediators may help to improve the quality and impartiality of environmental mediation in practice.

The process of mediation is a voluntary one and ultimately its success depends on the willingness of both parties to compromise in order to reach an agreement. As discussed in Chapter I, a party is unlikely to be willing to compromise if that party is able to unilaterally achieve its aims. This is a recurrent problem in the practice of environmental mediation in Indonesia. A small community's claim for compensation or environmental restoration may pose little threat to a well-connected industry quite capable of continuing operations despite the community's opposition. In several of the cases reviewed above, industries responded in a 'power-based' manner, seeking to 'resolve' the dispute by stonewalling, using government influence or intimidation rather than through an interest-based mediation process. For example, in the Tyfountex case the industry appeared to use mediation only as a temporary tactic of appeasement, before resorting to intimidation and power politics to undermine the community's position. The more powerful party is only likely to compromise where this power imbalance is redressed and there is some threat of an alternative sanction. This may be the threat of direct action by community members, adverse publicity in the mass media, a blockade by NGOs or pressure from a government agency. This was particularly evident in the Tapak River case where the long-running problem of pollution was only addressed through mediation after an organized boycott of the companies threatened adverse publicity. In the Naga Mas dispute, widespread publicity of the pollution prompted more rapid government action in facilitating a mediation process. In the Kelian Equatorial Mining case an international campaign by NGOs and accompanying publicity was an important step in initiating a mediation process. The willingness of polluting industries to compromise will of course be influenced by the wider administrative and legal context. Where continuing pollution from an industry is unlikely to result in either administrative sanction or judicial enforcement of environmental law then the polluting industry will be under little pressure to modify its behaviour.

In those cases where sufficient incentive has existed for both parties to reach an agreement, subsequent implementation of the agreement in the longer term has still frequently proven to be a problem. In some cases mediation appears to have been utilized merely as a tool of appeasement, as in the Tyfountex case where two agreements were reached yet never implemented. In other cases implementation of environmental monitoring is only partial, as in the Tapak River and Siak River disputes. Typically, demands of a more private or pecuniary nature, such as compensation or provision of drinking water, when agreed upon in a mediated agreement, tended to be implemented. More problematic was the public issue of pollution prevention and sustainability, which requires a continued commitment from industry in addition to governmental or industry monitoring. Yet to be truly successful as a path of environmental dispute resolution, mediation must address more than just the private pecuniary interests of the parties involved; mechanisms must also be created to ensure adequate implementation of all aspects of agreements, involving the participation of all stakeholders and invoking legal or administrative sanction where necessary. Thus, the implementation of mediated agreements is ultimately dependent on the efficacy and enforceability of legal and administrative sanctions for pollution and environmental damage.

CHAPTER V

Case studies of environmental mediation

This chapter presents two detailed case studies of environmental mediation in Indonesia that are intended to complement the overview of cases provided in the previous chapter. In each case study, the mediation process is contextualized in the broader dynamics and circumstances of the dispute, which are explored in substantial detail. The efficacy of the mediation process is then considered in relation to the principles of mediation theory outlined in Chapter I.

The Palur Raya dispute

History of dispute

PT Palur Raya is a factory that produces the food additive mono-sodium glutamate (MSG), having commenced its operations in 1987. Located in the regency of Karanganyar in the province of Central Java, the factory adjoins the village of Ngringo, the residents of which still primarily pursue a livelihood of wet rice agriculture.[1] Some local residents are employed by the factory, although the majority of the workforce is drawn from outside Ngringo village. The residents of Ngringo first reported the effects of pollution from PT Palur Raya in 1992. According to reports from the community, the environmental impact of the factory was severe and included the following (KKL 2000b):

- Residents' wells of a previous depth of 2-3 metres were now unable to draw water above a depth of 20 metres.
- The agricultural output of the surrounding rice paddies had dropped to 40% of their previous output in an area of 14 hectares surrounding the factory. In a 1.5 hectares area surrounding the factory no crops were able to be planted.

1 Sri Hardono and Widodo, interview, Padepokan Globlog, 23-1-2001.

- Discolouration of river water from liquid waste discharge, and the deaths of fishes which had been a food source for residents.
- Poor air quality, including offensive odours and acrid smoke, in the area surrounding the factory.
- The leaching of chemicals from hazardous, solid waste disposed on the western side of the factory.

Community representatives first voiced their opposition to the pollution in 1992, when they sent a letter to Post Box 5000 in Jakarta, a general purpose location to which complaints could be addressed to the government. The letter complained of the drop in the level of ground water subsequent to the factory's operation, and the consequent failure of residents' wells (Ngringo 1992). No solution to the ground water problem was forthcoming, however, and the residents were forced to use piped water for their everyday needs at their own expense. Demonstrations during this period also took place, in some cases prompting physical intimidation or repression by military or hired civilian thugs.[2]

In October 1998 a group of five residents conveyed a claim to PT Palur Raya regarding the impact of pollution and the loss of ground water. The complaints were also communicated to, and subsequently reported in, a local newspaper; the *Solo Post*. In the *Solo Post* article, the residents claimed that their rice harvest had declined from ten to 2.5 tonnes per hectare after the factory commenced operation. Furthermore, the quality of the rice produced was inferior to that of their previously healthy rice; a situation which the residents claimed to have endured for more than ten years. These complaints were also conveyed to a range of government agencies at the local, provincial and national levels. Yet, other than physical intimidation of residents by third parties, no concrete action was taken by either industry or government agencies to resolve these environmental problems (KKL 1999:2-4).

Negotiation

Several representatives of the community subsequently formed a 'team of nine' to represent community interests to PT Palur Raya and monitor the environmental impact of the factory's operations. In December 1998 discussions were held with representatives of PT Palur Raya, and agreement reached that the team of nine would participate in the process of waste management and environmental restoration. A formal agreement of cooperation was signed by the community representatives and PT Palur Raya, and

2 Sri Hardono and Widodo, interview, 23-1-2001.

witnessed by the regent (*bupati*) of Karanganyar. The agreement stated that the cooperation between the industry and the community would encompass the following activities:

- environmental audit;
- improvement of waste water treatment;
- employment of experts in environment and community health (with a priority also of employing residents from the adjoining areas in waste management efforts);
- creation of local health facilities (polyclinic), to monitor the health of local residents;
- preparation of a section of land to test the penetration of waste and monitor pollution levels;
- facilitation of community development through creation of a community meeting hall;
- regular meetings between community representatives and industry.

In the subsequent implementation phase, however, differences over implementation of this cooperative approach to environmental management emerged, leading to further conflict. According to community representatives, there were frequent attempts by factory representatives to either intimidate or, more frequently, bribe community leaders in a bid to maintain the status quo.[3] The agreement was subsequently repudiated by the team of nine, who felt the industry was no longer willing to allow them to participate in the environmental audit process. Community representatives also condemned the industry's alleged use of 'money politics' (KKL 2000b). By May 1999 the disillusioned members of the team of nine disbanded and community advocacy on the issue of Palur Raya's pollution lapsed.

Community organization

In May 2000, a year after the breakdown of the negotiated agreement with PT Palur Raya, community representatives held a series of meetings with several local NGOs to discuss possible responses and solutions to the continuing problems of pollution.[4] Subsequently, attention was directed toward raising

3 The leaders of the team of nine at the time stated they were offered Rp 5 million/month as 'peace money' (*uang damai*): Sri Hardono and Widodo, interview, 23-1-2001.

4 The local NGOs involved in the dispute were: Elpamas, LPTP, Studi Penelitian Lingkungan/ SPL, Merah Putih, and Lumut, all of which were based in the nearby city of Solo (Surakarta). As cited by Mutakin, head of advocacy organization Lembaga Studi Lingkungan (LSL), interview, 23-1-2001.

awareness of environmental issues and assisting community leaders to form a new environmental advocacy group: the Consortium of Waste Victims (Konsorsium Korban Limbah or KKL).[5] The consortium, which comprised eleven active members drawn from the Ngringo community and NGO workers, became a vehicle for the advocacy of environmental and residents' interests in relation to the dispute with PT Palur Raya.[6] From its formation, KKL was proactive in its advocacy of community and environmental interests, and made frequent use of a variety of advocacy techniques including press releases, lobbying and demonstrations. With the participation of various NGOs, the group was well resourced, having access to legal and environmental technical expertise. The cohesion of the group was also assisted by its authoritative leader, who was a policeman as well as an influential local religious leader.

One obstacle in the dispute resolution process was division within the Ngringo community between residents employed by the factory and those whose livelihoods were threatened by the factory's pollution. Conflict was further exacerbated by the industry's strategy of winning support amongst the community through gifts, monetary payments or offers of employment.[7] The fact that the village head (*kepala desa*) had tended to side with the factory also caused some division of leadership within the community.[8] Despite these divisions, community support for the advocacy of KKL, and overall community solidarity, remained relatively high throughout the dispute resolution process.

Partly as a result of environmental education carried out by NGOs, the community representatives were convinced of the necessity of an environmental rather than a monetary solution. Whilst the community did seek compensation for past environmental damage, this did not displace their primary concern of environmental restoration and prevention of further pollution by the factory. Frequent resort by the industry to 'money politics' did little to undermine community opposition to the factory's pollution. As one NGO worker involved with the community observed: 'Other environmental cases are often resolved with money. But I think this case will be different. The community aren't going to stop at compensation. They are determined to resolve the environmental problems at stake.'[9]

5 Not to be confused with Kerukunan Korban Limbah Kali Banger (KKLB), the Association of Banger River Waste Victims.

6 Mutakin (LSL), interview, 23-1-2001.

7 Tri Widono, interview, Bapedalda Karanganyar, 9-2-2000.

8 Mutakin, head of LSL, interview, 23-1-2001.

9 Mutakin (SLS), interview, 11-1-2000.

Mediation process

Following the Ngringo community's reorganization and renewed advocacy, a process of negotiation with PT Palur Raya was recommenced on 14 May 2000, in which community representatives conveyed the following demands (KKL 2000a):

- Cease air pollution including smoke and offensive odour from factory within three months;
- Cease pollution of water including groundwater, well water and irrigation water within three months;
- Undertake environmental rehabilitation of already damaged land and wells within one month;
- Pay compensation to residents affected by pollution;
- Allow residents to undertake monitoring of industry.

Negotiations continued during the latter part of May 2000, when a series of fractious meetings was held between KKL and PT Palur Raya. To the disappointment of community representatives, the meetings failed to produce any concrete result other than an informal agreement on the main environmental issues involved. PT Palur Raya showed little inclination to compromise, as had been the case in the past.

However, it was at this time that the industry received an administrative warning from the Karanganyar Environmental Impact Agency. The head of the agency recalled.

> On May 12, we told the factory to take a number of steps to clean up the environment. In response the industry promised to repair the waste management unit to an operational level, install a reception tank for solid waste, examine effluent outlets once every 3 months, work on improving relations with the community and undergo a general environmental audit. But the industry was too slow. The community lost its patience and started demonstrating. This was the impetus for the mediation process.[10]

The profile of the Palur Raya dispute was further raised as demonstrations against the factory received publicity in the mass media. Subsequent to this, an administrative directive was issued from the National Environment Minister, Dr Sonny Keraf, to the Environmental Impact Agency of Central Java, requesting resolution of the Palur Raya dispute via a mediation process. The mediation process was to involve all stakeholders, namely government agencies, community representatives, NGOs, parliamentary representatives and the industry

10 H. Hartono, Bapedalda Karanganyar, interview, 11-1-2001.

itself. Prompted by the ministerial directive, the Karanganyar Environmental Impact Agency assumed a more active role in facilitating, although not mediating, the dispute resolution process. With the consent of all parties, a third party mediator was agreed upon, Mr Goenawan Wibisono, the head of a local NGO focused on environmental issues and social development.

In the mediation process that followed, Wibisono's role as mediator was described favourably by a number of observers. In the words of one participant: 'His role was to bring the interests of the community, industry and the government together. He was quite independent and didn't side with anyone.'[11] Whilst lacking prior experience in mediation, Wibisono adopted an effective approach in promoting compromise and focusing on the key interests of both parties.

> This was my first time as a mediator, but I've been involved in environmental issues for a long time. I don't even know if you'd call this mediation or not. It doesn't really matter to me. I just wanted to avoid anyone feeling like they had won or lost. The principle I suggested at the beginning was that the industry not be closed as long as the community and the environment were not harmed.[12]

In the first mediation meeting between all stakeholders, representatives of both the army and police were also present. The mediator, however, discouraged this: 'I told them that this was a civil problem not a military problem. I said it shouldn't involve them and asked them not to come again.' In subsequent sessions government participation was limited to representatives from the Karanganyar environmental agency, and a member of the local parliament who lived near the factory also participated in the mediation process. The environmental agency representatives took a more passive role during mediation, although the comments they did make tended to support industry interests.[13] Nonetheless, on several occasions governmental representatives endeavoured to bring both sides to resolution on a number of critical issues, such as the matter of implementation time.[14] A primary concern of the agency, as made evident by a number of statements made in mediation, was to avoid escalation of the conflict into possible violence or broader social discord.[15]

PT Palur Raya's initial intransigence was maintained as the previous deadlock dragged on for a further four meetings. According to the mediator,

[11] Mutakin, head of LSL, interview, 23-1-2001.

[12] Goenawan Wibisono, leader of KKL, Solo, interview, 19-4-2001.

[13] Wibisono, interview, 19-4-2001.

[14] The industry wanted 2 years for implementation, whereas the community wanted 1 month. Eventually the agreement stipulated 3 months for the Independent Team's investigation, and 3 months for implementation of its resolution. As cited by Mutakin (LSL), interview, 23-1-2001.

[15] Mutakin (LSL), interview, 23-1-2001.

one obstacle was the legalistic and adversarial approach taken by the legal representative for PT Palur Raya.

> The industry used a lawyer which became a problem. He didn't understand environmental issues and just had a 'profit-loss' perspective. And he'd always stick to the law, whereas this was mediation. In the end, it was a weakness for them.[16]

However in the meantime the community was able to gain leverage in the negotiations, and during the fifth session an agreement was reached to resolve the dispute. Various theories were expressed by participants about the reasons for the success of the mediation process in reaching agreement. The outspoken leader of the Consortium of Waste Victims (KKL), Sri Hardono, emphasized the role of community pressure and threats of mass action.

> The agreement was reached because of our tactical strategy. I told them I would bring 7000 people to the street and we would close off their outlets or even burn their factory. Palur Raya had been brave to begin with but they soon were scared to death.[17]

Other observers confirmed Hardono's comments in this respect: 'The community pressure on the company was aggressive, even bordering on anarchy. Threats were made to burn the factory. The atmosphere of the negotiations was tense.'[18] Whilst the overt threats and community pressure in the mediation were significant, other observers emphasized the considerable witness and documentary evidence, confirming that PT Palur Raya had in fact been polluting for some years at the expense of both the environment and the local community.

> The facts of pollution couldn't be ignored – the colour of the river water, the stench in the air, the effluent discharged to the rice paddies [...] all of this caused much social unrest. These things couldn't be denied. I think it was this that pushed PT Palur Raya into compromise in the end.[19]

An alternative theory presented by another participant in the mediation process attributed the factory's 'capitulation' to other reasons.

> To begin with the factory's attitude was that they weren't in the wrong. They talked about how much they paid in taxes to the government and how many workers they employed. They said they were domestically owned (*pemilik modal dalam negeri*). But in fact this turned out to be false. The company actually was foreign

16 Goenawan Wibisono, leader of KKL, Solo, interview, 19-4-2001.

17 Sri Hardono and Widodo, interview, 23-1-2001.

18 Goenawan Wibisono, leader of KKL, Solo, interview, 12-2-2001.

19 Wibisono, second interview, 19-4-2001.

> owned (*pemilik modal asing*) – which meant they should be paying higher taxes and wages and its permits should be different. We got this information from a friend in the Central Environmental Impact Agency and once they [the company] knew we knew, they felt defeated. At that point the company acknowledged all its faults and wrongdoing.[20]

Other informants, whilst acknowledging the issue of the company's legal status, did not seem certain that it had influenced the final outcome of the mediation process to the same extent.

Mediated agreement

One of the most striking aspects of the agreement reached by the two parties was the comprehensive acknowledgement that pollution and other environmental damage of water, ground and air had occurred in the vicinity of the factory, as a result of waste produced, stored or discharged to the environment by PT Palur Raya. The pollution and environmental damage in question were, according to the agreement, caused by:

- liquid waste exceeding stipulated limits;
- unprocessed solid waste;
- poisonous gases;
- exploitation of shallow and deep ground water.

The agreement signed by the two parties went on to state that such pollution could not be tolerated from an ethical, ecological or legal perspective, and had furthermore damaged both residents and the environment at large. Consequently, the parties had agreed to resolve the dispute at hand, via mediation and legalization of the agreement.[21]

In addition to stipulating the nature of the pollution, the agreement promised the 'total cessation of pollution and environmental damage resulting from waste produced, stored or discharged by PT Palur Raya'. To this end articles 1-3 of the agreement required that PT Palur Raya cease pollution of air and water, whilst complying with stipulated waste parameters. The agreement stipulated the further guarantee that 'the interests of the community not [...] be compromised, whether their right to a healthy environment or their material interests'. Accordingly the agreement, in article 4, made provision for environmental rehabilitation of land damaged by polluting activities, whilst article 5 required PT Palur Raya to pay compensation (material or

20 Mutakin, head of Indonesian advocacy organization Lembaga Studi Lingkungan (LSL), interview, Solo, 23-1-2001.

21 Legalization in this respect meant authorization of the agreement by a public notary.

immaterial) to residents who had suffered loss as a result of the pollution or environmental damage.

On the issue of implementation, the agreement made relatively detailed provision. Article 7 required PT Palur Raya to cease all polluting activities in compliance with articles 1-3 within ninety days of the signing of the agreement. Implementation of environmental rehabilitation (article 4) and compensation (article 5) was to be facilitated by an Independent Team of experts. The team would be appointed by both parties, paid by PT Palur Raya, and would be required to finish its work within sixty days of the agreement's execution (article 10). The decision of the team in relation to these issues was to be absolute and binding. Some inconsistencies were evident in the implementation schedule, for example article 5 required compensation to be paid within thirty days whilst this was also a matter referred to the Independent Team to be achieved within a longer time frame. Similarly, article 9 provided for the creation of a 'working team' consisting of industry and community representatives to assist with implementation, whilst this task was also assigned to the Independent Team pursuant to article 10. Finally, the agreement made provision for a number of sanctions that would apply in the event that PT Palur Raya transgressed the provisions mentioned above. The stipulated sanctions included a range of fines, a publicized apology by PT Palur Raya to the community (in the event of continuing pollution) and, where transgression of the agreement continued, an obligatory relocation of the factory premises.

Independent Team investigation (ITI)

As discussed above, the matter of implementation was at first dealt with in the agreement itself, which specified a number of implementation 'deadlines'. Whilst sufficiently specific and enforceable on paper, in practice these implementation deadlines were for the most part disregarded; due to the involvement of the Independent Team, which became the practical focus of the dispute resolution process following the signing of the agreement.

The initial mandate of the Independent Team, as described above and as provided in article 10, was to assist with the implementation of environmental rehabilitation and compensation. In a subsequent addendum agreed to by the Ngringo community, PT Palur Raya management and Karanganyar Environmental Agency, this mandate was widened considerably to encompass:

- carrying out an environmental audit;
- calculating an appropriate level of compensation;
- recommending an appropriate model for environmental recovery to PT Palur Raya;

- carrying out further actions as considered important and necessary for preserving the environment.

Finally, in the work proposal formulated by the team members themselves and approved by both parties, the duties and objectives of the team during their investigation were further detailed:

- verify the existence of pollution and/or environmental damage;
- assess the extent of such pollution and/or environmental damage;
- locate sources of pollution;
- calculate compensation;
- make recommendations for implementation of environmentally friendly industry and community development.

This widened mandate was probably reflective of the significance that most parties placed on the participation of the Independent Team in this case. In the words of the chief officer of the Karanganyar Environmental Impact Agency:

> This is a new model of environmental dispute resolution. It's different from other cases. It will be based on objective scientific research, not subjective factors. It will tackle the actual environmental issues, rather than just giving a peppermint' [paying compensation].[22]

Other interviewees echoed his confidence in the 'scientific' nature of the dispute resolution process due to the involvement of the academically qualified Independent Team of researchers. Clearly, the involvement of an independent 'fact-finding' team was intended by the parties to clarify the environmental issues at stake and to provide a sound scientific basis for implementing a comprehensive solution to the dispute at hand. Nonetheless, some participants also considered strategic considerations to have influenced the decision to appoint the Independent Team.

> The industry representatives argued 'if we are accused of pollution, it must be proven'. Although they acknowledged as much in the agreement, they still wanted evidence to show the extent. For their part the community didn't want to 'sell' their environmental case [that is, only take compensation] and were happy for the environmental issues to be clarified by experts. Perhaps this was a trick by industry so they could repair their waste management unit before the tests were carried out.[23]

22 H. Hartono, Bapedalda Karanganyar, interview, 11-1-2001.
23 Goenawan Wibisono, leader of KKL, second interview, 19-4-2001.

The composition of the team was to be decided jointly by the two parties, with each appointing three members to form a total of six. The three industry-appointed researchers, from the Centre for Environmental Studies at the University of Gadjah Mada, examined issues of ecology (water and air quality), land/agricultural productivity and community health respectively.[24] The three community appointed researchers examined issues of hydrology, environmental law, and environmental economics respectively.[25] The team was given sixty days in which to complete its duties and report back to the parties involved. The team's research was carried out over a period of several months in the latter half of 2000, and the final results and report were presented in early March 2001.

ITI results 1: Ecology, Dr Sugiharto – appointed by Palur Raya

Dr Eko Sugiharto examined water and air quality in the vicinity of the factory location. His tests of residents' well water did not confirm pollution. Although samples from the Ngringo River were in excess of regulatory parameters, PT Palur Raya was considered to be only one of a number of possible sources for this decline in water quality. Tests of factory effluent produced ambiguous results; one sample of effluent discharged during the day satisfied stipulated parameters, however a second sample taken at night was not returned from the laboratory, whilst a third sample was seemingly the result of a possible pipe leak and was greatly in excess of stipulated parameters. The sampling method adopted by Dr Sugiharto was the subject of criticism by community representatives, who argued that more frequent testing of factory effluent was necessary to obtain accurate results. Community reports also indicated that the majority of effluent was discharged from the factory at night, and criticized the failure of Dr Sugiharto's research to satisfactorily examine this.[26] Gas emissions from the factory reportedly did not exceed stipulated parameters, although it may have been the source of unpleasant odours at times. Recommendations made by Dr Sugiharto included improved operation of the waste management unit to ensure future compliance with regula-

24 Note that PT Palur Raya did not individually appoint each researcher but rather requested the Centre for Environmental Studies provide three researchers with suitable qualifications. The three industry appointed researchers were Dr Eko Sugiharto (ecology/air and water quality), Dr Rachman Sutanto (land and agriculture), and Dr Doeljahman Moeljoharjo (community health).

25 The three community appointed researchers were Dr Setyo Sarwanto Moersidik (hydrology), Mr Heru Setyadi (environmental law), and Mr Nugroho Widiarto (environmental economics).

26 An official from the district Environmental Impact Agency recounted: 'the factory still disposes of waste at night, usually between 10pm-3.30am. The waste is like a torrent of black, foaming liquid. From the Independent Team, only Dr Setio (Moersidik – a community appointed member) witnessed this': Tri Widono, interview, Bapedalda Karanganyar, 11-1-2000.

tory standards, and additional treatment of gases emitted during the waste management process.

ITI results 2: Land and agriculture, Dr Sutanto – appointed by Palur Raya
Dr Rachman Sutanto found no evidence of chemical contamination or pollution of the agricultural land in the vicinity of the factory. Contrary to community claims, his research did not support a relationship between the decline in agricultural output and waste disposed from the factory. Damage that had occurred to newly planted rice seedlings was attributed to unusually high nitrogen levels in the soil. Despite noting this damage, Dr Sutanto considered that waste water from the factory could be potentially beneficial for crops, as it was high in nitrogen and contained beneficial micro-organisms, and would make it unnecessary for farmers to further fertilize their crops.

ITI results 3: Community health, Dr Moeljoharjo – appointed by Palur Raya
The third industry appointed researcher, Dr Doeljarman Moeljoharjo, examined the area of community health, confirming Dr Sugiharto's conclusion that residents' wells had not been polluted. Clinical examinations indicated some subjects (26.91%) suffered breathing disorders, a possible cause of which was polluting gases from PT Palur Raya, although the evidence was not conclusive in this respect. There were no reported cases of sickness or death due to pollution at the local health clinics. Recommendations by Dr Moeljoharjo were general in nature, including the further improvement and continued monitoring of the waste management unit, continued monitoring of residents' health by local clinics and future cooperation between factory and residents to maintain environmental health standards.

ITI results 4: Hydrology, Dr Moersidik – appointed by Ngringo community
Dr Setyo Sarwanto Moersidik's research focused on hydrology and the use of ground water by the factory. Research results confirmed the unauthorized use of ground water in excess of the factory's permit, causing a drop in the overall level of ground water by 7-10 metres and confirming the community's claims in this respect. The factory's actual use of water was calculated at 4000m^3 per day from seven bores, whereas the factory's permit allowed for only 700m^3 per day from four bores. In light of these findings, Dr Moersidik recommended a review of PT Palur Raya's licence for the use of ground water. Compensation was also recommended for residents adversely affected by the reduction in ground water levels. Further testing indicated that the volume of liquid waste produced by the factory exceeded the capacity of the waste management unit (by approximately 540m^3 per day), resulting in the discharge of untreated waste from the factory via a concealed bypass outlet – an occurrence which, again, had been alleged by the community previously. Given Dr

Moersidik's confirmation of this point, it is surprising that the existence of such an outlet was not discussed in the research presented by Dr Sugiharto, who had merely recorded one sample of untreated waste greatly in excess of stipulated contaminant levels. On the matter of liquid waste disposal, Dr Moersidik recommended a reduction in water intake to ensure the capacity of the waste management unit was not exceeded, in conjunction with the closure of the concealed waste outlet pipe.

Further research included a review of previous effluent tests from the factory during the period 1994-2000, which indicated frequent contravention of regulatory levels.[27] Despite recent improvements to the waste management unit, significant fluctuations in effluent contaminants were still evident; often exceeding stipulated levels – especially from effluent discharged between 10 pm and 4 am. This latter point confirmed community claims that untreated waste was discharged at night into the Ngringo River, a practice common amongst industries in Java, and lent more emphatic support to community allegations of water pollution. The findings of Dr Moersidik also confirmed the conclusion by Dr Sugiharto that 'at certain times liquid waste still exceeded standard regulated threshold limits'.

Contrary to Dr Sutanto's research, Dr Moersidik also considered that heavy metal pollution had occurred from solid waste stored in a location adjoining the factory, and accordingly recommended review of this potentially hazardous storage facility. Again in contrast to Dr Sutanto, Dr Moersidik cautioned against the use of liquid waste as fertilizer, recommending examination of the waste liquid fertilizer's potential environmental impact and compliance with relevant regulations.

ITI results 5: Environmental law, Mr Setyadi – appointed by Ngringo community

Mr Heru Setyadi's research examined PT Palur Raya's compliance with a range of environmental legislation and regulations. The research concluded that PT Palur Raya had contravened numerous environmental legal obligations relating to management of liquid waste, solid waste, extraction of ground water, and production and sale of liquid fertilizer. As a result, the company was liable to incur administrative sanctions, and legally obliged to pay compensation to residents who had been adversely affected by illegal or improper waste disposal. Mr Setyadi made a number of recommendations, including repair of the waste management system, implementation of a process of 'environmental recovery' through cooperation between industry, community and government agencies, closure of unauthorized sources of

27 Of tests reviewed, 50% indicated excessive BOD levels, 15% reported excessive COD levels, and 26% reported excessive TSS levels.

ground water, and further monitoring of ground water levels. Mr Setyadi further recommended payment of compensation by PT Palur Raya in accordance with the agreement, and an environmental impact analysis and review of licensing for liquid waste fertilizer, preceded by a temporary cessation of fertilizer production and sales.

ITI results 6: Environmental economics, Mr Widiarto – appointed by Ngringo community

The third community-appointed member of the Independent Team, Mr Nugroho Widiarto, examined the issue of compensation from the perspective of environmental economics. Compensation was calculated on the basis of research carried out by other members of the team regarding the nature and extent of pollution. In the areas of ecology (air/water quality), land and agriculture, and community health there was no conclusive evidence of pollution and hence no compensation was payable. Research in the areas of hydrology and environmental law, however, confirmed liquid waste pollution and illegal exploitation of ground water for which compensation could be calculated. Given much of the economic data required was not provided by the company, compensation was assessed on a rights basis (what should be paid) rather than a means basis (what the company actually could pay). In total the recommended compensation payment figure was Rp 7,299,569,706, comprising:[28]

Liquid waste pollution (environmental damages)	Rp	6,700,529,706
Ground water (unpaid tax)	Rp	157,248,000
Ground water (environmental damages)	Rp	441,792,000
Total compensation	Rp	7,299,569,706

The most visible achievement of the Independent Team's investigation, which spanned a period of some six months, was its compilation of a large body of scientific data on the environmental issues, which lay at the core of the dispute between PT Palur Raya and the Ngringo community.

Nonetheless, a number of disadvantages of the Independent Team's involvement in this case were also apparent. Firstly, the team's investigation prolonged the dispute resolution process by re-opening issues previously settled between the parties – in this case the matter of pollution and environmental damage.[29] During the period in which the team was carrying

[28] Dr Moersidik notes that, as much economic data was not provided by the company, compensation was assessed on a rights basis (what should be paid) rather than a means basis (what the company actually could pay). See Karanganyar 2001:137.

[29] See, for instance, the mediated agreement discussed above which explicitly recognized that

out its research, there was considerable anxiety amongst the community as to whether the team would in fact conclude there was pollution and would recommend suitable remedies. The team in effect became an expert 'judge and jury' rather than a technical advisory body on implementation as was originally envisaged.

The failure of the Independent Team to adequately address the matter of implementation was also evident in its final report, which failed to provide a detailed framework or timetable to properly facilitate the implementation process. The recommendations made by the majority of researchers were moreover mostly general or vague in nature, for example recommendations requiring 'improvement of the waste management unit' or a 'process of environmental recovery'.

Thirdly, the value of the data collected by the Independent Team was compromised to a considerable extent by the presence of significant ambiguities and contradictions between the conclusions of individual researchers. Conflicting opinions were evident on a number of issues, amongst others the effects on agriculture, contamination from solid waste and liability for river water quality decline. Thus, whilst the Independent Team's report presented a wealth of data on the disputed issues, the many contradictions among the research findings would most likely only fuel further dispute between the parties.

The report's potential to generate further dispute was also exacerbated by the discernable division in research results between those researchers appointed by the community and those appointed by the industry. Of the three industry appointed researchers, none found conclusive evidence of pollution, whereas of the three community appointed researchers, two found clear evidence of environmental damage and pollution, whilst the third awarded a record level of compensation for such damage on the basis of those conclusions.

The considerable variance in the team's research results, conclusions and recommendations highlights the ambiguity that may be present in scientific data, especially where a variety of research approaches and methodologies are adopted. The limited time span of some of the research may also account for some individual variances – most of the field tests by researchers were carried out over only a period of one or two months in 2000. In contrast, document-based research, such as that carried out by Mr Heru Setiayadi and Dr Moersidik, covered the period dating back to the factory's operation.

The ambiguous results of the investigation also raise the problematic

'pollution and environmental damage has occurred in the location of PT Palur Raya, caused by waste produced, stored or discharged into the environment by PT Palur Raya'.

issue of research independence and accountability. Whilst in this case three researchers each were appointed by the community and industry respectively, the costs of the research were paid solely by PT Palur Raya. Such an arrangement, whilst advocated by the community itself, also gave rise to some apprehension that the industry would be in a position to try to influence the research outcomes, although no evidence was presented that this had in fact occurred.

Implementation of agreement and team's recommendation

The final report of the Independent Team was presented in March 2001. The considerable variance in research results and recommendations appeared to create grounds for further conflict, which could potentially obstruct implementation of the original agreement.

Further conflict was in fact what followed. The report received a favourable response from the Ngringo community, with representatives quickly forming a new 'Implementing Committee' to facilitate implementation of the report's recommendations concerning compensation, waste monitoring, community health monitoring and ongoing compliance with environmental regulations. A less enthusiastic response, however, was forthcoming from representatives of PT Palur Raya, who rejected the team's conclusions. An arbitration process was suggested by several parties but ultimately not initiated.

In July 2001, lawyers for PT Palur Raya lodged a civil suit against the Independent Team in the district court of Yogyakarta, challenging the results of the team's investigation. In a rather farcical end to this phase of dispute resolution, the district court of Yogyakarta upheld the claim of the PT Palur Raya, declaring that the results of the Independent team were invalid and could not be used as a basis for resolving the dispute.[30] Accordingly, the Rp 7.3 billion compensation recommended in the team's report was also deemed invalid and disallowed. The decision of the court seems a strange one, which involved second guessing qualified experts in an area clearly outside the court's expertise. It is also unclear from the decision what grounds the court had for declaring that the Independent Team's report was an action contrary to law (*perbuatan melawan hukum*). The only action taken by the Team was to investigate and report on allegations of pollution in accordance with their instructions. Even if there was room for scientific differences over the Team's results, this was surely not grounds for declaring the actions of the Team contrary to law.

30 'PN Yogya kabulkan gugatan Palur Raya', *Suara Merdeka*, 14-10-2002.

Mediation recommenced

As little prospect of resolution appeared likely at the local level, representatives of the Ngringo community travelled to Jakarta to meet the Environment Minister, Nabiel Makarim. The Minister indicated his willingness to personally mediate the high profile dispute and subsequently met, accompanied by two senior officials, with industry and community representatives in Karanganyar on 19 January 2002. The mediation process proved to be quite lengthy and protracted, with a substantial part of the mediation carried out with each party separately.[31] Eventually the mediators were successful in guiding the parties to an interim agreement,[32] which encompassed the following:

- PT Palur Raya should comply with regulatory standards on waste emissions.
- Monitoring of waste management would be carried out by a team coordinated by the Environmental Ministry.
- PT Palur Raya would carry out a program of community development as defined by an independent third party after consultation with both parties.
- Both parties would discontinue their respective legal actions.

The legal actions commenced by either party were subsequently discontinued. Community representatives, however, expressed dissatisfaction with PT Palur Raya's implementation of improved waste management, and on 29 March 2002 around 200 community members blocked the factory's outlet pipes to the river (KKL 2002b:1). Following this incident, and in accordance with the previous interim agreement of January 2002, a second meeting was arranged by the Environment Minister to resolve the issue of a payment to the community (KKL 2002a). A further agreement, dated 1 April 2002, was the result of this mediation process. In this agreement, Palur Raya undertook to pay an amount of Rp 1.1 billion (termed a contribution rather than compensation) to the community and to improve relations with the community through appointment of a 'Communicator' and creation of a cooperative forum. The agreement stipulated that the funds of Rp 1.1 billion would be paid in three instalments: Rp 400 million in April 2002; Rp 400 million in August 2002 and Rp 300 million in December 2002. In addition the industry would comply with regulatory standards and both parties would discontinue

31 Widodo Sambodo, LH, Jakarta, interview, 6-6-2003.

32 *Hasil Kesepakatan Mediasi Antara Pt. Palur Raya Di Karanganyar Kimbah (KKL) Desa Ngringo* 2002.

any legal actions as stated in the original January agreement. The agreement, widely publicized in the local and national press, was witnessed by the regent (*bupati*) of Karanganyar and the National Environment Minister and legalized by a notary to give it force of a binding contract. Pursuant to the agreement, community representatives established a preliminary communication forum for the purpose of improving relations with PT Palur Raya, and a ceremonial event was planned for 30 April 2002 in which the first instalment of the industry funds would be paid to the community.

Ultimately, however, payment of the funds was frustrated once again. Whilst the community had formed a 'Team of 12' to receive and administer the funds in conjunction with other community leaders, the planned ceremony for payment of the first instalment in April 2002 did not actually take place. Community reports also indicated that pollution was continuing, and that the civil action of PT Palur Raya against the Independent Team had not been discontinued (KKL 2002c:3). A further meeting was held between industry and community representatives concerning the use and distribution of the funds, in which it was agreed that the funds would be used for environmental rehabilitation and community development purposes. The more precise use of the funds would be determined by a *musyawarah* (negotiation) process between the 'Team of 12' and other community leaders.

However, payment as agreed still did not occur. Correspondence from industry representatives to the Environmental Ministry indicated instead the industry's intention to determine the use and application of the funds itself. PT Palur Raya stated that Rp 600 million would be used to build a community meeting and sports building, for which contractors had previously submitted tenders. The remaining Rp 500 million would be reserved for the purchase of the necessary equipment and furnishings for the building's operation (Husein Ungai 2002). Community representatives objected to imposition of this condition, which had not been part of the negotiated agreement. Conflict over the matter created a division in the Ngringo community, between those – including the local village head (*kepala desa*) – who wanted to receive the payment regardless, and those (led by KKL) who wished to refuse the payment if its disbursement was controlled by PT Palur Raya.[33]

On 17 June 2002 a publicized meeting of all stakeholders was held at a hotel in Solo. Participants at the meeting included the national Environment Minister and senior Ministry officials, Karanganyar police and prosecutors, the Chief Justice of Karanganyar, district environmental officials and other district government officials. At the meeting the Minister emphasized that the

[33] This conflict was apparently exacerbated by industry attempts to 'buy support' among the local community: Widodo Sambodo, LH, Jakarta, interview, 6-6-2003.

role of the Ministry had already been discharged through its facilitation of the 1 April 2002 agreement between the parties. Implementation of the agreement was a technical issue to be resolved between the two parties, and if agreement was not possible on this issue then the parties should proceed to court. Any further action of the Ministry in relation to PT Palur Raya or this dispute would be toward ensuring proper implementation of the EMA 1997. Later that day a group of Ngringo residents again blocked the waste outlet pipes of PT Palur Raya in protest at the industry's failure to implement the agreement.[34] In July 2002 an investigation into PT Palur Raya' compliance with environmental regulations was commenced by the Karanganyar police, assisted by a team from the national environmental ministry and Karanganyar environmental officials. The police investigation was, however, later discontinued. A further attempt by the national Environment Ministry's team to carry out waste sampling at PT Palur Raya was refused by the industry, on the grounds that decentralization laws had transferred legal authority over environmental supervision from national to regional governments (KKL 2002c:5).

In April 2003 a series of meetings was held between the governor and vice-governor of Central Java, the head of the provincial environmental impact agency, the head of the Karanganyar district environmental agency, PT Palur Raya management and Ngringo community representatives, to faciliate implementation of the previous agreement. Following this, a payment of Rp 600 million was finally made by Palur Raya to the Ngringo community. This was supplemented by a Rp 500 million payment from the regional government. The money was distributed to those village members whose wells had dried up or rice fields had been polluted by liquid waste from the factory.[35] The remainder of the Rp 1,1 billion pledged by the industry, an amount of Rp 500 million, was reserved by the industry for the construction of the community building. The remaining money still has not been disbursed to date, as some community representatives are still opposed to the building's construction. Nonetheless, since the payment was made, conflict between the industry and the local community appears to have subsided, and no further demonstrations or actions have occurred.[36] From the perspective of environmental management, local residents have reported a general decrease in pollution levels from the factory. A new waste management unit has been reportedly effective in preventing offensive odours from the factory. Rice paddies in the factories' vicinity are also useable once again, although the rice is apparently of an inferior quality.

34 'PT Palur Raya ingkari kesepakatan, warga tutup saluran limbah', *Kompas*, 18-6-2002.
35 Sri Hardono, interview, 18-3-2003.
36 Sri Hardono, interview, 18-3-2003.

Conclusion

The Palur Raya case illustrates the potential complexity of environmental dispute resolution, encompassing as it did four distinct dispute resolution processes.

The first attempt at dispute resolution was through negotiation, and initially appeared successful, resulting in a detailed agreement. Cooperation between community and industry representatives broke down, however, and the agreement failed in the implementation phase.

Dispute resolution recommenced in June 2000 with a mediation process mediated by an independent third party. The mediation in this case succeeded in producing a detailed agreement between the parties, which formed the basis for the third process of dispute resolution, a fact-finding investigation by the 'Independent Team'. The team's ambiguous report then generated further conflict between the parties, including civil and criminal lawsuits.

The fourth and final attempt at dispute resolution was the mediation process most recently initiated by the national Environment Minister, Nabiel Makarim, which produced a written agreement and, after some problems with implementation, finally led to a compensatory payment from the industry to the Ngringo community.

The outcome of this lengthy and protracted process of dispute resolution has thus been mixed. In terms of the private interests of the Ngringo community, PT Palur Raya finally undertook to make a payment of Rp 1.1 billion, characterized as a contribution toward community development rather than as compensation. In itself this was a significant concession from the perspective of the community, obtained after years of advocacy and several attempts at dispute settlement. Part of the funds (Rp 600 million) has now been disbursed, whilst the remainder of the funds has been retained for the construction of a promised community facility, in a manner contrary to the original agreement. The fact that at least some of the payment has actually been made seems to have dissipated further conflict between the industry and the community.

From an environmental perspective, the outcome of the dispute resolution process has also been mixed. In the original mediated agreement between the community and PT Palur Raya, the industry acknowledged its operation had caused pollution, which it agreed to cease in addition to undertaking environmental rehabilitation. The subsequent Independent Team investigation appeared to confuse the matter, with some researchers confirming pollution claims whilst others claimed to have found no evidence of pollution. In the final mediated agreement PT Palur Raya undertook once again to comply with regulatory standards relating to waste management. According to the agreement, waste monitoring would also be carried out by a team coordinated by the

Environmental Ministry. Thus ultimately some provision for the prevention of further pollution was forthcoming from the dispute resolution process.

However, implementation of these provisions has also been inadequate. Despite the industry's agreement that the Environmental Ministry could conduct waste monitoring, it then refused access to a team from the Ministry on the grounds that the team did not possess the legal authority to do so. According to community reports, pollution also continued, prompting a group of Ngringo residents to block PT Palur Raya's waste outlet pipe for the second time on 17 June 2002.

Recent community reports tend to indicate a general decrease in pollution levels, however. Offensive odours from the factory, which were previously a common occurrence, are now prevented by an improvement in the factory's waste management procedures. The storage facility for solid waste from the factory has been moved, preventing further leakage of chemicals into nearby rice fields. Rice fields in close proximity to the factory have also been successfully planted again, although the quality of the rice is apparently less than average.[37]

The progress that was made toward dispute resolution in this case was facilitated by several factors. The first one was skilful mediation, which, on more than one occasion, was critical in enabling the disputing parties to overcome their differences. This was first evident in the formal mediation process commenced in June 2000. The outcome of that process was assisted by a capable mediator with considerable experience in environmental issues. Importantly, the mediator was acceptable to both parties from the outset and was able to remain sufficiently neutral during the dispute resolution process to successfully facilitate agreement between the parties. When disagreements re-emerged between the parties following the report of the Independent Team, intervention by a mediator was again significant in bringing the parties back to agreement. In the January-April 2002 mediation process, the environmental minister himself acted as mediator. According to a senior official from the Ministry, the personal intervention of the minister in this capacity was critical in influencing the management of PT Palur Raya to make a payment of the size it eventually did.[38] A series of meetings mediated by the governor of Central Java in April 2003 was also successful in facilitating implementation of the previous agreement.

The commencement of a mediation process on several occasions, and the respective outcomes of these processes, were also strongly influenced by the high level of community organization and mobilization in this case. Community

37 Sri Hardono, interview, 18-3-2003.

38 Widodo Sambodo, LH, Jakarta, interview, 6-6-2003.

organization was facilitated by the active participation of a number of NGOs, who assisted community representatives in clarifying issues, objectives and strategies as well as formulating a detailed advocacy strategy. An institutional forum, the Consortium of Waste Victims (KKL), provided a vehicle for the community's environmental advocacy. Implementation of various advocacy initiatives then followed, encompassing press releases, demonstrations, written complaints and delegations to both government agencies and industry. The advocacy campaign undertaken by community representatives and local NGOs was successful in raising the profile of the case, ultimately prompting the intervention of the national Environment Minister, Dr Sonny Keraf, and facilitating the start of the first mediation process.

Effective community organization enabled community representatives to apply sustained public pressure on PT Palur Raya at several critical points in the dispute resolution process. The effect of community or public pressure was amplified in this case by two main factors: the level of media exposure and the threat of direct action. The profile of the dispute was initially raised in May 2000 by KKL, whose claims were publicized in the regional and national press. This high level of media exposure was maintained and utilized by KKL during the course of the dispute resolution process. The threat of direct action was also utilized by community representatives on several occasions, and more recently actions to close factory outlets were carried out.

The threat of community direct action against the factory was arguably magnified in this case by the wider political context. Before the dissolution of the New Order in 1998, opposition to the factory's polluting activities had been relatively muted and, as in the case of many environmental disputes at the time, often the subject of physical repression by the state security apparatus. However, with the fall of President Suharto, the advent of reformasi and the consequent decline in military influence, community opposition to pollution had strengthened and become more overt. The widespread rioting and civil disorder that accompanied the fall of Suharto, particularly in the Solo area where this dispute was located, contributed to an apprehension expressed by several observers of potential 'mob violence' or 'anarchy' in the event the dispute was not resolved. This apprehension was heightened to an extent in this case, due to the potential for the environmental dispute to escalate into a racial or religious dispute, given the Indonesian-Chinese ethnicity of the factory owners. The mediator gave voice to the following concerns: 'My worry is that this environmental conflict will become a racial or religious conflict. We must not let this happen. It was this that pushed me to become involved.'[39]

The threat of community action, disorder or violence may thus have increased the motivation of PT Palur Raya to participate in mediation, if only

39 Goenawan Wibisono (leader of KKL), Solo, interview, 12-2-2001.

as a temporary appeasement of community sentiment. However, from the community's perspective, representatives did also emphasize that their intention was not to threaten violence or engender social anarchy. In fact, during the course of the May 1998 riots local residents claimed to have cooperated with factory workers to protect the factory site from damage by rioters (KKL 1999:2-4). When waste outlet pipes of PT Palur Raya were blocked on two occasions in 2002, community representatives also stressed that the action was limited in nature and was intended as a protest rather than an attempt to encourage social disorder or anarchy (MENLH 2002).

Another interesting aspect of this case is the somewhat ambiguous role played by scientific evidence in the dispute. According to the mediated agreement of 2000, the parties appointed an independent fact-finding team to clarify the nature and extent of the pollution, which would enable the team to determine the appropriate level of compensation and environmental rehabilitation. As discussed above, a number of the parties expressed their optimism in this 'scientific' and 'objective' approach to dispute resolution. Ultimately, however, the scientific research carried out by the Independent Team, whilst comprehensive, did not facilitate resolution of the dispute. The marked division in results between the industry-appointed and community-appointed researchers only exacerbated further conflict between the parties. Similarly, the notably high level of compensation recommended by one researcher prompted rejection of the report by PT Palur Raya and the further breakdown in relations between the parties. The case demonstrates the difficulty which may surround clarification of key factual matters in environmental disputes. Whilst clarification of such matters is often an important step in the dispute resolution process, it will not resolve the dispute of itself. Ultimately, resolution depends not upon scientific research but rather the willingness of the parties to compromise and reach agreement. However, it must be noted that most of the ambiguity of the data in this case could be explained by the failure to clearly stipulate the limits and procedures for their collection. In fact, such disparities in findings could have been predicted from the outset.

The role of government agencies in this case was also particularly significant in facilitating and guiding the dispute resolution process. At the local level, the Environmental Agency of Karanganyar at one stage issued an administrative warning to the factory to improve its environmental management, but otherwise seemed to lack the influence to facilitate resolution of the broader dispute. The intervention of the Environment Minister, Dr Sonny Keraf, appeared to strengthen the commitment of all parties to resolve the dispute, and acted as an important catalyst for the resolution process. The importance of high-level administrative support for the dispute settlement process was also evident in the more recent intervention by the Environment Minister, Nabiel Makarim, as mediator. His seniority and status added authority to the process and successfully motivated compromise between the parties. Likewise, the personal intervention of the Central Java governor was significant in facilitating implementation of the April 2002 agreement, particularly the promised payment to the Ngringo community.

Whilst the personal intervention of the Environment Minister certainly rescued the failing mediation process, and facilitated further agreement, implementation of the agreement still proved to be a problem. Indeed, implementation failure has been a repetitive theme in the course of this dispute. In 1998, the parties were successful in concluding an agreement through negotiation. However, the agreement was never implemented, and conflict between the parties quickly re-emerged. The subsequent mediated agreement of 2000 was implemented only to the extent that an investigation by an Independent Team was initiated. Yet the final report of the Independent Team itself was never implemented as required, and was challenged by PT Palur Raya through the courts. With the most recent agreement of 1 April 2002, implementation again proved to be a problem; at least initially. After further high level government pressure from the governor of Central Java, PT Palur Raya has now disbursed at least a part of the agreed sum. A significant part of the agreed payment, however, has been retained for the construction of a community building, contrary to the original agreement. The agreement also required ongoing monitoring of the industry's waste management practices, coordinated by the Environmental Ministry. Yet a team of investigators from the national Environment Ministry was recently refused access to the factory on legal grounds. Thus, the willingness of PT Palur Raya to enter mediation and conclude mediation agreements has often been accompanied by failure to actually implement those agreements. The fact that satisfactory implementation has failed to occur on several occasions in this case suggests the manipulation of mediation processes more to appease community opposition than to achieve a genuine position of compromise. In this case, PT Palur Raya's failure to implement mediated agreements also seems to have been facilitated by the inability of environmental agencies, including those at a national level, to effectively enforce environmental regulations. The threat of both civil and criminal judicial proceedings also seems to have been insufficient to compel the industry's compliance.[40] Thus, whilst mediation may indeed offer an alternative to administrative and judicial enforcement of environmental law, its effectiveness depends on the presence of prospective administrative or judicial sanctions, which provide an important incentive for polluters to comply with the terms of mediated agreements.

40 A recent criminal investigation by the Karanganyar police was discontinued as discussed above. In July 2002, community representatives indicated their intention to commence civil proceedings against the company.

The Kayu Lapis Indonesia dispute

History of the dispute

PT Kayu Lapis Indonesia (PT KLI) is a large wood-processing factory located near Semarang, Central Java. The factory produces plywood, blockboard, sawn timber and sawdust.[41] The considerable output of the factory, which employs over seven thousand workers, is exported to Europe, USA, Japan, Hongkong, China and Korea.[42] Construction of the factory premises, which currently cover some 100 hectares of land, commenced in 1976 and was completed around 1987. The raw materials for the factory's production are supplied from logging concessions controlled by the Kayu Lapis Indonesia Group, totalling some 3.5 million ha; which is reportedly the largest area of logging concessions held by one single entity in Indonesia.[43] Colloquially, PT KLI is known as one of the untouchable 'three gods' (*tiga dewa*) of industry in Central Java, holding immense political and economic influence (ICEL 1999a).

In the early 1990s, an environmental dispute (or rather disputes) emerged between PT KLI and several neighbouring communities of traditional fishpond farmers (*petani tambak*). Four neighbouring communities (Wonorejo and Mororejo, both in Kendal Regency; and Mangunharjo and Mangkang Wetan, both in Semarang municipality) claimed to have been adversely affected by environmental damage attributable to PT KLI. The damage suffered by the fishpond farmers in Wonorejo, Mangunharjo and Mangkang Wetan was of a similar nature, consisting of erosion and flooding of a number of fishponds, whilst in the area of Mororejo (to the west of the factory) the area of available land actually increased. In Mangunharjo and Mangkang Wetan the area of damaged or submerged fishponds amounted to some 110 ha, whilst in Wonorejo some 76 hectares of fishponds were affected.[44] The environmental damage suffered by these communities was attributed to a number of developments undertaken by PT KLI. Foremost in this respect was the factory's

41 Besides its primary products, the factory also produces side products of formaldehyde, urea formaldehyde and melamine formaldehyde. See LBHS 2001.

42 On average, production levels consist of 1,440,000 m^3/day for plywood, 230,000 m^3/day for blackboard, and 166,667 m^3/day for sawn timber. See LBHS 2001.

43 Suara Pembaharuan 31-7-1998 cited in LBHS 2001. In 1999, PT KLI still held 94 concessions, three of which had been closed on grounds of corruption: see Pagono 2000a:33. Much of the wood supply used by PT KLI is reputedly sourced from illegal logging, including logs with a diameter less than 40 cm and a size below 4 m. See Pagono 2000a:33.

44 The claims of the Wonorejo farmers only emerged in the late 1990s, whereas the claims of the Mangunharjo and Mangkang Wetan fishpond farming communities date to 1989. It is the claims, and their attempted resolution, of the latter two communities that form the subject of this case study.

redirection of the Wakak River. In 1987, as a result of flooding in a nearby area, the government agency responsible for irrigation in West Semarang (Pemimpin Proyek Irigasi Semarang Barat, PISB) entered into a cooperative agreement with PT KLI to 'normalise' the Wakak River so that it would not flood. Following negotiation, the agreement provided for the river's course to be altered within a maximum limit of 100 metres from the south-east corner of PT KLI's property. However, in transgression of the agreement and in the absence of the necessary government permits, PT KLI redirected the river some ninety degrees, thus enabling it to create a log pond where the previous mouth of the river had been. The redirected river was merged with the adjacent Plumbon River, finally entering the ocean some 1.6 kilometres from its original mouth. The fish and prawn ponds of the Mangunharjo farmers lie adjacent to the mouth of the Plumbon and redirected Wakak River. Some 53 hectares of the farmers' ponds have been flooded and submerged allegedly due to this redirection of the Wakak River.[45]

PT KLI's actions in redirecting the river without proper authorization did not go unnoticed by administrative authorities. In a letter to PT KLI dated 6 December 1989, the regent (*bupati*) of Kendal stated that the redirection of the river had adversely affected the interests of neighbouring communities by obstructing the river's flood-containment function, resulting in the inundation of neighbouring fishponds (ICEL 2000). Administrative sanction on the matter was also forthcoming from the governor of Central Java who, in a letter dated 28 February 1990, gave a strong warning (*peringatan keras*) to PT KLI. No further administrative action of a more substantive nature was, however, taken against PT KLI (ICEL 2000).

Redirection of the Wakak River enabled PT KLI to construct a log pond which served as a port and storage area for wood shipped from its logging concessions. Maintenance of the log pond, however, required considerable sand dredging, which was carried out by PT KLI without proper licence, in order to maintain the depth of the pond and allow boats to enter. The removal of large quantities of sand reportedly caused shifts in sand dunes in nearby areas, and the lowering in height of sand embankments bordering the ocean. Consequently, the sand embankments no longer offered adequate protection from ocean waves, which created further damage to the embankments and flooded the fish ponds. The log pond itself is the site for the unloading of logs from barges which, according to the community, number some five or six per day. This unauthorized traffic and unloading of barges is cited as another reason for the increased erosion of the coast and embank-

45 Research has confirmed that redirection of the Wakak River by PT KLI was a key cause of the erosion and submersion of the fishponds. See Sutrisno Anggoro and Slamet Hargono 2000:6-14.

ment protecting the farmers' ponds.[46]

The flooding and erosion caused by the Wakak River's redirection and maintenance of the log pond was worsened by further development undertaken by PT KLI in 1987. This development consisted of the reclamation of some 500 metres of land from the sea, for the construction of additional factory units. An environmental study (*studi evaluasi lingkungan*) conducted on PT KLI concluded that this coastal alteration by PT KLI caused changes in ocean current strength and direction and consequent alterations in sedimentation build-up (ICEL 2000). Weak currents have increased sedimentation on the western side, whilst on the eastern side (where the fishponds of the Mangunharjo and Mangkang Wetan communities are located) a lack of sediment build up has caused further erosion of the beach and consequent damage to the adjoining ponds.[47]

Whilst the substantive environmental changes wrought by PT KLI caused greatly exacerbated erosion in the areas of Mangunharjo and Mangkang Wetan (to the east of the factory), as noted above sedimentation build-up occurred in the area of Mororejo (to the west of the factory) and the area of available land actually increased. Although the build-up of sedimentation enabled the creation of some new fishponds, it also obstructed the access of existing fishponds to the sea by blocking the mouth of a river, into which the factory also disposed liquid waste. Consequently, the factory's waste flowed into the adjacent rice paddies and prawn ponds, causing pollution and damage to crops and fish stock. The productivity of fishponds near PT KLI also reportedly declined as a result of sawdust and smoke discharged from the factory which polluted the ponds (LBHS 2001:5). Communities of ocean-going fishermen had also been adversely affected by the factory's discharge of large volumes of inadequately processed waste into the ocean, resulting in a sharp decline in the typical daily catch of local fisherman. Liquid and solid waste discharged by the factory included chemical by-products used in glue production, such as urea, phenol, melamine, methanol, ammonia and formalin (Pagono 2000b:30). The nets, motors and boats of fisherman were also frequently damaged by waste wood disposed from barges and the factory itself. Other solid waste included free floating logs that frequently damaged both fishing vessels and fishponds.

46 Queries have also been raised concerning the legal status of much of the wood which passes through this informal, unauthorized port and is not subject to the usual permits and examinations. See LBHS 2001.

47 Further research has also confirmed that the land reclamation by PT KLI and its effect on sedimentation build-up resulted in increased erosion of the Mangunharjo coastline. See Sutrisno Anggoro and Slamet Hargono 2000:6-14; and Randiono, *Tinjauan secara kuantitatif perubahan volume sedimen gisik sepanjang pantai kecamatan Kaliwungu kabupaten Kendal*, Unpublished thesis, Facultly of Fisheries and Oceanography, UNDIP, Semarang, p. 34 cited in LBHS 2001.

Negotiation

Whilst the prawn farmers in the locality of PT KLI had suffered the industry's environmental impact since 1987, it was only following the fall of Suharto and the ensuing *reformasi* in 1998 that these communities were prepared to openly advocate their cause against the well-connected industry (Pagono 2000b:30). At this point, prawn farmers from several communities surrounding PT KLI, including Mororejo to the west as well as Mangunharjo and Mangkang Wetan to the east, sought compensation and environmental restoration for problems ranging from erosion and flooding to liquid waste pollution.[48] Subsequent to the farmers obtaining legal representation, a series of twelve negotiation meetings ensued between the farmers and PT KLI in 1998. One outcome of these meetings was an undertaking by PT KLI to construct a sea embankment 500 m-700 m wide and 2 km long. However, after PT KLI reviewed the actual conditions in the field it was considered too difficult and was not carried out (LBHS 1999b). The two parties were unable to reach agreement on the matter of compensation, with the farmers requesting Rp 5,000 per m^2 but PT KLI offering only Rp 900. PT KLI justified its position by claiming that the damage in question was due to natural phenomena and that the farmers had failed to produce evidence to support their claim that PT KLI was responsible. The industry reiterated that it was only prepared to help the farmers in a cooperative manner (*secara gotong royong*), by assisting with heavy machinery in the repair of damaged embankments and fishponds (KLI 1998). Further negotiations were stalled when PT KLI refused to participate on the basis that the farmers' representatives did not have proper legal authority from their respective communities.[49] Finally the negotiation process was overtaken when, outside of negotiations, a payment of Rp 110 million was offered by PT KLI to the sub-group of twelve Mororejo farmers (known as the 'Blok Wakak'), which was accepted.[50] Prawn farmers with fishponds in other areas, such as Mangunharjo and Mangkang Wetan, were not included in this payment, which caused some division among the broader community of farmers and suspicion as to PT KLI's intentions.

48 The claims of the Wonorejo farmers were only raised at a later date, around June 2000.

49 This stance was taken despite the representatives being accepted in previous negotiations.

50 All of the farmers who received compensation owned ponds in Mororejo, although some of them happened to live in Mangunharjo. This group was also known as the 'Blok Wakak'. The farmers who did not receive compensation were those who owned ponds in Mangunharjo, further to the east of PT KLI. This group of farmers was also known as the 'Blok Irigasi'.

Community organization

Following the failure of the negotiation efforts to resolve the problems of the Mangunharjo and Mangkang Wetan communities, contact was renewed with the Legal Aid Institute of Semarang (LBHS) in June 1999. With assistance from LBHS the farmers regrouped, forming an advocacy oriented body named the Kelompok Masyarakat Peduli Lingkungan (KMPL).[51] Further capacity building was carried out in a training workshop for the Mangunharjo community, conducted by the Indonesian Centre for Environmental Law (ICEL) and LBHS from 10-13 September 1999, in which 20 to 30 members of the Mangunharjo community, mostly members of KMPL, participated (ICEL 1999b). The workshop focused on raising community awareness of environmental laws, and building basic skills in techniques of advocacy, mediation and environmental dispute resolution. Other themes included the importance of addressing environmental issues in mediation and maintaining realistic expectations concerning the process of mediation, which could be lengthy and protracted.[52]

One successful outcome of the workshop was that members of the community and KMPL itself were able to clarify their interests and subsequently communicate their key claims through several media releases as well as through direct communications with PT KLI and a range of government agencies. The claims conveyed by the Mangunharjo farmers were:

- construction of a sea wall to prevent further erosion;
- repair of damaged embankments and ponds;
- restoration of coastal environment through removal of liquid and solid waste and stopping further disposal of unprocessed waste;
- compensation for lost income (1990-1998);
- compensation for ponds that have been totally lost (submerged).[53]

51 'Community Group of Environmental Carers'. Prior to the formation of KMPL, eight farmers (who had lost fishponds) had been organized in a group named Kelompok Masyarakat Korban Abrasi ('The Community Group of Erosion Victims'), however the farmers had felt the group was too small and under resourced to deal with the might of PT KLI. As the environmental effects of PT KLI's actions were also increasingly widely felt, there was a perceived need to make the group more representative. Thus the new KMPL was formed, which consisted of a wider cross section of the community including farmers directly affected by erosion, other farmers that potentially could be affected, community leaders, fishermen, youth and other interested persons. See ICEL 1999e.

52 Ari Mochammed Arif, Div Advocacy ICEL and Kasus PT Kayu Lapis Indonesia ICEL, Jakarta, interview, 17-11-1999.

53 'Pengaduan tak ditanggapi, temui dewan', *Suara Merdeka*, 5-11-1999.

From the description above it is apparent that the claims of the farmers had evolved over the period from when negotiation was first commenced with PT KLI, before the commencement of the formal mediation process. Whilst the farmers' initial concerns were primarily economic (obtaining compensation for lost income and lost capital in the form of submerged fishponds), subsequent to the training carried out by ICEL and LBHS at the community level, community representatives agreed it was equally important that environmental issues be addressed in any resolution of the dispute. Environmental solutions canvassed and adopted by community group KMPL included repair of damaged embankments and ponds, construction of a 'sea wall' to prevent future erosion, and stopping disposal of solid and liquid wastes responsible for pollution.[54]

The community and NGOs canvassed both litigation and mediation as possible paths for dispute resolution.[55] Certainly the legal position of PT KLI was, on paper at least, highly problematic. An analysis by ICEL concluded that the factory had contravened the following laws (ICEL 2000):

- Spatial Planning. According to the General Spatial Plan of Kendal Regency, the location of the factory is zoned as an area of fishpond farming not an industrial area, a fact recognized by an environmental study sponsored by KLI itself in 1992 (LBHS 2001);
- Environmental Impact Assessment (article 15,18 EMA 1997; Government Regulation 27 of 1999). No environmental impact assessment was carried out prior to redirection of the river by KLI, which also contravened a legal agreement with a government agency (PISB). KLI's actions in redirecting the river prompted a strong administrative warning (*peringatan keras*) from the governor, however, no further administrative action was taken;
- Government Regulation No. 35 of 1991 concerning Rivers. Article 25 prohibits redirection of a river without a proper licence, which KLI did not possess;
- Pollution/Environmental Damage of a Coastal Area (No. Kep45/ MENLH/11/1999 regarding Sustainable Coastal Program). Article 2 places an obligation on an enterprise to prevent pollution and/or environmental damage of coastal areas. Evidence indicates such pollution and damage had occurred due to KLI's activities;
- Prevention of environmental damage. Article 6(1) of the EMA 1997 states that 'each person is obligated to preserve environmental functions and pre-

54 Initially redirection of the Wakak River to its original course did not appear as a key demand, although this was adopted later as it was perceived by the farmers as necessary to prevent flooding of the fishponds.

55 Poltak Ike Wibowo and Tandiono Bawor Purbaya, interview, LBH Semarang, 24-11-2000.

vent and control pollution or environmental damage'. Evidence indicates that the developments carried out by KLI failed to preserve environmental functions and caused considerable pollution and environmental damage.

Nonetheless, most of the NGO workers involved considered a legal suit unlikely to succeed, given the practical difficulties of proving environmental damage or pollution in a court of law and, moreover, the prevalence of judicial corruption.[56] The prospects of a successful legal suit were also rated low due to the considerable political and economic clout of PT KLI. A further procedural and technical obstacle was the perceived difficulty of proving causation of pollution or environmental damage. Mediation, supported by a range of advocacy strategies, was thus considered the best available option for the Mangunharjo farmers to resolve the dispute. Support in lobbying government agencies and industry to commence a mediation process was provided by ICEL and LBHS, both of which had considerable experience in the mediation of environmental disputes.

Response of government agencies

Subsequent to the capacity building training undertaken at the community level, advocacy initiatives were undertaken including representations made to the provincial parliament and a media campaign to attract publicity to the farmers' cause (ICEL 1999f). Efforts to approach government agencies to resolve the problem were initially unproductive. Representatives of the Mangunharjo farmers, together with the Legal Aid Institute of Semarang (LBHS), initially requested assistance from the governor's office (of Central Java), but were redirected to the regional government level II of Semarang Municipality. The farmers and LBHS then met with a representative of the Semarang Mayor's office on 1 July 1999, along with representatives of other relevant agencies including the Environmental Impact Agency of Semarang. The mayor's representative was sympathetic to the farmers concerns, agreeing that the river should be redirected to its original course and undertaking to meet with the director of PT KLI.[57] The meeting with the mayoralty of Semarang and associated officials at least prompted a visit to Mangunharjo the following day, to view the damage in question. On 5 July a further meeting was held between the LBHS, community group KMPL, and the Environmental Impact Agency of Semarang. Representatives of the agency agreed with LBHS that the dispute resolution process should emphasize the

56 Ari Mochammed Arif, Div Advocacy ICEL and Kasus PT Kayu Lapis Indonesia ICEL, Jakarta, interview, 17-11-1999.

57 'Pemda Kodya akan panggil bos PT KLI', *Wawasan*, 2-7-1999.

matter of environmental restoration (as opposed to mere compensation). Whilst the Semarang Environmental Agency undertook to assist the community as much as possible, it stressed the dispute was the responsibility of the provincial level government (level I) as it encompassed two administrative areas: Semarang municipality and Kendal regency (LBHS 1999b). Subsequently, the Semarang regional government formally requested the assistance of the governor (of Central Java) in resolving the dispute.[58]

The request of the Semarang regional government was followed by a petition in August 1999 to the governor from the Mangunharjo community itself, to resolve the dispute with PT KLI. A formal complaint and request for assistance was also sent to the Central Environmental Control Agency. After several months, the lack of response from either government agency prompted thirty members of KMPL to undertake a widely publicized visit to the Central Java legislature.[59] A meeting with the governor's office was finally granted on 17 November. The meeting, however, produced little result; representatives of KMPL and LBHS were met only by administrative staff with no decision-making authority.[60] A legislative hearing was also held on 18 November 1999 by the Development Commission of the Central Java legislature, in response to the citizens' demands. The meeting was characterized by a heated exchange between representatives of the water management agency (PU Pengairan) and PT KLI over the redirection of the Wakak River, prompting the head of the commission to suggest resolution of the case via judicial channels.[61]

In early December 1999, community representatives met with the Environment Minister, Dr Sonny Keraf, and conveyed their concerns relating to the dispute with PT KLI.[62] Subsequent to this meeting, Dr Keraf publicly requested the governor of Central Java to resolve the long-running PT KLI dispute.[63] The Environment Minister's injunction added momentum to the dispute resolution process, prompting a visit of provincial legislative members and senior government officials the next day to view the environmental damage in Mangunharjo. The governor also pledged to form an independent team of government officials and NGO members, to investigate the contributing causes of the damaged fishponds in Mangunharjo and facilitate mediation between PT KLI and the Mangunharjo community. The team was to be headed by Dr Sudharto P. Hadi from the University of Diponegoro, Semarang.[64]

58 'Pemda Kodya minta bantuan gubernur, soal abrasi PT KLI', *Wawasan*, 30-7-1999.
59 'Pengaduan tak ditanggapi, temui dewan', *Suara Merdeka*, 5-11-1999.
60 'PT KLI Saling Tuding dengan Dinas Pengairan', *Kompas*, 20-11-1999.
61 'PT KLI Saling Tuding dengan Dinas Pengairan', *Kompas*, 20-11-1999.
62 'Rusaknya Tambak di Mangkang diloporkan kepada Menteri LH', *Wawasan*, 1-12-1999.
63 'Gubernur harus segera selesaikan kasus KLI', *Suara Merdeka*, 1-12-1999.
64 'Muspida pantau pertambakan di Mangkang lewat helikopter', *Wawasan*, 2-12-1999.

Response of PT KLI

As discussed above, the factory initially entered negotiations with several communities of farmers in 1998. Its conduct in the negotiations varied, with promised concessions often retracted later. When a payment was finally made by the company to the Mororejo farmers in 1998, it was described as a 'goodwill' payment (*tali asih*), rather than compensation. In addition, the farmers were pressured to sign an agreement prior to receipt of the money, which abrogated their rights to bring any future claim against PT KLI. The agreement was subsequently used by PT KLI as a defence against further environmental claims by the Mororejo community. Furthermore, from an early stage the company also consistently denied culpability for any environmental damage or pollution, attributing the erosion and flooding suffered by the Mangunharjo farmers to natural phenomena including the 'El Niño' effect.[65] More direct approaches had also been employed by PT KLI to discourage claims against it, including from time to time hiring 'third parties' (allegedly hired thugs) to intimidate the local populace. This occurred, for example, after the training program carried out by ICEL and LBHS in the Mangunharjo community.[66] Around the same time, the company also fired 600 workers from the Mangunharjo community and hired 600 workers from the Mororejo community. This was perceived by locals as an attempt to promote discord and conflict within the communities and prevent any 'united front' against the factory.[67]

Despite pressure from government agencies, PT KLI adamantly refused initial overtures to join a mediation process toward resolving the dispute. The factory justified its refusal by reference to the monetary payment (of Rp 110 million) made to the farmers (of Mororejo) in 1998.[68] Furthermore, the industry stood by its argument that the ponds of the Mangunharjo farmers had been submerged because of wider climatic changes and rising sea levels rather than any fault of its own. The stalemate persisted despite formal and informal requests from the governor of Central Java and the Ministry of the Environment to participate in discussions towards resolution of the

65 'Kali Wakak bukan dibuat PT KLI', *Suara Merdeka*, 7-12-1999.

66 Ari Mochammed Arif, Div Advocacy ICEL and Kasus PT Kayu Lapis Indonesia ICEL, Jakarta, interview, 17-11-1999.

67 Arif, Div Advocacy ICEL and Kasus PT Kayu Lapis Indonesia ICEL, Jakarta, interview, 17-11-1999.

68 Several government agencies also considered the case to be closed on this basis. After some lobbying by ICEL, it was recognised however that the separate plight of the Mangunharjo farmers had not been resolved, and that the environmental problems were in any case still continuing. See ICEL and Semarang 1999.

dispute.[69] The company finally acquiesced to the governor's request to participate in a mediation process following the formation, by the governor (at the Environment Minister's behest), of an independent team to resolve the dispute. Yet, whilst PT KLI had finally agreed to enter the mediation process, it was clearly a problematic start to an 'interest-based' dispute resolution process. PT KLI's commitment to the mediation process appeared shaky, and at least partially the product of administrative pressure rather than self-interest.

Mediation process; Mediation December 1999 – June 2000

A new phase of dispute resolution was entered into on 3 December 1999, when mediation commenced between the Mangunharjo community and PT KLI (LBHS 2001). In the first mediation session Dr Sudharto P. Hadi, the Third Assistant to the National Minister for the Environment, and Sri Suryoko, an academic from the Centre for Environmental Studies at the University of Diponegoro, were appointed as mediator and co-mediator respectively. Whilst Sudharto suggested ICEL as a potential co-mediator, this was rejected by PT KLI, who seemingly retained suspicions as to their neutrality (LBHS 1999c). There was some speculation as to the appropriateness of Sudharto because, as he himself acknowledged, he had previously had some interest in the matter as the author of an Environmental Evaluation Study of PT KLI in 1985 (ICEL 1999c; ICEL 1999d). Whilst the representatives of the community retained some suspicion toward him on this basis, it was not sufficient for them to oppose his appointment as mediator.[70]

In the first session (4 December 1999) an 'agreement to mediate' was reached, where both parties agreed to attempt resolution of the dispute via mediation rather than litigation. Mediation, as Dr Sudharto emphasized, should benefit both parties and therefore produce a lasting resolution of the dispute. This theme of an 'interest-based' approach was accentuated by the mediator at several points in the first session. For instance Dr Sudharto stated

> KLI has an interest to maintain a good image and continue its production without obstruction. Meanwhile, the farmers also have an interest that their fishponds and their livelihoods are not threatened. So it may be said that between KLI and the fishpond farmers there is a synergy of interests. [...] Here we will explore ways to allow KLI and the community to live side by side. The direction of the dispute resolution will be toward that which benefits both parties. (LBHS 1999c.)

69 Arif, ICEL and Kasus PT Kayu Lapis Indonesia ICEL, interview, 17-11-1999.

70 Poltak Ike Wibowo and Tandiono Bawor Purbaya, LBHS, interview, 24-11-2000.

Following classic interest-based approaches to mediation, the mediator thus stressed the need to 'separate between the people and the problem' and 'concentrate on attacking the problem rather than the people'. The parties were urged to 'focus on their respective interests rather than their respective positions' and brainstorm multiple solutions based on their shared interests (LBHS 1999c).

A further focus of the first mediation session was the identification of stakeholders who would participate in the mediation process. The main protagonists in the conflict, PT KLI and the Mangunharjo farmers, were represented by three spokespersons and an additional legal representative. Other parties identified as primary stakeholders in the dispute included the provincial Environmental Control Agency, the district (Semarang) Environmental Control Agency, the Environmental Bureau of Kendal, and the governor of Central Java (usually represented by its Legal Bureau), each of which was allowed two representatives. In addition, a number of other parties were also identified as having some stake in the dispute and thus a legitimate basis for involvement in the mediation process. These included:

- Water and Public Works Agency (PU Pengairan), which had originally contracted with KLI concerning the redirection of the Wakak River;
- Department of Mining, whose authority was invoked with respect to KLI's unlicenced sand excavation activities;
- Department of Fisheries, which held administrative authority over the activities of the fish-pond and ocean fishermen;
- ICEL, environmental NGO with expertise in environmental mediation;
- Local government officials from Mangunharjo and adjoining areas;
- The Development Commission of the Central Java legislative assembly (Dewan Perwakilan Rakyat Daerah, DPRD);
- Workers at KLI;
- Fishermen in Mangunharjo and adjoining areas;
- Other observers (including press, NGOs, university academics, and Mangunharjo farmers) to play a supportive or advisory role as needed.

The considerable representation of governmental agencies was a notable feature of the mediation process, due in part to the fact that the dispute crossed administrative boundaries, thus involving agencies from the provincial level (level I), Semarang municipality (level II) and Kendal regency (level II). The complexity of the environmental damage in question and the political and economic significance of PT KLI also ensured that an inclusive mediation process would need to include a wide range of stakeholders.

The main dispute over stakeholders occurred in the second session, when community legal representatives supported the inclusion of the Mororejo fishpond farmers as stakeholders in the mediation process.[71] As discussed above, the Mororejo farmers, whose fishponds were situated to the west of the factory, had experienced a number of problems relating to PT KLI's activities. The industry's land reclamation had obstructed a river mouth, which both restricted the flow of water into existing fishponds and channelled pollution from the factory into the ponds. Whilst some of the Mororejo farmers had received a 'goodwill' payment from PT KLI in 1998, the environmental problems had remained unresolved. However, the proposal to include the Mororejo farmers in the mediation process was firmly opposed by PT KLI, resulting in a deadlock in the third mediation session. Ultimately community legal representatives acquiesced to PT KLI's continuing opposition on this issue, and the mediation process continued without including the Mororejo farmers.

Some discussion was also held concerning the nature of the conflict between the Mangunharjo fishpond farmers and PT KLI. As the mediator noted, one aspect of this conflict was a difference in perception as to the causes of the environmental damage in question.

> Like it or not there is a problem between KLI and the prawn farmers. There is a difference of opinion or conflict. The difference of opinion is a difference of perception between the prawn farmers and KLI. The prawn farmers claim the damage is because of KLI, whereas KLI claims it is due to natural phenomena. (LBHS 1999c.)

Disagreement over the nature, extent and causes of the environmental damage in question emerged in the first mediation session and resurfaced frequently as the mediation process progressed. Shortly after the first session, conflict between the parties emerged when PT KLI publicly asserted that the damage to the fishponds and the coast was solely due to natural factors. In response, the legal representative for the Mangunharjo farmers, Poltak Ike Wibowo, accused PT KLI of provocation contrary to the agreement to mediate. Wibowo maintained that the coastal erosion and flooding of the fishponds was caused by PT KLI's development activities, as was confirmed by the administrative warning issued by the governor to PT KLI in 1990 concerning redirection of the Wakak River.[72]

The parties' positions on this issue shifted little in the second and third mediation sessions.[73] PT KLI refused 'to be blamed' for the environmental damage in question, which it maintained was due to natural phenomena,

71 Several of the Mororejo farmers had approached the Legal Aid Institute of Semarang after mediation had commenced and requested their inclusion in the process. See 'Giliran warga Mororejo gugat PT KLI', *Suara Merdeka*, 10-12-1999.

72 'PT KLI dinilai melakukan provokasi', *Suara Merdeka*, 8-12-1999.

73 Also held in December 1999.

while community representatives continued to assert PT KLI's responsibility for coastal erosion and flooding. The conflicting positions of the parties on the causes of the environmental damage influenced their respective views as to how discussion should proceed. Anxious to avoid further blame, PT KLI suggested that discussion in the sessions should focus on potential solutions: 'We are meeting here to solve a problem not a case. How can we repair and utilize the coast together' (LBHS 2000a:4).

Whilst PT KLI itself had not proposed a solution at this point, and was opposed in principle to the payment of compensation, it was seemingly prepared to undertake environmental restoration.[74] On the other hand, legal aid representatives, whilst having previously suggested construction of a sea wall (*sabuk pantai*) and compensation as suitable remedies, nonetheless insisted that discussion proceed on an 'issue by issue' basis. As one representative stated: 'We prefer to discuss issue by issue, because if we suddenly discuss solutions it will only obscure the causes'. In the fifth mediation session, held on 22 December 1999, the mediator suggested a focus on 'alternative solutions' or 'joint problem solving' consisting of coastal rehabilitation, community development and improved operation of industry (PT KLI). PT KLI and the participating government agencies agreed to this agenda, yet LBHS continued to insist the discussion proceed on an issue-by-issue basis. The issue of causation and blame resulted in further division between the parties with PT KLI becoming increasingly defensive.

> KLI: 'If we discuss issues we also have a requirement. The respective parties should show proof. The fact is there is a difference in opinion and a difference in evidence. [...] Then who will evaluate the validity of the evidence. This isn't a court. [...] And to clarify, if we discuss solutions it doesn't mean that the cause is PT KLI.'
> LBHS: 'We only have discussed one issue, but I think that PT KLI already doesn't want to be blamed'.
> LBHS: 'Its better we return to our early agreement to find the causes so that then we may find the solutions'.
> Mediator: 'Focusing on solutions in this forum doesn't mean leaving the sources of pollution. But it would be better if it were focused on solutions'.

Ultimately, discussion proceeded on an issue-by-issue basis, with the mediators' entreaty to 'not only discuss the problem but also the solution'.

Despite continuing disagreement over the causes of environmental damage, the parties were finally able to agree on an agenda of issues for further discussion. The five issues to be discussed were: redirection of the Wakak River, coastal reclamation, sand excavation, disposal of waste, and damage caused by free floating logs. On the mediator's suggestion, the parties began

74 'Alot, perundingan antara petani tambak dan PT KLI', *Wawasan*, 13-12-1999.

discussion on the least contentious issue: that of free floating logs causing damage to embankments. PT KLI acknowledged that some logs could dislodge and float free, although there was considerable difference with the Legal Aid Institute of Semarang (LBHS) over the number of logs involved and the culpability of PT KLI for the damage in question.[75] The Environmental Agency of Semarang also conveyed its concern that the free-floating logs were causing damage to mangrove plantations. Despite the disagreement over the extent of the problem, the parties were able to reach some consensus on this issue as to proposed solutions; in the form of an agreement in principle, encompassing coastal rehabilitation (tree planting, repair of fishponds and construction of breakwater), review of PT KLI's environmental management plan and operating procedures, and improved communication between farmers and PT KLI.

The next issue examined by the parties was the disposal of oil, solid and liquid waste. LBHS presented its claims, based on a range of written and oral evidence, that hazardous solid and liquid waste disposed of by PT KLI had caused environmental pollution and affected the livelihoods of local fishpond farmers and fishermen. In a continuation of the previous pattern of conflict, PT KLI responded belligerently, denying any culpability.

> KLI is an industry oriented toward business. All its actions are calculated by profit and loss. Used oil we sell, so it isn't possible we just dispose of it like that. Furthermore, for us solid waste [in this case woodchips] is money. We take that to RPI [an associated factory] to process it and sell. Then for other chemicals, it's expensive. [...] If we just throw them away it's inefficient. Then we'd like to ask if we bring a tissue and drop it does this pollute the environment? (LBHS 2000c.)

PT KLI's representative then proceeded to make his own counter accusations: 'I'd like to ask about the fisherman's operations. The fishpond farmers also use *Bristan* to kill small pests (*trisipan*) which is then thrown in the river. But they are never touched.' The mediator responded by suggesting a technical team be appointed to review the issue, as the two parties' animosity heightened.

> LBHS: 'The area where KLI is located is not industrial, according to spatial planning. You (KLI) are a guest who hasn't been invited.'
> KLI: 'This is the risk if we discuss issues. As for the problem of language, how can we use polite speech, how dare we be called an uninvited guest.'

The mediator's idea of a technical review (of both PT KLI and the farmers' operations) was well received by government agencies and PT KLI. LBHS,

75 According to LBHS and the farmers the logs could 'number in the hundreds', whereas PT KLI's estimates were much less than this.

however, opposed the review, arguing that what was required was the implementation of existing environmental management plans.

> LBHS: 'This is certainly a collective problem but the one that hasn't fulfilled its commitment is KLI so why is the community blamed? The fishpond farmers are already being examined by the Fisheries Department.'

Continuing to oppose the idea of a technical team, LBHS adhered to its proposed solutions of moving KLI's log pond to land to ensure no ship traffic near the factory, as well as stopping the use of hazardous materials and moving the location of methanol storage.

The positions of the parties were seemingly further hardened in the following, sixth, pleno forum on 28 January 2000. Conflict emerged over a press report which, according to PT KLI, contravened a previous agreement between the parties regarding restrictions on information given to the mass media about the case. PT KLI also reiterated its positions that any 'issues' raised for discussion should be subject to investigation and any 'accusations' made by LBHS should be supported by evidence. As the pattern of recrimination and counter-recrimination continued between the primary parties, the commitment of PT KLI to the mediation process began to visibly weaken. PT KLI demanded that the pleno session be postponed and that separate discussions be held between the mediator with the respective parties. In the event this was not carried out PT KLI threatened to withdraw from the mediation process. The parties agreed to the proposal and separate discussions were carried out, following which both parties affirmed separately their intention to continue with the mediation process.

In light of the increasing conflict between the primary parties in the pleno sessions, the mediation team changed tack in February and March 2000, embarking on an intensive series of separate meetings with the respective sides to facilitate progress toward agreement. The expressed intention of the mediation team was to convene a meeting of all parties only when there was sufficient indication of progress toward an agreement. Then a pleno session would be organized to bring all sides together and produce a comprehensive agreement. The separate meetings were designed to enable individual parties to discuss and elaborate their own potential solutions to the dispute. Given the state of animosity and conflict that had been reached in the pleno mediation sessions, this tactical change seems to have been appropriate, and did serve to minimize conflict between the parties. By April 2000, after seven separate meetings, the parties had at least reached an agreement in principle on the need for three broad solutions: coastal rehabilitation, improved environmental management of PT KLI, and community development; although the details of each had not been determined or agreed upon.[76]

Subsequent to the series of separate meetings and discussion of possible solutions, the mediation team presented a written proposal to all parties, for resolution of the dispute. The solution detailed a number of measures to be undertaken, including:

- construction of sea barrier;
- tree planting;
- repair of river embankments;
- normalization and restoration of Wakak River;
- no further disposal of solid or liquid waste to sea;
- compliance with stipulated levels waste disposal;
- enforcement of environmental law;
- compensation for lost income of farmers;
- payment for submerged ponds;
- exemption from land tax for submerged ponds.

The proposal by the mediation team was clearly an attempt to refocus the parties on a possible solution rather than continuing the increasingly acrimonious discussion of 'issues', as had occurred in previous sessions. Whilst the mediator's proposed solution attempted to cover all the issues raised by the parties, some of the proposed measures were insufficiently specific, such as 'enforcement of environmental law'. Even 'normalization' of the Wakak River sidestepped crucial questions about whether 'normalization' would mean returning the river to its original course, or only slightly readjusting its current course – a matter that would become a key issue in later discussions.

All parties were given a period of time to consider the mediator's proposed solution, and were required to respond by 14 April 2000. Whilst the Mangunharjo community and regional government responded favourably to the proposal, no reply was forthcoming from PT KLI, even after several extensions of the deadline by the mediation team. As the stalemate in negotiations dragged on, the community representatives publicly criticized the mediator and carried out several demonstrations, in conjunction with other communities that had experienced environmental damage or pollution in the vicinity of PT KLI.[77] A circular letter was issued by the Governor (of Central Java), which appealed to all parties to respond to the solution proposed by

76 A particular point of contention was whether the third solution 'community development' would encompass payment of compensation. See 'Tanggapan Sudharto P. Hadi', *Radar Semarang*, 6-4-2000.

77 'Demo KLI dan RPI, digiring polisi', *Radar Semarang*, 4-4-2000; 'Warga sekitar kli tak percaya Prof Soedhardo', *Radar Semarang*, 4-4-2000.

the mediator and resolve the dispute.[78] Despite this appeal, PT KLI refused to accept or even respond to the proposed solution. The deadlock continued, and the level of frustration in the Mangunharjo community increased, with one representative publicly warning that the community was 'ready to wage a holy war in fighting for their rights'.[79] By late May the mediator, Dr Sudharto P. Hadi, also expressed disillusionment with the industry's lack of response: 'Actually [the mediation team] is weary of the process, but we respect Governor Mardiyanto who still wishes to resolve the case through mediation'.[80]

In a further attempt to break the deadlock, the governor's office attempted to arrange separate negotiations with each of the respective parties, on three occasions. Despite the requests from the governor's office, PT KLI consistently refused to attend.

Mediation recommenced; June – September 2000

In June 2000, a group of one hundred Mangunharjo fishpond farmers visited the Central Java governor's office to request the assistance of the governor in resolving the mediation with PT KLI.[81] The governor confirmed his willingness to facilitate further negotiation and stated that PT KLI's management had also indicated their willingness to continue mediation. In response to the community's request, a further meeting was held on 29 June, chaired by the Vice-Governor and Sudharto, at which all parties were present. At this meeting PT KLI indicated it was only willing to continue mediation under a new format, according to which the primary parties (Mangunharjo community and PT KLI) would negotiate directly without legal representation, mediated by the governor or his representative. This 'small format' (*format kecil*) negotiation was agreed to by all parties in a subsequent pleno session on 10 July 2000, at which PT KLI was not present, although community representatives requested that the process be mediated by a member of the mediation team rather than the governor's office (Hadi 2000). At the pleno session the parties also agreed to continue the mediation process, which had originally been scheduled to end on 31 March 2000.

The first meeting of the 'small format' mediation was held on 15 July 2000 at the Centre for Environmental Studies, University of Diponegoro. PT KLI again failed to attend; however discussion proceeded between community representatives, the vice-governor and the Central Java Environmental

78 'Jika macet masyarakat siap jihad', *Wawasan*, 12-5-2000.
79 'Jika macet masyarakat siap jihad', *Wawasan*, 12-5-2000.
80 'Tim mediasi leleh urusi KLI', *Wawasan*, 27-5-2000.
81 'Kasus KLI, Gubernur akan pertemukan pihak pertait', *Kompas*, 17-6-2000.

Control Agency. The Mangunharjo farmers presented an offer for resolution of the dispute, which was discussed by government representatives. A broad consensus on the need for coastal rehabilitation was reached, with regional government representatives further agreeing to several initiatives, including:

- discharging submerged fishponds in Mangunharjo from further tax;
- supervision of industry operations;
- enforcement of environmental regulations;
- repair of Wakak (Beringin) River (contingent on approval of legislature);
- normalization of Santren and Paluh Rivers.

After PT KLI's failure to attend the 15 July mediation session facilitated by the governor, an administrative warning was issued to the company; which prompted its attendance at the subsequent session on 11 August.[82] At the meeting, the industry indicated its willingness to resolve the case by mediation, yet reiterated it was not prepared to pay compensation, although a 'good will' payment (*tali asih*) below Rp 110 million could be made. Yet, despite pressure from government representatives to reduce their demands, community representatives rejected what they saw as a 'manipulative' approach to resolving the dispute.[83]

A pleno session of all stakeholders, with the exception of PT KLI which did not attend, was held on 9 September 2000. At this meeting, it was agreed to form two separate forums for resolution of the dispute: the 'Small Format' mediation and the 'Consultation Forum', both of which are discussed below.

Small Format Mediation

The so-called 'Small Format' Mediation was originally proposed by participants in a meeting on 10 July 2000. This simplified form of mediation would be restricted to the Mangunharjo fishpond farmers and PT KLI, without legal representation. The process was to be facilitated by the mediation team and the governor's representative, with a particular focus on resolving the matter of compensation.

An initial meeting of the 'small format' group was held on 19 September 2000. Again, PT KLI failed to attend, and the farmers were therefore unable to gain clarification concerning PT KLI's willingness to give capital assistance

82 'Gubernur tegur keras KLI', *Wawasan*, 12-8-2000.
83 'Gubernur tegur keras KLI', *Wawasan*, 12-8-2000.

to the farmers. Due to PT KLI's lack of response, the farmers intended to formally request a direct audience with the governor to convey their concerns. The persistent failure of PT KLI to participate in mediation attracted public criticism from the mediator, Dr Sudharto P. Hadi, who speculated that the industry's lack of participation could provide a basis for the regional government to close down the industry.[84] Within the Mangunharjo community, PT KLI's refusal to negotiate caused increasing frustration and threats of direct action against the industry (KMPL/LBH 2000). A further meeting was held between PT KLI and the Mangunharjo farmers pursuant to the 'Small Format' in early February 2001, during which PT KLI reportedly offered the farmers some Rp 50 million in compensation.[85] This was rejected by the farmers, and no agreement was forthcoming.

More recently, the 'Small Format' Mediation between PT KLI and the Mangunharjo farmers has finally resulted in Rp 125 million being offered by PT KLI to the sixteen farmers whose fishponds had been completely submerged as a result of encroaching sea levels. The payment was supplemented by an additional sum of Rp 375 million, which was paid to the farmers by the provincial government.[86] Other farmers, whose ponds had suffered partial damage from erosion or flooding, were not compensated however.[87] The payment was also not described as compensation, but rather a goodwill payment to those farmers who had lost their fishponds because of 'natural disaster'. Whilst the payment satisifed the farmers' demands for compensation, it also resulted in conflict within KMPL, between those who wished to accept the payment and those who did not. Some within the group felt that payment should only be accepted if it were accompanied by a commitment to carry out environmental rehabilitation. However, for the sixteen farmers who had lost land because of erosion and flooding, the payment was a welcome compensation of their economic loss. The payment was ultimately accepted by the sixteen farmers and KMPL subsequently disbanded.[88]

Consultation Forum; September 2000 – March 2001

The second mediation process, termed the 'Consultation Forum', was intended to focus on discussing and elaborating on potential government programs connected with the above solutions. Participants in the forum would include

84 'Gubernor punya landasan UU 23/1997', *Wawasan*, 6-11-2000.
85 Andi, Director of LBHS, interview, 15-2-2001.
86 Wiwiek Awiati, ICEL, interview, 18-11-2003.
87 Wiwiek Awiati, ICEL, interview, 4-6-2003.
88 However, a number of members from the community continue to be active in environmental advocacy through other organizations: Tandiono Bawor Purbaya, interview, 18-11-2003.

Mangunharjo fishpond farmers (and their legal representatives from LBHS), relevant government agencies from Semarang, Kendal Regency and the Central Java Provincial government, and other experts. The Consultation Forum would be facilitated by the mediation team.

In the first session of the Consultation Forum, held on 20 September 2000, the parties present agreed to develop joint programs addressing coastal rehabilitation, operational improvement (of industry) and community development.[89] Participants agreed that programs should be based on the 'the common commitment [...] of community and regional government [...] to uphold environmental law'. Programs should also 'anticipate potential negative impacts' and 'be real and applicable and of benefit to both community and regional government' and hopefully become 'a planning model that will facilitate joint community/government decision making in the future also' (PPLH Undip Semarang 2000). The parties resolved to discuss operational improvement (*peningkatan kinerja*) first, referring to the five issues identified in previous meetings:

- redirection and restoration of river;
- reclamation;
- sand excavation;
- free-floating logs;
- disposal of oil, solid waste and other chemicals.

The second Consultation Forum, held on 12 October 2000, provided an opportunity for the respective parties and coordinating groups to present preliminary drafts of suggested programs, which for the most part were still couched in general terms.[90] The suggested program of the provincial coordinating group (headed by the Central Java Environmental Impact Agency) emphasized rehabilitation of damaged coast/ponds, re-evaluation of redirection of the river, and operational improvement of the industry. The suggested

89 These programs corresponded with the three broad categories of solutions agreed by PT KLI and the Mangunharjo farmers in previous mediation sessions. The parties present included representatives of: Mangunharjo farmers and legal representatives (from Semarang Legal Aid Institute); Kendal Environmental Bureau; Legal Bureau (provincial); Semarang subdistrict head; Fisheries Agency (Semarang); Environmental Agency (Semarang); Semarang Mayorality; Environmental Agency (Central Java); mediation team.

90 Several coordinating groups (*gugus tugas*) were formed to facilitate interaction between the large number of government agencies. Coordinating groups included the provincial coordinating group (headed by the Central Java Environmental Impact Agency), the Kendal coordinating group (headed by Kendal environmental bureau), the Semarang coordinating group (headed by the Semarang Environmental Impact Agency) and the community coordinating group (headed by representatives of the Mangunharjo community).

program of the Semarang coordinating group (headed by the Semarang Environmental Impact Agency) emphasized coastal rehabilitation, whilst the officials of Kendal regency were not present. The proposed programs of the community coordinating group focused on operational improvement of PT KLI. Community representatives stressed that PT KLI's operations to date had been illegal in a number of respects. The industry had never held a permit or licence for its reclamation of land, which had also contravened spatial planning requirements that development only be carried out a minimum of 100 metres from the waterline. PT KLI had also failed to carry out recommendations of a previous environmental review (*kajian SEL*) and still disposed of solid waste into the ocean. In the community's opinion there was still no evidence of a change in the industry's behaviour, and accordingly the community considered it necessary to carry out an environmental audit. The proposal of an environmental audit was supported by other government representatives, and all participants in the Consultation Forum endorsed the enforcement of environmental law as an element of a comprehensive solution, further noting that the application of sanctions to PT KLI did not imply closure of the industry.

The community also emphasized the need to ensure the suitability of coastal rehabilitation programs for conditions on the Mangunharjo coast, and requested government agencies coordinate program implementation with community members to this end.[91] The most essential programs, from the community's perspective, were the construction of a sea wall, redirection of the Wakak River to its original course, and reclamation of submerged coast. The Mangunharjo fishpond farmers considered the redirected river as the primary cause of the erosion and flooding of their fishponds, which research from several different sources had confirmed (Sutrisno Anggoro and Slamet Hargono 2000:6-14). Whilst re-evaluation of the Wakak River issue was included in the provincial coordinating group's program, the matter was a problematic one for several of the government agencies involved. The river had been illegally redirected by PT KLI and, in failing to act on the matter, the government agencies had been tacit accomplices. As a result, some of the agencies involved were reportedly apprehensive at the possibility of being sued in the administrative court over their role in the matter.[92] In subsequent meetings of the forum, redirection of the Wakak River would become one of the major issues of negotiation.

The third Consultation Forum was held on 2 November 2000. The forum commenced with the presentation of proposed solutions by the regional gov-

91 Previous rehabilitation measures, including tree planting, had failed due to a lack of suitability and knowledge of local conditions.

92 Tandiono Bawor Purbaya, LBHS, interview, 15-2-2001.

ernment agency of Kendal, which emphasized coastal rehabilitation and was supported by all participants. Regency officials also presented the proposed solutions of PT KLI, which were sent to Kendal regency on 29 September 2000.[93] Further discussions by the coordinating group for Semarang City had resulted in several additions to their proposed program, including creation of a basic map of the coastal area within Semarang Municipality, inventorying coastal problems and carrying out a Beach Preservation Program ('Program Pantai Lestari'). Redirection of the Wakak River was again a central issue for discussion. The Water/Public Works agency responsible argued that further redirection of the Wakak River would require a legal permit, and consequently would require a prior legal review to be undertaken. Representatives of the community criticized this position, maintaining that as the river had been illegally redirected in the first place a legal permit should not be necessary to return it to its prior course. Government representatives agreed that the matter should be the subject of further review, and a consensus was reached to form a team to carry out a legal and technical review on the matter.[94]

A further forum was held on 13 January 2001, at which the task of implementation was discussed, with some government agencies cautioning that legislative approval might be required to carry out their proposed programs. Legal representatives of the community feared the need for legislative approval could be used as an excuse for non-implementation of the programs and solutions, and requested that the relevant government agencies give some certainty that programs could be implemented as proposed. To facilitate implementation, the mediator proposed a joint working group to supervise execution of the agreement. The proposal to return the Wakak River to its original course was also the subject of further discussion. The Mangunharjo community agreed that diversion of the river, short of returning it fully to its original course, was acceptable provided no further negative environmental impacts occurred. It was agreed that a comprehensive technical review would be undertaken to determine the suitability of redirecting the river. Finally, an agreement was reached between all parties to hold a subsequent workshop to finalize solutions, which would then be put to the provincial legislative assembly and governor for agreement and immediate implementation.

On 16-17 February, 2 March and 9 March 2001, several last consultative workshops were held between the Mangunharjo community and various government agencies to finalize the proposed programs relating to the envi-

93 These included standard environmental management measures in accordance with regulatory requirements, and some physical development proposals, which were to be further monitored by the Kendal regency.

94 Tim pelurusan Sungai Wakak coordinated by the Agency for Public/Water Works.

ronmental issues in the PT KLI dispute. The conclusions of three working groups were combined into an agreement (*Cooperative agreement* 2001), signed on 9 March 2001, detailing the proposed solutions to be implemented.[95]

The two main areas covered by the agreement were coastal rehabilitation and operational improvement. Coast rehabilitation measures would address the problems of erosion and flooding caused by the redirection of the river, and land reclamation. Specific measures included restoration of the Aji and Wakak Rivers, to ensure they continued to fulfil drainage and irrigation functions properly in relation to the surrounding fish-ponds. Further erosion would be prevented by construction of a sea wall and groin. Operational improvements were intended to address the problems of free-floating logs, waste management and compliance with environmental standards. Specific measures included relocation of PT KLI's existing log-pond, and improvements in the transport of logs to prevent further damage by free-floating logs to fishponds. Waste management would be implemented by monitoring of PT KLI's waste (solid, liquid and gaseous) emissions, and improvement of its waste processing unit. An environmental audit of PT KLI's operations, including its use of hazardous chemicals, would also be carried out to ensure compliance with existing environmental regulations. The agreement also provided for community participation and access to results of audits or reviews at all stages of the program.

All parties present agreed that implementation of this program of solutions was possible, as it was within the authority of the Central Java, Kendal Regency and Semarang City regional governments. Nonetheless, the leader of the mediation team, Dr Sudharto P. Hadi, recognized that the program would certainly benefit from a corresponding commitment from PT KLI to its implementation. The participating parties also agreed that the details of the agreement should be incorporated into a decision of the Central Java governor, to further facilitate the process of implementation.[96]

By 2002 the program of solutions elaborated by the Consultation Forum was approved by the regional parliament of Central Java. To date, however, only partial implementation of the program has occurred. Environmental rehabilitation work so far undertaken includes the reclamation and rehabilitation of a beach. The provincial government of Central Java sponsored the work, which cost approximately Rp 500 million and was implemented by the local community. Rehabilitation of the beach is expected to reduce erosion

95 Kesepakatan perundingan penyelesaian kasus kerusakan tambak dan panti Mangunharjo kecamatan tugu kota Semarang dalam forum konsultasi.

96 Decision of the Central Java Governor No. 660.1.05/07/1999 had initially provided for formation of the mediation team and commencement of the mediation process to resolve the PT KLI dispute.

and flooding, although further work will be necessary in the longer term for a more lasting solution to these problems.[97]

Conclusion

Like the PT Palur Raya case discussed in the first half of this chapter, the dispute between PT KLI and the Mangunharjo fishpond farmers has been a protracted one, dragging out for over ten years without comprehensive resolution. In the late 1990s, a combination of factors contributed to the commencement of a mediation process. Chief amongst these were the broad political changes accompanying the demise of the Suharto regime and the advent of *reformasi,* which created the political space for a dispute with such a well-connected industry to emerge openly. A process of community education and organization facilitated by several NGOs also resulted in more effective advocacy and a subsequent higher profile for the dispute in the regional and national press. Whilst the industry at first paid little attention to the community's demands, a campaign by KMPL involving visits to government agencies and the provincial legislature gradually increased the public pressure on PT KLI. The final catalyst for the mediation process came from the national Environment Minister, Dr Sonny Keraf, who met with Mangunharjo community representatives and then requested the governor to resolve the long running dispute; leading to the formation of the independent team at the governor's directive to mediate the dispute. In this respect, the factors that facilitated access to a structured mediation process are directly comparable to the Palur Raya dispute, which only gained momentum in the post-New Order period, supported by effective community advocacy and, finally, intervention from the national Environment Minister.

In the initial mediation sessions the parties were at least able to agree on procedural matters and the use of mediation as a means to resolve the dispute. Progress on substantive issues was less forthcoming, and conflict between PT KLI and the community's legal representatives increased in the early phase of mediation. The mediation team accordingly chose to split the mediation process and negotiate separately with PT KLI and the Mangunharjo community. Whilst this strategy minimized conflict it did not prevent PT KLI's subsequent withdrawal from mediation, as evinced by the industry's failure to respond to the mediator's proposed solution or participate in further discussion. Despite PT KLI's withdrawal, the mediation process continued on two separate tracks – the 'Small Format' mediation focused primarily on

[97] Tandiono Bawor Purbaya, interview, 18-11-2003.

issues of compensation, and the 'Consultation Forum', which has focused on elaborating social and environmental solutions to the dispute in conjunction with government agencies.

Whilst mediation has certainly been protracted and hindered by PT KLI's frequent failure to participate, it now appears to have borne at least some concrete results. Through the 'Small Format' Mediation, compensation has been paid to those farmers whose land was lost as a result of encroaching sea levels. Through the 'Consultation Forum' mediation, a program of solutions to address issues of environmental rehabilitation, waste management and community development has now been elaborated and endorsed by regional government agencies. Whilst the program has yet to be properly implemented, one initiative of environmental rehabilitation has been carried out successfully. More substantive initiatives, including the proposed redirection of the Wakak River, are likely to require substantial commitment from both district and provincial agencies and, moreover, PT KLI itself.

Important progress has thus been made, not least of which is improved communication amongst the diversity of stakeholders involved in this dispute, particularly between the Mangunharjo community and numerous government agencies from the Central Java, Kendal regency and Semarang city regional governments. The most serious obstacle to progress toward resolving this dispute was PT KLI's withdrawal from mediation in March 2000, which caused a serious derailment of the process. Despite this withdrawal, progress toward resolution was maintained; however, PT KLI's lack of commitment to the process could continue to threaten comprehensive resolution of the dispute, in the event that PT KLI does not support implementation of the rehabilitation program.

Before the commencement of mediation in December 1999, PT KLI had displayed little willingness to compromise or even enter into discussions with the Mangunharjo farmers. PT KLI's position in this respect was strengthened by the marked imbalance of power between the parties. As a national political and economic heavy-weight with strong government backing, an industry of PT KLI's stature had seemingly little to fear from a small community of fishpond farmers. Ultimately, the participation of the otherwise recalcitrant industry in the mediation process was only secured by direct political pressure from the governor of Central Java.

The potential for compromise was also likely to be limited by the history of contentious relationships between the parties. The Mangunharjo community had suffered the effects of environmental damage for almost a decade without recompense from PT KLI. Furthermore, the community had been angered at the industry's supposedly manipulative resolution of the previous dispute with surrounding farmers in 1998.[98] Furthermore, a history of contentious relationship also existed between PT KLI and the Legal Aid Institute of Semarang (LBHS), who were appointed legal representatives for the Mangunharjo farmers and negotiated on their behalf during the mediation process. The same lawyers representing the Mangunharjo farmers in this dispute were frequent public critics of the industry and had acted against the industry in numerous environmental and labor disputes in the past.[99] An imbalance of power between the parties and a history of contentious relationships were thus factors mitigating against the success of mediation from an early stage.

Yet despite these factors, some potential for compromise did apparently exist at the commencement of mediation. Several mitigation measures were possible for the environmental damage in question; such as construction of a sea wall. Whilst refusing to accept responsibility for the environmental damage, PT KLI was still reportedly prepared to undertake some measures of environmental rehabilitation. The 'interest-based' approach to mediation that commenced in December 1999 was intended to build upon such areas of potential compromise with the hope of achieving, in the mediator's words, a 'resolution that benefits both parties' (LBHS 1999c). As explained in the first mediation session, an interest-based approach implied 'attacking the problem not the people', 'focusing on interests rather than positions', and 'brainstorming multiple solutions that reflect common interests' (LBHS 1999c). Yet in practice, the process of mediation was unable to shift the parties from their relatively entrenched positions to focus on areas of potential compromise.

One contributing factor in this respect was a lack of objective standards by which to assess the extent and causes of the environmental damage in question. PT KLI's often reiterated defence from the earliest stage in negotiation was that the environmental damage was not 'proven' to be PT KLI's responsibility. The company itself attributed the damage to natural phenomena, and so was prepared to help 'solve the problem', in the spirit of *gotong royong* ('mutual cooperation'), but was singularly unprepared to acknowledge any wrongdoing or obligation on its part. The company thus wished to focus on solutions rather than issues, as it was 'here to solve a problem not a case'(LBHS 2000c). In contrast, legal representatives for the Mangunharjo farmers argued vigorously that the damage to the fishponds was directly attributable to PT KLI's redirection of the Wakak River and associated activities, including sand dredging and land reclamation. Community legal repre-

98 The industry's payment of Rp 110 million to only a small group of Mororejo farmers was regarded as an attempt to split opposition to the factory.

99 Note in the subsequent process of 'Small Format' Mediation, legal representatives did not participate.

sentatives responded to PT KLI's position of denial by presenting evidence to clarify the 'causes' of the environmental damage, namely PT KLI's development activities. This approach, however, only elicited further denials from PT KLI, who stated bluntly: 'The fact is there is a difference in opinion and a difference in evidence. [...] Then who will evaluate the validity of the evidence. This isn't a court'. (LBHS 2000c.)

Both parties thus started the mediation process with fundamentally different views concerning the cause of the environmental damage; a conflict that was apparently not resolved during the mediation process. Clearly, the need in this case was for some objective, informed and independent standard by which the extent and causes of the environmental damage could be assessed. Whilst some research into the environmental damage had confirmed the farmers' claim, the research was not comprehensive in nature nor jointly arranged by (and thus acceptable to) both parties.[100] However, as discussed above, such jointly arranged research was undertaken in the Palur Raya dispute, and still did not resolve conflict over factual issues. In both disputes therefore, disagreement over issues of factual causation remained an obstacle to resolution.

The escalating dynamic of conflict that appeared in the early stages of mediation in this case was quite contrary to the mediator's initial intentions of an interest-based approach. The parties held to their respective positions rather than identifying potentially common interests, and increasingly attacked each other rather than the problem at hand. In retrospect, one informant regretted that further training in interest-based mediation had not previously been carried out with all stakeholders. Such training may indeed have further 'entrenched' an interest-based approach, which the mediator's brief initial overview seemed unable to do. In the face of escalating conflict the mediation team made the appropriate choice, probably somewhat overdue, to pursue a strategy of 'shuttle diplomacy': negotiating separately with each of the parties from mid-February 2000 onwards. The strategy was unsuccessful, however, in producing an agreement between the parties; as evinced by the parties' responses when, following the series of separate negotiations, the mediator presented a proposed solution as a basis for a potential agreement. Whilst favourable responses to the proposed solution were received from community representatives and government agencies, no response was forthcoming from PT KLI. The industry reportedly considered that the proposal demonstrated bias on the part of the mediation team, and effectively

100 In fact, more detail research was commissioned into the environmental damage much later in the dispute resolution process, subsequent to PT KLI's withdrawal. The research, which at March 2001 was still not available, was to provide a basis for government departments and agencies to implement their proposed solutions.

withdrew itself from the mediation process for several months.

PT KLI's withdrawal and its failure to even respond to the proposed solution was a tangible expression of the industry's lack of commitment to the mediation process as a whole. This poor commitment was evident from the pre-mediation phase, when PT KLI was willing to participate in the mediation process after only direct pressure from the governor of Central Java. Following renewed political pressure and an administrative warning from the governor in July 2000, the industry agreed to reopen negotiations with the Mangunharjo farmers without legal representation. Yet even in this revised 'Small Format' Mediation, which PT KLI itself had suggested, the company failed to attend subsequent scheduled meetings on several occasions. The industry's behaviour in this respect seemed to demonstrate intent to delay, obfuscate and manipulate, rather than actually resolve the dispute at hand. Similar behaviour was also evident from PT Palur Raya in the Palur Raya dispute, although this occurred more in the implementation rather than mediation phase. PT KLI's reluctance to negotiate and resolve the dispute constituted probably the most serious obstacle to resolution in this case. As stated by Dr Sudharto P. Hadi, mediator to the dispute: 'PT KLI did not demonstrate a willingness to negotiate. In contrast, the willingness of the community to negotiate was very high.'[101] The tenuous commitment of PT KLI to the dispute resolution process demonstrated not only the marked imbalance in power between the parties but also the absence of effective administrative or legal sanctions that could have acted as an incentive for the industry to persevere with negotiations. As discussed above, PT KLI had typically acted in a unilateral fashion in redirecting of the Wakak River, reclaiming land and carrying out sand dredging. The company displayed little concern for regulations, which it contravened, nor for administrative warnings issued to it by regional government agencies on several occasions. Evidently the company enjoyed government backing at high levels, and no regional government agency was prepared to go beyond an issuance of written warnings despite numerous breaches of environmental law. The threat of potential administrative sanction was thus too weak to provide a sufficient incentive for the company to either desist from environmentally damaging activities or resolve related conflict with neighbouring communities. Parallels may again be drawn with the Palur Raya dispute in this respect, where the inability or unwillingness of supervising administrative agencies to enforce environmental regulations ensured there was little pressure on the industry to comply with mediated environmental agreements.

Despite transgressing numerous environmental, spatial planning and

[101] 'Gubernor punya landasan UU 23/1997', *Wawasan*, 6-11-2000.

sectoral regulations in the course of its operations, PT KLI also seemingly had little to fear from legal suits brought by the neighbouring communities with which it was in conflict. In a letter to the Mangunharjo and Mororejo fishpond farmers in September 1998, the director of PT KLI stated that if the farmers were unwilling to accept the company's offers of limited cooperative assistance then 'the problem should be solved through legal channels' (KLI 1998). It is also telling that, despite PT KLI's withdrawal from mediation, the Mangunharjo community had not resorted to litigation to address its environmental and economic claims. As discussed above, the most salient reason for this choice was the perceived poor prospect of success within a court system that was inexperienced in dealing with environmental suits, formalistic and conservative in its application of laws and, moreover, riddled with corruption.

Thus, in both the PT KLI and Palur Raya cases, a lax environment of administrative and judicial enforcement enabled or contributed to the industries' contravention of environmental regulations and apparent lack of commitment to mediation. However, in both cases the industries eventually did make significant compensation payments to the respective claimants.[102] Thus, despite the weakness of administrative and judicial law enforcement, the industries apparently did have at least some incentive to make substantial payments toward resolution of the respective disputes. In the PT KLI case, part of this incentive was due to senior government pressure on the industry to resolve the high profile dispute. It was initially the intervention of the national Environmental Minister, Dr Sonny Keraf, in 1999, which prompted formal initiation of the mediation process by the Central Java governor in December 1999. The governor also exerted personal pressure on PT KLI's management on several occasions to participate in mediation and resolve the dispute.[103] Similarly, in the Palur Raya case, the national Environment Minister was a catalyst for the start of mediation and also brokered the final agreement between the parties.

The intervention of senior government figures to resolve the dispute was in turn related to the high level of public pressure evident in both the PT KLI and the Palur Raya cases. In the PT KLI case, community organization was facilitated initially by the involvement of local and national level non-government organizations. Subsequently the local community organization KMPL became the institutional focal point for advocacy, assisted by the Legal Aid Institute of Semarang (LBHS). Advocacy encompassed a range of approaches including press releases, seminars, demonstrations and lobbying. As in the

102 In the case of PT Palur Raya, Rp 1.1 billion. In the case of PT KLI, Rp 125 million.

103 Ari Mochammed Arif, Div Advocacy ICEL and Kasus PT Kayu Lapis Indonesia ICEL, Jakarta, interview, 17-11-1999.

Palur Raya dispute, focused community advocacy maximized exposure through print and electronic media. Both disputes developed quickly into high profile cases, ensuring that any developments regularly received wide coverage in national print and electronic media.

Whilst both these factors encouraged an industry payment to 'resolve' the dispute, there appears to be less incentive for industries in either case to comply with environmental agreements or regulations on an ongoing basis. In the PT KLI case, regional (district and provincial) agencies appear to have had very limited capacity to enforce compliance of the industry with environmental regulations. Similarly, in the Palur Raya dispute district and provincial agencies have been reportedly ineffective in ensuring the factory's compliance with waste management regulations. Thus, whilst both industries appeared prepared to make substantial payments to end the disruptive disputes, it is less certain whether the incentive exists in the longer term to implement solutions to the environmental problems underlying the disputes. Interestingly, in both cases the payments made by industry have had the effect of significantly muting community opposition, despite the failure to address environmental issues.

CHAPTER VI

Conclusion
Environmental justice in Indonesia

The cornerstone of President Suharto's New Order was economic development (*pembangunan*), which encompassed both the intensive development of the industrial sector and the exploitation of a range of natural resources. Whilst economic development brought benefits to the wider populace, the environmental cost was considerable and, more often than not, ignored. Since 1997, political, economic and social crisis has shaken the nation of Indonesia, relegating environmental issues to a relatively low position on the state's political agenda.[1] Ironically, these wider changes have only intensified the incidence of environmental disputes across the archipelago, as natural resources have come under increasing pressure from spiralling rates of illegal exploitation. The political liberalization that followed the demise of the New Order has also been a catalyst for the re-emergence of long suppressed environmental disputes. Long suffering victims of pollution and environmental damage have become increasingly prepared to voice their dissent in ways that would have attracted severe repression in years past. In this context of change, the need for reliable mechanisms for environmental dispute resolution is clear. As we have seen, the Environmental Management Act 1997 has endeavoured to create a legal framework for this purpose, encompassing both judicial and non-judicial environmental dispute resolution, the application of which has been the focus of this book. In this final chapter, we shall assess and compare the effectiveness of these two forums for environmental dispute resolution, with reference to the theoretical framework elaborated in Chapter I.

1 The slow and ultimately ineffective response of the Indonesian government to the forest fires of 1997-98 was one example of the lack of priority given to environmental issues at the time. See Dauvergne 1998:13-20.

Environmental litigation

As discussed in Chapter I, effective environmental litigation should facilitate access to justice in environmental matters in both a procedural and substantive sense. Ideally, litigation provides a mechanism for private interest claimants to enforce environmental rights, obtain compensation for environmental damage and resolve environmental disputes. Litigation may also provide an important mechanism through which the public interest in environmental sustainability may be protected. From a state perspective, effective environmental litigation should increase legal certainty, through the objective and impartial application of environmental law by the courts. In this concluding section, we consider the extent to which environmental litigation in Indonesia has fulfilled these functions. In answering this question, we shall draw upon the findings and conclusions of previous chapters and also refer to Appendix I, which summarizes all environmental litigation cases reviewed in this book.

As discussed in Chapter I, the extent to which environmental litigation fulfils these functions is influenced by a number of legal and non-legal factors or conditions. These conditions are diverse in nature, encompassing the procedural and substantive legal framework, the institutional resources of litigants, the independence of the judiciary and the wider social-political context. In this concluding chapter, we shall draw together our examination of these conditions and assess their influence on environmental litigation in the Indonesian context. Our concluding analysis of these conditions shall also provide a basis for a number of recommendations to improve the effectiveness of environmental litigation in Indonesia.

Access to litigation

This section provides an overview of factors that have impacted upon access to environmental litigation in Indonesia. Several of the factors mentioned in this overview, such as judicial and social/political context, are only introduced here and are explored in more substantive depth later in this chapter.

Access to litigation; Procedural access

As discussed in Chapter I, procedural access to justice is a key prerequisite for effective environmental litigation. In Chapter II we learnt that environmental standing was first introduced in Indonesia in the Inti Indorayon Utama case in 1989. Whilst the plaintiff in that case, WALHI, failed on substantive grounds, the court did recognize its procedural right to undertake legal action on behalf of environmental interests. The PT IIU case was followed in several subsequent cases until the principle of environmental standing received explicit legislative endorsement in article 38(1) of the EMA 1997.

Whilst the introduction of environmental standing in Indonesia has certainly facilitated environmental public interest litigation, it has hardly opened the 'floodgates' of environmental litigation as some critics feared. Over the twenty year period reviewed, there have been only ten environmental public interest cases, amounting to only one case every two years. Despite the flexibility of 'environmental standing', the right to bring environmental public interest claims appears to have been utilized by only a small number of well-resourced environmental organizations. Amongst environmental public interest litigants WALHI, the National Forum for the Environment, has been the most active litigant, acting as a plaintiff in eight of the ten cases to date. The Indonesian Legal Aid Foundation (YLBHI), and its various associated offices, have also played an integral role in the majority of public interest actions, providing legal representation and in some cases acting as co-plaintiff. In several other cases, public interest suits have been initiated by coalitions of environmental organizations; for instance in the Reafforestation Fund (IPTN) case in 1994 (five NGOs), the Reafforestation Fund (Kiani Kertas) case in 1997 (three NGOs), the Transgenic Cotton case in 2001 (six NGOs) and the Eksponen 66 case in 1998 (thirteen NGOs). Whilst the majority of public interest litigants have been larger, Jakarta-based organizations, some recent actions have been initiated by regional community or environmental organizations, as in the Eksponen 66 case and the Transgenic Cotton case.

Whilst traditional rules of standing did not preclude private litigants who had suffered some 'material' loss due to environmental pollution or damage, procedural obstacles did exist for litigants attempting to undertake a 'representative' or 'class' action. Representative actions were not regulated in the EMA 1982; although that EMA did contain a number of provisions that Indonesian courts could, but did not, use to allow a class action. This procedural obstacle was apparently removed with the introduction of article 37 of the EMA 1997, yet procedural confusion still surrounded the class action mechanism, further discouraging potential litigants, until the enactment of Supreme Court Regulation No. 1 of 2002 on Procedure for Class Action, which appears to have resolved the issue.

Like public interest actions, the actual number of environmental private interest suits has been relatively low. In the period reviewed, from 1982-2002, fourteen environmental private interest claims were brought, thus averaging around one case every 1.5 years; a figure only slightly higher than the number of environmental public interest cases. Given the population of Indonesia and the reported extent of environmental pollution and damage across a range of sectors, this small number of cases suggests that the legal framework for compensation and/or restoration of environmental damage has been significantly under-utilized. The remainder of this section explores some of the factors, other than that of procedural access, which have been obstacles for potential litigants seeking access to environmental justice.

Access to litigation; Lack of financial resources

In Indonesia legal aid centres, under the umbrella of the Indonesian Legal Aid Foundation (YLBHI), have played an important role in facilitating access to justice for individuals and communities in a range of disputes, including those in the environmental context.[2] Despite the contribution of legal aid, lack of financial resources remains a problem for many potential environmental claimants; many victims of pollution may not have access to a legal aid centre, which are usually only found in the larger cities. The financial and human resources of legal aid centres are also limited and spread across a wide range of areas, with the result that not all needy claimants can be provided with assistance.[3] In the absence of legal aid, the cost of privately funding legal representation is prohibitive for many poorly resourced victims of environmental damage. In addition to the cost of legal representation, the cost of obtaining scientific evidence, whether expert testimony or laboratory tests, may also be considerable. Such costs may be a significant obstacle to both private and public interest litigants, as highlighted in a recent statement by the director of WALHI, Emmy Hafild: 'The cost of just one sample can be hundreds of thousands (rupiah), so you can imagine what sort of cost WALHI had to pay to prove the Arafura sea was polluted by tailings (Arinto Wiryoto 2001)'. Larger NGOs such as WALHI are often largely funded by grants from foreign aid agencies, such as US AID or AusAid, or international donor organizations such as the Ford Foundation. This form of aid funding, however, sometimes comes with strings attached. In Indonesia, WALHI, the National Forum for the Environment, had its funding from USAID temporarily withdrawn after initiating another legal action against US mining giant Freeport's operations in Indonesia.

Access to litigation; Evidential obstacles

A number of commentators on environmental dispute resolution have noted the difficulties inherent in establishing legal proof of allegations of pollution or environmental damage in a court of law. This has certainly been the case in Indonesia, where the legal and technical difficulties associated with proving pollution in court have provided another obstacle to environmental litigants. Emmy Hafild, the director of WALHI, highlighted this problem, stating: 'WALHI has brought environmental cases to court nine times now and been

2 See discussion of the history of legal aid and the concept of 'structural' legal aid as a vehicle for social and political reform in Adnan Buyung Nasution 1981.

3 Rambun Tjaj, former internal director of LBH Jakarta, interview, 2-7-1997.

defeated every time. The judges' reason is usually a lack of evidence.' (Arinto Wiryoto 2001.) Eye-witness accounts of pollution are usually given little weight, whilst laboratory tests which indicate excessive levels of pollutants may still not satisfy legal elements such as causation. The Sari Morawa case (1996) illustrates this point. In that case, the Lubuk Pakam district court failed to uphold a claim for environmental compensation despite considerable eye-witness and laboratory evidence of pollution. Critical information and evidence may also be difficult to obtain from uncooperative government agencies, especially in the absence of established procedures facilitating access to government or public information.[4]

Conversely, the few successful environmental claims discussed in Chapters II and III generally featured evidence of a particularly strong and conclusive nature. For instance, in the Banger River case (1999) the plaintiffs' claims of pollution were confirmed by research from several government agencies. This was further verified by the undisputed fact that the industries in question did not even own waste management units before 1996. The allegations of pollution were also supported by expert witnesses, whose testimony proved influential during the case. Similarly, in the WALHI v. Freeport case (1995) the deaths of four men in the Lake Wanagon disaster were used as evidence of Freeport's negligence in the matter, which was further confirmed by government investigation. Given the legal and technical complexities of proving pollution or environmental damage, however, it is quite rare that such conclusive and incontrovertible evidence will exist. More commonly, significant ambiguities or contradictions may appear in evidence presented to the court, making a successful claim less likely. For instance, in the Babon River case (1998) the court was presented with laboratory evidence that showed significant levels of pollutants in the Babon River in March 1997, whilst other data showed the industries' effluent to comply with regulatory standards at that time. Moreover, although strong, conclusive evidence may increase an environmental claim's chances of success, it will by no means guarantee the outcome. In many cases, such as the Sari Morawa case discussed above, courts may reject apparently convincing evidence on grounds of a purportedly legal nature.

One legal solution to the problem of evidence in environmental cases is a reversed burden of proof, as discussed in Chapter II. A reversed burden of proof could be applied on the basis of the strict liability principle or through the discretion exercised by the court. Another important step in overcoming evidential difficulties in environmental cases is improving access to environmental information from both government agencies and private companies.

4 Eko Nuryanto 1995:7-9. This issue of evidence is discussed further below.

As discussed above, article 6(2) of the EMA 1997 imposes an obligation upon 'every person carrying out a business or other activity [to] provide true and accurate information regarding environmental management'. The decision in WALHI v. Freeport is an indication of the increasing willingness of Indonesian courts to apply this right. The planned enactment of freedom of information legislation should also further facilitate access to relevant information held by environmental and other government agencies.[5]

Access to litigation; Judicial independence

As noted in Chapter I, access to the courts only becomes access to 'justice' where judicial adjudication is both independent (of executive influence) and impartial. In Indonesia the perceived lack of judicial impartiality and independence is another significant disincentive for environmental litigants. Probably the most significant problem is that of judicial corruption, the frequent reports of which have contributed toward widely held attitudes of scepticism and suspicion towards judicial institutions. A recent opinion survey by Berlin-based Transparency International found that most Indonesians saw corruption in the courts, rather than in political parties or the police, as the problem needing the most immediate attention in Indonesia.[6] Other problems deterring the environmental litigant include lengthy delays in the administration of justice, particularly in the case of appeals to higher courts. In the Supreme Court alone there is currently a backlog of over 16,000 cases.[7]

Access to litigation; Social context

According to Jerold Auerbach, the American tendency to litigiousness expresses and accentuates the pursuit of individual advantage in a society founded on individualism (Auerbach 1983:10). In Indonesia, litigation occurs within a very different cultural context, where individualism and litigiousness are certainly not yet dominant features. Traditional cultural values in Indonesia tend to accentuate the need for harmony and compromise, rather than the assertion of individual rights.[8] For this reason, in Indonesia mediation may be a more 'comfortable' cultural choice than litigation. Victims of environmental damage or pollution are also in most cases the *rakyat kecil*

5 Freedom of information legislation is currently being considered by a special committee of the national legislature. See Ati Nurbaiti 2003.

6 The survey was based on around 1000 persons, and departed from the most common result found in other countries where respondents selected political parties as the institution most needing reform. See Bayuni: 'Corrupt courts seen as RI's greatest problem', *The Jakarta Post*, 10-7-2003.

7 'Lack of justices blamed for judicial corruption', *The Jakarta Post*, 2-8-2003.

8 See Takdir Rachmadi 1986. Takdir Rachmadi considers cultural attitudes such as these as a supportive factor in the use of mediation in environmental dispute resolution in Indonesia.

('little people'), who may be farmers, workers and others in the lower socio-economic strata of society. People from this stratum of society typically have minimal or no experience of navigating state institutions and processes such as litigation. Culturally, they may also be more accustomed to deferring to, rather than questioning, authority figures. Thus, the cultural attitudes and experiences of pollution victims may also not support the use of litigation as a dispute resolution option.[9] In addition, attitudes of cultural submissiveness may be strongly reinforced in an environment of political repression. In some cases, victims of environmental damage or pollution may be unwilling to undertake litigation due to the possible sanctions (whether legal or economic or extra-legal) that this might result in.

Case outcomes

Besides the issue of procedural access, effective environmental litigation implies access to environmental justice in a substantive sense. That is, environmental litigation should enable private litigants to enforce environmental rights and obtain redress for environmentally related damage. Litigation should also enable public interest litigants to protect the public interest in environmental sustainability through judicial enforcement of environmental law. To what extent have these more substantive objectives of environmental litigation been realized in Indonesia? An overview of environmental litigation cases reviewed in this book, and their outcomes, may be found in Appendix I. The overview divides the cases reviewed in Chapters II and III into public and private interest cases. In the 20-year period reviewed, from 1982-2002, there have been a total of ten environmental public interest cases reviewed; eight in the general courts and three in the administrative courts. Whilst the first environmental public interest case, Indorayon, was lost on substantive grounds, it achieved the significant procedural victory of environmental standing. This important precedent, together with the subsequent enactment of environmental standing in the EMA 1997, facilitated the series of environmental public interest suits that followed. The procedural success of environmental standing, however, was not matched by a high rate of success in a substantive legal sense. The first five environmental public interest cases were lost on substantive grounds. The sixth case was won at first instance, but lost on appeal. The seventh case was successful against only two of eleven defendants, and is pending appeal. The following two cases were both lost on substantive grounds, whilst the tenth case was partially success-

9 Note in many cases these social obstacles have been overcome by intervention and assistance by NGOs. This is discussed further below.

ful and is currently pending appeal. Overall, three out of ten cases were at least partially successful at the district court level, an initial success rate of 30%. As already stated, one of these partially successful cases was overturned on appeal; whilst at the time of writing the other two cases still had appeals pending. Thus, to date, environmental organizations have been unsuccessful in achieving substantive protection of environmental interests through public interest suits.

An interesting feature of this overview is that all the successful or partially successful public interest claims (three in total) have occurred from 1998 onwards, in the post-New Order period. All successful claims have also occurred in the general courts, with all three of the environmental public interest suits in the administrative courts failing. The three (partially) successful claims were also all granted at the district court level, in contrast to the lack of successful environmental public interest claims at the appellate level (high court or Supreme Court). The broader implications of these findings are considered in more detail below.[10]

As noted in the preceding section on access to justice, over the same period (1982-2002) the number of private interest environmental claims brought pursuant to the Environmental Management Acts of 1982 and 1997 was, at fourteen cases, slightly higher than the number of public interest claims. The proportion of private interest environmental claims that were successful was, however, similar to that for public interest claims. Of the fourteen private interest cases, ten were lost and four were at least partially successful at the district court level; an initial success rate of 28.6%, compared to an initial success rate of 30% for public interest claims. Also as with public interest cases, the success rate was lower at the appellate level, where only two claims have been partially successful. Furthermore, only one of these two claims (the Muara Jaya case) has resulted in an actual payment of compensation, whilst the other (the Banger River case) is still pending an appeal to the Supreme Court. Compensation was also paid in a third case (the Peat Land/Farmers Compensation case, 1999), but this was the result of a settlement rather than an actual decision of the court. Thus, private interest litigants have been no more successful than public interest litigants, and in particular their success in achieving substantive remedies has been limited, with compensation so far paid in only two out of fourteen cases.

Like public interest claims, successful private interest environmental claims have been concentrated in the post-New Order period (1998 onwards). All four successful claims at the district court level were decided in the post-

10 See particularly the discussion of judicial decision making, and the discussion of social/political context, both in this chapter.

New Order period. The one exception and successful claim during the New Order period was the Muara Jaya case (1991). Again like public interest claims, private interest claims have also had a higher success rate at the district court level (four cases), compared to the appellate court level (two cases).

In those environmental cases that were successful, the most common remedy was that of compensation, awarded in six cases, of which three were reversed on appeal. Environmental measures, relating to the prevention or remediation of environmental damage or pollution, were ordered by courts in only four cases. This tendency of courts to place somewhat more emphasis on pecuniary rather than environmental remedies was also noticeable in the litigation case studies examined in Chapter III. As mentioned above, claims that have actually been finalized and remedies implemented are found in only two cases, the Muara Jaya and Kalimantan Peat Land (Farmers' Compensation) cases, both of which involved only remedies of a pecuniary nature. There are therefore no examples of private or public interest cases where protective or restorative environmental measures have actually been implemented by a court, although the high court in the Banger River case did order optimization of the companies' waste management unit (but the case is still pending an appeal to the Supreme Court).

Substantive legal framework

One important determinant of the ability of potential environmental litigants to access environmental justice through litigation is the nature of the procedural and substantive legal framework governing environmental claims. The issue of procedural access to the courts has already been the subject of some discussion in Chapter VI. According to David Robinson, the substantive environmental legal framework should ideally consist of 'strong law', that is legislation with explicit objectives and substantive remedies that may be effectively adjudicated by courts, if it is to effectively facilitate environmental public interest litigation (Robinson 1995a:294-326). By contrast, 'weak law' is non-specific in nature and relies on the exercise of administrative discretion for its implementation.

On the whole, legislation in Indonesia (*undang-undang*) has tended to be very broad and general in nature, relying to a large extent upon implementing regulations and executive directives for its implementation (Damian and Hornick 1992). This was certainly a fault of the EMA 1982, for which many implementing regulations were never enacted (Niessen 2003:67). As discussed in Chapter II, this absence of implementing regulations was a contributing factor in Indonesian courts' apparent reluctance to enforce environmental law, such as the right to compensation for environmental damage.

The second EMA of 1997 was clearly an improvement in this respect, with a number of provisions being further elaborated, thus facilitating their enforcement without the need for implementing regulations. For instance, the right to compensation for environmental damage (article 34) and the principle of strict liability (article 35) were both sufficiently elaborated in the EMA 1997, so as to not refer to or require further implementing regulations. Whilst still intended as an 'umbrella act' for environmentally related legislation, the EMA 1997 was thus much less dependent on implementing regulations for its elaboration and enforcement, when compared to its more general predecessor, the EMA of 1982.

Moreover, the second EMA introduced several important new legal principles, including environmental standing (article 38[1] – a confirmation of the Indorayon precedent), community representative actions (article 37) and an action for environmental restoration (article 38). This improved legal framework has certainly been one element supporting access to environmental justice in Indonesia. Public interest litigants such as WALHI have utilized the principle of environmental standing on numerous occasions to initiate environmental suits. Private interest litigants were also more successful under the EMA 1997 than under the previous EMA, where the lack of implementing regulations was often a block to compensation claims. Nonetheless, the potential of the environmental legal framework does not appear to have been fully realized, when one examines the limited number of cases to date and the rather conservative application of potentially far-reaching legal principles by Indonesia courts. The actual application of environmental law by Indonesian courts is examined in more detail below.

As the current EMA 1997 is due for review in the near future, an opportunity to further improve the legal framework exists. Several improvements to the EMA could be made and have been discussed in some detail in Chapter II. Possible reforms include the following.

Legal framework; Broadening the scope of environmental standing

The application of environmental law has been facilitated by reform of traditional standing rules through the Inti Indorayon Utama case and article 38(1) of the EMA 1997. However, pursuant to the latter provision, the right of 'environmental standing' is restricted to environmental organizations which meet several criteria stated in the legislation. Whilst environmental standing provisions have been utilized by NGOs, the number of cases (approximately one every two years) is very limited for a rapidly developing country of around 200 million people with a plethora of environmental problems. Access to environmental justice could be further strengthened by the broadening of environmental standing to enable citizens, in addition to environmental organizations, to bring actions for the enforcement of environmental law. This broadening of environmental standing is logical, given the right of every person to a 'good and healthy' environment (article 5) and the obligation of every person to 'combat environmental pollution and damage' (article 6), and would make such rights and obligations enforceable.

Legal framework; Increasing remedies available to public interest litigants
Access for public interest litigants is only meaningful if litigants can obtain effective remedies to affect enforcement of environmental law. In Chapter II it was argued that the remedies in article 38(2) should be broadened to include claims for the cost of environmental restoration. This would increase the enforceability of article 34, which creates an obligation for polluters to pay compensation in the event of environmental pollution or damage. Damages awarded could be paid into an environmental trust fund to be used specifically for rehabilitation of the polluted site.

Legal framework; Legislative protection from SLAPP suits
As discussed in Chapter III, the defendants in the Babon River case launched a counter-claim for damages against the plaintiffs due to injury to their reputation resulting from the plaintiffs' allegations. Reference was also made in that chapter to the Tanah Lot dispute in Bali, where several farmers were successfully counter-sued by a developer and consequently were ordered by the court to pay US$35,000 damages. Claims of this nature have been described as 'SLAPP' suits (Strategic Lawsuits Against Public Participation) and are a phenomenon found in many jurisdictions where well resourced defendants seek to intimidate potential litigants from enforcing their environmental rights. The risk of such suits is relevant to environmental litigation, as it may prove a strong disincentive for victims of environmental pollution or damage to seek redress through the courts. SLAPP suits could be prevented through legislation aimed at protecting a well-defined right of public participation and which prohibits improper interference with this right through a range of means.

Legal framework; Clarification of the application of strict liability (article 35)
As discussed in Chapter II, Indonesian courts have largely failed to apply the potentially far-reaching principle of strict liability in environmental disputes to date. In the Laguna Mandiri case (1998), the only case to directly address article 35 and the issue of strict liability, the high court of Banjarmasin (in this writer's opinion) incorrectly interpreted the principle of strict liability by restricting its operation to cases involving hazardous and toxic materials. To enable the correct application of this important principle, it is important that clarification be made, either by way of Supreme Court circular letter or alternatively in the elucidation to article 35 of the EMA 1997, which endorses the correct and broader interpretation of that article's scope.

Legal framework; Legislative recognition of NGOs

Article 19 of the EMA 1982 originally gave specific legislative recognition of the role played by non-government organizations in environmental management. The article was omitted from the EMA 1997, although under that later law NGOs did receive explicit grounds for access to the courts in environmental matters through article 38(1). Nonetheless, it is argued that an article in a form similar to the old article 19 be reintroduced to the current EMA, to provide a legal foundation for the broader participation of NGOs in environmental management. As the EMA seeks to provide a framework for environmental management in Indonesia, it is appropriate that the role of NGOs be recognized and given satisfactory legal endorsement within such framework.

Legal framework; Strengthen citizen mechanisms of administrative enforcement

In many litigation cases reviewed in Chapters II and III, litigants turned to the courts partly because the response of administrative agencies to the environmental pollution or damage in question had been inadequate. The response of administrative agencies to environmental problems can do much to facilitate or obstruct access to environmental justice. Whilst citizens may often feel powerless to influence the response of government agencies, there is nonetheless existing legal provision in the EMA 1997 to facilitate citizen-initiated administrative enforcement. Article 25(3) states that a 'third party which has an interest has the right to submit an application to the authorized official to carry out an administrative sanction'. Similarly, article 37(1) gives a community 'the right [...] to report to law enforcers concerning various environmental problems which inflict losses on the life of the community'. Whilst these provisions facilitate the communication of environmental grievances to administrative agencies, the strengthening of these provisions could facilitate both access to justice and the administrative enforcement of environmental law. Article 25(1), for instance, could be strengthened by requiring a written decision on an application to an authorized official within a reasonable time frame, which, if contrary to law in the applicant's opinion, could be challenged in the administrative courts. The enforceability of article 37 could also be improved by imposing upon administrative agencies an obligation to act where environmental damage or pollution is established.

Judicial decision making

Our review of case outcomes (earlier in this chapter) indicates that the substantive success of litigation has been limited from the claimant's perspective, whether in facilitating environmental protection (public interest) or the compensation or restoration of environmental damage/pollution (private interest). The concluding review of the environmental legal framework in the preceding section indicates that, whilst improvements still could be made to the law, the EMA 1997 has overcome a number of legal deficiencies from the preceding EMA 1982. Since enactment of the EMA 1997, the legal framework in itself no longer appears to be a serious obstacle to effective environmental litigation. Rather, our review of case outcomes suggests the more serious obstacle at present to be the manner in which the legal framework is interpreted in practice, namely the nature and quality of judicial decision-making in environmental cases, which has been a major focus of discussion in Chapters II and III.

As discussed in Chapter I, the judicial process ideally involves an independent and impartial application of the law, which facilitates the final determination and resolution of a dispute. Yet, even where judicial decision-making is independent and impartial, it is still inevitably influenced by a range of factors, including the social and political character of the judiciary itself. As argued in Chapter I, environmental public interest law has tended to flourish more in countries where it is applied by an 'activist' judiciary that is prepared to value environmental sustainability as a matter of public interest comparable with economic growth or national security. What has been the nature and quality of Indonesian judicial decision-making in environmental cases, and how has it affected the efficacy of litigation as a process of environmental dispute resolution?

There have been probably only a few instances of judicial decisions at what might be called the 'activist' end of the judicial decision making spectrum. The PT IIU Indorayon case, as discussed above, is one such case. In that case the court took considerable initiative in revising traditional civil procedural law to allow an environmental organization standing to sue. In doing so the court emphasized the public interest in environmental preservation and argued that the environment was in itself a legal subject with an instrinsic right to be sustained. Yet the activism of the court in this case appeared limited to issues of a procedural, rather than substantive, nature. On the substantive issue of the legality of PT IIU's operating permits, the court took a much more conservative approach, essentially excluding application of the environmental impact analysis (EIA) regulations from activities commenced prior to its enactment. It is this latter, more formalistic and conservative approach, rather than the 'activist' attitude of the court toward environmental standing, that has characterized the application of environmental law in the majority of environmental cases, at least up until 1998.

Courts, for instance, have shown great reluctance to 'fill in the gaps' of the environmental legal framework, where, for instance, implementing regulations had not been enacted in relation to a specific provision. The absence of implementing regulations for article 20 of the EMA 1982, for example, was cited as a reason for refusing environmental claims in the PT SSS case (1991) and the Surabaya River case (1995). Whilst such a stance may be justified legally, courts also could also have found legal justification for a more activist approach. As discussed in Chapter I, article 27(1) of the Law on Judicial Authority No. 14 of 1970 provides some scope for judicial 'law-making', authorizing judges to 'uncover, follow and understand the principles of living law in the community'.

Inconsistency has also characterized judicial decision-making in environmental cases. For example, the absence of implementing regulations was not an obstacle for a claim for compensation of environmental damage in the Muara Jaya case, yet it was a basis for refusing claims in the PT SSS and Surabaya River cases. Inconsistency has also been apparent in environmental cases related to the administrative jurisdiction. In the two Reafforestation Fund cases, review of certain Presidential Decrees was refused, as they were not of a 'final' nature and hence did not fall within the specific jurisdiction of the administrative courts. Logically, Presidential Decrees that fell outside the jurisdiction of the administrative courts would still be reviewable in the general courts. An opportunity to test this proposition was presented in the Kalimantan Peat Land case, where a challenge to several Presidential Decrees was undertaken in the Central Jakarta district court. Yet this claim was also refused on jurisdictional grounds, with the result that Presidential Decrees are apparently not reviewable in either the administrative or the general courts.

As discussed above, the reticence of courts to uphold environmental claims may in some cases be explained by deficiencies in the legal framework, particularly in relation to the earlier EMA of 1982. There are, however, several examples of equally conservative decision making in environmental cases made on the basis of factual or evidential considerations rather than legal grounds. For example, in the Sari Morawa case, the court apparently did not consider the absence of implementing regulations for article 20 EMA 1982 an obstacle to that claim for environmental compensation. The court instead refused the claim on evidential grounds, despite the presentation of convincing laboratory, expert and witness evidence by the plaintiffs, a considerable part of which was not even considered by the court. Similarly, in the PT SSS case the main reason cited in the judgement for refusal of the claim was the fact that government facilitated mediation had not preceded the claim. In fact a government investigation and mediation had been carried out prior to the claim, yet this was not considered in the court's decision. The court also made no attempt to assist the environmental litigants by directing an appropriate government agency to facilitate the necessary investigation or mediation process. Similarly, in cases where jurisdiction has been a bar to adjudication of a claim, courts have made no attempt, through for instance an interim decision, to redirect litigants to an appropriate court prior to a full hearing of the claim.[11]

Even subsequent to the enactment of the more detailed EMA 1997, which depends to a far lesser extent on implementing regulations than its legislative predecessor, Indonesian courts continue to show reticence in applying potentially far-reaching environmental legal principles such as strict liability, as stipulated in article 35 of the EMA 1997. Despite numerous opportunities, the principle of strict liability has not been applied by any Indonesian court to date. In the Laguna Mandiri case, the strict liability principle was at least discussed by the high court of Banjarmasin but, in the opinion of this writer, incorrectly discounted. Representative actions, introduced in article 37 of the EMA 1997, were also initially under-utilized by the courts, although cases since 2000 illustrate the growing familiarity of the Indonesian judiciary with this Western-derived legal mechanism. The previous judicial ambiguity about the appropriate procedure for class actions appears to now be addressed by Supreme Court Regulation No. 1 of 2002 on Procedure for Class Action, which from a procedural perspective at least, should facilitate future representative actions.

There have, however, been important exceptions to the more conservative aspects of Indonesian judicial decision making in environmental cases. As discussed above, courts have been willing and consistent in applying the doctrine of environmental standing, even prior to its enactment in the EMA 1997. In the Muara Jaya case (1991) both the high court of Samarinda and the Supreme Court proved willing to award a significant sum as compensation for environmental damage caused by installation of an oil pipe. The most discernible change in the tenor of judicial making in environmental cases, however, has occurred in the post-New Order period, from 1998 onwards. Prior to 1998, no public interest environmental cases had succeeded on substantive grounds. In contrast, in the post-New Order period there have been three environmental public interest claims at least partially upheld at the district court level. A similar trend is evident in environmental private interest cases. Prior to 1998 only one claim for compensation of environmental damage or pollution had been upheld; while from 1998 onwards there have been four private interest environmental claims upheld at the district court level. This greater willingness to uphold environmental claims seems more apparent at the district court than the high court level. Two of the private interest environmental claims upheld at the district court level since 1998 have been rejected on appeal to the respective high courts. This was also the case with one of the

11 See for instance the Ciujung River case, the Reafforestation Fund cases and the Kalimantan Peat Land Development case.

successful public interest claims in the post New Order period.

In these more recent, successful claims, which include the Banger River and Babon River disputes examined in Chapter III, courts have appeared increasingly willing to actually apply the environmental legal framework. In the Banger River case, for instance, the decision of the district court of Pekalongan emphasized in its judgement that 'industrial development must be sustainable' and concluded that the defendant industries had polluted and were liable to pay compensation. In a surprising decision, given the more conservative tendency of appellate courts in environmental cases, the high court of Semarang also upheld this decision on appeal and, moreover, awarded a significant compensatory sum of Rp 750 million in addition to ordering improvements in waste management practices. A greater willingness to apply the environmental legal framework was also evident initially in the Babon River case, where a claim for compensation due to pollution was upheld at least in part by the district court of Semarang.[12] Similarly, in the recent Freeport v. WALHI case, an environmental public interest suit against the mining multinational Freeport was upheld in part by the district court of South Jakarta, which concluded the company had acted illegally in polluting the environment in the vicinity of the factory and making factually incorrect statements. It remains to be seen whether this progressive trend in judicial decision making will be encouraged by the Supreme Court, which is due to hear appeals in a number of the cases listed above.

Social-legal context of judicial decision making

As discussed in the previous section, judicial decision making in environmental cases has ranged across a spectrum from reactionary to conservative to progressive and even, in a few cases, activist. There are multiple variables which might have influenced and could serve to explain the decision-making patterns of Indonesian judges in environmental cases. Given that the purported objective of the legal process is an impartial application of law, then the letter of the law itself is clearly a significant factor influencing the outcome of an environmental claim. If a legal basis for an environmental claim does not exist, then naturally the claim is bound to fail. Accordingly, we have examined the legal framework and its adequacy in a preceding section, considering its impact on access to environmental justice. In this section, however, we go beyond the legal framework to consider the social-legal context within which environmental law has been applied in Indonesia, and the possible influence of several variables on the process of environmental litigation.

12 As discussed in Chapter III, however, the decision was later overturned by the high court of Central Java on appeal.

Social-legal context of judicial decision making; The judicial context

In Chapter I the notion of judicial independence was considered as a prerequisite for effective environmental litigation. It was suggested that effective judicial enforcement of environmental law requires a judiciary that is substantively impartial and independent from executive influence. In Indonesia the principles of judicial independence and the rule of law are given at least formal recognition in the Indonesian 1945 Constitutional Law (Undang-Undang Dasar 1945), which proclaims 'Indonesia is a state based on law (*rechtsstaat*), not merely based on power (*machtsstaat*)'. The elucidation to the Constitution further defines judicial authority as 'an independent authority, in the sense that it is beyond the influence of the government' (see Todung Mulya Lubis 1993).

Yet during the New Order period in Indonesia, legal rhetoric depicting Indonesia as a *negara hukum* ('state based on law') was criticized by many as little more than a transparent attempt to legitimize a political system built along authoritarian and corporatist lines. Throughout this period, the judicial system as a whole was directly responsive to the influence of a highly powerful executive. A frequently cited example of executive influence over judicial decision-making in an environmentally related matter is the Kedung Ombo case. In that case, a landmark Supreme Court decision in 1993 to award record levels of compensation to villagers displaced by a dam and irrigation project was reversed, following high-level political pressure and a reputed request by President Suharto that the ruling be reviewed (Nicholson 1994:84). Executive influence over judicial decision-making was supported by the structural integration of the legal and executive apparatus, which granted the Minister of Justice financial, administrative, and organizational supervision of the court.[13] Such authority was not infrequently used to influence the course of justice, through selective manipulation of judicial transfers and promotions (Pompe 1996:222). Over time, the political cooptation of the judiciary became more complete, until such overt mechanisms of control were no longer necessary. In a repressive political environment, the judiciary internalized the rules of political compliance for itself (Pompe 1996:101). For example, whilst not possessing powers of legislative review, the Supreme Court was nonetheless empowered to review regulations and executive directions, which in fact constituted the majority of substantive executive policy. Yet in practice the Supreme Court consistently refused to hear cases where it was asked to quash executive regulation, contributing to its image as a 'toothless court' (*mahkamah ompong*) (Pompe 1996:18-9). Pursuant to article

13 Law on the General Court No. 2 of 1986, article 5 (Indonesia). The term 'General Court' includes the district court and the court of appeal of the district court.

27(1) of the Basic Law on the Judiciary No. 14 of 1970, judges also have the authority and duty to 'discover' law as reflected in the changing legal mores in the community. Yet such authority has rarely been utilized in the context of environmental cases, where judges have generally adopted a formalistic and narrow interpretative approach.

The close linkages between the judicial and executive arms of government in Indonesia are also evident in the often close correlation of executive and administrative responses in environmental disputes. In a number of the environmental litigation cases reviewed in Chapters II and III, an apparently significant factor influencing judicial decision-making has been the previous response of executive or administrative bodies to the dispute in question. In a number of cases where environmental claimants were successful, the decision of the court was preceded by administrative or executive condemnation of the pollution or environmental damage in question. This point was evident particularly in the Banger River case, where the polluting companies had been the subjects of both criminal and administrative sanction, including the attempted withdrawal of the factories' operating permits. Indeed, in that case the high court of Semarang treated the fact of prior administrative sanction as sufficient evidence in itself of the defendants' culpability for the pollution. In the recent WALHI v. Freeport case, the decision of the court in upholding part of WALHI's claim was also preceded by high level political condemnation of Freeport's apparent negligence in the Lake Wanagon incident. Similarly, in the Babon River case, the six defendant industries had been identified as polluters by the regional government and in the Clean Rivers Program (Prokasih). Administrative sanction, in the withdrawal of 166 forest use permits from timber companies, was also an apparently strong consideration in the court's decision in the Eksponen 66 case. Thus, whilst prior executive or administrative sanction will by no means ensure a similar judicial decision, where it is more politically safe to uphold an environmental claim, Indonesian courts appear more prepared to do so.[14]

Judicial impartiality has also been significantly impaired by the incidence of corruption at all levels of the judiciary (Pompe 1996:343). Following a recent review of Indonesia's justice system, United Nations' special rapporteur Dato Param Cumaraswamy declared Indonesia's judiciary one of the most corrupt in the world.[15] Widespread corruption has produced an unsurprising correlation between the financial resources of a litigant, and their capacity to influ-

14 However, prior administrative sanction would not seem sufficient in itself to necessarily result in a favourable outcome for an environmental claim. In some cases reviewed, for example the Sari Morawa dispute, the court rejected the plaintiffs' claim despite the fact the regional government had clearly identified the defendant industry as a polluter.

15 'Hukum di Indonesia salah satu terburuk', *Suara Merdeka*, 22-7-2002.

ence the judicial decision-making process in their favour.[16] In environmental litigation, this places industry litigants at a significant advantage over public interest litigants or victims of environmental damage, who tend to be from socially and economically disadvantaged sections of society. Whilst it is difficult to identify corruption as a determining factor in particular cases, given its general incidence in Indonesian courts it is without doubt a contributing factor to the low success rates of environmental claims, and to the sometimes intransigent quality of judicial decision-making in certain cases where claims have failed despite clear legal grounds and strong evidence. As discussed above, the prevalence of judicial corruption has contributed to a deeply held skepticism in the community toward the integrity and capacity of judicial institutions, which in turn discourages potential environmental litigants (Hyronimus Rhiti 1998).

Whilst it is perhaps the lack of judicial independence and impartiality that produce the greatest distortions in the legal process, other factors also play a part. The failure of judges and other legal actors handling environmental disputes to understand and correctly apply environmental law has been evident in some cases discussed above. Judicial decision-making in environmental disputes has tended to interpret environmental legislation in a legalistic, narrow and conservative manner, to the frustration of environmental public interest litigants. Principles of environmental management and participation underlying environmental law are frequently not understood by the judges who seek to apply them. Whilst to some extent this may be the result of the institutional pressures discussed above, inadequate judicial education concerning environmental law may also be a contributing factor. Highlighting this problem, one Indonesian legal academic recently observed: '[Indonesian] judges don't fully understand environmental law. At the time they carried out their studies, senior judges never received material on environmental law.'[17] As this comment highlights, the need for specialized judicial training in environmental law is heightened in Indonesia, as many modern environmental legal principles, such as representative actions or strict liability, have their basis in common law jurisdictions. Such principles may appear quite foreign to some Indonesian jurists with a traditional, civil law training. Besides novel legal principles, environmental cases often involve complex scientific evidence, which may require specialized knowledge or handling.[18] For instance, in the WALHI vs. PT Pakerin case (1998), satellite photographs of fire 'hotspots' were presented as evidence, yet were apparently not considered by the court. Reforms have been undertaken to address the need for specialized

16 See discussion in Bedner 2000:289.

17 'Hakim kurang paham lingkungan hidup', *Suara Merdeka*, 23-6-2003.

18 'Rumit, pembuktian pencemaran lingkungan', *Suara Merdeka*, 13-7-2002.

judicial training in environmental law, and are discussed further below.

The issue of specialist training has recently been addressed by several initiatives in environmental law training and capacity building. In 1998 and 2001 a Course on Environmental Law and Administration (CELA) was undertaken in the Netherlands and Indonesia for a number of Indonesian judges and jurists. In 1999 an Australian sponsored program for the specialized training of Indonesian judges in environmental law was also initiated. Both programs were run in conjunction with the Indonesian Centre for Environmental Law, which has played a key role in the specialist training of Indonesian judges in environmental law. Ongoing programs include plans for selected judges to study environmental law and its application overseas in countries such as the United States and Australia.[19] Currently, around seven hundred judges at the district, high and Supreme Court levels have completed specialist training in environmental law.

The creation of a core of judges with specialized knowledge in environmental law has the potential to greatly improve the quality of judicial decision making in environmental cases. This potential could be more fully realized if the adjudication of environmental cases was restricted to judges certified to have received specialist environmental law training, as recently proposed by the Indonesian Centre for Environmental Law (Rino Subagyo 2002b). A core group of judges specially trained in environmental law could even form the basis for a separate judicial division for environmental (and potentially land related) cases. A similar, but more far reaching reform would see the creation of a specialist court for environmental cases (Stein 1995:256-73). Calls for an environmental court were backed by the Environment Minister, Nabiel Makarim, who proposed a plan named 'Formula 12', whereby environmental cases would be handled by twelve prosecutors and twelve judges specialized in environmental law.[20] A specialist court would not only ensure the necessary level of judicial expertise but could incorporate non-judicial technical assessors and, moreover, resolve the problems of defining jurisdiction in environmental matters between the general and administrative courts.

Wider judicial reform initiatives, including efforts to promote the rule of law, judicial independence and the eradication of corruption, have assumed at least a nominally high priority in the post-Suharto era of *reformasi*, prompted by both domestic and international pressure. Recent legislation amending the Basic Law on Judicial Authority No. 14 of 1970 has entirely transferred

19 According to a recent statement by the Environment Ministry, 12 jurists (including prosecutors and judges) were to be sent overseas to study environmental law. See 'DPU akan pasang tiga pompa', *Suara Merdeka*, 20-5-2000.

20 'Pembentukan peradilan khusus lingkungan jangan ditunda-tunda', *Media Indonesia*, 16-9-2002.

responsibility for judicial management (in matters such as promotions and transfers) from the Ministry of Justice to the Supreme Court.[21] Such administrative reform will potentially assist in demarcating the boundaries of executive and judicial power.[22] The amending legislation also has pre-empted further regulation establishing mechanisms of judicial supervision, including a Council of Judicial Honour (Dewan Kehormatan Hakim), which will establish a code of judicial conduct and review issues such as recruitment, promotions and judicial corruption. In 2002 a monitoring division of the Supreme Court was set up to establish a judiciary 'free of corruption, collusion and nepotism'.[23] In its first year the monitoring division recommended punitive action against eleven judges. Yet doubts over the capacity of the judiciary for self-monitoring have also led to calls for external supervision of the judiciary. Several non-government judicial supervisory bodies have been created, including the Indonesian Institute for an Independent Judiciary (Lembaga Kajian dan Advokasi untuk Independensi Peradilan) and Judicial Watch. Pompe (1996) has also made a number of recommendations toward strengthening the role and independence of the judiciary, particularly that of the Supreme Court, based on a detailed analysis of the history of that court over fifty years. Pompe's recommendations include increasing judicial income levels (to reduce the incentive for corruption); ensuring objective, high standards of recruitment and the broadening of recruitment beyond 'career judges'; increasing the quality of judicial training and education; improving the security and tenure of judges (ensuring judges are not subject to transfer by way of punishment); ensuring advancement in the judicial hierachy is according to public and objective criteria (rather than personal favour or influence); granting the Supreme Court the right of judicial (constitutional) review; and ensuring public access to all Supreme Court decisions and the publication of selected decisions through an independent authority (Pompe 1996:410). Following an equally detailed analysis of the administrative courts in Indonesia, Bedner has made recommendations of a similar nature, including the increase of judicial salaries, the clarification of transfer procedures, broader recruitment policies, specialized training for judges and improved publication of case law (Bedner 2000:330-2).

More specifically, the suspected prevalence of corruption in environmental cases has highlighted the need for greater scrutiny of judicial decisions in environmental cases. For instance, in July 2002 the Indonesian Centre for Environmental Law (ICEL) called for reforms to enable investigations into

21 See Law No. 35 of 1999 (Indonesia).

22 See Pompe (1996:109) who questions whether a transfer of court administration to the Supreme Court of Indonesia would in fact contribute to judicial independence.

23 'Lack of justices blamed for judicial corruption', *The Jakarta Post*, 2-8-2003.

environmental cases where there are indications that corruption may have occurred.[24] The environmental organization recommended investigations be carried out by the National Ombudsman Commission or, alternatively, jointly conducted by the Environment Ministry and the Supreme Court based on a memorandum of understanding. Certainly effective mechanisms of judicial monitoring will be required to combat the incidence of corruption. As discussed above, community pressure and scrutiny of the judicial process may in some cases fulfil this role in an informal manner. Effective monitoring, however, requires independent monitoring on a more permanent and institutionalized basis; such as that suggested by ICEL. Whilst comprehensive reform of the judiciary will no doubt be a protracted and challenging process, the prospects for its success have been greatly increased by the dramatic political changes in Indonesia, which include democratic elections in 1999 and the ongoing transition from a highly centralized authoritarian regime to a more politically diversified and pluralist polity.

Social-legal context of judicial decision making; Political context

The issue of judicial independence from the executive is closely related to the wider political and institutional context within which judicial institutions are embedded. For instance, during the 'Guided Democracy' years of President Sukarno, the concept of judicial independence was ridiculed by Sukarno, who firmly established executive influence over the appellate courts (Lev 1978:27-71). During the New Order era of President Suharto, judicial independence and the rule of law were promoted as part of the New Order's statist ideology, but in practice executive will dominated the upper echelons of the judiciary as discussed above. The relationship between judicial and executive decision-making will thus vary greatly according to social-political context; a fact that has led some commentators, such as Shapiro, to question the relevance of the traditional, universal 'prototype' of an 'independent' judiciary.[25] Yet, as argued in Chapter I, whilst the notion of judicial independence may be greatly qualified in its implementation in different societal contexts, this does not disqualify its utility as a principle of good governance underlying real legal certainty in modern societies. At the same time, however, we must openly acknowledge and closely examine the definite and tangible influence of the political and institutional context upon judicial decision-making.

The review of environmental cases in this book suggests that judicial decision-making in environmental cases has been strongly influenced by

[24] 'Peringatan ulang tahun ICEL ke-9', *Hukum dan Advokasi Lingkungan*, 9-2002:13.

[25] For instance, Shapiro argues that the 'universal pattern' is in fact that 'judging runs as an integral part of the mainstream of political authority rather than as a separate entity'. See Shapiro 1981:20.

the wider political context. As we have seen, there was only one successful environmental case in the period from 1982, when the first EMA was enacted, to 1998, when the New Order period came to an end following President Suharto's resignation. Thus, despite the introduction of an environmental legal framework purportedly intended to, amongst other things, facilitate every person's right to a 'good and healthy environment', actual access to environmental justice increased very little. Whilst deficiencies in the legal framework may have been one element contributing to this outcome, a more significant factor, as argued above, was the conservative and intransigent manner in which the legal framework was applied by Indonesian courts. As already noted, there have been a few exceptions to this trend of conservative judicial decision-making, the most celebrated of which was the granting of environmental standing to WALHI in 1989. This occurred at a time when environmentalism was being embraced by the New Order government (and championed by a dynamic Environment Minister, Emil Salim), both as a concession to international and domestic middle class concerns and as a means to further extend bureaucratic control over the economy in an era where there was continuing pressure to deregulate (Cribb 1987).

Nonetheless, whilst the New Order government was willing to adopt environmental policies and laws and to make some concessions of a symbolic nature, these were limited in a more substantive sense. Indeed, the lack of resources devoted to implementation of this policy and legislative framework suggests they were not seriously intended to impact significantly upon the political-economic interests of the ruling elite, which were closely intertwined with the forestry, mining, industrial and development sectors.[26] Similarly, the patterns of judicial decision-making in environmental cases demonstrate that the granting of symbolically important procedural concessions, such as environmental standing, was not matched by a willingness to allow substantive claims that may have jeopardized, or been perceived as jeopardizing, the political-economic interests of the state. The style of judicial decision-making in environmental cases in this period thus appears oriented to fulfilling the function of 'social control' and helping maintain the essential interests of political regime and its ruling elite. This close accordance of state interests and judicial responses in the environmental context in this respect matches Kanishka Jayasuriya's description of the close collaboration and consultation between the judicial and executive arms of government in East Asian countries, including Indonesia, which he describes as 'corporatist' (Kanishka Jayasuriya 1999:173-204).

26 The Environment Ministry lacked, and still lacks, a departmental structure; and thus lacks the institutional framework and resources necessary for effective implementation of environmental law and policy.

The one successful environmental claim during this period, the Muara Jaya case, is an exception to the otherwise consistent pattern of failed claims. Interestingly, that case was not brought by an activist NGO or a legal aid organization, but rather involved a group of middle-class housing estate residents suing a mining company for environmental damage to their estate. Whilst it is difficult to draw a definitive conclusion regarding the reasons for the success of this particular claim, it was certainly, in sociological and political terms, a claim that was more likely to succeed. Robert Cribb, for instance, has argued that legislative responses to pollution control in the 1980s were partly attributable to growing concern over the effects of pollution amongst the increasingly influential middle-class and ruling elite (Cribb 1990:1123-35). Other commentators have also drawn attention to the increasing influence of the 'new rich' on state policies in Indonesia and Southeast Asia generally, during the 1980s and 1990s (Robison and Goodman 1996). Yet, as numerous studies on the growing theme of environmental justice have highlighted, the distribution of environmental 'externalities' has tended to be skewed strongly toward poorer, marginalized communities (Hofrichter 1993). Whilst this has not been a subject of analysis in this book, it is fair to say that the victims of environmental pollution or damage in the majority of cases reviewed in this book, tended to be from communities at the lower end of the socio-economic spectrum. Cases of 'middle-class' environmental complaints are thus relatively few and far between.

Whilst the overall substantive failure of environmental litigation in the period 1982-2002 is an interesting reflection on the inter-relationship of judiciary and state, the fact that the legal framework was utilized and that claims were brought, especially by high-profile environmental organizations, is also a reflection of the dynamics of civil society at the time. The area of environmental management was one area among many that saw the proliferation and increasing influence of non-government organizations during the 1980s and 1990s.[27] As discussed in the preceding section on access to justice, NGOs such as WALHI and the Indonesian Legal Aid Foundation (YLBHI) have been particularly active in attempting to utilize the environmental legal framework since the late 1980s. Thus, although the fruits of this environmental legal activism were limited by the conservative approach of the courts, an important foundation of alliances between reformist lawyers and environmental activists was being established during this period. In this respect, Indonesia has differed markedly from countries such as India, where the development of environmental public interest law was spearheaded by an activist Supreme Court. In Indonesia, reformist lawyers together with environmental activists have taken the lead in attempting to utilize the legal framework for the

[27] For an in-depth discussion of this topic, see Elridge 1995.

protection of the environment.[28] As discussed in Chapter I, this in itself is an important condition for the successful development of environmental public interest law, and indeed the potential of these alliances and their efforts at utilizing environmental law have arguably begun to bear more fruit in the post-Suharto period.

Although the substantive legal success of environmental public interest litigation was limited by the conservative response of the courts, it is also important to view the outcome of these public interest cases from a wider political perspective. As discussed in Chapter I, public interest litigation can in some instances function as a catalyst for wider political change, regardless of the formal legal outcome of proceedings. Certainly, the litigants and activists responsible for bringing the environmental public interest suits in question were cognizant of this point and were not under any illusions as to the slim likelihood of a favourable political outcome. As noted in the conclusion to Chapter II, public interest litigants have consciously utilized the courts as a 'stage' for high profile environmental cases, in the context of wider campaigns on important environmental issues. Whilst this book has not attempted detailed evaluation of such an approach from a political science perspective, it is clear that this approach has been fruitful. In the Kalimantan Peat Land case, for instance, the suit against the President was a focal point for publicity in a broader political campaign to publicize the disastrous environmental effects of the project and pressure the government to abandon it. In the IPTN and PT Kiani Kertas cases, NGOs were also successful in publicly embarrassing the government and focusing considerable media attention on the government-sponsored misappropriation of monies from the Reaforrestation Fund. As noted in Chapter II, the political campaign was ultimately successful in this instance and, in the changed political circumstances of *reformasi,* government prosecutors convicted several influential figures involved in the embezzlement of considerable sums of money from the Reafforestation Fund. The WALHI v. Freeport case (2001) was also a political coup for WALHI in its ongoing campaign against Freeport's operations in West Irian Jaya. Whilst the substantive legal remedies ordered by the court were limited, the court's finding that the company had made factually incorrect statements to the public was symbolically potent. WALHI's subsequent press release publicly and triumphantly broadcasted the fact that Freeport 'had lied' to the public. Indeed, WALHI's political-legal campaign against Freeport was so apparently damaging to that company's reputation, that Freeport pressured USAID into

28 There are of course some important exceptions of state leadership in the environmental arena, including Emil Salim, the first Environment Minister who was an outspoken and widely respected advocate of environmental interests, and Paulus Lotulung, the judge (now a member of the Supreme Court) who initially recognized environmental standing in the PT IIU case.

withdrawing aid funding previously granted to WALHI.

Environmental public interest suits such as these can thus have a politically potent symbolic effect, despite the fact that the action ultimately fails legally. Even where the action does not legally succeed, the protracted court process offers numerous opportunities for publicizing the plaintiff's case in the national press and across the television networks. As noted above, even during the New Order period, when the executive strongly dominated judicial decision-making, the regime still purported to be a *negara hukum* ('state based on law'). The rule of law thus remained an important political symbol and a source of political legitimacy for the regime, both domestically and internationally. As Bourchier has noted, the desire of the New Order to improve its international image as a state based on the rule of law was one important factor contributing to the establishment of the administrative court system (Bourchier 1999:233-52). Public interest suits were arguably a successful means of appropriating this rule of law discourse so as to both successfully express opposition to the regime and publicly embarrass the regime by reference to the standards that it purported to uphold.[29]

The political context in Indonesia changed dramatically in May 1998, with the forced resignation of President Suharto amid a wave of demonstrations and riots. The political liberalization and decline in military control that accompanied the demise of the New Order has enabled the victims of environmental damage or pollution to become increasingly assertive and vocal. For instance, in both the PT KLI and the Palur Raya cases, environmental claims were only openly pursued in the post-Suharto period, although the communities had suffered the effects of environmental damage and pollution for a number of years. Correspondingly, it would seem judicial institutions in environmental cases have become somewhat more responsive to environmental public interest actions and community-based claims for compensation or environmental restoration. The overview of cases above has demonstrated the distinct change in judicial decision-making trends that occurred in the post-New Order period. Six of the seven successful environmental claims have occurred in the post-Suharto period. In the more open political context of *reformasi*, courts have thus appeared to be more willing to uphold both public interest and private interest environmental claims.

The two case studies examined in Chapter III were both examples of environmental compensation claims undertaken in the post-Suharto period

[29] Public interest suits also flourished in other areas following the introduction of the administrative courts in 1991. For instance the *Tempo* case, where the editor of the critical *Tempo* magazine Goenawan Mohamad challenged the decision of Information Minister Harmoko withdrawing his magazine's public permit, became a cause celebré in 1995 and transformed Judge Benyamin Mangkoeldilaga into an instant celebrity when he upheld the claim. See Bourchier 1999:233-52.

that were, in at least one court, successful. One noticeable aspect in both these cases was the role of community or social pressure, which appeared to have some influence on the presiding courts in both cases. This was particularly evident in the Banger River case, where court sittings at both the district court and high court level were attended by large numbers from the Dekoro community. Several participants considered that the high degree of community pressure to return a 'fair' verdict was a likely influence on the eventual decision of the courts. Indeed at one point, after two hundred or so observers had 'pounded their chairs in disappointment', the presiding judge conceded that he would 'in principle [...] defend the people's interests'.[30] A prominent and vocal community presence was also maintained in the district court hearing of the Babon River case, where the environmental claim was upheld. In contrast, no community presence was maintained during the high court hearings, when the initially favourable decision was overturned – a decision that several participants attributed partly to the lack of community scrutiny.

The vocal expression of community sentiments, particularly during the course of a hearing, is an expression of the more open and tolerant political context in the period immediately following Suharto's resignation. From one perspective, such pressure might be described as a 'power-based' approach, utilized in these cases by claimants to influence the outcome of the rights-based litigation process. Resort to power-based strategies to influence the outcome of litigation is certainly not unknown in the Indonesian context. Bribery and political interference in the judicial process are well-established traditions in the Indonesian political context and are discussed in more detail below. However, to equate community pressure of this nature with other, more covert power-based tactics such as bribery and political interference is probably to exaggerate its influence and also to unfairly denigrate its intent. Certainly, where community pressure contains a threat of violence it is a threat to the impartiality and integrity of the judicial process, which should not be condoned. Yet public attendance at hearings, and even the vocal expression of support, fall short of such a threat and may be accommodated within a public dispute resolution such as litigation.

Community pressure and strongly held public sentiments may thus play an important role in environmental disputes, which are often public and highly controversial. For instance in the Eksponen 66 case, strong community sentiments of a more general nature were an apparent influence on the court's decision making. The plaintiffs in that case were a diverse collection of community organizations representing a wide cross-section of society. The public interest action undertaken by the plaintiffs articulated a widespread sense of anger at

30 'Pengunjung sidang gebrak kursi', *Suara Merdeka*, 29-6-1999.

the unprecedented environmental, social and economic damage caused by the uncontrollable forest fires. The district court's decision in upholding the claim appeared to be influenced more by these articulated social sentiments than by the specific factual and legal circumstances of the claim.

In cases such as Eksponen 66, the relational distance between the court as a social control agent and the community represented by the public interest suit appears to have narrowed significantly.[31] The closer relational distance between court and claimants may be one factor contributing to the greater success of environmental claims at the district court level than at the appellate court level. As discussed above, ten environmental cases were (at least partially) successful at the district court level, compared to only two at the high court or Supreme Court levels. Appellate courts are geographically further removed from their district constituencies; high courts are located in the capital cities of provinces, whilst the Supreme Court is located in the national capital Jakarta. The appellate process is also generally less open and accessible to the public and usually will not involve more extensive public hearings, as may occur at the district court level. There are therefore fewer opportunities for claimant communities to attend, view or participate in the appellate process, as may be possible at the district court level. If public participation in or scrutiny of the judicial process tends to narrow the relational distance between environmental claimants and judicial decision-makers, this may be one explanation for the different outcomes at the district court level compared to the high court or Supreme Court levels.

Environmental mediation

To complement our concluding discussion of environmental litigation, in this section we begin with an overview and analysis of outcomes in the environmental mediation cases reviewed in Chapters IV and V, and conclude with an examination of the conditions, introduced in Chapter I, which have been most influential in shaping the process and outcome in environmental mediation cases. This discussion will refer particularly to the two detailed case studies – the Palur Raya and the Kayu Lapis Indonesia cases – presented in Chapter V, and will provide a comparison for the concluding discussion of environmental litigation in the previous section. Finally, our comparative and concluding analysis of environmental mediation will form the basis for a number of recommendations to improve the effectiveness of such mediation in Indonesia.

31 See discussion of the concept of relational distance in Chapter I.

Cultural basis and legal framework for mediation

Consensually-based forms of dispute resolution (*musyawarah*) have a strong cultural base and a long history in Indonesia. At the village level, various forms of consensual deliberation have been utilized for dispute resolution and community decision-making throughout the archipelago. Group deliberation toward consensus (*musyawarah untuk mufakat*) is even enshrined as one of the five basic principles (Pancasila) of the Indonesian Republic, reflecting the high priority afforded to values of compromise, consensus and harmony within Indonesian culture. As discussed in Chapter IV, several commentators have considered the traditional practice of *musyawarah* as a solid foundation and cultural precedent for the use of mediation in environmental disputes. Nonetheless, the social-political context of modern environmental disputes is very different from the traditional cultural context of *musyawarah.* Furthermore, the ideology of *musyawarah* has itself been utilized in the modern political context as a pretext for stifling dissent, rather than achieving true consensus. Thus, whilst the *musyawarah* tradition remains an important cultural base for modern forms of mediation, comparison between the two approaches should be cognizant of the social and political complexities of modern environmental disputes.

The cultural basis for mediation in Indonesia has been supplemented by legislation institutionalizing mediation as a channel of dispute resolution in environmental disputes. In comparison to the legal framework for environmental litigation, the framework for environmental mediation established by Part Two, Chapter VII of the EMA 1997 is succinct and relatively basic. Most importantly, the provisions in Part Two provide formal, legal recognition to 'out of court' environmental dispute settlement. The legal bottleneck created by article 20 of the EMA 1982, which made mediation via a government tripartite team compulsory prior to litigation, has been resolved by article 30 of the EMA 1997, which has confirmed the voluntary nature of mediation. Article 30 has ensured that mediation constitutes an alternative, but not an obstacle to environmental litigation and does not compromise the parties' rights to civil process. Furthermore, mediation may be initiated by the disputing parties themselves, and – unlike under the EMA 1982 – mediation is not dependent upon government facilitation, which may or may not eventuate.

Access to mediation

The cultural familiarity and procedural informality of mediation has tended to increase its accessibility to potential environmental claimants in Indonesia. Certainly in the majority of environmental disputes at least some types of non-judicial dispute settlement, such as negotiation or mediation, have been attempted. In many cases, the first response of community members is to approach either factory management or local government figures to discuss the problem of pollution and attempt to negotiate a solution. Such informal attempts at negotiation or mediation are not usually successful however, and are often met by indifference or inaction on the part of industry or government. For instance, in both the PT KLI and Palur Raya cases, early attempts at negotiation were made, but these were unsuccessful in providing a comprehensive resolution to the disputes. Cases in which a more structured, independently facilitated and inclusive process of mediation has occurred to resolve a dispute appear to be few. Although more affordable and procedurally informal than litigation, a structured mediation process is not always immediately accessible to environmental disputants. In both the Palur Raya and PT KLI cases, for example, a structured mediation process was undertaken only after an extensive process of community campaigning and high-level government intervention. Mediation is a voluntary choice and is predicated upon the willingness of all parties to participate, a precondition which is not always fulfilled.

Access to properly facilitated and structured mediation processes would be improved by a proper institutional framework to facilitate the implementation of environmental mediation. Although the Central Environmental Impact Agency (Bapedal) and a number of its regional counterparts have on several occasions encouraged or initiated mediation processes in environmental disputes, the agency has recently been dissolved. Devolution of environmental management responsibilities to the district level, pursuant to decentralization laws, is unlikely to facilitate access to environmental mediation. In both the KLI and Palur Raya cases, the district governments were ineffective in facilitating a mediation process themselves. A structured mediation process was only initiated in both cases following ministerial intervention from the national level and, in the case of PT KLI, strong support from the provincial governor. Access to mediation could certainly be improved by implementation of the recently enacted Government Regulation No. 54 of 2000 concerning Environmental Dispute Settlement Providers. This regulation provides a legal basis for all central or regional governments to create an environmental dispute resolution service provider, pursuant to article 33 of the EMA 1997. To date, such dispute resolution providers have not been created, and thus the proper institutional support for an independent, well facilitation mediation process is still lacking. In the absence of this formal support, environmental mediation is often a sporadic and ad hoc process, dependent largely on informal support from influential government figures for its success.

Case outcomes

In Chapters IV and V of this book, seventeen environmental mediation cases were reviewed in total, two of which were the subjects of detailed case studies in Chapter V. The outcomes of the cases are summarized in Appendix II. The majority of the cases reviewed were industry related disputes located in Java; the exception was the KEM mining dispute (2001) in Kalimantan. Agreements were reached in a high percentage (80%) of the cases reviewed. Yet, as the discussion in the previous chapters indicates, a written agreement in itself does not necessarily result in either the cessation of further pollution or the resolution of the dispute. In several instances, mediated agreements were concluded but were not subsequently implemented. Where implementation did occur, one of the most common outcomes was the payment of some form of compensation. In the cases summarized above, a payment of some form was made by industry to the environmental claimants in eleven out of seventeen cases (65%). In the majority of cases, however, these payments were framed as 'contributions' to community development, rather than as compensation for pollution or environmental damage. In the Palur Raya case, for instance, the payment ultimately made to the Ngringo community was described as a contribution to community development, despite the industry's earlier acknowledgement of pollution in the mediation agreement of June 2000. Similarly in the PT KLI case, despite independent research confirming the impact of PT KLI's development activities, the payment made by the industry to the sixteen farmers was described as a goodwill rather than compensatory payment. There was thus, in both cases, no explicit acknowledgment that pollution or environmental damage had in fact occurred. The cases illustrate a preference, on the part of industry, to address or 'solve' environmental problems by direct payments made to complainants rather than by acknowledging the environmental damage or pollution itself and taking appropriate steps to remedy the problem.[32] For instance, in a number of cases, a monetary payment by industry was used to install a piped water supply, so that the community was no longer dependent on polluted river or ground water in their daily lives. The 'solution' to the environmental dispute in such cases is only limited in nature, and fails to adequately address environmental considerations. In many cases, such measures have apparently allowed industries to continue their operations in a polluting manner, thereby increasing the likelihood of future conflict.

Not surprisingly, the continuation of pollution and environmental dam-

[32] As one industry owner put it: 'Give the money, the conflict is finished' (*Kasih uang, konflik selesai*): Sindu Dharmali, interview, 18-11-2003.

age has been a problem in a number of the environmental mediation cases reviewed. Although mediated agreements frequently included provisions pertaining to improved environmental management, in practice pollution remained a problem even after mediation, in nine out of seventeen cases (53%). In most cases, the problem in this respect has been one of implementation. Whilst industries pledged, pursuant to written agreements, to improve environmental management or undertake environmental restoration, this did not occur to the satisfaction of the community in the subsequent implementation phase. Nonetheless, of the cases reviewed, there were several in which significant improvements in environmental management occurred through the mediation process. For example in the Samitex (1995), Palur Raya (2002) and Kanasritex (2000) cases, waste management systems were repaired, improved and constructed respectively. Where improved environmental management measures were not adequately implemented, this led to further conflict between the disputing parties in a number of cases; even when compensation for prior environmental damage had been paid. In eight out of fifteen (53%) of the cases reviewed, conflict reoccurred after mediation.

Social-legal context of mediation 1: relational distance, balance of power and BATNAs

In Chapter I, we discussed Black's styles of social control, which may also be understood as approaches to conflict management. The 'conciliatory' style described by Black was a remedial approach, such as negotiation or mediation, where both parties sought to negotiate a mutually acceptable resolution to the dispute. Black makes the point that this style of conflict management is most suited where the relational distance, or social distance, between parties is close. Where relations are close, there is less 'law' involved, and both parties themselves will have sufficient incentive to seek resolution of the conflict. It is precisely in this manner that traditional mediation approaches (*musyawarah*) were applied at the village level in Indonesia, where social bonds were close and conflict could not easily be ignored. In contrast, the social context of environmental disputes in Indonesia is very different. In all the cases reviewed in Chapters IV and V, the relational distance between disputants was considerably greater than the relational distance likely to have existed between disputants at the village level. In the majority of cases the industry owner or CEO lived in a city some distance from the factory and surrounding villages, and was from a very different social-economic stratum of society. Also, in the Palur Raya and PT KLI disputes, the majority of village plaintiffs were not employed by the respective industries, and many had livelihoods that were directly threatened by the industries' operation. Unsurprisingly in this context, in both disputes the relations between disputants were characterized by a considerable degree of hostility. The natural inclination to seek a harmonious restoration of social bonds was absent, given the lack of pre-existing close social bonds.

Nonetheless, as noted in Chapter I, the literature on environmental mediation makes it clear that conciliatory approaches such as mediation have been applied with success to a range of modern environmental disputes where the relational distance between disputants may be great. What this literature does note, however, is that certain conditions should exist if attempts at mediation are to bear fruit. One of these conditions, which we discussed in Chapter I, was that a relative parity or balance of power exist between the disputants in a mediation process. In the case studies reviewed in Chapters IV and V, however, this condition was often not present, at least initially. In the two case studies reviewed in Chapter V, for instance, the alleged 'polluters' were large industries with significant political and economic clout at the provincial and national levels. In contrast, the 'victims' of environmental damage and pollution were villagers of relatively simple means, with limited economic and political resources at their disposal. This is by no means an atypical pattern, as studies in a number of countries have demonstrated the uneven distribution of adverse environmental impacts which tend to be inflicted disproportionately upon the marginalized or poorer sectors of society.[33]

Such a significant power disparity between disputants presents a considerable obstacle to the success of mediation, due mainly to the likelihood that the more powerful party will have several 'Better Alternatives to a Negotiated Agreement' (BATNAs) at its disposal. As the literature reviewed in Chapter I suggested, the success of mediation depends in part upon the absence of a BATNA. In essence, neither party should be able to achieve its aims unilaterally, through either power-based (lobbying, intimidation, bribery, political influence, etcetera) or rights-based (litigation) approaches. When both parties reach this 'point of impasse' then it is more likely that each party will be sufficiently motivated to commit to a negotiated settlement, which will inevitably involve some compromise.

The 'better alternative' for industries in many of the cases reviewed was, at least initially, the stone-walling or denial of pollution claims, particularly in the New Order period prior to 1998. In a number of cases, community complaints were voiced for several years before industry representatives became willing to negotiate. In the Palur Raya case, community complaints over pollution were first expressed in 1992, but were met with indifference and intimidation until 1998 when industry representatives agreed to enter a negotiation process. In the PT KLI case, residents of Mororejo and Mangunharjo

[33] For a comprehensive bibliography of environmental justice studies, see http://www.epa.gov/compliance/resources/publications/ej/ej_bib.html.

had suffered the effects of PT KLI's development activities since 1987, yet only felt safe to voice their claims openly after the political changes of 1998. In the Tapak River case (1991), residents tried unsuccessfully to resolve pollution problems for fourteen years before a mediation process was commenced.

In these cases, maintenance of the status quo was the better alternative to negotiation as far as industry was concerned. This alternative was possible in these and other cases for three main reasons. Firstly, in these cases the enforcement of environmental law by administrative agencies was inadequate or non-existent. This was certainly the case in both case studies examined in Chapter V, where local and regional authorites were unable or unwilling to enforce administrative sanctions despite obvious breaches of legal requirements. Secondly, neither was there any real threat of law enforcement through the courts. In the PT KLI case, on more than one occasion industry representatives invited the community to sue them if it had a claim for damages. Legal representatives for the community, however, advised against this course given the legal and technical difficulties of proving pollution and the vulnerability of the courts to corruption. Thirdly, in some cases, particularly during the New Order period prior to 1998, the security forces of the state actually helped industries maintain the status quo by directly repressing protests against the effects of environmental pollution. A notorious example of such a repressive response was the Nipah tragedy, when security forces opened fire on a peaceful demonstration over the Nipah dam construction on the island of Madura in 1993, killing four people and injuring three (Amnesty International 1994:58). Whilst the Nipah case attracted widespread publicity, it was commonplace during this time for large scale developments to be accompanied by a deliberate program of intimidation by police, military or civilian hired thugs. It was the threat of this kind of response that suppressed conflicts such as the PT KLI and Palur Raya disputes prior to 1998, despite the fact that pollution had been ongoing for years, as noted earlier in the PT KLI case study.

Yet, as is evident from the overview of case outcomes in the previous section, mediation was successful in at least partially resolving disputes in a number of cases. In our two case studies, the intransigence of industry was finally overcome in both disputes, and mediation was at least commenced. What was the catalyst for the commencement of mediation in these cases, and in other cases reviewed in Chapter IV? The main catalyst appeared to be a shift in the power balance between the disputing parties, with a corresponding reduction in the 'better alternatives' to mediation that were available to industry. In each case it became harder for industry to stonewall or suppress environmental claims, and as a result mediation presented itself as a more viable option for resolving the situation. In the cases reviewed in Chapters IV and V, there have been two main mechanisms through which this has occurred: increased community pressure and increased government pressure and/or intervention. We shall discuss each of these in turn.

Social-legal context of mediation 2: community organization

The capacity of a community involved in an environmental dispute to effectively organize and advocate their interests was one important condition which influenced both access to a structured mediation process and the outcome of that process. An initial function of effective community organization is that it may help facilitate access to a mediation process. If a community suffering pollution is to proceed beyond the indifference, denial or intimidation from industry and government agencies that greet many initial environmental claims, a sophisticated level of organization and campaign skills may be necessary to raise the profile of their case. For example, in the Palur Raya case, community organization and strategic planning were undertaken in collaboration with several NGOs. Subsequent to this, a public campaign was conducted which raised the profile of the case and finally prompted the intervention of the National Environment Minister, who ordered the initiation of a mediation process. In this case the Consortium of Waste Victims (KKL), formed by community representatives and NGO workers, provided an important vehicle for communication of environmental and community concerns to the mass media and government agencies. A similar process was evident in the Kayu Lapis Indonesia case, where formation of the community forum KMPL provided a vehicle for the clarification of community demands and their communication to the mass media, government agencies and industry. In this case, the community of fishpond farmers was forced to undertake extensive lobbying of district, provincial and finally national government representatives, before a mediation process was eventually undertaken. Effective community organization such as the creation of representative forums also served, in these case studies, to clarify internal decision-making within a community, and enabled more effective representation of community interests during the mediation process. In both the PT KLI and Palur Raya cases, the intervention of non-government organizations skilled in advocacy and organization was also critical to the ability of each community to effectively organize and advocate their interests.

Similar trends are evident in some of the other environmental mediation cases reviewed in Chapter IV. In the Tapak River case, a community boycott appeared to influence the willingness of the polluting industries to negotiate. Increased community pressure and the blocking of a factory waste outlet in the Indo Acidatama case (1997) prompted the formation of a fact-finding team to resolve the dispute. Similarly, in the Kanasritex case widespread publicity and government support for the community's claims prompted a change in the industry's stance and the commencement of an ultimately successful mediation process. In these examples, community organization and advocacy was usually facilitated by non-government organizations working closely with community members, to raise their awareness of environmental rights and to train community representatives in key advocacy skills.

More effective community organization and advocacy is not an end in itself, but rather a tool to assist communities in clarifying and communicating their demands in key public forums such as the legislature, media and executive decision-making offices at the regional and national levels. In particular the regional and national media may play a significant role in raising the profile of an environmental dispute, and by doing so may escalate the public pressure on government and corporate decision makers (Lucas and Arief Djati 2000:19). In both the PT KLI and Palur Raya disputes, the communities were relatively skilled in coordinating advocacy efforts with media coverage. Even in earlier disputes during the New Order period, such as the Tapak River case, media coverage has played an important role. Despite the tight rein held by the government over the media during the New Order period, environmental disputes were still publicized and popular opinion often expressed through cartoons critical of pollution's effects on local people (Warren 1994). The scope of media coverage of environmental disputes was, nonetheless, sometimes limited by editorial censorship, industry or government pressure, or bribery of journalists assigned to report environmental issues (Lucas and Arief Djati 2000:19). Now, in the very different political context of post-Suharto Indonesia, there appear to be few restrictions on media coverage; a fact which is likely to amplify the role of the media and its use by communities and environmental organizations in environmental disputes.

The ability of a community to mobilize public support, communicate their claims to the mass media and lobby senior government agencies may thus go some way towards redressing the power imbalance that usually exists between the polluter and the victims of pollution in most environmental disputes. This ability may not only serve to facilitate access to a structured mediation process but also increase the willingness of industry or government agencies to compromise, thus influencing the final result. For example in the Palur Raya case, the ability of community representatives to mobilize public support, utilize the media and effectively advocate their interests was a strong influence on the final outcome of the initial mediation process. Yet, whilst effective community organization may serve to redress a power imbalance and potentially influence the outcome of the mediation process, this of course will not always be the case. In the Kayu Lapis Indonesia case for example, whilst community advocacy facilitated the commencement of a structured mediation process it did little to influence the intransient attitude of industry management, which led to PT KLI's withdrawal from mediation. Continued community advocacy, however, facilitated the later resumption of mediation with government agencies, and the reopening of negotiation with PT KLI on the matter of compensation.

Social-legal context of mediation 3: government intervention

The review of cases in Chapters IV and V also demonstrates the importance of the roles and responses of government agencies and influential government figures to the commencement and outcome of a structured mediation process. As noted above, government intervention or administrative pressure may also play a significant role in increasing the committment and willingness of industry to negotiate. Whilst industries such as Kayu Lapis Indonesia (KLI) and Palur Raya possessed considerable political and economic clout, they do not operate independently of government patronage, and their operations are ultimately dependent upon the support of key government decision makers. Thus, in the PT KLI case personal pressure exerted by the governor of Central Java was essential in drawing the industry into the mediation process. In the Palur Raya case, the personal intervention of the Environment Minister in the final phase of the mediation process was a critical factor in the agreement that was ultimately reached.

In a number of cases the national Environmental Impact Agency (Bapedal), in particular, has played a key role in initiating and supporting environmental mediation. For instance, in the Palur Raya case the intervention of the national Environment Minister prompted the regional environmental agency to take a more active role in facilitating a mediation process between the disputing parties. The same Environment Minister was also a catalyst for the mediation process in the Kayu Lapis Indonesia case. Several other cases have followed a similar pattern, including the Kanasritex, Sambong River (1993) and Siak River (1992) disputes. Yet whilst support from the National Environmental Agency has facilitated mediation in some instances, in other cases it has failed to do so, particularly when support was not also forthcoming from the regional government concerned. For instance in the Ciujung River case (1995), pollution was confirmed by research from the National Environmental Agency, which also supported an initiative to resolve the case via mediation. The mediation ultimately failed, however, in the absence of support from the regional government of Serang.

In other cases, where support from regional authorities has been evident, environmental mediation has resulted in a more successful outcome. For example, in the Samitex case the regional Yogyakarta Environmental Bureau was responsible for mediating the ultimately successful conflict resolution process. Similarly in the Naga Mas case (1994), district government officials successfully mediated an environmental dispute at the instigation of Batang regent. In the PT KLI case, the support of the Central Java governor was key not only in starting mediation but also in compelling PT KLI to re-enter the mediation process following its initial withdrawal.

Whilst the response of regional administrative or executive authorities has been significant in mediation cases, regional legislative assemblies have also played an important role in several cases. In the Kayu Lapis Indonesia case, a widely publicized visit to the regional legislature and a subsequent legislative hearing on the dispute facilitated commencement of the dispute resolution process in the following month. Similarly, in the Naga Mas case a complaint conveyed by community representatives to the legislative assembly facilitated an investigation into the community's pollution claims. In the Tawang Mas case (2000), a permanent committee of the legislative assembly actually mediated the dispute and brokered the final agreement to redirect the Tawang Mas river. For mediation, the degree of administrative and/or legislative support appears to play an essential role in both facilitating access to a mediation process and influencing its final outcome.

Given the relevance of the administrative context to the environmental dispute resolution process, it is likely that the recent moves toward decentralization in Indonesia will have a significant impact. The decentralization laws in question provide for a significant devolution of administrative authority from the national to the district (regency/city municipality) level.[34] In the mediation cases reviewed in Chapters IV and V, district environmental agencies played the least significant role in facilitating the mediation process, when compared to agencies at the provincial and national levels. In both the PT KLI and Palur Raya case studies, mediation only commenced after intervention and support from the provincial and/or national levels. In the Ciujung River case the Serang district government actively opposed attempts to commence a mediation process. The generally supportive position of district governments toward industry in environmental disputes is understandable, given the reliance of district governments on revenue from this sector. In this context, devolution of environmental management authority to the district level is unlikely to support the objectives of environmental dispute resolution.

Social-legal context of mediation 4: role of the mediator

Whilst effective community organization and government support may facilitate the commencement of mediation, the outcome of the process is by no means pre-determined. As discussed in Chapter I, the ability and impartiality of the mediator may strongly influence the potential course and outcome of mediation. The academic literature on mediation has tended

34 The laws in question are Law 22 of 1999 on Regional Governance and Law No. 25 of 1999 on the Fiscal Balance between the Central Government and the Regions.

to emphasize the need for a mediator who is both neutral and impartial. Government Regulation No. 54 of 2000 reiterates this principle, stating that a mediator should possess the appropriate skills and experience and have no interest in the dispute at hand. Despite the enactment of this regulation, however, this has not been the case in the majority of environmental mediation cases to date. In practice, mediators are often government officials who, by virtue of their office, have a clear interest in the dispute. In some cases, this interest has been apparent from the attempts of mediating officials to influence the outcome of the mediation. For example in the Tembok Dukuh case (1991), regional government officials acting as mediators pressured residents to compromise and accept the industry's offer of compensation. In other cases however, government appointed mediators have mediated in a sufficiently neutral and effective manner. For example in the Sambong River dispute, the government appointed mediator was not only sufficiently neutral but was able to minimize animosity between parties through 'shuttle diplomacy'[35] and overcome a deadlock on the matter of compensation. In the Siak River dispute, a senior official from the Environmental Control Agency acted as mediator and facilitated an agreement in principle between the disputing parties. Similarly in the Samitex case, officials from the Yogyakarta Environmental Bureau successfully performed the task of mediation.

Indeed, in some cases, the position and influence of a senior government mediator may be an important catalyst to facilitate compromise between the disputing parties, especially where a deadlock exists. For instance, in the Palur Raya case, the personal intervention of the national Environment Minister as a mediator was a key factor in overcoming an impasse, influencing industry and bringing the parties to agreement. Similarly, the intervention of the governor of Central Java in April 2003 facilitated implementation of the agreement. In the PT KLI case, the influence of the governor of Central Java was significant in initially bringing PT KLI to the negotiating table and in facilitating the eventual payment of compensation to the fishpond farmers. A government mediator with senior status may thus also be effective and may be particularly appropriate where the parties need a more directive approach.

One disadvantage of a government mediator is that he or she is probably at a greater risk of appearing biased. For instance, in the PT KLI case, community representatives reported considerable pressure from regional government authorities during the 'Small Format' Mediation process to accept industry offers of compensation. A high status mediator is also more likely to dominate the process and outcome of mediation, playing more of a directive rather than a facilitative role. Nonetheless, use of a high status or

35 Negotiating separately with each of the parties.

'vested interest' mediator may well increase the likelihood of an industry's participation in the mediation process. As argued above, key government figures have played an important role in facilitating mediation through their personal and political influence on industry. Sometimes this intervention has included acting as mediator, as was the case in the Palur Raya case in the final stage of mediation. It is also interesting that in the PT KLI case, the apparently 'neutral' mediator agreed to by both parties was ultimately rejected by the industry, who agreed to negotiate only through the mediation of the vice-governor.

Whether a 'vested interest' mediator is necessary or not is likely to depend on the circumstances of each case. If the 'threshold' issue of industry participation is already resolved, then a neutral and independent mediator would be preferable, as this would ensure impartiality towards both parties. Yet at present the use of government mediators is often a necessity, due to the lack of an institutional base for or source of independent, qualified mediators. Government Regulation No. 54 of 2000 addresses this problem by authorizing regional governments or communities to establish environmental dispute resolution service providers, and stipulating criteria which such providers must meet. To date, however, the regulation has not been implemented, and thus the issue of sourcing a mediator is still dealt with on an ad hoc, case by case basis. Implementation of this important regulation would at least increase the available options for choosing a mediator in environmental disputes, ensuring that a neutral and independent mediator is available where that is the most appropriate choice.

Social-legal context of mediation 5: implementation of mediated agreements

In a number of cases, the factors discussed above – effective community organization, government support, a skilled and sufficiently impartial mediator – combined to facilitate both mediation and a successful resolution of an agreement between the disputing parties. However, an agreement in itself does not constitute a resolution of the dispute. As noted in Chapter I, effective implementation of mediated agreements is necessary for a successful resolution in the longer term. Implementation of compensatory remedies is usually not a problem in practice, although it certainly proved problematic in the Palur Raya case, where the industry attempted to control disbursement of the funds. However, in the majority of cases reviewed, if industry agreed to pay compensation (or a 'contribution') then payment did occur. A more problematic issue has been implementation of measures to rehabilitate or prevent environmental damage or pollution. For example, in the Palur Raya case, the final agreement stipulated ongoing monitoring of the factory's compliance with environmental regulations, which was to be carried out by a regulatory team from the National Environmental Agency. Yet, in practice this did not happen, as the team from the Environment Ministry was refused access to the factory site. Continuing problems with environmental pollution were in fact reported in ten of the seventeen (59%) mediation cases reviewed. In some cases, such as the Palur Raya dispute, industry undertakings to improve environmental management appear mostly symbolic, and designed to appease community sentiment in the short term rather than achieve actual changes in industry practice in the longer term.

The problem of enforcing environmental measures is closely related to problems of administrative enforcement of environmental regulations. Indeed, a common term in the mediated agreements reviewed was 'ongoing compliance with environmental regulations'. To ensure such compliance it is necessary for the relevant government agencies to carry out regular monitoring and apply administrative sanctions in the event of non-compliance. Alternatively, mediated agreements could be legalized as a decision of the court and thus made enforceable through judicial mechanisms. This occurred in the Kalimantan Peat Land (Farmers' Compensation) case, where the agreement reached through settlement was legalized as a decision of the court. Yet judicial mechanisms of law enforcement are not likely to be any more effective than administrative mechanisms. Where law enforcement, whether judicial or administrative, is inadequate and sporadic, there will be little incentive for industry to comply with environmental standards in the longer term. Unfortunately this is often the case in Indonesia, where available evidence suggests administrative enforcement is, at best, only partially effective. In the worst cases, companies may operate with blatant disregard for environmental regulation. For instance, in the Banger River case, the polluting factories continued operations despite the withdrawal of their operating permit by the district government.[36] Similarly in the PT KLI case, the industry redirected the Wakak River and excavated a log pond without the required permits to do so. This situation has been highlighted by a recent statement from a senior Environment Ministry official, who noted that only 50% of chemical industries in Indonesia comply with regulations governing the disposal of hazardous waste.[37] Inadequate enforcement of environmental standards not only undermines the prospect of implementing mediated agreements or judicial decisions in environmental disputes, but also increases the number

36 At the time of writing the factories were still reportedly operating without an operating permit. According to a lawyer for the Dekoro community, the situation was tolerated due to the considerable number of workers employed by the factory: Lusila Anjela Bodroani, interview, 18-11-2003.

37 According to the statement by Masnillyarti Hilman, Deputy VII (Area for Technical Development in Environmental Management), the worst offenders were small-scale industries that lacked the financial or technical capacity to adequately manage hazardous waste. See 'Cuma 50% industri kimia ramah lingkungan', *Media Indonesia*, 13-3-2003.

of environmental disputes requiring resolution in the first place.[38] Efforts to improve the effectiveness of mechanisms for environmental dispute resolution are thus closely correlated with parallel efforts to improve the effectiveness of administrative enforcement of environmental law.[39]

Comparison of environmental litigation and mediation

As discussed in Chapter I, litigation and mediation are in many ways quite distinct approaches to dispute resolution. In litigation, dispute resolution is achieved through a court's authoritative determination of the rights, remedies and relationship of disputing parties, through the application of legal norms. In mediation, by contrast, dispute resolution is achieved via a voluntary and consensual process of facilitated negotiation, in which the parties attempt to reach a harmonious reconciliation of their conflicting interests. Nonetheless, for our purpose litigation and mediation may be seen as different means to a common end: that of environmental justice. In the EMA 1997, litigation and mediation are presented as two options available to a claimant seeking some remedy for an environmental wrong. How do these two channels of dispute resolution compare in practice? What are their respective strengths and weaknesses? Can either be said to have been 'more effective'?

Access

As previously discussed, there is a myriad of factors that mitigate access to a dispute resolution procedure, including social values, economic resources, legal framework and political context. As we have seen, access to litigation has been facilitated by the reform of procedural law but has in practice been limited by a number of factors, including: a cultural reluctance to litigate (especially against 'social superiors'); the expense of litigation and the limited availability of legal aid; the technical and legal difficulties of proving pollution in court; and the institutional problems, especially corruption, which have undermined public confidence in the judiciary. Notwithstanding these problems, the legal framework has been utilized in over twenty cases,

38 This point was made by the Environmental Ministry quoted in the note above who, given the lack of law enforcement, expressed 'no surprise that environmental pollution cases around industry cannot be avoided'. See 'Cuma 50% industri kimia ramah lingkungan', *Media Indonesia*, 13-3-2003.

39 Whilst this subject is outside the scope of this book it has been addressed by other researchers in the Indonesia Netherlands Study on Environmental Law and Administration (INSELA) project. See, for instance, Bedner and Van Rooij 2001.

although this number appears relatively limited given the scope of environmental problems and the population size of Indonesia.

At first glance, mediation appears significantly more accessible than litigation. As we have seen, mediation has a strong cultural antecedent in Indonesia, as consensual forms of negotiation and decision-making (*musyawarah*) are an established feature of traditional cultures at the village level. Unlike America, where the cultural imperative of individualism underlies the litigiousness of that society, in Indonesia the cultural value placed on consensus and harmony makes mediation a more culturally familiar and comfortable choice. Mediation also lacks the legal and technical obstacles of 'proving' pollution and does not involve the cost of legal representation. It is, as a result, very common in environmental disputes for at least some rudimentary form of 'consensual' dispute settlement to be attempted outside of court, usually in the form of negotiation, although the success rate of such rudimentary attempts is low. However, access to a formally structured mediation process is often more problematic, and essentially depends upon the willingness of key government officials and industry representatives to cooperate. In this respect, the absence of independent dispute resolution providers (as provided for in Government Regulation No. 54 of 2000) is an ongoing problem. Ultimately, where access to mediation fails and where industry or government agencies are not willing to negotiate, then litigation may prove a more accessible option; as citizens always have the right to file a legal suit, at the hearing of which the attendance of any defendant will be compulsory.

Case outcomes

When considering case outcomes, mediation has had a higher success rate than litigation in terms of disputants actually obtaining compensation for environmental damage or pollution. Of the fourteen private interest cases in the courts, ten were lost and four were at least partially successful at the district court level. However, only two of these were finally successful at the appellate level and one of those is still pending an appeal to the Supreme Court. The strong likelihood of appeal against any award of compensation by a court, combined with the extremely protracted nature of the appeal process – due in part to a severe backlog of cases at the appellate level – is another problematic aspect of litigation. In the Banger River case, for instance, the legal action of the Dekoro community was commenced in November 1998 and was still pending an appeal (to the Supreme Court) more than five years later.

In contrast, compensation payments were made in eleven of the seventeen mediation cases reviewed in this book, a considerably more frequent outcome than in litigation. Additionally, whilst mediation processes can also be lengthy, the delays involved usually do not approach anything like the protracted nature of litigation proceedings. For the most part, where payments were the subject of agreement in mediation cases they were generally made within a period of several months. Certainly, mediation appears to be a more probable and direct way of obtaining compensation for environmental damage than does litigation.

However, it is worth noting that when payments were made following mediation, they were frequently described not as 'compensation' but rather as 'good will payments' (*tali asih*) or 'contributions' to community development. This highlights the general tendency in environmental mediation cases to emphasize pecuniary rather than environmental remedies, although as noted some definite improvements in environmental management were evident in several cases. A similar emphasis was evident in environmental litigation cases. As noted above, compensation was the most common remedy ordered by courts, and in some cases, such the Babon River case, the failure of the court to address the issue of environmental management was clearly evident. Even in cases where orders to address environmental management were made by the courts, none of these orders have ever been implemented, as the decisions were either overturned on appeal or are still pending appeal.

Generally speaking, mediation appears to have been utilized in private interest, rather than public interest disputes. As discussed above, public interest suits have fulfilled an important political function even where substantive legal outcomes have not been achieved. The open and public nature of the judicial forum lends itself more readily to use as a 'public stage'. In comparison, the mediation process is usually restricted to the immediate participating parties and deliberately kept private and confidential. For instance, in the PT KLI case, the mediation process stalled early on following an alleged breach of confidentiality by one of the parties, who had provided a commentary of the mediation process to the regional press. Due to its private nature the mediation process is of only limited utility to activist environmental organizations, which may wish to publicize the broader issues of public policy that lie at the centre of the dispute. Public interest litigants like WALHI are also concerned not so much with the resolution of particular disputes, but rather with the ongoing political struggle to influence policy so as to ensure environmental protection, which we may characterize as a process of conflict rather than disputing.[40] A mediated dispute, even if successfully mediated, offers little benefit to an environmental organization engaged in such a broader political struggle, whereas any court case, even if unsuccessful, will bring an environmental dispute into the public spotlight – and a successful or partially successful case (like the PT IIU case) will not only provide public

40 See discussion of this point in Chapter I.

vindication for a cause but may establish a favourable precedent for future cases. As a result, public interest litigants may actually avoid resolving a dispute through mediation, even where this is a possibility. For instance in the WALHI v. Freeport case (2001), legal representatives for the environmental organization specifically rejected the chief magistrate's invitation to settle the dispute through mediation.[41]

Social-legal context

Our analysis of environmental litigation and mediation in the preceding chapters demonstrates the large extent to which both are contingent upon and responsive to the surrounding social-legal context. In litigation we saw how the adjudication of environmental cases has been strongly influenced by the political character of the judiciary, which in turn has been strongly influenced by the wider political context. We have also discussed how the institutional problems of judicial corruption and lack of judicial independence have influenced the administration of justice in environmental cases. Whilst the institutional problems affecting litigation in Indonesia are a well recognized problem, this is less the case with mediation. Advocates of environmental mediation in Indonesia had hoped that mediation would provide a means of 'bypassing' these institutional problems, thus improving the adjudication and resolution of environmental disputes. Similarly, advocates of mediation in Western countries have presented it as an 'alternative' to the inefficiencies and detractions of the court system. Yet, whilst mediation is undertaken outside the judicial institutional context and may thus bypass some of the problems therein, it is certainly apparent from this study that it cannot transcend the social-political context within which it is located. In this respect, much of the 'rhetoric' of mediation tends to accentuate and sometimes exaggerate the ability of state-of-the-art mediation techniques to resolve disputes, whilst failing to comprehend the significance and potential consequences of the wider social-political context within which these techniques operate.

As discussed above, one of the major obstacles to environmental mediation in Indonesia has been the significant power disparities between disputants. Typically, the more powerful, polluting party is not compelled nor motivated to mediate because there are better alternatives to a negotiated agreement (BATNAs). The most obvious of these is maintenance of the status quo, a logical choice in the face of inadequate administrative and judicial law enforcement. This dilemma illustrates the interrelation and inter-dependence of mediation with those processes of 'rights-based' and 'power-based' dis-

41 'Tolak berdamai, Walhi tetap tuntut Freeport minta maaf', *Suara Karya*, 22-8-2000.

pute resolution, which some writers have argued it should substitute. It is precisely due to the failure of rights-based and power-based ('command and control') enforcement mechanisms that the necessary conditions for mediation often do not exist. Fortunately, this type of situation has not been an absolute obstacle to the use of mediation. As discussed, a combination of factors, such as community pressure and government intervention, may create the necessary conditions for a successful mediation process. Yet this in itself demonstrates the interdependence of 'power-based' approaches with an 'interest-based' approach such as mediation. An interest-based approach only becomes possible where power-based approaches, such as advocacy, lobbying and political pressure, have brought the parties to a point of relative impasse. This approach may work on an ad hoc basis, especially in high profile cases where there is the necessary media exposure, prolonged campaigning or personal intervention of senior government figures. However, where these conditions are not present, it is less likely that mediation will succeed in the absence of judicial and administrative mechanisms for the enforcement of environmental law. In this way, the more 'legalistic' methods of dispute resolution need to be effective as a 'backstop' to mediation. There can be no 'bargaining in the shadow of the law' when the law itself casts no shadow.[42] Litigation and mediation thus should not be seen as autonomous or exclusive 'alternatives', but rather are interrelated and interdependent in their operation. To this end, reforms to improve environmental dispute resolution should simultaneously address all mechanisms of dispute resolution and law enforcement, namely administrative, judicial and consensual modes of environmental dispute settlement.

Our analysis of environmental litigation and mediation also demonstrates that these alternatives modes of dispute resolution are not only interdependent, but best regarded as complementary choices dependent upon the context of each dispute. Mediation may be an appropriate choice where the parties are at a point of impasse and are willing to pursue a negotiated agreement. Indeed, the efficiency of litigation could be greatly improved by the integration of mediation processes into the court system so as to ensure that cases that are susceptible to mediation are resolved consensually between the parties. On the other hand, where the interests of the disputants are in fact incompatible, where either party is unwilling to pursue a negotiated agreement or where a public interest claimant wishes a dispute to be resolved in a public forum, litigation may be a more appropriate choice.

[42] The phrase 'bargaining in the shadow of the law' comes from Mnookin and Kornhauser 1979:950.

Summary of recommendations[43]

1 Broadening of environmental standing
Broaden procedural access to the courts for environmental public interest litigants by introducing a 'citizen suit' provision where any interested citizen, or community organization, could undertake legal action for a breach of environmental law. This would remove existing restrictions on public interest standing provisions and facilitate enforcement of the EMA 1997.

2 Environmental compensation in public interest cases
Broaden the remedies available to public interest litigants to include compensation for environmental damage to cover the cost of environmental restoration. This would facilitate the enforcement of article 34 of the EMA 1997 in particular, which creates an obligation for polluters to pay compensation in the event of environmental pollution or damage.

3 'Polluter-pays' environmental trust fund
If public interest litigants were able to sue parties responsible for pollution or environmental damage for compensation (see recommendation 2), that compensation could be paid into an environmental trust fund for disbursement toward environmental restoration.

4 Protection of right to participate in environmental management
Enact legislation protecting the citizen's right to participate in environmental management, including the exercise of their civil rights to litigate breaches of environmental law. This would minimize the prospect of potential environmental litigants being intimidated by the risk of a 'SLAPP' suit undertaken by defendants.

5 Clarification of strict liability
Strict liability is, as discussed above, a legal doctrine with considerable potential to increase access to environmental justice through the courts. The significant potential of this doctrine has not been realized by Indonesian courts and in one case, has been attributed a scope much narrower than legislative intent arguably would allow. The strict liability doctrine and its application should therefore be clarified through several means to ensure its correct application in the future. These could be achieved through ongoing specialized training of judges in environmental law (see recommendation

43 More detailed explanations for these recommendations relating to the legal framework for litigation are discussed in Chapter VI above.

8), clarification of the doctrine's application by a Supreme Court regulation (as occurred with class actions) or, alternatively, legislative clarification or elucidation of the wider scope of strict liability to enable its correct application in future cases.

6 Legislative recognition of NGOs
Reintroduction of an article, similar in terms to article 19 of the EMA 1982, which originally gave specific legislative recognition of the role played by non-government organizations in environmental management. This would provide a clearer legal foundation for the broader participation of NGOs in environmental management.

7 Strengthen citizen initiated mechanisms of administrative enforcement
Strengthen citizen initiated mechanisms of administrative enforcement of environmental law through legislative amendment of article 25(1) of the EMA 1997, requiring a written decision on an application to an authorized official within a reasonable time frame, which, if contrary to law in the applicant's opinion, could be challenged in the administrative courts. The enforceability of article 37 could also be improved by imposing an obligation to act upon administrative agencies where environmental damage or pollution is established. Improved administrative enforcement of environmental law would indirectly improve the prospect of environmental dispute resolution through litigation and mediation, both of which have been shown to be directly influenced by administrative enforcement of environmental law.

8 Adjudication of environmental cases by specially trained judges
As discussed above, judicial decision making has been compromised in some environmental cases by a lack of judicial familiarity or expertise in environmental matters. One basic initiative to address this problem and improve competency in environmental judicial decision making would be to restrict the adjudication of environmental cases to judges certified to have received specialist environmental law training, such as the training carried out to date in the AusAid or Indonesia-Netherlands Course on Environmental Law and Administration (CELA) program.

9 Creation of a separate environmental division or environment court to handle environmental cases
A further, and more far reaching reform in this direction would be for the core group of judges specially trained in environmental law to form the basis for a separate judicial division for environmental (and potentially land related) cases. A similar, even broader reform would see the creation of a specialist court for environmental cases. A specialist court would not only ensure the

necessary level of judicial expertise but could incorporate non-judicial technical assessors and, moreover, resolve the problems of defining jurisdiction in environmental matters between the general and administrative courts.

10 Improved institutionalization of mediation

Access to structured mediation should be improved by providing an institutional basis within which environmental mediation processes can occur, rather than having to provide 'ad hoc' institutional support on a case-by-case basis. There are two main bases upon which this could occur. Firstly, Government Regulation No. 54 of 2000 has provided a legislative basis for the creation of mediation service providers by the public or government. Proper implementation of this regulation at national, provincial and district levels is necessary to ensure the effectiveness of environmental mediation. Secondly, mediation processes could be annexed to court proceedings, which would have the effect of not only improving access to mediation but also improving the efficiency of the court system by filtering out cases that could be satisfactorily resolved by mediation. At the time of writing, a regulation on court-annexed mediation was being considered by the Supreme Court.

11 Creation of an environmental investigating office

The incidence of corruption in environmental court cases and also in cases of inadequate administrative enforcement could be reduced if administrative and judicial enforcement of environmental law were more effectively supervised. This could be achieved through the creation of a supervisory body, such as an 'Environmental Rights Commission' or an 'Environmental Ombudsman', to investigate cases where administrative or judicial enforcement of environmental law has failed to remedy serious breaches of environmental rights or where corruption is alleged to have occurred.[44]

12 Continued judicial reform to strengthen judicial independence and impartiality

This study has emphasized the influence of the judicial institutional context upon the adjudication of environmental cases in court and indirectly on the mediation of environmental disputes outside of court. Accordingly, to ensure effective environmental dispute resolution it is essential that resources be devoted to reform programs designed to improve and strengthen judicial independence, impartiality and efficiency. The nature of such reforms has been discussed in detail above.

44 The Indonesian Centre for Environmental Law has previously made a similar recommendation for supervision.

Appendices

APPENDIX 1

Overview of environmental litigation cases

Environmental public interest cases 1982-2002

No	Case name	Year	Category of dispute	Plaintiffs
1	Indorayon (PT Into Indorayon Utama)	1989	industry (pulp and paper)	1 WALHI
2	Reafforestation Fund (IPTN)	1994	forestry; administrative	1 WALHI 2 Indonesia Institute for Tropical Nature 3 Forum for Study of Population and Environment 4 Institute for Environment and Natural Resource Development 5 Indonesian Centre for Environmental Law 6 Indonesia Rainbow Foundation
3	Surabaya River/ Meka Box	1995	industrial; water pollution	1 WALHI
4	Freeport	1995	mining	1 WALHI
5	Reafforestation Fund II (PT Kiani Kertas)	1997	forestry; administrative	1 WALHI 2 Legal Aid Foundation 3 Women's Legal Aid Association for Justice

Defendants	Summary of claim	Outcome
1 Central Agency for Coordination of Investment (BKPM) 2 Governor of North Sumatra 3 Minister for Industry 4 Minister for Environment 5 Minister for Forestry 6 PT IIU	issue of government permit contrary to environmental legislation	LOST – Substantive claim rejected yet environmental standing accepted (Central Jakarta district court)
1 The President of the Republic of Indonesia	Presidential Decree No. 29 of 1990 contrary to legislation	LOST – Substantive claim rejected. Environmental standing also recognized in administrative context (Jakarta administrative court)
1 PT Surabaya Mekabox 2 PT Surabaya Agung Industri Pulp dan Kertas 3 PT Suparma	claim for compensation and environmental restoration	LOST – Substantive claim rejected due to lack of implementing regulations (Surabaya district court) LOST – on appeal (East Java high court) PENDING – appeal to Supreme Court
1 Secretary general of the Department of Mining and Energy	challenge to decision to approve Freeport's environmental management plan (GR No. 51 of 1993; AJA) forestry; administrative	LOST – (Jakarta administrative court)
1 President of the Republic of Indonesia	challenge to Presidential Decree No. 93 of 1996 (AJA)	LOST – (Jakarta administrative court)

No	Case name	Year	Category of dispute	Plaintiffs
6	Eksponen 66 v. APHI	1998	forestry; land clearing; fires	A group of 13 community, religious and student organizations based in North Sumatra
7	PT Pakerin et al.	1998	forestry; land clearing; fires	1 WALHI
8	Peat Land (WALHI)	1999	agriculture; peat swamp development	1 WALHI
9	Transgenic Cotton	2001	agriculture, genetic modification	1 ICEL 2 Indonesian Consumers' Institute 3 National Consortium for Nature and Forest Conservation 4 Foundation for Biodynamic Agriculture 5 Southern Sulawesi Consumers' Foundation 6 Community Research and Capacity Building Institute
10	WALHI v. PT Freeport	2001	mining	1 WALHI

TOTAL NUMBER OF CASES 10
General courts 7
Administrative courts 3

Defendants	Summary of claim	Outcome
6 national and regional timber and wood-processing industry associations	representative action for compensation/environmental restoration (article 37 EMA 1997)	WON – Compensation of US$6.5 million awarded (Medan district court) LOST – on appeal (North Sumatra high court)
1 11 forestry/plantation companies located in South Sumatra	claim for environmental restoration (article 38[2] EMA 1997)	WON – 2 defendants – ordered to implement an effective fire management system LOST – 11 defendants (Palembang district court) PENDING – appeal to Supreme Court
President of the Republic Indonesia, 10 national Ministers and 10 other senior government officials	challenge to Presidential Decree No. 82 of 1995	LOST – Case rejected on jurisdictional grounds (Central Jakarta district court)
1 Agricultural Minister 2 PT Monagro Kimia	administrative challenge to legality of Agricultural Minister's decision to approve planting of GM cotton	LOST – Jakarta administrative court
1 PT Freeport Indonesia	right to accurate environmental information	WON (partially) – Court ordered improved environmental management (South Jakarta district court) PENDING – appeal to high court
		CASE OUTCOMES: 7 cases lost at district court level 3 cases won (partially) at district court level 0 cases won at appellate level

Environmental private interest cases 1982-2002

No.	Case name	Year	Number of plaintiffs
1	Indorayon II (Samidun Sitorus v. PT IIU)	1989	1
2	Pupuk Iskandar Muda	1989	602
3	Sulae	1992	8
4	Sarana Surya Sakti	1991	18
5	Muara Jaya	1991	23
6	Singosari SUTET	1994	92
7	Ciujung River	1995	17 class representatives 5000 class members
8	Sari Morawa	1996	260
9	Banger River	1999	79
10	Babon River	1998	9
11	Laguna Mandiri	1998	106

Category of dispute	Summary of claim	Outcome
industrial; pulp and paper; water pollution/deforestation	claim for compensation due to environmental damage	LOST – district court of Medan, North Sumatra
industrial; gas leak	claim for compensation	LOST – district court of Lhokseumawe LOST – high court of Aceh
forestry; plantation; deforestation;	compensation and environmental restoration	LOST – district court of Makale, South Sulawesi
industrial; water and ground pollution	claim for compensation (article 20 EMA 1982)	LOST – district court of Surabaya LOST – high court of East Java PENDING – Supreme Court
energy (oil)	claim for compensation	LOST – district court of Balikpapan WON – Compensation of Rp 677.4 million awarded (high court of Samarinda) WON – Compensation claim upheld (Supreme Court)
electricity	claim for compensation	LOST – central district court of Jakarta
industrial; pulp/paper; water pollution	claim for compensation and environmental restoration	LOST – district court of North Jakarta
industrial; water pollution	claim for compensation and environmental restoration (article 20 EMA 1997)	LOST – district court of Lubuk Pakam
industrial; water pollution	claim for compensation and environmental restoration (article 34 EMA 1997)	WON – Rp 49 million compensation (district court of Pekalongan) WON – Rp 750 million compensation and improvement in environmental management ordered (high court of Semarang) PENDING – Supreme Court
industrial; water pollution	claim for compensation (article 34 EMA 1997)	WON – Rp 4.4 million (district court of Semarang) LOST – high court of Central Java PENDING – Supreme Court
forestry; land clearing; fires	claim for compensation (article 34, 35 EMA 1997)	WON – Rp 150 million compensation. Order for implementation of fire control management system (district court of Kota Baru) LOST – high court of Banjarmasin PENDING – Supreme Court

No.	Case name	Year	Number of plaintiffs
12	Peat Land Farmers' Compensation	1999	49
13	Pekanbaru Smog	2000	1 class representative 600,000 class members
14	Way Seputih River	2000	27

TOTAL NUMBER OF CASES 14

COMBINED PUBLIC AND
PRIVATE INTEREST CASES

TOTAL NUMBER OF CASES 24

Category of dispute	Summary of claim	Outcome
agriculture; peat swamp development	compensation for environmental damage	WON – compensation Rp 649 million – (district court of Kuala Kapuas) SETTLED – high court
forest fires	representative claim for compensation and environmental rehabilitation	LOST – district court of Pekanbaru
industrial; water pollution	representative action for compensation	LOST – district court of Metro
industrial 8 forestry 3 mining 1 agriculture 1 other 1		CASE OUTCOMES: 10 lost at district court level 4 won at district court level 2 won at appellate level 1 settled COMBINED PUBLIC AND PRIVATE INTEREST CASE OUTCOMES 17 lost at district court level 7 won (partially) at district court level 2 won at appellate level

APPENDIX 2

Overview of environmental mediation cases

No.	Name of case	Year	Agreement reached	Compensation / monetary payment
1	Tapak River	1991	Yes	Yes
2	Tembok Dukuh	1991	No	No
3	Tyfountex	1992	Yes	No
4	Sambong River	1993	Yes	Yes
5	Siak River	1992	Yes	Yes
6	Sibalec	1994	Yes	Yes
7	Naga Mas	1994	Yes	Yes: payment of drinking water supply
8	Ciujung River	1995	No	No
9	Samitex	1995	Yes	Yes
10	Indoacidatama	1997	Yes	Yes
11	PT Pura	1999	Yes	Yes
12	PT Sumber Sehat	1999	Yes	No
13	Kanasritex	2000	Yes	No
14	Tawang Mas	2000	Yes	No
15	KEM	2001	Yes	Yes
16	Kayu Lapis Indonesia	2001	No	Yes
17	Palur Raya	2002	Yes	Yes
TOTAL NUMBER OF CASES 17			Agreement reached: 14 No agreement: 3	Payment: 11 No payment: 6

Continuing pollution and/or environmental damage	Significant further conflict
Yes: continuing pollution despite industry pledges to improve waste management	Yes
Yes	Yes
Yes	Yes
Yes: rehabilitation of dikes not undertaken	No
Yes: continuing pollution despite industry pledges to improve waste management	Yes
Yes: repair of waste management facilities but some continuing problems regarding monitoring of water quality	Minimal
Yes	Yes
No	No
Yes: environmental restoration/management not addressed by agreement. Continuing pollution problems	Yes
No	No
No	No
No: permanent waste channel constructed for waste disposal minimizing impact on adjacent rice paddies	No
Yes	Yes
No	No
Yes	Yes
No	No
Continuing pollution and/or environmental damage: 10	Further conflict: 8

Bibliography

Adam, Siti Megadianty

1997 'Kasus Sibalec 1', in: M.A. Santosa, T. Rahmadi and S.M. Adam (eds), *Mediasi lingkungan di Indonesia; Sebuah pengalaman*, pp. 31-9. Jakarta: ICEL.

Adam, Siti Megadianty and Takdir Rahmadi

1997 'Kasus PT. Samitex', in: M.A. Santosa, T. Rahmadi and S.M. Adam (eds), *Mediasi lingkungan di Indonesia; Sebuah pengalaman*, pp. 47-51. Jakarta: ICEL.

Aden, Jean Bush

1975 'The relevance of environmental protection in Indonesia', *Ecology Law Quarterly* 4:987.

Adiati, Hanni

1998 'Ambisi swasembada yang menghancurkan ekosistem dan ekonomi rakyat', *Tanah Air* 18:14-8.

Adicondro, George and David Kowalewski

1994 'Damning the dams in Indonesia; A test of competing perspectives', *Asian Survey* 34:381-95.

Aditjondro, George J.

1979 'Industriawan dan petani tambak; Kisah polusi di Dukuh Tapak', *Prisma* 7:66-81.

1998 'Large dam victims and their defenders; The emergence of an anti-dam movement in Indonesia', in: P. Hirsch and C. Warren (eds), *The politics of environment in Southeast Asia; Resources and resistance*, pp. 29-70. London: Routledge.

Adjie, Puspo

1993 'Pencemaran Kali Sambong', in: A.L. Hutapea (ed.), *Beberapa penanganan kasus lingkungan hidup*, pp. 49-52. Jakarta: Wahana Lingkungan Hidup Indonesia (WALHI).

Agreement to resolve dispute between Denmaan Village

1999 Agreement to resolve an environmental dispute between residents of Demaan Village, Kudus and cattle and milk processing factory PT Sumber Sehat.

Amnesty International

1994 *Power and impunity; Human rights under the New Order Indonesia and East Timor*. London: Amnesty International.

Anderson, Michael
1996 'Human rights approaches to environmental protection; An overview', in: Alen E. Boyle and Michael R. Anderson (eds), *Human rights approaches to environmental protection*, p. 21. Oxford: Clarendon.

Andri, M. Ramdan
1999 'Masalah ganti kerugian dalam penegakan hukum lingkungan secara perdata', *Jurnal Hukum Lingkungan* 5-1:1-13.

Anggoro, Sutrisno and Slamet Hargono
2000 *Kerusakan pantai Mangunharjo dan Mororejo; Faktor penyebab dan alternatif penanggulangannya*. Semarang: UNDIP.

Arimbi Heroepoetri
1994a *Unrevealed things in the Indorayon case*. Jakarta: Walhi.
1994b 'Penggunaan mediasi dalam sengketa lingkungan di Indonesia'. Paper, Alternatif Penyelesaian Sengketa dalam Kasus-Kasus Tanah, Perburuhan, dan Lingkungan, Jakarta, 11 August.

Astor, Hilary and Christine M. Chinkin
1992 *Dispute resolution in Australia*. Sydney: Butterworths.

Auerbach, Jerold S.
1983 *Justice without law?* Oxford: Oxford University Press.

Balai Teknik Kesehatan Lingkungan
1997 Pemeriksaan kimia di laboratorium (Sungai Babon). Yogyakarta: Balai Teknik Kesehatan Lingkungan.

Baldwin, Pamela L.
1978 Environmental mediation; An effective alternative? Foreword by Russell E. Train and John Busterud. Palo Alto, CA: Resolve. [Report, Conference, Reston, VA, January 11-13.]

Barber, Charles V.
1989 *The state, the environment and developmen; The genesis and transformation of social forest policy in New Order Indonesia*. PhD thesis, University of California, Berkeley.

Barker, Michael L.
1996 'Standing to sue in public interest environmental litigation; From ACF v commonwealth to Tasmanian Conservation Trust v Minister for Resources', *Environmental and Planning Law Journal* 13-3:186-208.

Becker, Theodore L.
1970 *Comparative judicial politic; The political functionings of courts*. Chicago: Rand McNally.

Bedner, Adriaan W.
2000 *Administrative courts in Indonesia; A social-legal study*. PhD thesis, University of Leiden.

Bedner, Adriaan and Benjamin van Rooij
2001 'Environmental disputes and enforcement'. Paper, INSELA Conference on Environmental Disputes and Enforcement of Environmental Law - Indonesia in Comparative Perspective, Leiden.

Biaro, Endi
2000 'KEM; Cerita di balik perundingan', *Gali-Gali* 2(September):9-10.

Bingham, Gail

1986 *Resolving environmental disputes; A decade of experience*. Washington, DC: The Conservation Foundation.

Black, Donald J.

1976 *The behaviour of law*. New York/London: Academic Press.

1989 *Sociological justice*. New York: Oxford University Press.

Blackburn, J. Walton

1990 'Theoretical dimensions of environmental mediation', in: M. Afzalur Rahim (ed.), *Theory and research in conflict management*, pp. 151-70. New York: Praeger.

1995 'Environmental mediation theory and practice; Challenges, issues, and needed research and theory development', in: J.W. Blackburn and W.M. Bruce (eds), *Mediating environmental conflicts; Theory and practice*, pp. 267-80. Westport, CT: Quorum Books.

Blackburn, J. Walton and Wila Marie Bruce

1995 'Introduction', in: J.W. Blackburn and W.M. Bruce (eds), *Mediating environmental conflict; Theory and practice*, pp. 1-2. Westport, CT: Quorum Books.

Boulle, Laurence

1996 *Mediation; Principles, process, practice*. London: Butterworths.

Bourchier, David

1999 'Magic memos, collusion and judges with attitude; Notes on the politics of law in contemporary Indonesia', in: Kanishka Jayasuriya (ed.), *Law, capitalism and power in Asia; The rule of law and legal institutions*, pp. 233-52. London: Routledge.

Bowden, Paul

1995 'Citizen suits; Can we afford them and do we need them anyway?' in: David Robinson and John Dunkley (eds), *Public interest perspectives in environmental law*, pp. 172-88. London: Chancery.

Brown, Henry J. and Arthur L. Marriott

1999 *ADR principles and practice*. Second edition. London: Sweet and Maxwell. [First edition 1993.]

Budiardjo, Carmel and Liem Soei Liong

1988 *West Papua; The obliteration of a people*. Third, revised and substantially re-written edition. Thornton Heath: Tapol. [First edition 1983.]

Burgess, Guy and Heidi Burgess

1995 'Beyond the limits; Dispute resolution of intractable environmental conflicts', in: J.W. Blackburn and W.M. Bruce (eds), *Mediating environmental conflicts; Theory and practice*, pp. 101-20. Westport, CT: Quorum Books.

Cappelletti, Mauro and Bryant Garth

1978 'Access to justice; The worldwide movement to make rights effective', in: Mauro Cappelletti and Bryant Garth (eds), *Access to justice; Volume 1: A world survey*, pp. 6-10. Alphen aan den Rijn: Sijthoff. [Florence access-to-justice project.]

Cassels, Jamie
1989 'Judicial activism and public interest litigation in India; Attempting the impossible?', *American Journal of Comparative Law* 37:495-519.

Chopra, Shambhu
1992 *Public interest litigation; An appraisal of its scope and potential as a litigational strategy, and of the emerging issues in public interest activism.* Allahabad: [Chopra].

Cooperative agreement
1999 Kesepakatan bersama, antara kelompok petani dengan pihak management PT Indo Acidatama.
2000 Perjanjian bersama tentang upaya bersama pengelolaan lingkungan antara PT. Pura Nusapersada dan warga masyarakat desa Pladen.
2001 Kesepakatan perundingan penyelesaian kasus kerusakan tambak dan panti Mangunharjo kecamatan tugu kota Semarang dalam forum konsultasi.

Cotterrell, Roger
1992 *The sociology of law; An introduction.* Second edition. London: Butterworths. [First edition 1984.]

Cottrell, Jill
1993 'Third generation rights and social action litigation', in: Sammy Adelman and Abdul Paliwala (eds), *Law and crisis in the Third World*, pp. 102-26. London: Hans Zell. [African Discourse Series 4.]

Cranston, Ross
1997 'Access to justice in South and South-Eeast Asia', in: Julio Faúndez (ed.), *Good government and law; Legal and institutional reform in developing countries*, pp. 233-55. New York: St. Martin's.

Cribb, Robert
1987 *The politics of environmental protection in Indonesia.* PhD thesis, Centre of Southeast Asian Studies, Monash University, Clayton, VIC.
1990 'The politics of pollution control in Indonesia', *Asian Survey* 30:1123-35.

Crouch, Harold
1979 'Patrimonialism and military rule in Indonesia', *World Politics* 31:571-87.

Crowfoot, James E. and Julia M. Wondolleck
1990 'Environmental dispute settlement', in: James E. Crowfoot and Julia M. Wondolleck (eds), *Environmental disputes; Community involvement in conflict resolution*, pp. 17-31. Washington, DC: Island Press.

Damian, Eddy and Robert N. Hornick
1992 *Indonesia's formal legal system; An introduction.* Bandung: Alumni. [First edition 1976.]

Dauvergne, Peter
1994 'The politics of deforestation in Indonesia', *Pacific Affairs* 66:497-518.
1998 'The political economy of Indonesia's 1997 forest fires', *Australian Journal of International Affairs* 52:13-20.

Davis, A. and R. Salem
1984 'Dealing with power imbalances in the mediation of interpersonal disputes', *Mediation Quartely 6(December)*:17-26.

Deimann, Sven and Bernard Dyssli (eds)
1995 *Environmental rights; Law, litigation and access to justice*. London: Cameron May.

Denvir, John
1976 'Towards a political theory of public interest litigation', *The North Carolina Law Review* 54:1133.

Desai, Bharat
1993 'Enforcement of the right to environment protection through public interest litigation in India', *Indian Journal of International Law* 33:27-40.

District court Kota Baru
1998 Laguna Mandiri I. In *PT Laguna Mandiri dkk.*, 18-39. District court of Kota Baru: No. 09/Pdt.G/1998/PN.KTB.

District court North Jakarta
1995 Ciujung River. vol. No. 176/PDT/G/1995/P.N. JKT.Ut. West Java.

Du Bois, Francois
1995 '"Well-being" and "the common man"; A critical look at public interest environmental law in South Africa and India', in: David Robinson and John Dunkley (eds), *Public interest perspectives in environmental law*, pp. 144-6. London: Wiley Chancery.

Eksponen 66 v. APHI
1998 Eksponen 66 v. APHI. 41-5. District court of Medan: No. 425/Pdt.G/1997/PN.Mdn.

Elridge, Philip J.
1995 *Non-government organizations and democratic participation in Indonesia.* Kuala Lumpur/New York: Oxford University Press.

Environesia
1988 *Environesia* 2:1.

Felsteiner, W., R. Abel and A. Sarat
1980 'The emergence and transformation of disputes; Naming, claiming and blaming', *Law and Society Review* 15:631-54.

Fernandes, Edesio
1995 'Collective interests in Brazilian environmental law', in: David Robinson and John Dunkley (eds), *Public interest perspectives in environmental law*, p. 118. London: Wiley Chancery.

Fisher, Roger and William Ury
1991 *Getting to yes; Negotiating agreement without giving in*. Second edition. New York: Penguin. [First edition published under the same title. Boston: Houghton Mifflin, 1981.]

Fiss, Owen M.
1984 'Against settlement', *Yale Law Journal* 93:1073-90.

Fuhr, Martin, Betty Gebers, Thomas Ormond and Gerhard Roller
1995 'Access to justice; Legal standing for environmental associations in the European Union', in: David Robinson and John Dunkley (eds), *Public*

interest perspectives in environmental law, pp. 77, 89. London: Wiley Chancery.

Galanter, Marc
1974 'Why the "Haves" come out ahead; Speculations on the limits of legal change', *Law and Society* (Fall):95.

Galanter, Marc and John Lande
1992 'Private courts and public authority', *Studies in law, politics and society* 12:398.

Geddes, Andrew
1992 'Locus Standi and EEC environmental measures', *Journal of Environmental Law* 4:29-39.

Ginting, Longgena
1998 'Mega proyek lahan gambut sejuta hektar, sejuta masalah', *Tanah Air* 4:2-3.

Gita Pertiwi
2000a Melawan Naga Mas. 4. Solo: Gita Pertiwi.
2000b Menggugat pencemaran Kali Babon. 1. Solo: Gita Pertiwi.
2000c Rakyat meradang, Tyfountex diterjang. 6. Solo: Gita Pertiwi.

Golten, Bob
1980 'Confessions of an environmental litigator', *Environmental Consensus* (Spring):2-3.

Gomez, Mario and Jill Cottrell
1994 'In the public interest; Essays on public interest litigation and participatory justice', *International and Comparative Law Quarterly* 43:237.

Griffith, J.A.G.
1985 *The politics of the judiciary*. Third edition. London: Fontana. [First edition 1977; Fontana Original 6020.]

Gunawan, Eddy
1999 'Persepsi perusahaan terhadap masyarakat lingkungan'. Paper, Seminar Nasional Yayasan Alumni Universitas Diponegoro, Universitas Semarang.

Hadi, Sudharto P.
2000 Perkembangan perundingan kasus kerusakan tambak dan panti Mangunharjo, kecamatan Tugu kota Semarang. 28-7-2000.

Hadjon, Philipus M.
1993 *Pengantar hukum administrasi Indonesia*. Yogyakarta: Gadjah Mada University Press.

Hamacher, W.
1996 *Environmental conflict management; An environmental policy instrument in developing countries*. Eschborn: Deutsche Gesellschaft für Technische Zusammenarbeit (GTZ).

Hamzah, A.
1995 *Penegakan hukum lingkungan*. Jakarta: Arikha Media Cipta.

Harding, Andrew
1992 'Public interest groups, public interest law and development in Malaysia', *Third World Legal Studies* 1992:231-43.

Hardiyanto, Andik
1999 *Kendala penyelesaian sengketa lingkungan di luar pengadilan*. Semarang: LBH Semarang.

Hardjasoemantri, Koesnadi
1991 *Hukum perlindungan lingkungan; Konservasi sumber daya alam hayati dan ekosistemnya*. Yogyakarta: Gadjah Mada University Press. [Seri Hukum Lingkungan 2.]
1993 *Hukum tata lingkungan*. Fifth edition. Yogyakarta: Gadjah Mada University Press. [Seri Hukum Lingkungan 1; First edition 1983.]
1998 'Strict liability (tanggung jawab mutlak)'. Paper, Lokakarya legal standing and class action, Hotel Kartika Chandra, Jakarta, 7 December.

Hardjono, Joan
1986 'Environmental crisis in Java', *Prisma* 39:3-13.

Hartanto, Edith
2001 'Indonesia forests dwindling rapidly by the year', *The Jakarta Post*, 27-12-2001.

Hibani, Hidayat (ed.)
1994 *Delapan perusahaan perusak lingkungan*. Jakarta: SKEPHI.

Hill, Hal
2000 *The Indonesian economy*. Second edition. Cambridge: Cambridge University Press. [First edition 1996.]

Hirsch, Philip and Carol Warren (eds)
1998 *The politics of environment in Southeast Asia; Resources and resistance*. London: Routledge.

Hofrichter, Richard (ed.)
1993 *Toxic struggles; The theory and practice of environmental justice*. Philadelphia: New Society.

Holland, Kenneth M. (ed.)
1991 *Judicial activism in comparative perspective*. Basingstoke, Hampshire: Macmillan.

Horwitz, Alan V.
1990 *The logic of social control*. New York: Plenum.

Hurst, Phillip
1990 *Rainforest politics; Ecological destruction in South-East Asia*. London: Zed Books.

Hutapea, Anthony L.P. (ed.)
1993 *Beberapa penanganan kasus lingkungan hidup*. Jakarta: Wahana Lingkungan Hidup Indonesia (WALHI).

Hutchinson, A. and P. Monahan (eds)
1987 *The rule of law; Ideal or ideology*. Toronto: Carswell.

ICEL
1999a Buletin informasi; Hukum dan advokasi lingkungan. Jakarta: ICEL.
1999b Buletin informasi; Kasus kasus lingkungan 1996. Jakarta: ICEL.
1999c Laporan kegiatan on-site training. Jakarta: ICEL.
1999d Laporan kunjungan ke Mangunhardjo. Jakarta: ICEL.
1999e Laporan on site training. Semarang: ICEL.

1999f Penyelesaian sengketa lingkungan berdasarkan pendekatan perundingan interest based, partisipatif and komprehensif. Jakarta: ICEL.

2000 Analisa hukum; Kasus perusakan pantai akibat kegiatan PT KLI. Jakarta: ICEL.

ICEL and Bapedalda Tk. II Semarang

1999 Rapat Bapedalda Tk II Semarang. Semarang.

Indonesian Centre for Environmental Law, Legal Aid Institute of Jakarta and Association of Ciujing Water Users

1995 Menabur limbah menuai tanggung jawab. 35. Jakarta: Indonesian Centre for Environmental Law, Legal Aid Institute of Jakarta and Association of Ciujung Water Users.

Indroharto, S.H.

1993 *Usaha memahami undang-undang tentang peradilan tata usaha negara.* Jakarta: Pustaka Sinar Harapan.

IPTN

1995 IPTN - Appeal. No. 33/B/1995/PT.TUN. JKT.

Jakarta state administrative court

1997 *Reafforestation Fund (Pt Kiani Kertas).* Decision No. 037/G. TUN/1997/ PTUN-JKT.

2001 *Transgenic Cotton Case.* Decision No. 107/Kpts/KB.430/2/2001.

Jayasuriya, Kanishka

1999 'Corporatism and judicial independence within statist legal institutions in East Asia', in: Kanishka Jayasuriya (ed.), *Law, capitalism and power in Asia; The rule of law and legal institutions,* pp. 173-204. London: Routledge.

Karanganyar, Bapedalda

2001 Research report of Independent Team Re Palur Raya. 137.

Kedaulatan Rakyat

2000 'Warga tawang Mas Ngamuk; Bioskop dirusak, polisi babak belur'. *Kedaulatan Rakyat,* 17-5-2000.

Kelian Equatorial Mining

2003 Compensation Issues - May 2003. 2: Kelian Equatorial Mining.

Kiani Kertas - Appeal

1997 Kiani Kertas - Appeal. Jakarta administrative high court: No. 113/B/ 1997/PT.TUN JKT.

KLI

1998 Sikap PT. KLI terhadap kasus tambak. 22-9-1998.

KKL

1999 Sejarah berdirinya team sembilan dan perjuangan terhadap keseriusan PT. Palur Raya untuk masalah penanggulangan cemaran limbah. 2-4: Konsorsium Korban Limbah.

2000a Pernyataan sikap; Hentikan pencemaran sekarang juga. Konsorsium Korban Limbah.

2000b Berita acara. Konsorsium Korban Limbah.

2002a Kesepakatan penyelesaian sengketa lingkungan antara PT. Palur Raya dengan masyarakat desa Ngringo yang diwakili oleh Konsorsium Korban Limbah. Konsorsium Korban Limbah.

2002b Kronologi proses mediasi dan advokasi penyelesaian sengketa lingkungan antara masyarakat desa Ngringo dengan PT. Palur Raya. 1. Ngringo. Konsorsium Korban Limbah.

2002c Kronologis kasus PT. Palur Raya. 3. Konsorsium Korban Limbah.

KMPL/LBH

2000 Dalam 1 tahun KLI pasti jadi milik rakyat. Semarang: KMPL and LBH Semarang.

Kramer, Ludwig

1996 'Public interest litigation in environmental matters before European courts', *Journal of Environmental Law* 8:1-18.

Kritis

2000 'Tawang Mas; Tragedi salah urus tata ruang kota', *Kritis* 2:5-6

Kritis, Team

1999 'Menggugat (Dewa) perusak', *Kritis* 1:5-7.

Lau, Martin

1995 'The right to public participation; Public interest litigation and environmental law in Pakistan', *Review of European Community and International Environmental Law* 4:49-50.

LBHS

1999a Diskripsi kasus pencemaran limbah PT Indo Acidatama. Semarang: LBH Semarang.

1999b Deskripsi perusakan pantai desa Mangunharjo kec. Mangkang kabupaten Semarang. LBHS (Legal Aid Institute of Semarang).

1999c Notulensi perundingan 1. University of Diponegoro, Semarang.

2000a Laporan live in di desa Mangunharjo. 4. Semarang: LBHS (Legal Aid Institute of Semarang).

2000b Kasus Kanasritex; 'Catatan perjuangan petani'. Semarang: LBHS (Legal Aid Institute of Semarang).

2000c Notulensi perundingan V. LBHS (Legal Aid Institute of Semarang).

LBHS, Environmental Division

2001 Gugatan dari pesisir Pantura (Tragedi perusakan pantai oleh PT KLI). Semarang: LBHS (Legal Aid Institute of Semarang).

Lev, Daniel S.

1978 'Judicial authority and the struggle for an Indonesian rechtsstaat', *Law and Society* 13:27-71.

1990 *Hukum dan politik di Indonesia; Kesinambungan dan perubahan*. Jakarta: Lembaga Penelitian, Pendidikan dan Penerangan Ekonomi dan Sosial.

Lotulung, Paulus Effendie

1991 *Penegakan hukum lingkungan oleh hakim perdata; Melalui penerapan pasal 1365 KUHAP sipil*. Universiteit Leiden: Faculteit der Rechtsgeleerdheid.

1993a 'Masalah perijinan yang berkaitan dengan bidang lingkungan hidup', *Gema Peratun* 1:1.

1993b *Penegakan hukum lingkungan oleh hakim perdata*. Bandung: Citra Aditya Bakti.

1995 'Aspek hukum perdata dalam pengelolaan lingkungan'. Paper, Semiloka Litigasi Lingkungan, Malang, 9-11 September.

Lubis, Todung Mulya
1993 *In search of human rights; Legal-political dilemmas of Indonesia's new order, 1966-1990.* Jakarta: Gramedia Pustaka Utama.

Lucas, Anton
1998 'River pollution and political action in Indonesia', in: P. Hirsch and C. Warren (eds), *The politics of environment in Southeast Asia; Resources and resistance*, pp. 181-209. London: Routledge.

Lucas, Anton and Arief Djati
2000 *The dog is dead so throw it in the river; Environmental politics and water pollution in Indonesia; An East Java case study.* Clayton: Monash Asia Institute, Monash University. [Monash Papers on Southeast Asia 51.]

Lukman, Hakim
2000 Way Seputih River. 1-5. District court of Metro: No. 04/Pdt.G/2000/PNM.

Lynch, Owen J. and Emily Harwell
2002 *Whose resources? Whose common good?; Towards a new paradigm of environmental justice and national interest in Indonesia.* Washington: Centre for International Environmental Law, Jakarta: Lembaga Studi dan Advokasi Masyarakat (ELSAM).

MacAndrews, Colin
1994 'The Indonesian environmental impact agency (Bapedal); Its role, development and future', *Bulletin of Indonesian Economic Studies* 30:85-103.

Maimunah, Siti
2002 'Membongkar paradigma ganti-rugi', *Gali-Gali* 4:20.

Makmun, H.A. Nasoha
2000 Komisi A DPRD II melanjutkan rapat tuntutan warga Tawang Mas tanpa menghadirkan warga. Forum Komunikasi Masyarakat Tawang Mas.

Marr, Carolyn
1993 *Digging deep; The hidden costs of mining in Indonesia.* London: Down to Earth [International Campaign for Ecological Justice in Indonesia; DTE Special Report 2.]

Mayell, Hillary
2001 'Study links logging with severity of forest fires'. *National Geographic News*, 3-12-2001.

Menkel-Meadow, Carrie
1995 'The many ways of mediation; The transformation of traditions, ideologies, paradigms, and practices', *Negotiation Journal* 11(July):217-42.
2001 'Introduction', in: Carrie Menkel-Meadow (ed.), *Mediation; Theory, policy and practice*, pp. 12-33. Burlington, VT: Ashgate Publishing.

MENLH, Asdep 5/IV
2002 Penyampaian laporan hasil pertemuan bapak menteri negara lingkungan hidup tentang kasus PT. Palur Raya di Surakarta tanggal 17 Juni 2002. B.M.N.L. Hidup (ed.).

Micklitz, Hans-W. and Norbert Reich (eds)
1996 *Public interest litigation before European courts*. Baden-Baden: Nomos. [Schriftenreihe des Vereinigten Instituts für Europäisches Wirtschafts- und Verbraucherrecht e.V 2.]

Mnookin, R. and L. Kornhauser
1979 'Bargaining in the shadow of the law', *Yale Law Journal* 88:950.

Moore, Christopher W.
1996 *The mediation process: Practical strategies for resolving conflict*. Second edition. San Francisco: Jossey-Bass Publishers. [The Jossey-Bass Conflict Resoulution Series; First edition 1986.]
1998 'The practice of cooperative environmental conflict resolution in developing countries', in: Christopher Napier (ed.), *Environmental conflict resolution*, pp. 160-95. London: Cameron May.

Moore, Christopher and Mas Achmad Santosa
1995 'Developing appropriate environmental conflict management procedures in Indonesia; Integrating traditional and new approaches', *Cultural Survival Quarterly* 19:23-9.

Muara Jawa
1991 Muara Jawa. No. 2727K/Pdt/1991.

Muhaimin, C.S.
1998 Babon River Case: PT Condro Purnomo Cipto CS. 35. District court of Semarang: No. 42/Pdt.G/1998/PN.Smg.

Muhammed, Chalid
2002 Penghianatan Rio Tinto dan Kelian Equatorial Mining terhadap kesepakatan-kesepakatannya dengan masyarakat Kelian. Jaringan Advokasi Tambang.

Nasution, Adnan Buyung
1981 *Bantuan hukum di Indonesia*. Jakarta: Lembaga Penelitian, Pendidikan dan Penerangan Ekonomi dan Sosial.

Ngringo, Warga Desa
1992 Pencemaran PT Palur Raya. Kotak Pos 5000.

Nicholson, David
1994 *Environmental litigation in Indonesia*. PhD thesis, Faculty of Law, Murdoch University, Perth.

Niessen, Nicole
2000 'Indonesia's Environmental Management Act of 1997; Comprehensive and integrated?' in: Adriaan Bedner and Nicole Niessen (eds), *Towards integrated environmental management in Indonesia?* p. 67. Leiden: CNWS Publishers.

Nugroho, Adi
1998 *Pemantauan lingkungan kasus pencemaran Sungai Banger, Pekalongan, Jawa Tengah*. Solo: Gita Pertiwi.

Nurbaiti, Ati
2003 'Freedom of Information Act should set precedent', *The Jakarta Post*, 18-3-2003.

Nurbianto, Bambang and Fitri Wulandari

2001 'Kalimantan's forests could disappear in 5 years', *The Jakarta Post*, 10-12-2001.

Nurchayo, Bagyo

2000a 'Pemasukan minim, biaya perawatan tinggi', *Jateng Pos*, 8-2-2000.

2000b 'Dituduh antek pki, penghasut, dijebloskan penjara', *Jateng Pos*, 29-3-2000.

2000c 'Ganang Ismail Sumber Masalahnya'. *Jateng Pos*, 28-3-2000.

Nuryanto, Eko

1995 'Kendala dan peluang pendayagunaan hukum perdata dan hukum acara perdata indonesia dalam kasus lingkungan; Refleksi atas penangan kasus lingkungan'. Paper, Semiloka Litigasi Lingkungan, Malang, 9-11 September.

Nusatara

1989 'Sengketa lingkungan dan masalah beban pembuktian'. Paper, Prosiding Diskusi Dua Hari 'Masalah-Masalah Prosedural dalam Penyelesaian Sengketa Lingkungan', Jakarta, 19 June.

O'Leary, Rosemary

1995 'Environmental mediation; What do we know and how do we know it?', in: J.W. Blackburn and W.M. Bruce (eds), *Mediating environmental conflicts; Theory and practice*, pp. 17-36. Westport. CT: Quorum Books.

Otto, Jan Michiel

1991 *Conflicts between citizens and state in Indonesia; The development of administrative jurisdiction*. PhD thesis, Van Vollenhoven Instituut, Leiden.

1997 'Implementation of environmental law; Harmonisation, environmental management and enforcement by the courts, with references to Indonesian and the Netherlands by executive summary', *Indonesian Journal of Environmental Law* 2:21-62.

2002 'Toward an analytical framework: Real legal certainty and its explanatory factors', in: Jianfu Chen, Yuwen Li and J.M. Otto (eds), *Implementation of law in the People's Republic of China*, pp. 23-34. The Hague: Kluwer Law International. [The London-Leiden Series on Law, Administration and Development 8.]

Pagono, Franz

2000a 'Profil (Sang Dewa) PT KLI', *Ozon* (January):33.

2000b 'PT KLI Berulah, petani kena tulah', *Ozon* (January):30.

Parnwell, Michael J.G. and Raymond L. Bryant (eds)

1996 *Environmental change in South-East Asia; People, politics and sustainable development.* London: Routledge. [Global Environmental Change Series.]

Peiris, G.L.

1991 'Public interest litigation in the Indian subcontinent; Current dimensions', *International and Comparative Law Quarterly* 40:66-90.

Poffenberger, Mark

1997 'Rethinking Indonesian forest policy; Beyond the timber barons', *Asian Survey* 37:453-69.

Pompe, S. van Hoeij Schilthouwer
1996 *The Indonesian Supreme Court; Fifty years of judicial development*. PhD thesis, Faculty of Law, Leiden University.

Potter, David
1996 'Democratisation and the environment; NGOs and deforestation policies in India (Karnataka) and Indonesia (North Sumatra)', *Journal of Commonwealth and Comparative Politics* 34:9-37.

PPLH Undip Semarang
2000 Laporan; Hasil kegiatan tim dalam format kecil dan forum konsultasi. Semarang: PPLH, Undip Semarang.

Prihartono, R. Dwiyanto
1995 'Kendala dan peluang mendayagunakan hukum perdata dan hukum acara perdata Indonesia dalam kasus Indonesia'. Paper, Semiloka Litigasi Lingkungan, Malang, 9-11 September.

Purwadi, Trias and Syam Dakrita
1999 'Pembuangan Limbah Lumpur ke Kali Banger dihentikan', *Suara Merdeka*, 15-3-1999.

Rahmadi, Takdir
1986 Mekanisme alternatif penyelesaian sengketa dalam konteks masyarakat Indonesia Masa Kini. Faculty of Law, University of Andalas.
1993 Efforts to resolve a dispute over industrial pollution in Surabaya, Indonesia; The Tembok Dukuh Dispute. 1-5. Jakarta: ICEL.
1997a 'Kasus Kali Sambong', in: M.A. Santosa, T. Rahmadi and S.M. Adam (eds), *Mediasi lingkungan di Indonesia; Sebuah pengalaman*, p. 55. Jakarta: ICEL.
1997b 'Kasus Kali Tapak', in: M.A. Santosa, T. Rahmadi and S.M. Adam (eds), *Mediasi lingkungan di Indonesia; Sebuah pengalaman*. Jakarta: ICEL.
1997c 'Kasus PT Naga Mas', in: M.A. Santosa, T. Rahmadi and S.M. Adam (eds), *Mediasi Lingkungan di Indonesia; Sebuah pengalaman*, pp. 65-73. Jakarta: ICEL.
1998 *Teknik perundingan tradisional dalam masyarakat adat mingan kabau Sumatra Barat*. Jakarta: Indonesian Centre for Environmental Law.

Rangkuti, Siti Sundari
1995 'Beberapa problematika hukum lingkungan', *Jurnal Hukum Lingkungan* 1:52-4.

Report Lord Chancellor
1989 Report to the Lord Chancellor on the costs and effectiveness of conciliation in England and Wales. University of Newcastle upon Tyne.

Rhiti, Hyronimus
1998 'Penyelesaian sengketa lingkungan menurut UUPLH', *Suara Pembaruan*, 22-1-1998.

Robbins, Deidre H.
1995 'Public interest environmental litigation in the United States', in: David Robinson and John Dunkley (eds), *Public interest perspectives in environmental law*, pp. 5-37. London: Wiley Chancery. [Environmental Law Series.]

Roberts, E. and J. Dobbins
1992 'The role of the citizen in environmental enforcement'. Paper, International Conference on Environmental Enforcement, Budapest, Hungary, September 22-25.
Robinson, David
1995a 'Public interest environmental law commentary and analysis', in: David Robinson and John Dunkley (eds), *Public interest perspectives in environmental law*, pp. 294-326. London: Wiley Chancery. [Environmental Law Series.]
1995b 'Public interest environmental law firms in the United States', in: David Robinson and John Dunkley (eds), *Public interest perspectives in environmental law*, pp. 40-69. London: Wiley Chancery. [Environmental Law Series.]
Robinson, D. and J. Dunkley (eds)
1995 *Public interest perspectives in environmental law*. London: Wiley Chancery.
Robinson, N.A.
1998 'Principles of environmental justice; A foundation for dispute prevention and resolution', *Asia Pacific Journal of Environmental Law* 3-4:349.
Robison, Richard and David S.G. Goodman (eds)
1996 *The new rich in Asia; Mobile phones, McDonald's and middle-class revolution*. London: Routledge. [The New Rich in Asia Series.]
Romsan, Achmad
1998 *Mediasi tradisional dalam masyarakat adat di dataran Tinggi Sumatera Selatan*. Jakarta: Indonesian Centre for Environmental Law.
Santosa, Mas Achmad
1988 'Standing atau locus standi; Persoalan pokok dalam gugatan lingkungan', *Forum Keadilan* 6:100.
1990 *Citizen participation in environmental administrative decision-making; A case study of Indonesia*. PhD thesis, York University, Toronto.
1995 'Internalization of environmental ADR into a national institution; An Indonesian case study'. Paper, Environmental Mediation and Negotiation Workshop 'Sharing Experiences through Case Studies', International Academy of the Environment, Geneva, 13-15 November.
1996 (ed.) *Resolving environmental disputes through cooperative dispute resolution; A case evaluation*. Jakarta: ICEL.
1998 'HAM dan lingkungan hidup', *Bisnis Indonesia*.
Santosa, Mas Achmad and Antony L.P. Hutapea
1992 'Mendayagunakan mekanisme alternatif penyesesaian sengketa (MAPS) di Indonesia; Sebuah pengalaman'. PhD thesis, ICEL, Jakarta.
Santosa, Mas Achmad and Christopher Moore
1997 'Kasus yang gagal menghasilkan kesepakatan; Kasus tembok dukuh', in: M.A. Santosa, T. Rahmadi and S.M. Adam (eds), *Mediasi lingkungan di Indonesia; Sebuah pengalaman*, pp 84-7. Jakarta: ICEL.

Santosa, Mas Achmad, Takdir Rahmadi and Siti Megadianty Adam
1997 *Mediasi lingkungan di Indonesia; Sebuah pengalaman*. Jakarta: ICEL.

Santosa, Mas Achmad and Sulaiman N. Sembiring
1997 *Hak gugat organisasi lingkungan*. Jakarta: ICEL.

Santosa, Mas Achmad and Indro Sugianto
2002 'Class action; Sekedar trend atau senjata ampuh (Refleksi atas putusan pengadilan)', *Hukum dan Advokasi Lingkungan* 4(September):3.

Santosa, Mas Achmad and T.M. Luthfi Yazid
1997 'Kasus pencemaran sungai Ciujung', in: M.A. Santosa, T. Rahmadi and S.M. Adam (eds), *Mediasi lingkungan di Indonesia; Sebuah pengalaman*, pp. 91-102. Jakarta: ICEL.
1998 'Kasus pencemaran sungai Ciujung', in: M.A. Santosa, T. Rahmadi and S.M. Adam (eds), *Mediasi lingkungan di Indonesia; Sebuah pengalaman*, pp. 5-15. Jakarta: Lembaga Pengembangan Hukum Lingkungan Indonesia: ICEL.

Sarana Surya Sakti
1993 Sarana Surya Sakti. District court of Surabaya: No. 373/Pdt.G/1991/PN. Sby.

Satyoga, Joko Hadi
1992 'Kali Tapak; Sebuah perjalan advokasi kasus pencemaran lingkungan hidup'. Paper, Lokakarya Pengetahuan Hukum dan Advokasi Lingkungan Hidup bagi Pekerjaan Bantuan Hukum dan Pola Penganganan Kasus-Kasus Lingkungan, Surabaya, 18-22 June.

Schubert, Glendon
1975 *Human jurisprudence; Public law as political science*. Honolulu: The University Press of Hawaii.

Shapiro, Martin
1981 *Courts; A comparative and political analysis*. Chicago: The University of Chicago Press.

Shetreet, Shimon and Jules Deschênes
1985 *Judicial independence; The contemporary debate*. Dordrecht/Boston, MAS: Nijhoff.

Shrybman, Steven
1983 *Environmental mediation; From theory to practice*. Ottawa: The Canadian Environmental Law Association.

Silalahi, Daud
1992 *Hukum lingkungan; Dalam sistem penegakan hukum lingkungan Indonesia*. Bandung: Alumni.

Simpson, Tony and Vanessa Jackson
1997 'Human rights and the environment', *Environmental and Planning Law Journal* 14:268-81.

Stein, Paul
1995 'A specialist environmental court; An Australian experience', in: D. Robinson and J. Dunkley (eds), *Public interest perspectives in environmental law*, pp. 256-73. London: Wiley Chancery.

Stone, Christopher D.
1974 *Should trees have standing?* Los Altos, CA: Kaufman.
Subagyo, Rino
2002a 'Menggugat kebijakan pengembangan kapas transgenik di Indonesia', *Hukum dan Advokasi Lingkungan* 4(September):5.
2002b 'Peradilan lingkungan di Indonesia', *Hukum dan advokasi lingkungan* 4(September):6.
Sudarsono, Yuyun
1999 'Hak atas informasi lingkungan hidup'. Paper, Hak Atas Informasi Lingkungan Hidup, Jakarta, 4 March.
Sumardja, Effendy
1999 'Kebijakan hak atas informasi lingkungan'. Paper, Lokakarya Hak Atas Informasi Lingkungan, Jakarta, 4 March.
Sundari, E.
1999 *Implementasi prinsip class action dalam wacana sistem hukum acara perdata Indonesia.* PhD thesis, University of Gadjah Mada: Yogyakarta.
Sunoto and Takdir Rahmadi
1997 'Kasus pencemaran sungai Siak', in: M.A. Santosa, T. Rahmadi and S.M. Adam (eds), *Mediasi lingkungan di Indonesia; Sebuah pengalaman.* Jakarta: ICEL.
Suparni, Niniek
1992 *Pelestarian, pengelolaan dan penegakan hukum lingkungan.* Jakarta: Sinar Grafika.
Supriyatna, Akhmad
1998 'Menggugat proyek sejuta hektare', *Panji Masyarakat* 14(22 July).
Surabaya Public Prosecutor
1991 Hasil evaluasi penuntut umum terhadap berkas perkara dari penyidik polwitabes Surabaya dalam kasus tindak pidana pencemaran sumur penduduk oleh limbah dari PT Sarana Surya Sakti. Surabaya: Surabaya Public Prosecutor.
Surabaya Sekretaris Kotamadya
1992 Laporan penyelesaian kasus PT. Sarana Surya Sakti dengan Warga. W.K.D.T.I. Surabaya: Sekretaris Kotamadya Daerah Tk. II.
Susman, Susan D.
1994 'Distant voices in the courts of India; Transformation of standing in public interest litigation', *Wisconsin International Law Journal* 13:57-103.
Susskind, Lawrence E. and Joshua Secunda
1998 'Environmental conflict resolution; The American experience', in: Christopher Napier (ed.), *Environmental conflict resolution*, pp. 160-95. London: Cameron May.
Tamanaha, Brian Z.
1995 'The lessons of law and development studies (review article)', *The American Journal of International Law* 89:470-3.
Tate, C. Neal
1987 'Judicial institutions in cross-national perspective; Toward integrating courts into the comparative study of politics', in: John R. Schmidhauser

(ed.), *Comparative judicial systems; Challenging frontiers in conceptual and empirical analysis; Advances in political science*, pp. 1-28. London: Butterworths. [Advances in Political Science 6.]

Thorburn, Craig C.
1992 'Consumer boycott of polluting industries in Central Java; A case study in the development of a modern environmental conciousness'. [Unpublished paper.]

Toha, M.
1993 'Sulitnya menjerat sang pencemar', *Forum Keadilan*, 2-9-1993.

Tomasic, Roman
1985 *The sociology of law*. London: Sage. [Current Sociology 33.]

Trisasongko, Dadang
1998 'Sungai Siak terus terkoyak', in: S.N. Sembiring (ed.), *Hukum dan advokasi lingkungan*, pp. 28-30. Jakarta: ICEL.

Ungai, Husein
2002 Letter from Husein Ungai S.H. to Minister for Environment W W Sambodo, dated 4 June 2003.

Ury, William L., Jeanne M. Brett and Stephen B. Goldberg
1986 *Getting disputes resolved; Designing systems to cut the cost of conflict*. San Francisco: Jossey-Bass. [Jossey-Bass Management Series; Jossey-Bass Social and Behavioral Science Series.]

Usman, Rachmadi
1993 *Pokok-pokok hukum lingkungan nasional*. Jakarta: Akademika Pressindo.

Vayda, Andrew P.
1999 *Finding causes of the 1997-98 Indonesian forest fires; Problems and possibilities*. Jakarta: World Wildlife Fund for Nature.

WALHI
1991 *Gugatan dan jawaba; Proses peradilan masalah-masalah lingkungan*. Jakarta: WALHI.
1995a 'Surabaya River (First instance)', in: WALHI (ed.), *PT Surabaya mekabox, PT Surabaya agung industri pulp dan kertas, PT suparma*. Surabaya district court: Decision No.: 116/PDT.G/1995/PN.SBY.
1995b *Kembalikan dana pelestarian hutan; Memori banding and putasan dalam perkara pembatalan Surat Keputusan Presiden No. 42/1994 tentang bantuan pinjaman kepada PT. IPTN*. [Jakarta]: WALHI. 1999 7 anak perusahaan Salim Group terbukti membakar hutan.
2001 PT Freeport bohong.

WALHI and President
1999 Kalimantan Peat Swamp (Central Jakarta district court: 427/Pdt.G/1999/PN.Jkt.Pusat, 1999). 14. Jakarta: WALHI.

WALHI v. PT Pakerin et al.
1998 WALHI v. PT Pakerin et al. district court of Palembang: 8/Pdt.G/1998/PN.Plg.

Walker, David M.
1980 *The Oxford companion to law*. Oxford: Clarendon.

Warga RT 02/VII desa Demaan, Kudus and PT Sumber Sehat
1999 Perjanjian kesepakatan dalam penyelesaian sengketa lingkungan.
Warren, Carol
1998 'Tanah Lot; The cultural and environmental politics of resort development in Bali', in: Philip Hirsch and Carol Warren (eds), *The politics of environment in Southeast Asia; Resources and resistance*, pp. 229-61. London: Routledge.
1994 (ed.) 'Bali sing ken-ken!?; Tourism, culture and the environment in Balinese political cartoons'. Paper, ASAA Biennial Conference, Fremantle Arts Centre and Murdoch University, Perth, Western Australia, 30-31 September.
Warren, Carol and Kylie Elston
1994 *Environmental regulation in Indonesia*. Nedlands: University of Western Australia.
Wijoyo, Suparto
1999 'Penyelesaian sengketa lingkungan menurut UUPLH', *Jurnal Hukum Lingkungan* 5:32-3.
Wiryoto, Arinto
2001 'Walhi minta pembuktian terbalik buat perusakan lingkungan', *Tempo Interatkif*, 21-4-2001.
YAPHI
1998 Pencemaran lingkungan sungai Babon-Demak. YAPHI.
2000 Narasi penyelesaian kasus pencemaran kali Banger, Pekalongan. YAPHI.
Yazid, T.M. Luthfi
1995 Ciujung River pollution case; Some obstacles to set up the ADR mechanism in Indonesia. 5: ICEL.
Yeazell, Stephen C.
1987 *From medieval group litigation to the modern class action*. New Haven: Yale University Press.

Index

www.ingramcontent.com/pod-product-compliance
Lightning Source LLC
Chambersburg PA
CBHW031320230926
51848CB00001B/23
9789067183260